Meaning Making in International Criminal Law

Leiden Studies on the Frontiers of International Law

VOLUME 12

The titles published in this series are listed at *brill.com/lsfi*

Meaning Making in International Criminal Law

A Normative Account of the Acts that Constitute International Crimes

By

Ciara Laverty

BRILL | NIJHOFF

LEIDEN | BOSTON

Cover illustration: Come to this side. Book cover picture by Fernanda Martinez (www.latintaart.com).

The Library of Congress Cataloging-in-Publication Data is available online at https://catalog.loc.gov
LC record available at https://lccn.loc.gov/2024002816

Typeface for the Latin, Greek, and Cyrillic scripts: "Brill". See and download: brill.com/brill-typeface.

ISSN 2212-4195
ISBN 978-90-04-68783-7 (hardback)
ISBN 978-90-04-68784-4 (e-book)
DOI 10.1163/9789004687844

This book is printed on acid-free paper and produced in a sustainable manner.

I Mamgu

Contents

Acknowledgments

This book is an adaptation of the PhD thesis that I defended at Leiden University in December 2022. It could not have been written without the support of many colleagues and friends. I am firstly grateful to Prof. Carsten Stahn and Assoc. Prof. Joe Powderly for their support for and supervision of this research. I also express my thanks to Prof. Mark Drumbl, Dr. Kiran Grewal, Dr. Barrie Sander, Prof. Larissa van den Herik and Dr. Letizia Lo Giacco for serving on my doctorate committee and for their thoughtful comments on the manuscript.

I owe a significant debt of gratitude to the extended PhD community at the Grotius Centre for International Legal Studies and beyond. Many thanks in particular to Sofia Poulopoulou, Sophie Starrenburg and Thea Coventry for being rocks and keeping me going while we were all stuck at home, to Emma Irving for being an oracle of wisdom, and to Tinia De Bruycker, Kritika Sharma and Raam Dutia for all the chats and the moral support. Without Dieneke de Vos this project would never have been started or completed. I am especially grateful to her for being such a great friend, a source of advice, feedback and support, and basically a second brain. To those friends who have been supporting me from long before this journey began, diolch, thank you and dzięks panis.

Finally, and most of all, I am grateful to my family, to my parents Sandra and Patrick and to my sister Siona, for their constant and unwavering support, and to Ianto, Gruff and Dyfi for keeping me cheerful.

Introduction

Foundational aspects of international criminal law, concerning the field's origins, its essence and its rationales, are disputed.[1] A central question to which there remains no settled answer relates to the definition of the concept of international crime.[2] The contemporary catalogue of four core crimes, namely war crimes, crimes against humanity, genocide, and the crime of aggression, has been described as characterised by a 'lack of normative connectivity'[3] in the sense that no clear shared normative basis has been identified to justify or restrict the concept in these terms. A variety of views have nevertheless been offered to explain the essence of this collection of crimes, in particular on the issue of what characterises them as specifically 'international' crimes. The international character of these crimes has been variously interpreted as rooted in how they are understood to transcend borders, to be especially grave because of their scale or seriousness, to affect humanity as a whole, to undermine international peace and security, or to violate the organising principle of the system of sovereign states at different periods in history.[4]

While a variety of answers have in this way been offered to the question of what constitutes the international essence of international crimes, the nature of the acts of violence that make up these wider crime categories have remained somewhat peripheral to this theorising. A generalised perspective on the normative dimensions of the individual acts that constitute international crimes situates international criminal law within broader human rights discourses promoting the 'protection of life, dignity and freedom from discrimination.'[5]

1 For an overview of debates in this area see Sarah Nouwen, 'International Criminal Law: Theory All Over the Place' in Ann Orford and Florian Hoffman (eds), *The Oxford Handbook of the Theory of International Law* (Oxford University Press 2016), 738–761.

2 *Ibid.*, 751.

3 Asad G. Kiyani, 'International Crime and the Politics of Criminal Theory: Voices and Conduct of Exclusion', (2015) 48(1) *New York University Journal of International Law and Politics*, 133.

4 See Larry May, 'Mass Rape and the Concept of International Crime' in Carol A. L. Prager and Trudy Gover (eds), *Dilemmas of Reconciliation: Cases and Concepts* (Wilfrid Laurier University Press 2003), 152–156; Robert Cryer, 'The Doctrinal Foundations of International Criminalization' in M. Cherif Bassiouni (ed), *International Criminal Law, Volume 1: Sources, Subjects and Contents* (Martinus Nijhoff 2008), 125; Ryan Liss, 'Crimes Against the Sovereign Order: Rethinking International Criminal Justice', (2019) 113(4) *American Journal of International Law*, 727–771.

5 Frédéric Mégret, 'What Sort of Global Justice is 'International Criminal Justice'?', (2015) 13(1) *Journal of International Criminal Justice*, 86.

 | DOI:10.1163/9789004687844_002

International crimes are in this way popularly conceived as 'gross'[6] violations of human rights, meaning that international criminal justice is understood as 'the use of criminal law to enforce basic human rights.'[7] The 'basic' or 'fundamental' human rights in question are usually conceived as those that are 'necessary to enjoy any other rights – physical security rights.'[8] The notion that the nature of the acts of violence that constitute international crimes can be understood in terms of violations of basic human rights, commonly understood as rights to life, physical security and subsistence, also characterises the more philosophical literature on international crimes.[9] This conceptualisation of the type of violence at the heart of international criminal law has also featured centrally in critiques of the field as a whole, which have problematised its focus on kinetic, physical violence that falls within the framework of violations of civil and political rights for how this naturalises structural forms of violence or those that violate economic, social and cultural rights.[10]

This book nevertheless challenges the notion that the criminal acts that constitute international crimes can be straightforwardly boiled down to violations of physical security and subsistence rights. It posits that the nature of the individual acts that constitute international crimes are more normatively complex than their generalised treatment in these terms suggests. Identifying a lack of systematic analysis of the normative dimensions of these acts in the scholarship on international criminal law, beyond their conception in broad terms as involving violations of basic security rights, this research sets out to

6 David Luban, 'Fairness to Rightness: Jurisdiction, Legality, and the Legitimacy of International Criminal Law' in Samantha Besson and John Tasioulas (eds), *The Philosophy of International Law* (Oxford University Press 2010), 574; Robert Cryer et al., *An Introduction to International Criminal Law and Procedure* (Cambridge University Press 2014), 3.

7 Luban (n 6), 574. See also Nouwen (n 1), 749.

8 Kirsten Fisher, *Moral Accountability and International Criminal Law – Holding Agents of Atrocity Accountable to the World*, (Routledge 2013), 24.

9 See for example Larry May, *Crimes Against Humanity: A Normative Account* (Cambridge University Press 2005), 64; Massimo Renzo, 'Crimes Against Humanity and the Limits of International Law', (2012) 31(4) *Law and Philosophy*, 452.

10 For examples of these types of critiques see Tor Krever, 'International Criminal Law: An Ideology Critique', (2013) 26(3) *Leiden Journal of International Law*, 701–723; Kiyani (n 3), 129–208; Zinaida Miller, 'Anti-Impunity Politics in Post-Genocide Rwanda' in Karen Engle, Zinaida Miller, D. M. Davis (eds), *Anti-Impunity and the Human Rights Agenda* (Cambridge University Press 2017), 169; Mark Drumbl. 'Accountability for Property Crimes and Environmental War Crimes: Prosecution, Litigation, and Development', International Center for Transitional Justice, November 2009; Evelyne Schmid, *Taking Economic, Social and Cultural Rights Seriously in International Criminal Law* (Cambridge University Press 2015).

develop a more particularised account of how the normative dimensions of these acts can be understood.

The book takes as its point of departure the idea that, without a clearer or more systematic accounting for the normative dimensions of the specific forms of violence criminalised as international crimes, it is difficult to have a wider conversation about what is included in and what is excluded from the sphere of international criminalisation. At present, ad hoc challenges to the inclusion of specific acts, such as crimes against property or apartheid, within the normative universe of international criminal law illustrate that the answer to the question of why particular acts are criminalised under international law, and whether this is justified or legitimate, is far from settled.[11] A more granular accounting for the normative dimensions of the acts that make up the categories of international crimes would therefore facilitate more transparent discussion of what is actually captured by international criminal law, how this has been justified, and its possible implications.

In this respect, from a more representational perspective, analysing the normative dimensions of the individual forms of violence criminalised under international law would contribute to the development of a more precise account of 'what work international criminal justice does in the world.'[12] This research departs from a theoretical understanding of criminal law as both 'generated by and productive of social order.'[13] It understands law in socially constitutive terms, which draws to the fore the representational facets of international criminal justice in constructing and shaping the world in its own image.[14] From this perspective, the tendency to characterise the nature of the

11 See on crimes against property and apartheid respectively Fisher (n 8), 41–42; Kiyani (n 3), 131–133.

12 Anette Bringedal Houge, 'Narrative expressivism: A criminological approach to the expressive function of international criminal justice', (2019) 19(3) *Criminology and Criminal Justice*, 279.

13 Lindsay Farmer, 'Criminal Wrongs in Historical Perspective' in R.A. Duff et al. (eds), *The Boundaries of the Criminal Law* (Oxford University Press 2010), 237.

14 For examples of scholarship that reflects this concern with the representational dimensions of international criminal justice see Krever (n 10), 701–723; Sara Kendall and Sarah Nouwen, 'Representational practices at the International Criminal Court: the gap between juridified and abstract victimhood', (2013) 76(3–4) *Law and Contemporary Problems*, 235–262; Frédéric Mégret, 'In whose name? The ICC and the search for constituency' in Christian De Vos, Sara Kendall and Carsten Stahn (eds), *Contested Justice: The Politics and Practice of International Criminal Court Interventions* (Cambridge University Press 2015), 23–45; Christine Schwöbel-Patel, 'Spectacle in international criminal law: the fundraising image of victimhood', (2016) 4(2) *London Review of International Law*, 247–274; Maria Elander, *Figuring Victims in International Criminal Justice: The Case of the Khmer Rouge Tribunal* (Routledge 2018); Nesam McMillan, *Imagining the International: Crime,*

acts that constitute international crimes in generalised, non-specific terms as violations of physical security and subsistence rights risks overlooking the representational work and productive effects of the criminalisation and prosecution of acts that don't conform straightforwardly to this framework.

For these reasons, this book seeks to explore the normative dimensions of international crimes at this more granular level. It leaves aside the grander question of the normative basis of the four core crimes to examine instead the normative nature of the criminal acts that form the building blocks of these wider categories. The book seeks in this respect to address the question of how the normative dimensions of the individual acts that constitute international crimes can be understood. The 'normative' dimensions of these crimes here refers straightforwardly to their value implications. Criminal law can be understood as 'unavoidably normative in character in the sense that it is a major site of moral politics and moral enterprise.'[15] In this respect, the criminalisation of acts as crimes inherently imply value judgments in the sense that crimes proscribe wrongs. Put simply and in general terms, the criminalisation of an act makes a certain statement about what is good or bad, what actions are right or wrong.[16] This book examines the individual acts that constitute international crimes from this perspective; it seeks to consider how the criminalisation of these acts can be understood in terms of what they proscribe in value terms as wrong.

The first section of this introductory chapter provides a more precise overview of the different approaches to theorising international crimes that have been developed to date. It demonstrates how the normative dimensions of the individual acts of violence that constitute international crimes have not featured centrally in these dominant theorisations. In addition, it highlights how, in those instances where the normative dimensions of these criminal acts are addressed, they have been primarily understood in terms of violations of or harms to physical security and subsistence rights. The second section of this introduction makes the general case that many individual criminal acts under international criminal law can be understood in more multi-dimensional

Justice, and the Promise of the Community (Stanford University Press 2020); Sofia Stolk, *The Opening Statement of the Prosecution in International Criminal Trials: A Solemn Tale of Horror* (Routledge 2021).

15 David Brown, 'Criminalisation and Normative Theory', (2013) 25(2) *Current Issues in Criminal Justice*, 620.

16 Kimmo Nuotio, 'Theories of Criminalization and the Limits of Criminal Law: A Legal Cultural Approach' in R.A. Duff et al. (eds), *The Boundaries of the Criminal Law* (Oxford University Press 2010), 242.

terms than what is captured by existing normative accounts of international crimes. The final section of this introduction identifies the research question and aims of this study, and provides an outline of the structure of the book as a whole.

1 Theories of International Crimes

The literature addressing the normative basis of international crimes has focused predominantly on theorising the nature of the categories of war crimes, crimes against humanity, genocide, and more recently, the crime of aggression. Many of these philosophical accounts approach the question of the normative nature of international crimes primarily from the perspective of analysing the distinction between domestic and international crimes, focussing therefore on questions of jurisdiction and authority to prosecute. They have, for instance, suggested justifications for international, as opposed to domestic criminalisation,[17] have analysed the normative basis for intervening in the sovereign affairs of a state in order to conduct international prosecutions,[18] and have considered the implications of international punishment for the relationship between authority, community and punishment in the criminal law.[19] The normative nature of the crimes themselves, in terms of the forms of violence they criminalise independent of questions of jurisdiction or authority to prosecute, have remained peripheral to many of these accounts.

In his normative-philosophical analysis of crimes against humanity, for instance, Larry May proposes a justification for the violation of state sovereignty involved in prosecuting perpetrators of such crimes by reference to two principles.[20] May's first principle, the security principle, holds that only certain types of violations of human rights, namely basic rights to security and subsistence, when perpetrated by the state against its own population, or permitted to occur by the state, justifies violating state sovereignty in order to protect victims and prosecute perpetrators.[21] May combines this principle

17 Kai Ambos, *Treatise on International Criminal Law: Volume 1: Foundations and General Part* (Oxford University Press 2013), 57–60.

18 Alejandro Chehtman, *The Philosophical Foundations of Extraterritorial Punishment* (Oxford 2010).

19 Antony Duff, 'Authority and Responsibility in International Criminal Law' in Samantha Besson and John Tasioulas (eds), *The Philosophy of International Law* (Oxford University Press 2010), 589–604.

20 May (n 9), 5.

21 *Ibid.*, 21.

with an international harm principle, which holds that, in order to justify international, as opposed to domestic prosecutions, crimes must be in some way group-based in terms of the nature of the victims or the perpetrators.[22] According to May, this group-based dimension of international crimes can be understood to harm the international community itself, which is what characterises them specifically as international crimes.[23]

May explains that crimes against humanity can be understood to cause harm to the international community in this way because they 'react [not] to the individual features of a person, but rather to those features that the individual shares with all, or very many others, or if the perpetrator of the harm is, or involves, a state or other collective entity rather than being merely perpetrated by an individual human person.'[24] In this sense, May's theorisation of crimes against humanity suggests that, fundamentally, international crimes are best understood as assaults on security and subsistence targeted at or perpetrated by groups. Beyond describing them as constituted by violations of 'those human rights that protect physical security and subsistence,'[25] May proposes no further analysis of the acts that constitute crimes against humanity beyond the broader requirements that they be perpetrated by or directed at groups.

In his theorisation of crimes against humanity, David Luban similarly focuses on their group-based nature to conclude that crimes against humanity are 'crimes against humanness as such.'[26] In his view, just as domestic criminal law distinguishes between crimes against persons, property, public order or morals, humanity itself is the legal value that the criminalisation of crimes against humanity is intended to protect.[27] Luban suggests that the characteristics of crimes against humanity that reflect their nature as assaults on humanity relate to the fact that they have 'a double character: they simultaneously assault individuals and groups.[28] This leads Luban to his principal argument, that crimes against humanity target the nature of humans as political animals, in that 'group diversity accounts for half of the double nature of humanness represented in the conception of us as political animals [...] individual

22 *Ibid.*, 80.
23 *Ibid.*
24 *Ibid.*, 83.
25 *Ibid.*, 35.
26 David Luban, 'A Theory of Crimes Against Humanity', (2004) 29(1) *Yale Journal of International Law*, 87.
27 *Ibid.*
28 *Ibid.*, 117.

diversity or, more simply, individuality composes the other half of the political animal's double nature.'[29]

On the question of the acts that constitute crimes against humanity, Luban's account is more circumscribed. He suggests that the underlying acts criminalised as crimes against humanity are 'singled out not because they violate our nature as political animals, but because they violate basic moral decency.'[30] Without expanding on his conception of basic moral decency, Luban argues that 'great depravity by itself does not distinguish crimes against humanity from the cruellest deeds that municipal systems criminalize. Rather, what makes crimes against humanity distinctive lies in the fact that they are atrocities committed by governments and government-like organizations toward civilian groups under their jurisdiction and control.'[31] While Luban may be right to centralise this aspect of crimes against humanity as that which distinguishes them from domestic crimes, his account nevertheless provides limited normative explanation of why it is that these acts, as opposed to others, when committed by governments or similar authorities, are classed as crimes against humanity. Indeed, Luban makes this explicit by stating 'I suspect that no underlying principle explains [...] the atrocities and humiliations that count as crimes against humanity [they] are, in effect, the ones that turn our stomachs, and no principle exists to explain what turns our stomachs.'[32]

Similar to Luban's conclusion that crimes against humanity are crimes against humanness,[33] many theoretical accounts of crimes against humanity centralise the notion of 'humanity' in their normative conceptions of the crime. They nevertheless offer different interpretations of how the 'humanity' protected by the criminalisation of crimes against humanity can be understood. On one reading, humanity refers to humankind, the collective entity of all people.[34] This interpretation of humanity, similar to May and Luban's accounts, captures the focus on large-scale or group-based violence as normatively constitutive of the crime.[35] From another perspective, humanity is understood to refer to human nature, making crimes against humanity 'all acts running contrary to those basic values that are, or should be, considered inherent in any human

29 *Ibid.*, 114–115.
30 *Ibid.*, 119.
31 *Ibid.*, 120.
32 *Ibid.*, 101.
33 *Ibid.*, 87.
34 Christopher Macleod, 'Towards a Philosophical Account of Crimes Against Humanity', (2010) 21(2) *European Journal of International Law*, 283.
35 *Ibid.*

being (in the notion, humanity did not mean "mankind" or "human race" but "the quality" or concept of human being).'[36] This conception of humanity as rooted in humanness, or the quality of being human, places more focus on the nature of the acts themselves and how they deny their victims' humanity, than on the contextual requirement that the violence be large-scale or group-based.

Massimo Renzo forwards a normative account of crimes against humanity that reflects this conception of humanity, ultimately arguing that the nature of the individual act should be determinative of what a crime against humanity is understood to be. Departing from Antony Duff's theory of criminal responsibility as rooted in the notion of 'answerability', which justifies criminal law on the grounds that citizens of a political community are answerable to one another for those wrongs that violate the foundational values of that community, Renzo conceives of international crimes as constituting those harms to which the individual is answerable to the broader human community by reason of their membership in it.[37]

From this perspective, Renzo understands the harms caused by the acts that constitute crimes against humanity as violations of fundamental human rights which deny the victims' status as a human being, meaning that the perpetrator is therefore answerable to the whole of the human community. This leads him to conclude that 'the list of acts that constitute crimes against humanity is limited to violations of basic human rights (i.e. crimes such as torture, rape and murder) [because] only when the rights to the conditions necessary for a minimally decent life are violated is the human status of the victim denied.'[38] Centralising in this way the nature of the harm to individual victims as providing the normative basis for the criminalisation of crimes against humanity at international level, the result of Renzo's argument is that he considers the nature of the act to be determinative of a crime against humanity, meaning that, normatively speaking, every individual act of this type constitutes a crime against humanity.[39]

However, even an account such as this, which centralises the acts that constitute the broader crime to the extent that it ultimately rejects the contextual elements as relevant to the normative basis of crimes against humanity, nevertheless also relies on a conception of the acts themselves as violations of 'basic human rights'.[40] While this account provides a clearer normative

36 Antonio Cassese, *International Law* (Oxford University Press 2005), 440.
37 Renzo (n 9), 456.
38 *Ibid.*, 453.
39 *Ibid.*, 461.
40 *Ibid.*, 452.

basis for the criminalisation of the individual acts, in relying on a conception of basic human rights as those conditions 'that are necessary for a minimally decent life'[41] and listing acts such as torture, rape and murder in this regard,[42] it remains tied to a life and bodily integrity conception of such acts. As a normative account of how crimes against humanity should be defined, Renzo's account similarly does not address the fact that many of the acts reflected in the existing definition of crimes against humanity, such as persecution, apartheid, or acts of reproductive violence, while they may also involve violations of such fundamental rights, also seem to go beyond a simplistic understanding of 'basic' human rights and bodily integrity harms in terms of what could be considered to provide their normative basis.

The normative underpinnings of the criminalisation of war crimes have received more limited analysis than that of crimes against humanity. In his reflection on this question, Larry May suggests that 'it is possible that the laws of war have no underlying principle of justification. Indeed, it sometimes seems as if what we have is merely a list of rules from different eras, cobbled together into increasingly lengthy instruments, where there is [...] little agreement about what their basis is.'[43] May nevertheless proposes that war crimes are ultimately best understood as violations of the principle of humaneness, requiring soldiers to act humanely, which he defines in terms of acting with mercy and compassion, even while they are permitted to kill the soldiers of the enemy.[44] May argues that the normative principle of humaneness ultimately underpins the more commonly recognised structure of international humanitarian law as resting on the legal principles of necessity, distinction and proportionality. He interprets this legal structure as giving practical form to the principle of humaneness's requirement of inflicting minimal suffering and acting with mercy and honour.[45]

On the question of the criminalisation and prosecution of certain violations of international humanitarian law as war crimes, May identifies the justification for undertaking prosecutions at an international level in how the soldiers responsible for committing war crimes represent states. In other words, in how war crimes are often committed with the involvement or facilitation of states.[46] From this perspective, May argues that the international community

41 *Ibid.*, 453.

42 *Ibid.*

43 Larry May, *War Crimes and Just War* (Cambridge University Press 2007), 74.

44 *Ibid.*, 1–2.

45 *Ibid.*, 85.

46 *Ibid.*, 41.

has an interest in prosecuting war crimes at an international level because, without international intervention, the state itself is unlikely to do so, resulting in impunity and a failure to deter such crimes in future.[47] This focus on the justification for international enforcement as rooted in the need to ensure accountability in the absence of domestic prosecutions nevertheless provides no answer to the question of why certain violations of international humanitarian law, and not others, should be subject to criminalisation i.e. to be prosecuted as war crimes, whether at domestic or international levels.

In this way, beyond the broad normative analysis of international humanitarian law as rooted in the principle of humaneness, and the general deterrence-based justification for international level prosecutions of crimes perpetrated or facilitated by states, May's account of war crimes engages in a more limited way with the nature of the specific violations of international humanitarian law that constitute war crimes. Choosing to focus primarily on the normative basis of war crimes involving killing or assaults on persons,[48] which he describes as the 'paradigmatic form of harm in war',[49] May explains that other types of war crimes, such as attacks on property or the environment, 'may not seem as important'[50] as attacks on persons. He goes on to argue that 'a conceptual difficulty arises in attempts to compare these crimes to [crimes involving attacks on persons], especially in those situations where it seems unavoidable that one choose either loss of life or loss of property.'[51] Without expanding on the types of situations that would involve unavoidable choices between loss of life or loss of property, and their relevance to the question of criminalisation, May's account leaves unaddressed the normative nature of many of the prohibitions in international humanitarian law that do not involve assaults on persons. As a result, this account leaves open the question of the possible normative underpinnings of the criminalisation of these types of violations of international humanitarian law as war crimes.

May's focus on violence to persons is also characteristic of the wider legal-philosophical literature on war crimes and international humanitarian law. For instance, in his analysis of the correlation between moral norms and the rules of international criminal and humanitarian law, Ahmad Adil Haque focuses on norms applicable specifically to killing during armed conflict.[52] Similarly, in

47 *Ibid.*, 41–42.

48 *Ibid.*, 17–18.

49 *Ibid.*, 18.

50 *Ibid.*, 19.

51 *Ibid.*, 20–21.

52 Adil Ahmad Haque, 'Criminal Law and Morality at War' in R.A. Duff and Stuart Green (eds), *Philosophical Foundations of Criminal Law* (Oxford University Press 2011), 482.

his account of the morality of action in war and its relationship to criminal law, Jeff McMahan centralises the question of the moral justification for killing, arguing that combatants are legitimate targets for attack in war since, by virtue of being a threat to others, targeting them is morally justified on the grounds that doing so is to engage in self-defence.[53] While not exhaustive of the legal-philosophical literature on war crimes, what these examples serve to illustrate is that, taken together, this body of literature tends to leave unaddressed the normative dimensions of prohibitions in international humanitarian law, and the criminalisation of their violation, that do not involve killing or violence to persons.

Lastly, the relationship between the criminalisation of particular acts of violence and the wider crime categories of genocide and aggression is somewhat distinct to those of war crimes and crimes against humanity. The normative dimensions of the individual acts that constitute genocide reflect how genocide 'is a form of instrumental violence in which the constituent acts serve as means to an end.'[54] The essence and structure of this crime, and the normative dimensions of the individual acts that constitute it, can therefore be understood more straightforwardly as being structured towards protecting a defined interest, namely the existence of particular types of human groups.[55] While structurally distinct, the crime of aggression can be understood in similar terms, in the sense that it is explicitly structured towards protecting a clearly defined interest, in this case, the prevention of aggressive war.[56] Despite their different structural forms, Kai Ambos has nevertheless sought to offer a holistic theorisation of the four categories of international crimes taken together. This theorisation seeks to capture the similarities in form of each of the categories, and goes some way towards capturing those features of international crimes that remain unaddressed by the accounts outlined above, namely the normative significance of the criminal acts that constitute the categories of international crimes.

Ambos proposes a theoretical model of international crimes that captures their collective-individualist nature by combining the two primary theories of criminalisation at domestic level; the theory of legal goods and the

53 Jeff McMahan, 'War Crimes and Immoral Action in War' in R.A. Duff et al. (eds), *The Constitution of the Criminal Law* (Oxford University Press 2013), 153.

54 Adil Ahmad Haque, 'International Crime: In Context and In Contrast' in R.A. Duff et al. (eds), *The Structures of the Criminal Law* (Oxford University Press 2011), 118.

55 *Ibid.* See also Larry May, *Genocide a Normative Account* (Cambridge University Press 2012), 62.

56 See Larry May, *Aggression and Crimes Against Peace* (Cambridge University Press 2009).

prevention of harm. Ambos argues that international criminal law purports to protect collective and supra-national interests, such as humanity as a whole, international peace and security or the well-being of the world, at the same time as protecting the individual interests of victims, in that it is violations of their fundamental rights, and therefore the material harm that is experienced by individuals, that constitute the core international crimes.[57] For this reason, he suggests that a theory of international crimes must recognise this dual nature since, 'the only way to account for the concrete sociological harm and for its two value-implications is by combining a theory of harm with a *Rechtsgut*-theory.'[58]

In this respect, his model goes further than those theorisations discussed above, by revealing the relevance of analysing the normative nature of the specific criminal acts, since it is the specific acts that constitute international crimes that are ultimately inflicted on individuals, and are therefore reflective of the individual interests these crimes can be understood to protect. Ambos begins this analysis by identifying, for example, that genocide protects the existence of national, ethnical, racial or religious groups as a legal good. At the same time, violence inflicted on individuals is what constitutes this crime, meaning that genocide also protects fundamental individual rights such as life and human dignity. Similarly, the acts constituting crimes against humanity protect the life, human, dignity and liberty of individuals, at the same time as the requirement of a widespread or systematic attack refers to the protection of collective interests such as international peace and security. Finally, war crimes protect the life, human dignity and physical integrity of individuals while simultaneously protecting the broader humanitarian goal of containing conflict and contributing to peace and security.[59] While Ambos' account in this way offers a conceptualisation of international crimes that captures the normative relevance of the individual acts of violence that constitute the wider crime categories, he nevertheless limits his analysis to fundamental and well-established individual interests that fall within the basic security rights paradigm, such as life, human dignity and physical integrity.

57 Kai Ambos, 'The Overall Function of International Criminal Law: Striking the Right Balance Between the Rechtsgut and the Harm Principles', (2015) 9(2) *Criminal Law and Philosophy*, 319–320.

58 *Ibid.*, 321.

59 *Ibid.*, 66.

2 Beyond Life, Physical Security and Bodily Integrity

When considered from the perspective of their normative dimensions, the individual acts criminalised as war crimes, crimes against humanity or genocide nevertheless reveal a more normatively complex picture than the generalised life, physical security and bodily integrity paradigm that is centralised in each of these theoretical accounts. War crimes can be understood to contain protections for, for instance, various types of property, for the environment or for the right to a fair trial.[60] Similarly, many of the acts criminalised as crimes against humanity, such as persecution, deportation or forcible transfer, apartheid, or crimes of sexual or reproductive violence, do not reflect an exclusive or one-dimensional account of well-established protections for basic security rights.

A non-exhaustive overview of some of the case law reveals the degree of normative variety identified in practice in this respect. For instance, in its first case, the ICTY articulated its conception of the crime against humanity of persecution as 'the violation of the right to equality in some serious fashion.'[61] The ICTR has described the criminalisation of rape as having 'the objective of protecting individual sexual autonomy'[62] while the ICC has articulated an understanding of the crime of forced pregnancy as being 'grounded in the woman's right to personal and reproductive autonomy and the right to family.'[63] In a similar manner, the ICC has stated that the crime of forced marriage violates 'the independently recognised basic right to consensually marry and establish a family […] This basic right is indeed the value (distinct from e.g. physical or sexual integrity, or personal liberty) that demands protection through the appropriate interpretation of article 7(1)(k).'[64]

The ICC Office of the Prosecutor (OTP) has also sought to identify the normative basis of certain individual criminal acts in its submissions. In its opening statements in the *Al Mahdi* case, the OTP described the war crime of attacking cultural objects as a crime 'against that which constitutes the

60 Tianying Song, 'Legal Goods Protected by War Crimes', Centre of International Law Research and Policy Conference Paper, 26 August 2017 [available at https://www.cilrap.org/cilrap-film/170826-song/ – accessed 11 February 2022].

61 *Prosecutor v. Duško Tadić*, IT-94-1-T, ICTY, Opinion and Judgment, 7 May 1997, para 697.

62 *Prosecutor v. Tharcisse Muvunyi*, ICTR-00-55, ICTR, Judgment and Sentence, 12 September 2006, para 521.

63 *Prosecutor v. Dominic Ongwen*, ICC-02/04-01/15, ICC, Trial Judgment, 4 February 2021, para 2717.

64 *Prosecutor v. Dominic Ongwen*, ICC-02/04-01/15, ICC, Decision on the confirmation of charges against Dominic Ongwen, 23 March 2016, para 94.

richness of whole communities. And it is thus a crime that impoverishes us all and damages universal values we are bound to protect [...] to protect cultural property is to protect our culture, our history, our identity, and our ways of expressing faith and practicing religion for current and future generations.'[65] Similarly, in submissions on the distinction between the crimes against humanity of deportation and forcible transfer, the OTP has asserted that it is necessary to distinguish between the two crimes in order to 'give effect to the different values protected' by them.[66] The OTP noted that while both crimes 'safeguard the right of individuals to "live in their communities and homes", deportation also protects a further set of important rights: the right of individuals to live in the particular State in which they were lawfully present – which means living within a particular culture, society, language, set of values, and legal protections.'[67]

The language used in each of these examples is not consistent in terms of whether the basis of the act is framed as a legal right, a value, or a more general interest. At the same time, each of these statements identifies a normative basis for the criminalisation of a particular act that is not captured by conceptions of international crimes as characterised exclusively by group-based violations of rights to physical security and subsistence. While some of these acts may also involve violations of such physical security and subsistence rights, these statements reveal that there may be significant additional dimensions to the nature of these crimes that have received limited attention from a normative perspective. The relatively limited normative analysis of the variety of individual criminal acts reflected in the scholarship, which has tended to characterise such acts in broad-brush terms as involving violations of basic security rights, in this sense overlooks the variety and complexity of these acts, ultimately providing a somewhat loose and imprecise account of their normative natures.

65 ICC, Statement of the Prosecutor of the International Criminal Court, Fatou Bensouda, at the opening of Trial in the case against Mr Ahmad Al-Faqi Al Mahdi, 22 August 2016 [available at https://www.icc-cpi.int/Pages/item.aspx?name=otp-stat-al-mahdi-160822 – accessed 9 February 2022].

66 Application Under Regulation 46(3), Prosecution's Request for a Ruling on Jurisdiction under Article 19(3) of the Statute, ICC, 9 April 2018, para 17.

67 *Ibid.*

3 Structure of the Book

This book therefore seeks to explore the normative nature of international crimes from this more granular perspective. It addresses the question of how the normative dimensions of the individual acts that constitute international crimes can be understood. In responding to this question, the book first aims to develop a theoretical framework through which the normative dimensions of these criminal acts can be examined. On the basis of this theoretical framework and the methodology derived from it, the book seeks to provide an account of the normative dimensions of four types of criminal acts that appear on the face of it to be more complex than the traditional life, bodily integrity and physical security paradigm, namely attacks on cultural property, pillage, sexual violence, and reproductive violence. By developing and applying a novel theoretical and methodological lens to this question, this book seeks to develop both a deeper understanding of the normative dimensions of these discrete criminal acts as well as a more conceptual account of how the normative dimensions of the criminal acts that constitute international crimes can be understood more widely.

The book is structured around the crimes analysed, with Chapter 1 outlining the theoretical framework and methodology applied to the subsequent analysis of the crimes of attacks on cultural property (Chapter 2), pillage (Chapter 3), sexual violence (Chapter 4), and reproductive violence (Chapter 5). Chapter 1 seeks to develop a theoretical approach to the research question that draws on a Durkheimian conception of the co-constitutive relationship between criminal law and society, advancing the argument that the normative dimensions of the acts that constitute international crimes are best understood from a constitutive and politically-productive rather than a declarative perspective. The chapter then goes on to propose a practice-based approach to how the normative meaning attached to the criminalisation of these acts is produced. This draws on expressive and discursive approaches to law and theorises the normative dimensions of these acts as processes of construction and meaning making.

On this basis, the final section of Chapter 1 justifies the selection of crimes for analysis and outlines a methodological approach that responds to the theoretical framework developed in this chapter. This methodological approach involves a four-step analysis of each crime, consisting of an account of the crime's historical-normative roots, a conceptual analysis of its legal definition, followed by a discourse analysis of the normative themes articulated in decisions involving charges for these crimes and the narratives that emerge around the crime during the course of proceedings. Through the different aspects of the analysis, this methodological approach seeks to capture the elements of how crimes and their normative dimensions are historically, socially and politically situated, can be understood as constitutive of certain normative principles in what their legal definitions invoke at an abstract, conceptual level, and are further discursively constructed through the processes of meaning making that take place during prosecution and judgment. The remainder of the book consists of the application of this four-step process to the crimes selected for analysis.

Chapters 2 and 3 examine crimes against property. Chapter 2 addresses the crime of attacks on cultural property, tracing the historical roots of this crime in the emergence of Renaissance and Enlightenment ideas about the value of art, history and culture. It considers how the different definitions of this crime in international criminal law conceptually invoke a civilian use and a cultural value rationale for the protection of cultural property during armed conflict. The chapter goes on to reveal how the discourse around these crimes in the case law and during the course of proceedings has evolved to construct an increasingly complex and multifaceted conception of the cultural value of protected buildings and the wrong therefore invoked by this crime. Chapter 3 examines the crime of pillage. It demonstrates how this crime's historical roots are situated in the rise of liberalism in Europe with its ideological valorisation of rights to private property, which continues to dominate contemporary definitions of the crime in international criminal law. The analysis of the case law and the discourse during proceedings nevertheless suggest a move away from these normative roots, towards a contemporary discourse that centralises the use value of property in ensuring the subsistence and survival of civilians during armed conflict.

Chapters 4 and 5 examine crimes widely understood as crimes of gender-based violence. Chapter 4 analyses crimes of sexual violence, tracing the normative roots of these crimes through their historical evolution from being conceived as crimes against property and honour, to their incorporation in international criminal law as crimes of physical violence that violate victims' bodily integrity and sexual autonomy. The chapter goes on to reveal a complex normative discourse around crimes of sexual violence in practice, which is dominated by a conception of such crimes as acts of violence and aggression that violate bodily integrity, but nevertheless continues to contain echoes of some of the more archaic honour-based conceptions of sexual violation. Chapter 5 addresses crimes of reproductive violence. This chapter traces the more recent codification of these crimes to the emergence of an international discourse on individual rights to sexual and reproductive health, identifying a tension in the definitions of these crimes between the nascent notion of an individual right to reproductive choice and ongoing resistance to this principle. The analysis nevertheless exposes an emphatic turn in practice towards a conception of these crimes as rooted in protections for reproductive rights and the principle of reproductive autonomy. The conclusion to this book seeks to draw together the theoretical framework developed in Chapter 1 with the substantive insights from the analysis of these four criminal acts. It ultimately offers a dynamic, pluralist and socially constructed account of wrong in international criminal law, which is produced through an ongoing process of meaning making in practice and captures the relationship between criminal wrong and transformations in the wider social and political order.

CHAPTER 1

Theoretical Framework

Having sought to demonstrate how it may be possible to understand many of the criminal acts that constitute international crimes in more multi-dimensional terms than the normative accounts outlined in the introduction to this book suggest, this chapter sketches a theoretical framework within which the normative dimensions of these individual acts are examined in this study. This theoretical framework is rooted in a Durkheimian conception of the co-constitutive relationship between criminal law and society. It advances the argument that the normative dimensions of these individual criminal acts are best understood from a constitutive rather than a declarative perspective. The first section of this chapter seeks to bring together this Durkheimian sociological approach to criminal law with elements of the philosophy of criminal law developed at the domestic level, to highlight the particular relevance of understanding the normative dimensions of crimes and criminalisation at the international level in constitutive, politically productive terms.

On this basis, the second section of the chapter goes on to advance a practice-based approach to conceptualising the normative meaning attached to the criminalisation of particular acts of violence in international criminal law, which draws on expressive and discursive approaches to (international criminal) law and the growing concern with the representational facets of international criminal justice. Conceptualising the normative dimensions of the individual criminal acts in this way as a process of construction and meaning making, this section proposes an approach which centralises the narratives and discourses that emerge around particular crimes as central to how they are given normative content, or 'made to mean',[1] in practice. Lastly, the final section of the chapter builds on this theoretical framework to outline the methodological approach which is applied to the analysis of each of the crimes discussed in the following chapters from this theoretical perspective.

1 Nesam McMillan, *Imagining the International: Crime, Justice, and the Promise of the Community* (Stanford University Press 2020), 11.

 | DOI:10.1163/9789004687844_003

1 International Criminalisation as Constitutive Process

In terms of its history, international criminal law has been described as 'essentially reactive'[2] in the sense that its evolution has been driven not through the pursuit of particular policy prescriptions but through responses to particular events. This has meant that the development of international criminal law has not taken place in a 'linear, cohesive, consistent, or logical fashion.'[3] As a category that has in this way 'grown out of ad hoc creation and application in response to specific crises',[4] Sarah Nouwen has argued that it may be challenging to identify in the concept of international crime 'an essence that it may never have had.'[5] Recognising the nature of international criminal law, and the crimes that it has codified, as in this way reactive and contingent brings to the fore how international criminal law is inherently 'socially, politically, historically, and legally located and produced.'[6] This conception of international criminal law reflects a central idea in the sociology of crime and deviance; that crime is socially constructed and is constituted through social processes. Such an understanding of crime has some of its historical roots in a Durkheimian conception of the relationship between criminal law and society.

1.1 *Durkheim and the Productive Politics of Criminal Law*

Durkheim conceived of criminal law as a manifestation of a society's collective consciousness, which he defined in terms of 'the totality of beliefs and sentiments common to the average members of a society.'[7] In Durkheim's view, crime 'disturbs those feelings which in any one type of society are to be found in every healthy consciousness.'[8] A crime therefore consists fundamentally of 'an act contrary to strong, well-defined states of the common consciousness.'[9] Understanding criminal law as emanating in this way from a collective consciousness, Durkheim did not approach crime as an intrinsic quality of a certain category of actions. Instead, he articulated the relationship between crime

2 Mark Drumbl, 'Introduction to International Criminal Law by M Cherif Bassiouni', (2005) 99 *American Journal of International Law*, 289.
3 M. Cherif Bassiouni, *Introduction to International Criminal Law* (Martinus Nijhoff 2014), 28.
4 Sarah Nouwen, 'International Criminal Law: Theory All Over the Place' in Anne Orford and Florian Hoffman (eds), *The Oxford Handbook of the Theory of International Law* (Oxford University Press 2016), 751.
5 *Ibid.*
6 McMillan (n 1), 10.
7 Emile Durkheim, *The Division of Labour in Society* (Palgrave Macmillan 2013), 63.
8 *Ibid.*, 59.
9 *Ibid.*, 81.

and the collective consciousness as one where collective sentiment 'far from deriving from the crime, constitutes the crime.'[10] Durkheim for this reason argued that 'we should not say that an act offends the common consciousness because it is criminal, but that it is criminal because it offends that consciousness. We do not condemn it because it is a crime, but it is a crime because we condemn it.'[11]

Durkheim's articulation of the relationship between criminal law and society in these terms has nevertheless been criticised for offering a static and somewhat reified conception of collective consciousness. David Garland argues, for instance, that Durkheim's account overlooks how 'the forms of social relations and moral beliefs that come to dominate in any society are [...] the outcome of an ongoing process of struggle and negotiation.'[12] He suggests that the collective consciousness that is purportedly manifested in criminal law may therefore be better understood in terms of a dominant ideology that has been established by certain social forces.[13] Despite this shortcoming, in highlighting how crime is ascribed its character not by an intrinsic quality to a particular act but through the importance attributed to it by the collective consciousness, Durkheim's account of criminal law is nevertheless valuable for how it exposed the nature of crime and criminalisation as fundamentally 'the outcome of a process of social definition.'[14]

From this perspective, criminologists have therefore argued that 'the category of crime [...] has no ontological reality [...] crimes and criminals are fictive events and characters in the sense that they have to be constructed before they can exist.'[15] Expanding on the nature of this process, Nils Christie has explained that '[c]rime does not exist. Only acts exist, acts often given different meanings within various social frameworks. [...] Our challenge is to follow the destiny of acts through the universe of meanings.'[16] Outlining in this vein how what has come to constitute the category of international crimes has changed over time and how, even at the doctrinal level, the legal definitions of international crimes are recognised as being the products of social and political

10 *Ibid.*, 64.

11 *Ibid.*

12 David Garland, *Punishment and Modern Society: A Study in Social Theory* (University of Chicago Press 1990), 51.

13 *Ibid.*, 53.

14 Immi Tallgren, 'The Durkheimian Spell of International Criminal Law', (2013) 71(2) *Revue interdisciplinaire d'études juridiques*, 145.

15 Paddy Hillyard and Steve Tombs, 'Beyond Criminology?' in Paddy Hillyard et al. (eds), *Beyond Criminology: Taking Harm Seriously* (Pluto Press 2004), 11.

16 Nils Christie, *A Suitable Amount of Crime* (Routledge 2004), 3.

dynamics at a given point in time,[17] Nesam McMillan has similarly highlighted in the context of international criminal law that '[n]otions of international crime and justice are constructed, contested, and socio-politically negotiated [...] the category of international crime, as well as what behaviour is placed in this category is thus a product of socio-political processes of criminalization.'[18]

Recognising in this way that 'acts *are* not, they *become*',[19] this perspective firstly highlights the relevance of asking the question; 'what are the social conditions that encourage or prevent giving the acts the meaning of being crime?'.[20] In other words, recognising how crimes are inherently constructed and socio-politically negotiated foregrounds firstly the question of the process through which the individual criminal acts under international criminal law came to constitute crimes i.e. from what normative environment they emerged and the political and legal processes that contributed to their inclusion as acts constituting international crimes.

In addition to highlighting the nature of criminalisation as inherently socially situated, Durkheim's account of the role and function of criminal punishment lays the foundations for conceptualising the socially and politically productive dimensions of criminal law. In identifying the normative substance of criminalisation as constituted by acts that violate the deeply held beliefs of a society's collective consciousness, Durkheim understood punishment as the expression of a collective emotional response to this violation; 'punishment constitutes essentially a reaction of passionate feeling, graduated in intensity, which society exerts through the mediation of an organised body over those of its members who have violated certain rules of conduct.'[21] Questioning more retributive or deterrence-based rationales for the institution of punishment, Durkheim instead identified a social role to this emotional response, describing the real function of punishment as being:

> to maintain inviolate the cohesion of society by sustaining the common consciousness in all its vigour. If that consciousness were thwarted so categorically, it would necessarily lose some of its power, were an emotional reaction from the community not forthcoming to make good that loss. Thus there would result a relaxation in the bonds of social solidarity. The consciousness must therefore be conspicuously reinforced the moment

17 McMillan (n 1), 67.
18 *Ibid.*, 10.
19 Christie (n 16), 6.
20 *Ibid.*, 3.
21 Durkheim (n 7), 74.

> it meets with opposition. The sole means of doing so is to give voice to the unanimous aversion that the crime continues to evoke, and this by an official act, which can only mean suffering inflicted upon the wrongdoer. Thus, although a necessary outcome of the causes that give rise to it, this suffering is not a gratuitous act of cruelty. It is a sign indicating that the sentiments of the collectivity are still collective, that the communion of minds sharing the same faith remains absolute, and in this way the injury that the crime has inflicted upon society is made good. [...] Without this necessary act of satisfaction what is called the moral consciousness could not be preserved. Thus, without being paradoxical, we may state that punishment is above all intended to have its effect upon honest people. Since it serves to heal the wounds inflicted upon the collective sentiments, it can only fulfil this role where such sentiments exist, and in so far as they are active.[22]

In other words, Durkheim understood the infliction of punishment as an expression of a society's condemnation of the violation of its deeply held beliefs, which, in turn, functions to reassert those beliefs and therefore, importantly, to reassert the collective consciousness of which they are part. In this sense, the collective consciousness not only defines what constitutes crime and is the source of the emotional response to it – manifested in the institution of punishment – the collective consciousness is itself 'the beneficiary of the punitive process, being strengthened and reaffirmed by the social response to crime.'[23]

Frédéric Mégret has highlighted how this conception of the function of punishment 'fundamentally shapes the dialectical relation of the criminal law to society in a novel way: The criminal law does not exist because society (pre) exists; rather society exists because criminal law exists.'[24] The Durkheimian understanding of the function of punishment suggests how criminal law is in this way inherently socially and politically productive. The criminalisation, prosecution and punishment of acts that violate a society's collective consciousness not only functions as an expression of the blameworthiness that the society assigns to those acts but also functions as 'a way of constituting the society that assigns this blameworthiness.'[25]

22 *Ibid.*, 83.

23 Garland (n 78), 49.

24 Frédéric Mégret, 'Practices of Stigmatization', (2013) 76 *Law and Contemporary Problems*, 290.

25 *Ibid.*, 290.

This understanding of the co-constitutive relationship between criminal law and society has particular productive potency at the international level because the existence and nature of a society or community that can be conceived of as 'international' in some way, and how to understand it, is complex and remains a subject of significant debate.[26] In the context of international criminal law, the specific challenges of transposing criminal law theory developed at the domestic level, which takes the state as its centrepiece, to the international level is therefore well-recognised. The distinct international context has given rise to various debates on the justification for punitive power in the absence of a supranational sovereign, on the nature of international criminal jurisdiction, and on the link between crime, citizenship and community for explaining aspects of criminal law in the absence of the structuring framework of a state.[27] A Durkheimian conception of criminal law's constitutive function therefore has particular relevance at the international level precisely because the sovereign of international criminal law and the society which it is understood to represent 'must be actively constituted in legitimation processes that far exceed its domestic counterpart.'[28]

In this respect, Immi Tallgren has highlighted how a Durkheimian approach reveals the co-constitutive dynamic between international criminal law and the international community or society for which it is understood to speak. She argues that, in the context of international criminal law, the 'we' of the international community 'continuously reconstitutes itself in expressing its punitive feelings, those shared feelings being part of the conditions of its existence in the first place. If, on the contrary, 'we' remains silent on crime, the collective beliefs and sentiments fade, endangering the existence of an

---

26 From an international relations perspective see for instance Hedley Bull, *The Anarchical Society: A Study of Order in World Politics* (Columbia University Press 2012). For an overview of the normative implications of invocations of international community in the context of international criminal law see Immi Tallgren, 'The Voice of the International: Who is Speaking?', (2015) 13 *Journal of International Criminal Justice*, 135–155.

27 See for instance Kai Ambos, 'Punishment without a Sovereign? The Ius Puniendi Issue of International Criminal Law: A First Contribution towards a Consistent Theory of International Criminal Law', (2013) 33(2), *Oxford Journal of Legal Studies*, 293–315; Alejandro Chehtman, *The Philosophical Foundations of Extraterritorial Punishment* (Oxford University Press 2010); Darryl Robinson, 'International Criminal Law as Justice', (2013) 11(3) *Journal of International Criminal Justice*, 699–711; Ryan Liss, 'Crimes Against the Sovereign Order: Rethinking International Criminal Justice', 113(4) (2019) *American Journal of International Law*, 732–734.

28 Kjersti Lohne, 'Penal welfarism 'gone global'? Comparing international criminal justice to The Culture of Control', (2021) 23(1) *Punishment and Society*, 12.

audible 'we'.'[29] International criminal law can be understood, therefore, in these terms as 'the manifestation of an international society's will to exist [...] It seeks to affirm fundamental values of an international society in the making through international trials that embody an evolving international "collective consciousness".'[30]

Zooming in, then, on the individual acts criminalised as international crimes, this perspective on the nature of criminal law as both declarative and constitutive of a society's collective consciousness is illuminating for how it underscores the value of 'think[ing] fundamentally backwards'[31] about the normative dimensions of these criminal acts. Rather than asking what principle, interest or value explains or underlies the criminalisation of these acts, the constitutive perspective encourages making the inductive methodological move of asking instead how particular norms, principles or values are constituted through the criminalisation and prosecution of these acts. The particular significance of this approach in the context of international criminal law, in particular for the criminal acts it proscribes, is reinforced by considering the traditional criminal law theory conception of crimes as 'public' wrongs against the absence of a defined community that acts as referent for the 'public' character of international criminal wrongs.

1.2 *Crimes as Public Wrongs: Thinking Backwards*

Durkheim's sociological approach to criminal law as both animated by and constitutive of the deeply held beliefs that form a society's collective consciousness resonates with the traditional criminal law theory conception of crimes as 'public' wrongs. In his influential theory of domestic criminal law, in which he understands trial and punishment as the forum in which citizens of a shared political community call each other to account for the violation of the public values of that community, Antony Duff explains how crimes are public wrongs 'not in the sense that they harm 'the public' as distinct from any individual victims, but in the sense that they are wrongs that concern 'the public', i.e. all members of the polity, in virtue of their shared membership.'[32] On this account, the 'public' nature of criminal wrongs derives from the fact that, while criminal offences also constitute wrongs to the victims of the offence,

29 Tallgren (n 26), 148.

30 Mégret (n 24), 292.

31 *Ibid.*, 290.

32 Antony Duff, 'Authority and Responsibility in International Criminal Law' in Samantha Besson and John Tasioulas (eds), *The Philosophy of International Law* (Oxford University Press 2010), 595.

criminal wrongs are also wrongs committed against the community, since the offender delegitimises and undermines its system of social and legal norms by violating them.[33]

Offering a normative argument that echoes Durkheim's sociological conception of criminal punishment as contributing to reaffirming the deeply held beliefs of a society that have been violated through crime, Duff argues that wrongs of a 'public' nature require identification and condemnation 'in that for a polity not to condemn them, or not to make efforts to identify and condemn their perpetrators, would be to fail to take seriously both the wrongs as they impact on their victims, and the values to which the polity is supposedly committed.'[34] With respect to the justification and normative contents of criminalisation, Duff's account in this way illustrates how criminalisation is grounded in an understanding of the public nature of the wrongs to be criminalised. He explains that:

> A justification of criminalisation will need to begin by specifying some value(s) that can be claimed to be public, as part of the polity's self-definition; show how the conduct in question violates that value or threatens the goods that it protects; and argue that that violation or threat is such as to require or demand a public condemnation.[35]

On this account, criminalisation therefore ultimately reflects 'what kinds of wrongs should be seen as wrongs against 'us'; [...] which values are [...] so central to a community's identity and self-understanding, to its conceptions of its members' good, that actions which attack or flout these values are not merely individual matters which the individual victim should pursue for herself, but attacks on the community.'[36] Put simply, criminal wrongs are understood as public wrongs in the sense that they are wrongs that are seen to violate the values that define a community.[37]

When taken in the context of a Durkheimian conception of international criminal law, which, as articulated by Frédéric Mégret, would see international

33 Paul McGorrey, 'The Philosophy of Criminalisation: A Review of Duff et al.'s Criminalisation Series' (2018) 12(2) *Criminal Law and Philosophy*, 188; R.A. Duff, *Answering for Crime: Responsibility and Liability in the Criminal Law* (Hart 2007), 143.

34 Duff (n 32), 143.

35 *Ibid.*

36 S.E. Marshall and R.A. Duff, 'Criminalisation and Sharing Wrongs' (1998) 11(1) *Canadian Journal of Law and Jurisprudence*, 21–22.

37 Lindsay Farmer, 'Criminal Wrongs in Historical Perspective' in R.A. Duff et al. (eds), *The Boundaries of the Criminal Law* (Oxford University Press 2010), 222.

criminal law as 'constitutive of what some traditionally thought it could merely be declarative of',[38] this understanding of crime as specifically and inherently 'public' wrong underscores the particular value of 'thinking fundamentally backwards'[39] about the normative dimensions of the individual acts criminalised as international crimes. Mégret identifies the macro-level relation between international society and criminal justice from a Durkheimian perspective as 'dialectical: [i]nternational society exists only inasmuch as it can react sufficiently strongly, through criminal justice, to what challenges it at its core; and the more it does so, the more it can be said to actually betray that it really exists.'[40] At the more granular level, the normative dimensions of the acts that constitute international crimes can be understood as politically productive in the same way; reacting through criminal justice to the violation of norms that are understood to constitute the core of an international society not only betrays that that society really exists, but also betrays that there are norms that in fact constitute the core of that society, and that these similarly really exist. Understood in these terms, Durkheim's sociology of criminal law taken together with the public understanding of criminal wrongs makes visible 'an informal constitution of ruling morality and outrages, which stand beneath the formal stem of the Rome Statute and inscribe selected outrages as exemplars of "international" solidarity.'[41]

Sinja Graf has offered a conceptualisation of crimes against humanity in precisely these terms, illustrating how understanding criminal law as acting on behalf of a public interest calls into being a corresponding polity to act as its referent. Graf departs from the position that the public nature of criminal law is politically productive because of how it in this way addresses 'society in its entirety and [...] endow[s] an authority with the power to speak justice in the name of this political community'.[42] On this view, by prosecuting a wrongdoer because they have violated the values that are understood to define a particular political community, the criminal law and its enforcement also implicitly invokes the existence of that political community[43] and therefore, in the same way, the values that are understood to define it. This act of invocation can be

38 Mégret (n 24), 292.

39 *Ibid.*, 290.

40 *Ibid.*, 291.

41 Nikolas M. Rajkovic, 'What is a "grave" international crime? The Rome Statute, Durkheim and the sociology of ruling outrages', (2020) 16(1) *Loyola University Chicago International Law Review*, 85.

42 Sinja Graf, 'To Regain Some Kind of Human Equality: Theorizing the Political Productivity of "Crimes Against Humanity"', (2019) 15(3) *Law, Culture and the Humanities*, 757.

43 *Ibid.*, 758.

understood as politically productive because 'invoking is an act of creation; by calling on a community, that community is, at least partly, constructed.'[44]

Bringing together the nature of international criminal law as unmoored from a clearly defined political community with her analysis of political community as nevertheless the inherent referent of the 'public' nature of criminal wrongs, Sinja Graf therefore argues that 'if we take seriously the connection between criminal law and community "as a whole," the pronouncement of crimes against humanity by legal authorities involves the claim to humanity as a global political community.'[45] Graf's analysis in this way highlights how, while this invocation of humanity does not refer to any empirically identifiable 'global political community', the category of crimes against humanity nonetheless functions, in Durkheimian fashion, as a 'performative claim that calls into existence a global political community by positing an injury to it via the term "crimes against humanity."'[46]

Returning, then, to the question of the normative dimensions of the individual acts criminalised as international crimes, Graf's analysis of crimes against humanity offers two important insights. First, it reveals how the criminalisation of the individual acts that make up the wider categories of international crimes may also be understood to function in a politically productive manner, in terms of how the nature of crimes as 'public' wrongs that violate the defining values of a polity inherently invokes not only the existence of a political community as the referent of criminal law, but also, at a more granular level, the existence therefore of those values that are understood to define that community. In this way, the nature of the individual criminal wrongs that constitute international crimes, in their character as 'public' wrongs, similarly therefore conjure the existence of values that are 'so central to a community's identity and self-understanding, to its conceptions of its members' good, that actions which attack or flout these values are [...] attacks on the community.'[47]

Second, Graf's account in this way reinforces the value of the shift in perspective offered by thinking backwards, i.e. thinking constitutively, about the normative dimensions of international criminal acts, rather than approaching

---

44 Sofia Stolk, *The Opening Statement of the Prosecution in International Criminal Trials: A Solemn Tale of Horror* (Routledge 2021), 9. See also Luigi D.A. Corrias and Geoffrey M. Gordon, 'Judging in the Name of Humanity: International Criminal Tribunals and the Representation of a Global Public', (2015) 13 *Journal of International Criminal Justice*, 97–112.

45 Graf (n 42), 759.

46 *Ibid.*, 760.

47 Marshall and Duff (n 36), 21–22.

them from the explanatory or justificatory perspectives offered by traditional criminal law theory, with their concern with the 'underlying principles'[48] that explain the criminalisation of particular acts or the 'real underlying rationale for an offence.'[49] The particular relevance of this shift in perspective in the context of international criminal law can be further illustrated by considering the nature of domestic theories of criminalisation and how they function in the domestic context.

1.3 *Domestic Theories of Criminalisation: Form without International Content*

In broad terms, the two basic theories of criminalisation at the domestic level are the Anglo-American harm principle and the continental law concept of the protection of legal goods (*Rechtsgüter*). These theories have been developed to address the legitimate scope of criminalisation and therefore the limits on the state's power to criminalise conduct.[50] Both the harm principle and the theory of legal goods are in this way conceptually embedded within the framework of the state. This has implications for how their normative contents are determined.

In general terms, the theory of legal goods understands criminalisation as justified by the 'violation of or threat to a good, which the state is to guarantee equally to everyone and which is attributable to the human will.'[51] While approaches to identifying legal goods vary, in order to function as a tool for assessing the legitimacy of particular criminal offences, approaches to legal goods that go beyond a descriptive account of the legally protected interests reflected in existing criminal offences require an independent normative existence against which the criminal law can be evaluated.[52] Where to locate the independent values that provide the normative content of the concept of legal

48 David Luban, 'A Theory of Crimes Against Humanity', (2004) 29(1) *Yale Journal of International Law*, 101.

49 Kai Ambos, 'The Overall Function of International Criminal Law: Striking the Right Balance Between the Rechtsgut and the Harm Principles', (2015) 9(2) *Criminal Law and Philosophy*, 323.

50 For an overview see Nina Peršak, *Criminalising Harmful Conduct: The Harm Principle, its Limits and Continental Counterparts* (Springer 2007).

51 Johann Michael Franz Birnbaum as cited in Peršak (n 50), 107.

52 Carl Constanin Lauterwein, *The Limits of Criminal Law: A Comparative Analysis of Approaches to Legal Theorizing* (Routledge 2010), 9. See for instance Bernd Schünemann, 'The System of Criminal Wrongs: The Concept of Legal Goods and Victim-based Jurisprudence as a Bridge between the General and Special Parts of the Criminal Code', (2004) 7(2) *Buffalo Criminal Law Review*, 553; see also Peršak (n 50), 107.

goods is nevertheless contested. Some conceptions of legal goods identify the content of the goods to be protected outside of the framework of the criminal law yet remaining with the broader system of positive law. For instance, Claus Roxin argues that in order for the concept of legal goods to function as a constraint on the state's power to criminalise conduct, its content must be found in constitutional principles.[53] Other approaches derive the content of legal goods from the concept of rights, frequently constitutional rights.[54] In attempting to give autonomous substance to the concept of legal goods, these approaches in this way refer for the substance of the legal goods protected through criminal law to the contents of other areas of a state's legal framework.[55]

A further variation on the evaluative conception of legal goods locates their contents outside of the legal system. This conception of legal goods makes appeals to ethical or value-based foundations to provide the contents of the legal goods to be protected by criminal offences. These types of approaches place more emphasis on the normative nature of the concept of legal goods, as opposed to its legal nature.[56] In terms of substantive content, these conceptions of legal goods have typically referred back to liberal theories of social contract, defining legal goods along the lines of the 'conditions or chosen ends, which are useful either to the individual and his free development within the context of an overall social system based on this objective, or to the function of this system itself.'[57]

Beyond the broad contractualist criteria of legal goods as those preconditions fundamental for social life and individual development, this conception provides limited guidance as to what these preconditions can be considered to be, and therefore of which legal goods ultimately warrant protection.[58] In this way, a theory of legal goods does not ultimately provide 'substantive (normative) criteria to decide which goods or interests should be protected by criminal law and which should not.'[59] Rather, the theory of legal goods provides the

53 Claus Roxin, *Strafrecht Allgemeiner Teil Band I: Grundlagen. Der Aufbau der Verbrechenslehre* (Beck 1997), 15.

54 Otto Lagodny, 'The Case of Substantial Criminal Law before the Bars of Constitutional Law – An Overview from the Perspective of the German Legal Order', (1999) 7(3) *European Journal of Crime, Criminal Law and Criminal Justice*, 283.

55 Peršak (n 50), 108.

56 *Ibid.*, 110–111.

57 Claus Roxin as cited in Markus Dirk Dubber, 'Theories of Crime and Punishment in German Criminal Law', (2005) 53(3) *American Journal of Comparative Law*, 685.

58 Santiago Mir Puig, 'Legal Goods Protected by the Law and Legal Goods Protected by the Criminal Law as Limits to the State's Power to Criminalize Conduct', (2008) 11(3) *New Criminal Law Review: An International and Interdisciplinary Journal*, 414.

59 Ambos (n 49), 306.

conceptual framework through which the pre-determined values, understood to provide the preconditions for coexistence in a given society, are then protected through criminalisation.[60] In this way, in both its positivist and more normative forms, the theory of legal goods relies on its embeddedness within the legal or other normative structure of a state or defined political community for its substantive content.

In a similar manner, the harm principle, which provides the principal justification for criminalisation in Anglo-American legal systems, is intended to function as a check on the scope of the state's power to criminalise conduct. The harm principle originates in the liberal political theory of John Stuart Mill, who argued that state intervention with the autonomy of individuals requires strict justification:

> That principle, that the sole end for which mankind is warranted, individually or collectively, in interfering with the liberty of action of any of their number, is self-protection. That the only purpose for which power can rightfully be exercised over any member of a civilized community, against his will, is to prevent harm to others.[61]

In broad terms, the harm principle is therefore a more consequentialist theory of criminalisation than the theory of legal goods, requiring that 'conduct should be criminalized only if it is harmful.'[62] While inherently rooted in liberal theory, in relying on a more naturalistic or tangible understanding of the effects of the conduct to be criminalised, the harm principle is less obviously dependent on an external legal or normative framework to supply its substantive content than the theory of legal goods. At the same time, the harm principle has been subject to similar critiques to that of the theory of legal goods for failing to provide an evaluative limit on the scope of criminal liability. In this respect, some scholars have argued that the harm principle is insufficiently limiting because 'nearly any result that anyone has ever wanted to prevent could be construed as harmful.'[63]

---

60 *Ibid.*

61 John Stuart Mill, 'On Liberty' in Joel Feinberg and Jules Coleman (eds), *Philosophy of Law* (Thomson Wadsworth 2008), 251.

62 Hamish Stewart, 'The Limits of the Harm Principle', (2010) 4(1) *Criminal Law and Philosophy*, 18.

63 Douglas Husak, *Overcriminalization: The Limits of the Criminal Law* (Oxford University Press 2008), 71.

The most influential account of the harm principle has been advanced by Joel Feinberg who, in seeking to develop this limiting function, defined harm as a 'thwarting, setting back, or defeating of an interest' through wrongful conduct.[64] In this respect, Feinberg offered an account of harm as being a necessary, but not a sufficient condition for criminalisation, rejecting the notion that the harm principle can be understood in simple, determinate, or empirical terms.[65] Instead, he argued that:

> harm is a very complex concept with hidden normative dimensions, and that partly because of this, the harm principle cannot be applied in a plausible way in large ranges of circumstance without supplementary criteria (or 'mediating maxims'), some of which are provided by independent moral principles.[66]

The necessity of appealing to independent moral principles to develop a functional notion of harm is in this way revealing of how, similar to the notion of legal goods, some of the normative substance of the harm principle must be derived extrinsically. For instance, in his discussion of the relative importance of different harms for the purpose of determining the scope of criminalisation, Feinberg identifies three relevant characteristics for weighing the importance of different harms. One of the characteristics he identifies is the 'inherent moral quality' of the interest that is set back through wrongful conduct.[67]

Highlighting how Feinberg's definition of harm as the setting back of an interest relies in this way on an understanding of certain 'inherent moral qualities' to that interest, Bernard Harcourt has raised the question of what those inherent qualities can be considered to be, arguing that the harm principle itself cannot provide an answer to this question.[68] In this respect, Harcourt argues that 'we inevitably must look beyond the harm principle. [...] We must access larger debates in ethics, law and politics – debates about power, autonomy, identity, human flourishing, equality, freedom and other interests and values that give meaning to the claim that an identifiable harm matters.'[69] For

64 Joel Feinberg, *Harm to Others* (Oxford University Press 1984), 33.

65 *Ibid.*, 214.

66 *Ibid.*

67 Joel Feinberg, *The Moral Limits of the Criminal Law: Harm to Others* (Oxford University Press 1984), 217.

68 Bernard Harcourt, 'The Collapse of the Harm Principle', (1999) 90 *Journal of Criminal Law and Criminology*, 183.

69 *Ibid.*

this reason, and in a similar manner to scholarly debates on the contents of legal goods, critics have stressed the 'essential indeterminacy of the concept of harm, and its potential to be under or overinclusive',[70] with the result that the literature on the harm principle also reflects 'an intense struggle for the meaning of harm.'[71] This ultimately leads back to the sociological reality that the harm principle necessarily also relies on some kind of social agreement about what constitutes harm in order to construct a system of criminal law on this basis.[72]

Taken together, the theory of legal goods and the harm principle in this way illustrate how domestic theories of criminalisation inherently and necessarily require an external normative structure from which to derive their substance, whether through reliance on the legal framework within or the political theory of a state to supply them with normative content, or through the simple fact that criminal law necessarily emerges from and therefore embodies in legal form a socially situated conception of harm in a given societal context. As Nina Peršak explains; 'every type of criminalisation requires an underlying public moral theory, since it is connected to the values and morality of society.'[73] In this sense, as theories developed in the domestic context to determine the legitimate scope of the state's power to criminalise conduct, extracting the harm principle or the theory of legal goods from the structure of the state or a coherent social framework that gives them their substance arguably leaves them empty of normative content.

This illustrates, therefore, the particular relevance of adopting a constitutive approach to the normative dimensions of the individual acts criminalised as international crimes. Precisely in the way that the invocation of political community through criminal law has particular potency at the international level because it performatively calls into being the existence of an international political community, so the invocation of particular acts as crimes conjures the existence of particular normative principles that attach to them, however these are understood, where there is no clearly defined external social or legal referent to supply their normative content.

In other words, to return to the discussion of the politically productive character of criminal law, the nature of international crimes as public wrongs not

70 Farmer (n 37), 215.

71 Harcourt (n 68), 129.

72 Ed Gibney and Tanya Wyatt, 'Rebuilding the Harm Principle: Using an Evolutionary Perspective to Provide a New Foundation for Justice', (2020) 9(3) *International Journal for Crime, Justice and Social Democracy*, 102.

73 Peršak (n 50), 1.

only invokes the existence of an international community or society as a referent of the 'public' nature of the wrong, it also calls into existence those norms or values that are so central to the identity and self-understanding of that society that they constitute public wrongs in this way, and therefore warrant criminal protection. This shift in perspective from the domestic criminal law theory approach of seeking to identify substantive principles that provide the legitimate parameters of the state's power to criminalise illuminates the relevance of examining instead how the acts criminalised under international criminal law, in the absence of such an extrinsic framework to supply their normative content, are in this way politically productive and constitutive of the norms or values that they invoke through their criminalisation and prosecution.

2 International Criminal Law as Discursive Project

This ultimately leads to matters of practice and representation. In order to examine the nature of the norms, principles or values that are in this way constituted through the international criminalisation and prosecution of particular acts of violence, it is necessary to pay attention to how this process of constitution takes place. As noted previously, a limitation of Durkheim's conception of the relationship between criminal law and society is its static, structural conception of the collective consciousness, which is treated as an inherent, apolitical and ahistorical property of a homologous society, with the result that the Durkheimian conception of criminal law is 'blind to how moral orders are established temporally and spatially rather than just given'.[74] This critique of Durkheimian theory is evidently particularly relevant in the context of international criminal law, as a product of and operating as it does within an unequal and Western-dominated international order.[75] As one way of addressing this shortcoming, Frédéric Mégret has emphasised the importance of supplementing a Durkheimian conception of international criminal law with attention to its practices. Highlighting how Durkheim's static conception of the collective consciousness evades the issue of 'the power that lies behind

74 Rajkovic (n 41), 74–75.

75 See for instance Antony Anghie and B.S. Chimni, 'Third World Approaches to International Law and Individual Responsibility in Internal Conflicts', (2003) 2(1) *Chinese Journal of International Law*, 77–103; Wolfgang Kaleck, *Double Standards: International Criminal Law and the West* (Torkel Opsahl Academic EPublisher 2015); Asad G. Kiyani, 'International Crime and the Politics of Criminal Theory: Voices and Conduct of Exclusion', (2015) 48(1) *New York University Journal of International Law and Politics*, 129–208.

and constitutes the criminal-justice system, often treating it as one that has a sort of abstract will of its own, with the "collective consciousness" as the linchpin of a quasi-religious system',[76] Mégret underscores the necessity of examining the practices of the actual actors and institutions of international criminal justice in shaping and producing those norms or values that are understood to emanate from the 'collective consciousness'.

This view also ties in with some of the sociologically-oriented scholarship on international courts as social actors,[77] which highlights how 'courts often perform broader functions than just applying general norms or creating individual norms: courts also present general images of community goals, identities, principles, ways of life, etc.'[78] In this respect, the sociological recognition that 'only individuals – not institutions and laws – have intentions'[79] centralises the practices of the actors involved in the international criminal process in shaping these broader functions. On this view, the practices of these actors 'become key to understanding the development of these [...] institutions and laws.'[80]

While Mégret outlines a number of perspectives from which the role of practice can in this way be incorporated into a constitutive understanding of the relationship between international criminal law and society, Nesam McMillan has highlighted in particular the centrality of discourse and representation for understanding how international criminal law concretely functions as a process of 'socio-legal construction, with powerful effects.'[81] She explains that:

---

76 Mégret (n 24), 293.

77 See for example Mikael Rask Madsen, 'The Sociology of International Law: An Introduction' in Richard Nobles and David Schiff (eds), *Law Society and Community: Socio-Legal Essays in Honour of Roger Cotterell* (Routledge 2014), 241–253; Mikkel Jarle Christensen, 'The emerging sociology of international criminal courts: Between global restructurings and scientific innovations', (2015) 63(6) *Current Sociology*, 825–849; Vera Willems, 'International Courts and Tribunals and Their Linguistic Practices: A Communities of Practice Approach', (2017) 30 *International Journal for the Semiotics of Law*, 181–199; Nicole De Silva, 'International Courts' Socialization Strategies for Actual and Perceived Performance' in Theresa Squatrito et al. (eds), *The Performance of International Courts and Tribunals* (Cambridge University Press 2018), 288–321; Kjersti Lohne, 'Towards a Sociology of International Criminal Justice' in Morten Bergsmo et al. (eds), *Power in International Criminal Justice* (Torkel Opsahl Academic EPublisher 2020), 47–78; Moshe Hirsch, 'Introduction: Sociological Perspectives on International Tribunals', (2020) 34(2) *Temple International & Comparative Law Journal*, 193–201.

78 Wouter G. Werner, 'Speech Act Theory and the Concept of Sovereignty: A Critique of the Descriptivistic and the Normativistic Fallacy', (2001) 14 *The Hague Yearbook of International Law*, 73–84.

79 Lohne (n 77), 54.

80 *Ibid.*

81 McMillan (n 1), 125.

> [I]deas of international crime and justice are vivid and emotive as well as productive, figuring and enacting the spaces and subjectivities of which they speak. These discourses and representations of internationalized crime and justice are thus ethically significant, as they do not simply reflect the consolidation or existence of an already existing global community or common humanity with established norms and values. Rather, it is in and through representations and discourses of international criminal justice that such global subjectivities and modes of global responsibility and interconnection are productively imagined.[82]

Understanding international criminal justice in this way as a 'process of meaning making',[83] McMillan emphasises the importance of examining how notions of crime and justice are 'given content in practice.'[84] In general terms, the notion of 'meaning' can be understood to refer to 'the contested social and cultural processes by which situations are defined, individuals and groups are categorized, and human consequences are understood. [...] an ongoing, everyday process of sense-making, symbolic communication, and contested understanding.'[85] Meaning making can be understood in these terms as a foundational process in human culture through which situations and actions are categorised and defined by drawing patterns of relations on the basis of which people decide how to interpret and respond to different situations.[86] The practices of international criminal justice in this sense function as processes of discursive meaning making in how they contribute to structuring processes of categorisation which 'give meaning, sense and order to the world thus influencing how phenomena are experienced as reality.'[87]

---

82 *Ibid.*, 22.

83 *Ibid.*, 11.

84 *Ibid.*, 5.

85 Jeff Ferrell, 'Cultural Criminology and the Politics of Meaning', (2013) 21(3) *Critical Criminology*, 258.

86 Jay L. Lemke, *Textual Politics: Discourse and Social Dynamics* (Taylor and Francis 2005), 141–142; Reiner Keller and Adele E. Clarke, 'Situating SKAD in interpretive inquiry' in Reiner Keller, Anna-Katharina Hornidge and Wolf J. Schünemann (eds), *The Sociology of Knowledge Approach to Discourse Investigating the Politics of Knowledge and Meaning-making* (Routledge 2018), 48.

87 Hella von Unger, Penelope Scott and Dennis Odukoya, 'Using SKAD to analyse classification practices in public health: methodological reflections on the research process' in Reiner Keller, Anna-Katharina Hornidge and Wolf J. Schünemann (eds), *The Sociology of Knowledge Approach to Discourse Investigating the Politics of Knowledge and Meaning-making* (Routledge 2018), 172.

From this perspective, examining the normative dimensions of the acts that constitute international crimes requires attention not only to the normative environment from which they emerged and to what their legal definitions invoke, but also to the meanings generated by the discourses that are constructed around them through the practices of trial and punishment. Sociological approaches to international criminal justice have in this respect demonstrated how 'international criminal justice is 'brought into being' by analysing the 'products' of courts, such as documents, discourses, and other legal artefacts as empirical data rather than as legal statements.'[88] This brings to the fore the significance of the discourses and language that emerge through judicial practices as a central dimension of the 'process of meaning making'[89] involved in constituting the normative dimensions of the individual acts criminalised as international crimes. As Immi Tallgren has argued, international criminal law 'is a universe constructed in language, not predetermined by some necessary, natural order.'[90] Frédéric Mégret has similarly explained that 'the practices of international criminal justice are, fundamentally, logorrheic and hortatory, and involve the constant attempt to characterize situations and persons through the appropriate use of words.'[91]

This dimension of international criminal justice features centrally in expressivist approaches to international criminal law, which focus on the socially communicative features of law from a number of disciplinary and normative perspectives. Expressive theories of law can further enrich an understanding of international criminal justice as a process of meaning making in how they centralise in particular the performative, rhetorical and discursive features of law and the process of trial and punishment.

2.1 *Expressive Theories of International Criminal Law*

Theories of expressivism capture a number of ideas that have their roots in different disciplinary and normative perspectives. In general terms, expressive theories locate the value of law in its ability to convey social meaning, in addition to its ability to control behaviour directly.[92] Such theories are based on the fundamental assumption that 'actions are expressive; they carry meanings.'[93]

88 Lohne (n 77), 64.
89 McMillan (n 1), 11.
90 Tallgren (n 26), 138.
91 Mégret (n 24), 300.
92 Cass R Sunstein, 'On the Expressive Function of Law', (1996) 144 *University of Pennsylvania Law Review*, 2024.
93 *Ibid.*, 2021.

Reflecting its sociological foundations in Durkheimian sociology, from an expressivist perspective law is understood to carry meaning in that it reflects and communicates the norms and values of the society in which it exists.[94] Expressive theories of law vary in the way that they conceptualise the expressive function. The dominant approach has focussed on the concrete sociological effect of law on social norms.[95] These types of expressive theories focus on questions relating to the circumstances in which law is likely to produce social effects, such as issues relating to the law's perceived legitimacy as a factor in contributing to its ability to motivate behaviour, or consider how law can be employed as a tool for actively seeking to change values or morals among the public.[96]

Expressive theories of law have enjoyed particular prominence in the field of criminal law. Drawing on Durkheim's sociological conception of the relationship between criminal law and society, theories of criminal law that centralise its communicative or expressive function focus on its capacity to articulate societal censure for behaviour that violates a society's norms. Often identified as central to the communicative capacity of criminal law is the social function of punishment, whose purpose is not only to impose hardship on the criminal because this is what they deserve, or in order to deter future crimes, but serves as a 'device for the expression of attitudes of resentment and indignation, and of judgments of disapproval and reprobation, on the part either of the punishing authority himself or of those 'in whose name' the punishment is inflicted. Punishment, in short, has a symbolic significance largely missing from other kinds of penalties.'[97] This symbolic significance to punishment has been conceptualised from a variety of perspectives. Some approaches have centralised the messages sent to different actors within the criminal process, with, for instance, the perpetrator or victims of crimes understood as the primary targets of expressive messaging, while others have focused instead on the norm-affirming role of the message sent by punishment to the wider public.[98] Understood in these terms, the target audience of punishment at the international level includes 'not only the current and potential perpetrators

94 Carsten Stahn, *Justice As Message: Expressivist Foundations of International Criminal Justice* (Oxford University Press 2020), 26.

95 Sunstein (n 92), 2025–2026.

96 Richard McAdams, *The Expressive Powers of Law: Theories and Limits*, (Harvard University Press 2015), 3–4.

97 Joel Feinberg, 'The Expressive Function of Punishment' in Joel Feinberg (ed), *Doing and Deserving: Essays in the Theory of Responsibility* (Princeton University Press 1970), 98.

98 Stahn (n 94), 19.

of international crimes and the current and potential victims of international crimes, but any other person in the world community.'[99]

Expressive theories of and justifications for criminalisation and punishment have found particularly fertile ground in the field of international criminal justice.[100] Barrie Sander has identified an 'expressive turn'[101] in the scholarship on international criminal law, arising partly in response to the perceived failings of more common retributive and deterrence-based justifications for criminal law at an international level, while at the same time responding to some of the unique features of international criminal justice, which are understood as being particularly well-suited to expressive justification.[102] In this respect, the international stature and purported global audience of international criminal trials have been seen to lend them particular expressive value; international trials have been described as having 'a better chance of becoming the kinds of 'popular trials' that define a debate, remind us of the content and value of law, or serve as intergenerational 'signposts' in history.'[103]

---

99 *Ibid.*, 180.

100 See for instance Diane Marie Amann, 'Group Mentality, Expressivism, and Genocide', (2002) 2(2) *International Criminal Law Review*, 93–143; Mark Drumbl, *Atrocity, Punishment and International Law* (Cambridge University Press 2007); Robert D Sloane, 'The Expressive Capacity of International Punishment: The Limits of the National Law Analogy and the Potential of International Criminal Law', (2007) 43(1) *Stanford Journal of International Law*, 39–94; Margaret deGuzman, 'An Expressive Rationale for the Thematic Prosecution of Sex Crimes' in Morten Bergsmo (ed), *Thematic Prosecution of International Sex Crimes* (Torkel Opsahl Academic EPublisher 2012), 13–44; Margaret deGuzman, 'Choosing to Prosecute: Expressive Selection at the International Criminal Court', (2012) 33(2) *Michigan Journal of International Law*, 265–320; Maria Elander, 'The Victim's Address: Expressivism and the Victim at the Extraordinary Chambers in the Courts of Cambodia', (2013) 7 *International Journal of Transitional Justice*, 95–115; Saira Mohamed, 'Deviance, Aspiration and the Stories We Tell: Reconciling Mass Atrocity and the Criminal Law', (2015) 124(5) *Yale Law Journal*, 1628–1689; Tim Meijers and Marlies Glasius, 'Trials as Messages of Justice: What Should Be Expected of the International Criminal Court?', (2016) 30(4) *Ethics and International Affairs*, 429–447; Barrie Sander, 'The Expressive Limits of International Criminal Justice: Victim Trauma and Local Culture in the Iron Cage of the Law', (2019) 19(6) *International Criminal Law Review*, 1014–1045; Barrie Sander, 'The expressive turn of international criminal justice: A field in search of meaning', (2019) 32 *Leiden Journal of International Law*, 851–872; Stahn (n 96).

101 Sander 'The expressive turn' (n 100), 852.

102 Amann (n 100), 115–116; Drumbl (n 100), 61; Mark Drumbl, 'The Expressive Value of Prosecuting and Punishing Terrorists: Hamdan, the Geneva Conventions, and International Criminal Law', (2007) 75(5–6) *George Washington Law Review*, 1195; David Luban, 'Fairness to Rightness: Jurisdiction, Legality, and the Legitimacy of International Criminal Law' in Samantha Besson and John Tasioulas (eds), *The Philosophy of International Law* (Oxford University Press 2010); deGuzman (n 100), 33–34.

103 Drumbl (n 100), 175.

While early expressive approaches to international criminal law focussed on the social function of the institution of punishment, the scholarship in this area has developed to reflect a wider concern with 'the symbolic and aesthetic meanings generated by the broader range of social practices that comprise and surround international criminal proceedings.'[104] For instance, a study of the language employed in judgments at international criminal tribunals has revealed how judges often seek to move beyond simply making legal determinations, to reach out past the legal community and address broader audiences in moral or philosophical terms, reflecting their understanding of their role 'in the larger scope of the international judicial community and international relations.'[105]

Similarly, the performative dimensions of international criminal trials have been identified as contributing to their communicative function; trials are seen to be able to 'educate the public through the spectacle of theatre – there is, after all, pedagogical value to performance and communicative value to dramaturgy.'[106] The legal process itself, with the presentation of evidence by prosecution and defence, and its adjudication by a judge, is further seen to establish the facts of a crime as incontrovertible. By doing so, the legal process is understood to support a process of truth-telling, narrating history, and developing shared understandings of the origin and consequences of collective violence.[107] In these ways, the expressive functions of trials are seen to contribute to a much broader didactic process, which goes beyond the adjudication of guilt to address history and memory.[108] In general terms, then, expressive approaches to international criminal justice centralise its perceived ability to communicate, 'to share and declare – an ideal and aspiration'[109] and conceive of trial and punishment 'primarily as a normative, didactic endeavour.'[110]

Various limitations to and critiques of expressive theories of and justifications for international criminal justice have nevertheless been identified. In normative terms, critics have for instance highlighted how wider norm-expression oriented justifications for punishment run the risk of instrumentalising the

104 Sander 'The expressive turn' (n 100), 852.

105 Rosa Aloisi and James Meernik, *Judgment Day: Judicial Decision Making at the International Criminal Tribunals* (Cambridge University Press 2017), 198.

106 Drumbl (n 100), 175.

107 Drumbl (n 100), 174–175.

108 Lawrence Douglas, *The Memory of Judgment* (Yale University Press 2001).

109 Anette Bringedal Houge, 'Narrative expressivism: A criminological approach to the expressive function of international criminal justice', (2019) 19(3) *Criminology and Criminal Justice*, 281.

110 *Ibid.*

defendant by 'using the accused as an object in a didactic exercise rather than respecting autonomy and fairness.'[111] Similarly, the expressive function of punishment has been problematised for how it serves and empowers primarily the speaker or communicator, raising questions as to the legitimacy and validity of the perspective that is being expressed as universal by international criminal justice.[112]

From a more empirical perspective, the assumption that trials are necessarily articulating coherent and unified messages, rather than varied and conflicting narratives advanced by different parties to proceedings, has also been problematised,[113] while the complexity of conceptualising who the 'audiences' of international criminal trials may be and whether they are receptive to the messages that trials articulate has also been highlighted.[114] Similarly, limited empirical evidence exists to support the notion that anything resembling communication, in the sense of an audience or recipient who is 'an active participant in the process [and] will receive and respond to the communication',[115] is taking place between international criminal institutions and their purported audiences.[116] The wider truth and history-telling role of international criminal courts and tribunals has similarly been problematised in terms of how the legal process structures and shapes the nature of the truth that is constructed, which 'streamlines causality, draws individuals out of collectives and categorizes both them, the acts, victims and contexts.'[117]

Within this body of more critical scholarship on expressivism in the context of international criminal law, Barrie Sander has identified a strand that is concerned in particular with 'the illumination of the expressive limits of international criminal courts [in terms of] the configurations of power that underpin the messages and narratives constructed within such courts in different institutional contexts.'[118] These more critical approaches to the idea of an expressive function to international criminal law not only question the

111 Darryl Robinson, 'The Identity Crisis of International Criminal Law', (2008) 21 *Leiden Journal of International Law*, 931. See also Stahn (n 94), 81–82.

112 Stahn (n 94), 78–80.

113 Marlies Glasius, 'It Sends a Message': Liberian Opinion Leaders' Responses to the Trial of Charles Taylor', (2015) 13(3) *Journal of International Criminal Justice*, 423.

114 Meijers and Glasius (n 100), 433, 443; Glasius (n 113), 423.

115 Antony Duff, *Punishment, Communication and Community* (Oxford University Press 2003), 79.

116 See for instance Glasius (n 113), 419–447.

117 Houge (n 109), 283. See also Barrie Sander, *Doing Justice to History: Confronting the Past in International Criminal Courts* (Oxford University Press 2021).

118 Sander 'The expressive turn' (n 100), 853.

normative desirability of justifying punishment in these terms or the limits of expressivism in empirical terms, but also engage more fundamentally with the productive power of international criminal justice and the 'dynamics of power that underpin the messages and narratives that are constructed within such courts in practice.'[119]

Of particular relevance from the perspective of examining how practices of international criminal justice construct the normative meaning of the individual acts criminalised as international crimes is Anette Bringedal Houge's theorisation of a narrative approach to expressivism. Houge conceives of expressivism not in normative terms, as a justification for international criminal justice, but rather from the perspective of knowledge production – in terms of how international criminal legal processes contribute to the juridification of extra-legal knowledge in a way that feeds into and shapes wider societal understandings of violence.[120] Broadening the focus of expressive approaches to international criminal law from the concern with the communicative function of punishment, Houge instead centralises the narrative dimensions of international criminal law and criminal proceedings to capture 'all the acts and perspectives of the different actors that get voiced throughout proceedings on the international stage that the court provides.'[121]

In this respect, she understands legal decisions as well as the arguments of the different parties to proceedings, the testimonies of witnesses and the statements of defendants as narratives that form part of a discursive battle over how crimes are explained, understood and responded to.[122] From this perspective, Houge highlights how legal processes and decisions do not construct an objective or complete account of the events and acts to which they are applied, but instead offer a narrative that is necessarily filtered through the constraints and possibilities of the legal framework.[123] Criminal proceedings and the practices that surround them are in this sense understood as 'a process of inclusion and exclusion of different voices and […] the leveraging and silencing of some stories over others.'[124] Houge's approach in this way shifts the focus of legal expressivism from punishment towards stories, processes and description, to reveal how international criminal legal frameworks and processes function to promote 'a particular structuring of thought'[125] in relation to the violence

119 *Ibid.*, 863–864.
120 Houge (n 109), 288.
121 *Ibid.*, 282.
122 *Ibid.*
123 *Ibid.*, 283.
124 *Ibid.*
125 *Ibid.*, 277.

to which they are applied. Taken as a whole, then, Houge describes a narrative expressivist approach to international criminal justice as one that:

> emphasizes its *stories*, not its truths, its *understandings*, not its punishments, its descriptions and explanations, not its normative evaluation and judgment. That is, [narrative expressivism] looks at how laws generate and enable, constrain and silence, knowledge about complex collective violence.[126]

Importantly, Houge emphasises how in this way international legal frameworks and processes operate as a form of discursive power, in how they produce juridified understandings of the events to which they are applied, which, in turn, feed into and shape wider social and political discourses.[127] This dimension of international criminal justice has similarly been described by others as having representational power because of how it can 'affect collective representations and memories [...] and thereby [...] impress on a global public a particular understanding of mass violence as a form of criminal violence.'[128] As noted by Nesam McMillan, international criminal legal frameworks and processes in this way 'produce meaning themselves, shaping which events of harm come to external attention, which are seen to be important, and who and what they are seen to affect and implicate.'[129] Houge's conception of narrative expressivism in this way identifies the narrative functions of international criminal legal frameworks and processes as a central dimension of how they function as 'knowledge producers beyond the development of legal doctrine.'[130]

2.2 *Law as Discourse and Narrative*

In highlighting the discursive power of the narratives constructed by international criminal justice in this way, Houge's approach draws on a theoretical understanding of law as a discourse as well as on scholarship on the relationship between language, narrative and law. With its roots in social constructivism, the fundamental theoretical assumption that is central to a conception of law as a discourse is that language, or any system of meaning, does not simply

126 *Ibid.*, 284. Emphasis in the original.
127 *Ibid.*, 285.
128 Joachim J. Savelsberg, 'The Representational Power of International Criminal Courts' in Morten Bergsmo et al. (eds), *Power in International Criminal Justice* (Torkel Opsahl Academic EPublisher 2020), 287.
129 McMillan (n 1), 14.
130 Houge (n 109), 285.

reflect the world as it is, but functions to constitute social life. In this sense, discourses 'build objects, worlds, minds and social relations. It doesn't just reflect them.'[131] As some discourses gain prominence and become increasingly widely shared, they become in this way a part of social reality.[132] In its more post-structuralist form, discourse is therefore understood to be intrinsically linked to questions of power in the social world.[133] By constructing reality in a certain way, a discourse does not 'simply represent the world but signifies, constitutes and constructs social identities, (power) relations between people and systems of knowledge.'[134]

While this understanding of discourse is not limited to the role of language in the constitution of social reality, but is intended to capture a wider range of social practices, language nevertheless plays a central role in understanding how discourses define and produce objects of knowledge in how it governs how 'a topic can be meaningfully talked about and reasoned about. [It] 'rules in' certain ways of talking about a topic, defining an acceptable and intelligible way to talk, write, or conduct oneself [and] 'rules out', limits and restricts other ways of talking, of conducting ourselves in relation to the topic or constructing knowledge about it.'[135]

As a linguistic and symbolic discourse that determines how particular forms of violence can be named and imagined, international criminal law can in this sense be understood as 'a perfect reflection of discursive power floating within society while constructing particular subjects and identities, and shaping the very society it claims to act on behalf of.'[136] From this perspective, the discursive practices of international criminal legal proceedings in relation to the acts of violence criminalised as international crimes function as a site in which the normative meaning of these crimes and the acts of violence to which they are applied, are actually produced. Examining the normative dimensions of these criminal acts from a discursive perspective does not, for this reason, require

131 Margaret Wetherell, 'Themes in Discourse Research: The Case of Diana' in Margaret Wetherell et al. (eds), *Discourse Theory and Practice: A Reader* (Sage Publications 2002), 16.

132 *Ibid.*

133 Adele E. Clarke, *Situational Analysis: Grounded Theory After the Postmodern Turn* (SAGE Publications 2005), 149.

134 Johanna Niemi-Kiesiläinen, Päivi Honkatukia and Minna Ruuskanen, 'Legal Texts as Discourses' in Åsa Gunnarsson, Eva-Maria Svensson (eds), *Exploiting the Limits of Law: Swedish Feminism and the Challenge to Pessimism* (Routledge 2007), 82.

135 Stuart Hall, 'The Work of Representation' in Stuart Hall (ed), *Representation: Cultural Representations and Signifying Practices* (SAGE Publications 2003), 44.

136 Gözde Turan, 'Responsibility to prosecute' in an age of global governmentality: The international criminal court', (2016) 51 *Cooperation and Conflict*, 21.

consideration of the truth or falsity of the discourse or narrative constructed around the events in question. Instead, of primary importance is 'the process of construction itself, how 'truths' emerge, how social realities and identities are built and the consequences of these.'[137]

In this respect, Houge's conception of narrative expressivism brings to the fore how narrative plays a central role in this process of construction. Narrative has increasingly come to be understood as 'a basic part of legal discourse and legal interpretation'[138] which 'pervade[s] all law and, in a sense, constitute[s] law.'[139] In the context of international law, Anne Saab has highlighted the centrality of narrative and storytelling for an understanding of the work that international law does in the world, arguing that 'law, including international law, is not only a set of rules and principles, but also a way of engaging with and perceiving the world – that is, a force in telling stories and constituting the reality to which it subsequently responds.'[140]

Houge defines narrative broadly as 'a story that orders experience, renders experience meaningful or tentatively explains acts and events, always for a particular audience.'[141] As a particular representation of reality, a particular telling or ordering of acts and events, narratives are understood as central to the social construction of reality; 'rather than referring to "reality," [narratives] may in fact create or constitute it, as when "fiction" creates a "world" of its own.'[142] For this reason, narratives are inherently value-laden:

> [Narratives] tell one story to the detriment of others by silencing voices, setting characters aside, and – most importantly – by providing the authority of what is natural, what goes without saying. Over time, narratives are internalized and their authority and explanatory force are taken for granted.[143]

137 Wetherell (n 131), 16.

138 Greta Olson, 'On Narrating and Troping the Law: The Conjoined Use of Narrative and Metaphor in Legal Discourse' in Michael Hanne and Robert Weisberg (ed), *Narrative and Metaphor in the Law* (Cambridge University Press 2018), 19.

139 Paul Gewirtz, 'Narrative and Rhetoric in the Law' in Peter Brooks and Paul Gewirtz (eds), *Law's Stories: Narrative and Rhetoric in the Law* (Yale University Press 1996), 3.

140 Anne Saab, *Narratives of Hunger in International law: Feeding the World in Times of Climate Change* (Cambridge University Press 2019), 33–34.

141 Houge (n 109), 279.

142 Jerome Bruner, 'The Narrative Construction of Reality', (1991) 18(1) *Critical Inquiry*, 13.

143 Andrea Bianchi, *International Law Theories: An Inquiry into Different Ways of Thinking* (Oxford University Press 2016), 295.

In this sense, the legal, factual and normative narratives that are constructed during international criminal proceedings are best understood as 'reflections of particular discursive formations that determine what counts as the truth.'[144] Conceptualising the narratives constructed during international criminal proceedings in these terms is not to suggest that they are in some way fictions, or inaccurate representations of reality, but seeks instead to capture how, through the processes of construction, inclusion and exclusion inherent in narrativising events through legal processes, international criminal justice functions as 'a representational project as much as a practical endeavour.'[145]

Understanding the representational dimensions of the practice of international criminal justice in these terms also highlights how the 'process of meaning making'[146] that takes place with respect to the acts that constitute international crimes can also be understood as continuous and ongoing, taking place through the profusion of narratives that emerge throughout the continuum of the legal process and each new case and decision. In this respect, in addition to the processes of construction, inclusion and exclusion inherent in representing events in the form of discrete factual and legal narratives, Jan Blommaert has highlighted the role of processes of decontextualisation and recontextualisation in how legal frameworks and procedures function discursively as meaning making practices.[147] Blommaert offers the concept of text trajectory to capture how texts and discourses undergo transformations in meaning when they move around and are recontextualised in different interpretive spaces.[148] In the context of legal proceedings, Blommaert reveals in this way how narratives of events are not constructed 'in one act of communication; [they are] constructed through a sequence of re-entextualisations, involving far-reaching reinterpretations of the story, summarising and rewording practices, and the reframing of a story in a legal and procedural framework.'[149] For instance, in the context of criminal proceedings, trial testimony is often transplanted into other communicative events within the legal process; it can be recounted in the closing statements of lawyers, discussed by juries, or cited in the decisions of judges.[150] Susan Ehrlich and Tanya Romaniuk explain that

144 Carine M. Mardorossian, 'Toward a new feminist theory of rape', (2002) 27 *Signs*, 766.

145 McMillan (n 1), 22.

146 *Ibid.*, 11.

147 Jan Blommaert, *Discourse: A Critical Introduction* (Cambridge University Press 2005), 62–76; Susan Ehrlich, 'Text trajectories, legal discourse and gendered inequalities', (2012) 3(1) *Applied Linguistics Review*, 47–73.

148 Blommaert (n 147), 46.

149 *Ibid.*, 63.

150 Ehrlich (n 147), 49.

the transplantation of a text or discourse into a different context in this way can have 'transformative effects: once a stretch of talk is 'lifted out of its interactional setting', segmented, and turned into a 'text' [...] it may bring something from its earlier context, but may also take on different meanings as it is 'recentred' (i.e. recontextualised) in a new context.'[151]

The notion of text trajectories in this respect captures the idea that 'meaning-making practices are never exhausted after one speech event; rather they occur over a series of interconnected speech events and often involve far-reaching re-interpretations of that initial communicative event.'[152] Drawing also on the notion of text trajectories, the 'process of meaning making'[153] surrounding the criminal acts analysed in this book is therefore conceptualised as a continuum of discursive and narrative construction through which the normative meaning attributed to criminal acts are continually reconstituted through different dimensions of the legal process and through numerous decisions engaging with each other.

For the purposes of examining the individual acts that constitute international crimes from a normative perspective, a discursive and narrative expressivist approach in this way provides a means of complementing and operationalising the wider Durkheimian conception of the constitutive function of criminal law in relation to the norms or values invoked by the criminalisation of particular acts of violence. Such an approach brings to the fore not only the significance of the socially and politically situated roots of the criminalisation of certain acts of violence, and the normative dimensions of their legal definitions with the values or principles these conceptually invoke, but also the significance of how such crimes are constructed discursively in the factual and normative narratives forwarded about them both in judgments and during the course of criminal proceedings. Combining a Durkheimian conception of the constitutive function of criminal law with an analysis of the discourses that emerge through the practices of international criminal justice in this way seeks to capture how courts and legal practices 'do not just reflect common conscience, but also help to shape it. They become the agent of and substitute for values.'[154] The discourses that emerge through decisions, trial

151 Susan Ehrlich and Tanya Romaniuk, 'Text Trajectories and Gendered Inequalities in Institutions' in Jo Angouri and Judith Baxter (eds), *The Routledge Handbook of Language, Gender, and Sexuality* (Routledge 2021), 355.

152 Ehrlich (n 147), 69.

153 McMillan (n 1), 11.

154 Marlies Glasius, 'Do International Criminal Courts Require Democratic Legitimacy?', (2012) 23(1) *European Journal of International Law*, 56.

proceedings and other legal practices therefore provide one way of examining how the practices of international criminal justice produce and invoke these values. The narrative expressivist approach in this way provides a framework for examining how the practices of international criminal justice function concretely as a 'process of meaning making'[155] with respect to the normative dimensions of the individual acts of violence criminalised as international crimes and for conceptualising the productive effects of this process.

3 Methodological Approach

The methodological approach applied to the analysis of the crimes discussed in the rest of this book draws on the theoretical framework outlined in this chapter. Through the different aspects of the analysis, this methodological approach seeks to capture the elements of how crimes and their normative dimensions are historically, socially and politically situated, can be understood as constitutive of certain normative principles in what their legal definitions invoke at an abstract, conceptual level, and are further discursively constructed through the processes of meaning making that take place during prosecution and judgment.

3.1 *Selection of Crimes*

The four crimes analysed in each of the following chapters are those of attacking cultural property, pillage, crimes of sexual violence and crimes of reproductive violence. These four crimes have been selected for analysis because they fall outside or appear more normatively complex or multi-dimensional than the generalised life, physical security and bodily integrity framework that is relied upon in much of the scholarship on international crimes outlined in the introduction to this book. In this respect, two of the crimes constitute crimes against property while the other two are crimes that have emerged in the more recent history of international law, attach to less well-established international norms and capture forms of conduct that remain, to varying degrees, normatively contentious at an international level. In this sense, posing the question of 'what might be the normative basis of the criminalisation of this act?' in relation to the crimes selected would be likely to elicit a more complex response than might be the case for other crimes such as murder or torture, which fit more straightforwardly into the basic security rights paradigm previously

155 McMillan (n 1), 11.

discussed. These crimes have therefore been selected on the assumption that they are likely to reflect more richly the process of normative meaning making outlined in the theoretical framework proposed in this chapter.

Evidently, numerous other individual acts criminalised as international crimes could also fit these criteria. In addition to the limited scope of this study, which precludes an exhaustive investigation into all of the forms of violence criminalised as international crimes and required that a limited number be selected, it was necessary to select crimes for which there was sufficient material for analysis. For the purposes of this theoretical framework, this required the selection of crimes which have formed part of the charges in at least one case at an international tribunal in order to be able to analyse its treatment in decisions as well as the discourse that emerges around the crime during the course of proceedings. In other words, it was necessary to select crimes where some level of normative meaning making has taken place in practice. This therefore also ruled out crimes that meet some of the criteria outlined above but that have not been charged or prosecuted at an international tribunal to date such as, for instance, persecution on grounds of gender or apartheid.

Lastly, two crimes against property and two gender-related crimes were selected on the grounds that their normative dimensions have been understood as significant in some way; they have elicited a degree of normative controversy and/or have enjoyed celebration in normative terms. In this respect, some of the philosophical scholarship on international criminal law has reflected an uneasiness with the inclusion of crimes against property within the normative universe of 'the most serious crimes of concern to the international community as a whole'[156] that international criminal law claims to represent.[157] This uneasiness similarly manifested in the domestic and international response to the *Al Mahdi* case at the ICC, which involved a sole charge of intentionally directing attacks against religious and historic buildings. Various responses to this case questioned the normative legitimacy of focussing on this charge, with a Malian media source stating, for instance, that 'there are more important things than monuments. The human person is sacred and inviolable. Crimes of blood must come before crimes against monuments.'[158] The art critic for *The Guardian* newspaper notoriously also argued that:

156 Preamble to the Rome Statute of the International Criminal Court, 18 July 2002 [hereafter Rome Statute].

157 See for instance Larry May, *War Crimes and Just War* (Cambridge University Press 2007), 20; Kirsten Fisher, *Moral Accountability and International Criminal Law – Holding Agents of Atrocity Accountable to the World,* (Routledge 2013), 41–42.

158 Original: 'mais il ya plus important que les monuments. La personne humaine est sacrée et inviolable. Les crimes de sang doivent passer avant les crimes sur les

> The most precious work of art in the world is still worth less than a single human life. War crime as a category must be kept distinct. It needs to be highly specific. The destruction of art is vile and offensive to many – but it is not mass murder and we should not pretend it is the same, nor that it belongs in the same court. There is potential for absurdity and moral confusion if artistic vandalism becomes a matter for The Hague. […] Culture can be renewed, remade, reinvented. Human life cannot. The organised torture and murder of human beings is what war crime should always, and unmistakably, mean. So while we mourn the loss of art or cultural artefacts, we need to keep a moral perspective in which the true crimes of war can be seen for what they are, and eradicated from the world.[159]

The codification of crimes of sexual and reproductive violence under international law was, by contrast, celebrated precisely in normative terms, being understood to reflect a significant development in wider international attitudes to violence against women.[160] The normative dimensions of the criminalisation of forms of sexual violence, in particular, have nevertheless also been contested. Feminist scholarship has, for instance, questioned the dominant normative conception of such crimes primarily as violations of bodily integrity for how this overlooks the autonomy or discrimination harms attached to such acts, and for how this constructs women's bodies and sexualities as violable and submissive.[161] While the criminalisation of forms of reproductive violence has enjoyed less scholarly analysis, the normative dimensions

---

monuments.' – Maliweb, 'Détention d'un Malien à la CPI: De la poudre aux yeux?'', 2 October 2015 [available at https://www.maliweb.net/societe/justice/detention-dun-malien-a-la-cpi-de-la-poudre-aux-yeux-1179012.html – accessed 11 February 2022].

159 The Guardian, 'Destroying priceless art is vile and offensive – but it is not a war crime', 22 August 2016 [available at https://www.theguardian.com/artanddesign/jonathanjonesblog/2016/aug/22/ahmad-al-mahdi-war-crimes-the-hague-destroying-mausoleums-timbuktu#comment-81652909 – accessed 11 February 2022].

160 Karen Engle, *The Grip of Sexual Violence in Conflict: Feminist Interventions in International Law* (Stanford University Press 2020), 44–47.

161 See for instance Chiseche Salome Mibenge, *Sex and International Tribunals: The Erasure of Gender from the War Narrative* (University of Pennsylvania Press, 2013); Fionnuala Ni Aoláin, 'The Gender Politics of Fact-Finding in the Context of the Women, Peace and Security Agenda', University of Ulster Transitional Justice Institute Research Paper No. 14-08 (2014), 1–3; Vasuki Nesiah, 'Missionary Zeal for a Secular Mission: Bringing Gender to Transitional Justice and Redemption to Feminism' in Sari Kouvo and Zoe Pearson (eds), *Feminist Perspectives on Contemporary International Law: Between Resistance and Compliance?* (Oxford: Hart, 2014), 143; Kiran Grewal, 'International Criminal Law as a Site for Enhancing Women's Rights? Challenges, Possibilities, Strategies', (2015) 23(2) *Feminist Legal Studies*, 157–158; Engle (n 160), 151.

of these crimes were some of the most heavily contested during the drafting of the Rome Statute[162] while matters related to reproduction, in particular female reproductive choice, remain highly controversial internationally.[163]

Taken together, the normative contestation and debate that surrounds each of these four crimes for this reason makes for particularly fertile ground for examining how the practices of international criminal law seek to explain or justify their criminalisation and prosecution, and in this way engage with and construct their normative dimensions.

3.2 *Methodology*

The analysis of each crime will consist of four steps that reflect the theoretical framework outlined in this chapter. These steps consist of an account of the crime's historical-normative roots, a conceptual analysis of its legal definition, followed by a discourse analysis of the normative themes articulated in the case law and the narratives that emerge around the crime during the course of proceedings. While the project of international criminal justice is broader than the activities of international criminal courts and tribunals, and includes for instance domestic trials for international crimes and universal jurisdiction cases, this research focusses on the decisions and transcripts of proceedings of international courts and tribunals. This focus is due partly to the methodological constraint of selecting a feasible number of cases for which to examine decisions and transcripts, but is also due to the project's approach to examining the normative dimensions of the acts that constitute international crimes from the perspective of asking how certain internationally shared norms, principles or values are performatively invoked through their criminalisation and prosecution.

In this respect, the practices of international criminal courts and tribunals, as compared to their domestic counterparts, can be understood to more straightforwardly involve a performative invocation of internationally shared norms or values due to international courts' claim to speak on behalf of a notional international community, as distinct from the domestic political communities on whose behalf domestic courts claim to act as representative.[164] From

162 Michael Cottier and Sabine Mzee, 'Article 8(e) War crime of forced pregnancy', in Otto Triffterer and Kai Ambos (eds), *Rome Statute of the International Criminal Court: A Commentary* (2016 Beck/Hart), 499.

163 Lucía Berro Pizzarossa, 'Here to Stay: The Evolution of Sexual and Reproductive Health and Rights in International Human Rights Law', (2018) 7(3) *Laws*, 13–14.

164 Harmen van der Wilt, 'On Regional Criminal Courts as Representatives of Political Communities: The Special Case of the African Criminal Court' in Kevin Jon Heller

this perspective, trials at international courts and tribunals, by virtue of being internationalised, may send different signals about what they are doing and who they claim to represent than those that take place in domestic jurisdictions.[165] For this reason, while the nature of the political community invoked by domestic courts when prosecuting international crimes may not always be straightforward or bounded by the domestic political community in which a court is embedded, this book focusses on the practices of international courts and tribunals as the clearest starting point for examining how the processes of criminalising and prosecuting the acts that constitute international crimes performatively invoke a set of norms and values shared by an international community on whose behalf these institutions claim to speak.

In addition, while this book focusses on the normative dimensions of the acts that constitute international crimes due to the tendency in the scholarship to conceptualise them in generalised terms, it is important to note that it is not possible to entirely separate the normative dimensions of the acts that constitute international crimes from the wider crime categories to which they belong. The normative dimensions of these acts, in terms of their historical roots, their contemporary definitions and how they are constructed discursively in practice, will necessarily have been shaped in part by the context required by the category of crime in which they are embedded, be that a situation of armed conflict, a widespread or systematic attack against a civilian population or a situation involving the destruction of a national, ethnic, racial or religious group. In this sense, while this book focusses on the normative dimensions of the acts that constitute international crimes independent of the wider categories of international crimes, what is ultimately being examined is how these acts have been attributed with normative meaning within these contexts.

Taken together, the theoretical orientation of the different dimensions of this methodological approach is primarily inductive and intended to be descriptive, rather than normative. It seeks to capture the processes of normative meaning making that take place through the criminalisation and prosecution of the crimes under discussion. It is concerned in this sense with how the crimes are 'actually made to mean',[166] and the possible effects of this process of

---

et al. (eds), *The Oxford Handbook of International Criminal Law* (Oxford University Press 2020), 194.

165 Frédéric Mégret, 'In Defense of Hybridity: Towards a Representational Theory of International Criminal Justice', (2005) 38(3) *Cornell International Law Journal*, 743.

166 McMillan (n 1), 11.

construction and representation, rather than seeking to advance a normative argument about how crimes should be conceptualised or treated in practice.

3.2.1 Historical-Normative Roots

Responding to the theoretical recognition that, as products of processes of social definition, crimes are inherently historically, socially and politically situated, this section of the analysis examines the historical-normative roots of the crimes in question. This includes both a straightforward account of the historical development of the legal norms which provide the basis for their contemporary criminalisation as well as consideration of the wider social, political and normative environment that gave rise to these norms. This section of the analysis draws on the existing scholarship on the historical roots of these crimes as well as the wider historical literature relating to the practices that subsequently came to constitute acts criminalised under international criminal law. In relying on existing scholarship on the historical origins of these crimes, this analysis reflects the dominant linear historical narratives contained in these accounts. While recognising that this approach is limited in how it may omit a more plural account of the historical roots of these norms and their contestability,[167] it is ultimately beyond the scope of this project to undertake a more critical historical analysis of the origins of these crimes. Instead, the aim is to offer a general overview of the normative roots of these crimes as captured in the development of the legal norms that historically underpin them and how these were justified or normatively conceptualised at the time in order to expose some of the social, historical and conceptual conditions from which they emerged.

3.2.2 Legal Definitions

Departing from the theoretical position outlined in this chapter that crimes conceived as public wrongs inherently invoke a set of publicly shared norms, principles or values as their referent, this section examines the normative dimensions of the contemporary legal definitions of these crimes from a conceptual perspective, considering the nature of the principles or values invoked by the definitions of these crimes. This conceptual analysis considers both the drafting history of the crime, where this is normatively illuminating, as well as taking into account the nature and form of the conduct that the legal definition can be understood to capture. The focus of this analysis is not, therefore,

167 For an overview of debates emerging from the 'historical turn' in international law scholarship see Jean d'Aspremont, 'Critical histories of international law and the repression of disciplinary imagination', (2019) 7(1) *London Review of International Law*, 89–115.

on the nature of the legal interpretation, understood as the determination or the construction of the content of the law,[168] that has produced these definitions, but is instead on developing a descriptive account of their normative implications. In other words, this analysis provides an abstract account of the normative implications of what the definition of a crime includes or excludes in terms of conduct and the implications of this in terms of what norms or values, understood in general terms, it can therefore be understood to invoke. The definitions discussed are those included in the statutes of the international criminal tribunals, including the ICC's Elements of Crimes, and any definitions or elements of crimes further developed in the case law.

3.2.3 Normative Themes in the Case Law

Reflecting the narrative expressivist conception of the significance of the discourses constructed in legal decisions and more widely through the practices of international criminal justice, the next two sections turn to a more discursive account of the normative character of the crimes as constructed in the case law and during the course of proceedings, in order to examine the nature of the meaning making processes that take place in practice. It is important to note that the meaning making processes that construct the normative dimensions of these criminal acts may not be confined to practices internal to international criminal legal processes, but may also be shaped and informed by the practices of other actors involved in the international criminal justice system, such as states, civil society, the media or actors involved in domestic accountability efforts. The methodology applied in this research cannot therefore claim to capture the entirety of the meaning making processes that may shape the normative meanings of the acts that constitute international crimes. Instead, it focusses on judicial decisions and the transcripts of proceedings as a starting point for examining how practices internal to the legal process contribute to constructing, but are nevertheless not exclusive of, the normative meanings of these acts.

This section of each chapter therefore conducts a discourse analysis of the case law concerning the selected crimes at each of the international criminal tribunals. Importantly, and distinct from the previous section's conceptual analysis of the definitions of the crimes in legal terms, the analysis of the normative themes in the case law focuses on the nature of the language used in

168 For discussion of different approaches to the nature of legal interpretation see Gleider I. Hernández, 'Interpretation' in Jörg Kammerhofer and Jean D'Aspremont (eds), *International Legal Positivism in a Post-Modern World* (Cambridge University Press 2014), 317–348.

decisions to describe and interpret these crimes in both normative and factual terms. This analysis therefore captures both explicit normative statements that engage directly with the normative dimensions of a crime and articulate a chamber's understanding of it in normative terms, as well as the normative implications of broader legal findings that relate to the crime and wider normative themes reflected in the factual narratives constructed around them.

This section of each chapter is based on a discourse analysis of all trial and appeals judgments for cases involving the selected crimes at the ICTY, ICTR, ECCC, SCSL and ICC.[169] In addition, Confirmation of Charges, Sentencing and Reparations decisions from ICC cases, where available, and Sentencing decisions from ICTY and SCSL cases, where relevant, were also analysed on the grounds that they often contain substantial additional discussion of the normative dimensions of crimes. Taken together for each of the crimes, a total of 241 decisions were analysed. These are listed in Appendix I. In order to facilitate identification of the relevant sections of the decisions under analysis, they were searched for key words and coded using the qualitative analysis software ATLAS.ti. The list of key words used to search the decisions and identify relevant sections is included in Appendix II. This methodology of using key words to search the decisions for relevant text was not intended to be exhaustive, and some relevant sections may not have been identified if they did not contain any of these key words. However, the key words were intended to be sufficiently comprehensive to identify the vast majority of the relevant sections of the decisions, and often captured significantly more than was relevant to the analysis. This suggests that the majority of relevant sections were identified through the use of key word searches. The identified sections of the decisions were then read and coded according to the normative themes they reflected. Codes were identified both inductively and deductively, with some being informed by existing literature on the crimes and case law, while others emerged through the process of conducting the discourse analysis. Finally, the selected sections of text were organised according to the code they had been allocated and were re-read to identify particularly representative or illustrative examples, which then formed the basis of the discussion contained in the chapter.

169 As at November 2021. Following the completion of this research project, Chapter 5 was updated to include relevant discussion of the Appeal Judgment in the *Ongwen* case at the ICC, issued in December 2022.

3.2.4 Narratives During Proceedings

Capturing narrative expressivism's concern with the discourse that emerges through the practices and performative dimensions of international criminal trials, in addition to that which is contained in the decisions themselves, the final section of each of the chapters consists of a discourse analysis of the transcripts of the same trials, the decisions of which were analysed in the previous section. The discourse analysis of the trial transcripts was intended to capture the wider variety of narratives about these crimes that may have been forwarded by different parties to proceedings, prior to being condensed into, included in or excluded from a judgment or decision.

The transcripts of the trials analysed are listed in Appendix III. With the exception of the analysis of crimes of sexual violence, all transcripts of all trials included in Appendix I were analysed.[170] Due to the high number of cases involving charges for sexual violence, an exhaustive analysis of the transcripts of all trials involving such charges at the international criminal tribunals was not possible. The transcripts of those trials that featured charges of sexual violence most prominently, according to the previous analysis of the case law, were therefore selected and analysed for this chapter. The transcripts of the trials analysed for the chapter on crimes of sexual violence are also listed in Appendix III. In total, for all of the crimes, 19,157 trial transcripts were analysed. It is important to note the nature of publicly-available trial transcripts as a record of those sections of trial proceedings that have been conducted in open session. Some relevant sections of proceedings entered closed session, in particular those involving testimony of sexual and reproductive violence, meaning that the record of these sections of proceedings was not available for analysis. However, sufficient data from each trial was identified to ensure that an overview of the themes and narratives contained in them was captured.

A similar methodology to that outlined in the previous section was applied for the discourse analysis of the trial transcripts. Key words were again selected and searched for in order to identify those sections of transcripts where the crimes were likely to have been discussed during proceedings. These are listed in Appendix II. Identification of the relevant sections of proceedings where the crimes were discussed will similarly not have been exhaustive and some relevant sections may have been overlooked if the key words searched for did not appear. However, similar to the results of the key word searches of the decisions, significantly more text was identified by the key word search than was relevant to the analysis, which suggests that the majority of relevant sections

170 As at November 2021.

were captured using this method. The sections of the transcripts identified using the key word search were then read and coded according to the narratives or themes they reflected. Codes were again identified both inductively and deductively. Coded sections of text were subsequently organised according to theme or narrative and again re-analysed to identify illustrative or representative examples which formed the basis of the discussion contained in the chapter.

CHAPTER 2

Attacks on Cultural Property

In international criminal law, crimes against buildings or property are those that depart most explicitly from the paradigm of physical security or bodily integrity harms that are commonly identified as providing the core normative basis for international criminalisation.[1] The nature of the buildings and property protected in international criminal law, particularly within the category of war crimes, is varied. Some of these crimes, such as the prohibitions on directing attacks at civilian objects, humanitarian assistance or peacekeeping installations or at hospitals and medical facilities, may be linked at a normative level to the core concepts of the protection of the life and physical integrity of the human person, in that they function directly to spare civilian lives.[2]

The link between the criminalisation of acts targeting other types of property and this normative basis is less evident. For instance, the war crimes of appropriation or seizing of property and pillage expand the protection of different types of property beyond those linked with medical, humanitarian or civilian protection functions, to encompass a more general protection for the property of the adversary during situations of armed conflict. For this reason, some moral philosophical accounts of international criminal law question the criminalisation of acts of this nature on the grounds that they do not 'seem as important'[3] as attacks on persons. Others go further, to explicitly oppose the inclusion of these war crimes in the Rome Statute. According to this view, such acts are insufficiently grave to be criminalised under international law since they do not involve violations of physical security rights.[4]

The normative basis of the criminalisation of attacks on buildings dedicated to culture, as a specific category within broader protections for property under international criminal law, is similarly contested.[5] The response to the *Al*

1 Larry May, *Crimes Against Humanity: A Normative Account* (2005 Cambridge University Press), 21; Massimo Renzo, 'Crimes Against Humanity and the Limits of International Law', (2012) 31(4) *Law and Philosophy*, 453; Kirsten Fisher, *Moral Accountability and International Criminal Law – Holding Agents of Atrocity Accountable to the World,* (Routledge 2013), 41–42.

2 Micaela Frulli, 'The Criminalization of Offences against Cultural Heritage in Times of Armed Conflict: The Quest for Consistency', (2011) 22(1) *European Journal of International Law*, 207.

3 Larry May, *War Crimes and Just War* (Cambridge University Press 2007), 20.

4 Fisher (n 1), 41–42.

5 The term 'buildings dedicated to culture' or 'cultural property' are used in this chapter as a catch-all for the categories of buildings attacks on which are criminalised in the ICTY and

 | DOI:10.1163/9789004687844_004

Mahdi case at the ICC, which involved the first charges for attacks on cultural property at the Court, is illustrative of this contestation. Civil society actors expressed concerns at the limited scope of the trial, in which Al Mahdi was prosecuted and convicted on the sole charge of intentionally directing attacks against religious or historic buildings in Timbuktu, for excluding crimes involving violence against persons. Interviews among residents of Timbuktu similarly suggest a generally negative response to the focus on the destruction of cultural property over 'more serious crimes' that have taken place during the conflict in Mali.[6]

While not directly contesting the normative justification for conducting a prosecution for the destruction of cultural property per se, these responses nevertheless reflect a sense of unease with the perception that the destruction of a building could be placed on the same moral footing as crimes that involve violence against persons. This contestation over the normative validity of protecting or prioritising property in situations where human life is at risk is not new, and has long historical roots in debates over the legal doctrine governing the protection of cultural property in armed conflict.[7] At the heart of these debates, and how they have manifested in international criminal law, lies the question of what justifies the criminalisation of attacks on cultural property in the same normative universe as large-scale violence to life and person?

This chapter examines how this question has been navigated in the doctrine and through the practice of international criminal law. The chapter first sketches the legal-historical roots of the protection of cultural property in armed conflict, outlining its dual normative roots in the emergence of the doctrine of necessity in the law of war alongside wider ideas about the importance of the arts, history and culture that emerged in Europe during the Enlightenment. The chapter goes on to trace the legal developments in international humanitarian law as well as in specialised treaty regimes that provide the legal basis for the contemporary criminalisation of attacks on or destruction of cultural property during armed conflict. It identifies a degree of fluctuation between a civilian-use versus a cultural-value based rationale for the protection of cultural property during armed conflict invoked by these

---

Rome Statute, namely buildings dedicated to religion, education, art, science, charitable purposes, historic monuments and works of art and science.

6 See Oumar Ba, 'Contested Meanings: Timbuktu and the prosecution of destruction of cultural heritage as war crimes', (2020) 63(4) *African Studies Review*, 743–762.

7 John Henry Merryman and Albert E. Elsen, *Law, Ethics and the Visual Arts* (Kluwer Law International 2002), 1–111.

norms, which subsequently manifests in the definitions of this crime applied at the ICTY and the ICC.

Analysing the normative themes constructed around this crime in the case law of the ICTY and the ICC, the chapter nevertheless goes on to demonstrate how the cultural value rationale for the protection of cultural property has overwhelmingly dominated the normative discourse around the crime in practice. The chapter identifies a number of different conceptions of how the nature of cultural value is constructed in these cases in both the legal decisions as well as during the course of proceedings, which draw variously on the wider theoretical traditions of internationalist, object-centric, functionalist and anthropocentric approaches to cultural property. While these cases as a whole in this way offer a multifaceted account of the value of cultural property, and therefore of the justification for the criminalisation of its destruction, the chapter also identifies a pronounced shift towards a more emphatically anthropocentric, people-oriented conception of cultural value in the *Al Mahdi* case at the ICC.

1 Historical-Normative Roots in International Law

The international legal regime governing the protection of cultural property during armed conflict has its normative roots in early writing on the law of nations during the 16th and 17th centuries and the attempts to articulate norms regulating the plunder and destruction of property.[8] At this point in its development, contemporary notions of just war permitted the use of any violence necessary to advance the cause of a war whose end was considered just. In principle, the destruction of any of the enemy's property could therefore be considered permissible.[9] While permitting necessary violence, the dual nature of this doctrine of necessity nevertheless also therefore proscribed actions unnecessary for the advancement of the cause of a just war, such as the killing of civilians or the destruction of their property.[10] At this time, objects or property with cultural significance could therefore be considered to enjoy some degree of protection during war to the extent that their destruction did not contribute to the military strength or advantage of the enemy.

8 Roger O'Keefe, *The Protection of Cultural Property in Armed Conflict*, (Cambridge University Press 2009), 5.

9 *Ibid.*, 6.

10 *Ibid.*, 5–6.

While objects of cultural value were from this perspective not regarded as a category distinct from other types of property, by the 17th century, Hugo Grotius, and a number of other scholars, were alluding in a limited fashion to protections for some specific types of property that would fall within a modern understanding of 'cultural' property. Grotius, for instance, argued that 'those things which, if destroyed, do not weaken the enemy, nor bring gain to the one who destroys them' such as 'colonnades, statutes, and the like', namely 'things of artistic value', ought not to be destroyed.[11] By the mid-18th century Emmer de Vattel, in his treatise on the law of nations, made explicit that:

> For whatever cause a country is ravaged, we ought to spare those edifices which do honour to human society, and do not contribute to increase the enemy's strength, – such as temples, tombs, public buildings, and all works of remarkable beauty. What advantage is obtained by destroying them? It is declaring one's self an enemy to mankind, thus wantonly to deprive them of these monuments of art and models of taste.[12]

From an historical perspective, the normative roots of the protection of cultural property during armed conflict in this way lie in the general doctrine of necessity, requiring that only violence or destruction necessary for harming the enemy's ability to wage war be permitted, while acts unnecessary for achieving this aim were proscribed. At the same time, this early scholarship on the law of nations already attributed additional normative significance to a particular class of objects and property; those that 'do honour to human society.'[13] In this way, protections for cultural property during armed conflict can be understood to have emerged from a combined normative basis, rooted both in the protection of 'civilian' property (i.e. property that did not contribute to the enemy's military strength) as a general category, as well as in the understanding of cultural property as something distinct.

Wayne Sandholtz has outlined how the confluence of two sets of emerging trends in European society underpinned the development of this approach to cultural property. He identifies the attempts to humanise and rationalise war by limiting its use to that which is necessary for victory, combined with the wider cultural transformations of the Renaissance and the Enlightenment, in which European elites came to confer upon art 'an almost sacred status that

11 Hugo Grotius, *De Jure Belli ac Pacis* as cited in O'Keefe (n 8), 6.

12 Emer de Vattel, *The Law of Nations, Book 3* (Liberty Fund Inc. 2008), para 168 at 571.

13 *Ibid.*

separated works of art from other kinds of property, like horses and shoes',[14] as the catalysing normative developments that lie at the historical root of the modern legal regime governing the protection of cultural property during armed conflict.

The cultural transformations that gave rise to this veneration of art and culture originated during the Renaissance, which saw the emergence of a new humanism, a nostalgia for classical antiquity and the rapid expansion of interest in literature, architecture and the fine arts.[15] A new sense of historicity, brought about by the rejection of the medieval notion of a universal, religious history, reinforced the interest in the study of ancient monuments and works of art,[16] while the emergence of humanism, with its focus on the accomplishments of individual human beings, engendered a transformation in the concept of art. The medieval artisan tradition, in which painting and sculpture were viewed as crafts or trades, was replaced by the emergence of the concept of the work of art in its aesthetic dimension, attached to notions of innate beauty and understood in terms of having 'qualities surpassing those embodied in the works of ordinary craftsmanship, a unique character, marking the individual genius of its creator.'[17] Acquiring and restoring antiquities, works of art and collections became fashionable among the wealthy and educated European elite, whose shared experience of the 'grand tour' of Europe, which shaped their tastes and ideas through exposure to the cultural legacy of classical antiquity, reinforced the cosmopolitan ties among them and contributed to an understanding of the arts and sciences as something of a transnational common good.[18] Roger O'Keefe identifies the roots of later internationalist approaches to cultural property in this cultural moment. He explains that:

> the vision of a transnational commonwealth of the learned became the vision of a transnational commonwealth of what they were learned in: artworks, architecture and antiquities – that is, the actual paintings and sculptures, grand buildings and monuments, ruins and

14 Wayne Sandholtz, *Prohibiting Plunder: How Norms Change* (Oxford University Press 2007), 32.

15 Jukka Jokilehto, *A History of Architectural Conservation* (Butterworth-Heinemann 2002), 15.

16 *Ibid.*

17 Stanisław Edward Nahlik, 'Protection of Cultural Property' in Henry Dunant Institute (ed), *International Dimensions of Humanitarian Law* (Brill Nijhoff 1988), 203. See also Jokilehto (n 15), 15.

18 Jokilehto (n 15), 16. See also Sandholtz (n 14), 39; O'Keefe (n 8), 8.

> relics – themselves came to be viewed as a universal metaphysical estate whose wellbeing was a common human concern.[19]

The valorisation of culture, history and the arts expanded during the Enlightenment, as divine values came to be increasingly contested and the faith in human-directed progress through science and reason produced profound changes in the concepts of art, history, heritage and human beings' relationship to nature and the universe.[20] History came to be understood as a 'collective, social experience, recognizing that cultures of different ages and regions could have their own style and guiding spirit.'[21] With growing knowledge of this diversity of customs and values emerged an appreciation of cultural pluralism and the recognition that different nations had different cultures and attitudes.[22] This new approach to history and culture transformed how art, architecture and historic buildings were understood and led to consideration of works of art and historic buildings 'as unique, and worthy of conservation as an expression of a particular culture and a reflection of national identity.'[23]

The change in the understanding of history that took place during the Enlightenment in Europe, in which the past became 'intellectualised and valorised',[24] was central in the emergence of the concept of the historic monument in particular. Where previously past, present and future, sacred and secular were understood as interwoven, the new understanding of history and the growing separation of the sacred from the secular provided the conditions for the emergence of the concept of the historic monument as 'something unambiguously secular and tied to a strong sense of historical progress and authenticity, especially under the authority of the nation-state.'[25] Similarly, the centrality of individualism for Enlightenment thought and the displacement of God and religion as the centre of the universe by man's mastery over nature through science and creativity further elevated the status of art and artists. Art came to be revered 'not just because collecting it was a sign of wealth, power, and taste, but because art was seen as the most transcendent product of human genius and creativity. [...] The arts performed, for Enlightenment

19 O'Keefe (n 8), 9.
20 Jokilehto (n 15), 17.
21 *Ibid.*
22 *Ibid.*
23 *Ibid.*
24 Miles Glendinning, *The Conservation Movement: A History of Architectural Preservation Antiquity to Modernity* (Routledge 2013), 46.
25 *Ibid.*, 47.

thinkers, some of the roles previously associated with faith and devotion, in elevating and improving the spirit.'[26] It is this reverence for art and cultural treasures, characteristic of the Enlightenment, that is reflected in Emer de Vattel's appeal for the sparing during war of 'those edifices which do honour to human society [...] – such as temples, tombs, public buildings, and all works of remarkable beauty.'[27]

Against this wider societal context, the French Revolution and the Napoleonic wars marked a pivotal moment in attitudes to the protection of monuments and art during peace as well as during war.[28] During the French Revolution, buildings and monuments that represented religious or aristocratic power, as symbols of past oppression, became targets for destruction.[29] Replacing the absolutist state and its legitimacy based on divine right, secular notions such as national identity and class solidarity came to be venerated, with secular monuments representing the past achievements of the people who constituted the new nation taking on an 'almost sacred character, as a stabilising force that could offset the iconoclastic excesses of the revolution.'[30] The ensuing process of nationalising cultural assets gave rise to the emerging notion of relics and monuments as constituting a shared national 'heritage' that could anchor a nation's identity and future in its past.[31]

During the wars that followed, French armies across Europe systematically confiscated and appropriated collections of artworks from their enemies on a vast scale, prompting a continent-wide debate on the protection and restitution of looted cultural treasures.[32] From a normative perspective, Wayne Sandholtz has explained how the outcry engendered by this systematic looting sprang from the particular exalted position that art and culture had come to enjoy in society by the late 18th century. He argues that:

> Only in the context of this veneration of art and artists, developing since the Renaissance, is it possible to understand the meaning of wartime plunder both for those who engaged in it and for those who suffered it during the wars of the French Revolution and Empire. For neither group was art a simple possession, like cattle. Depriving a people of its great art

26 Sandholtz (n 14), 36.

27 de Vattel (n 12), para 168 at 571.

28 O'Keefe (n 8), 13.

29 Jokilehto (n 15), 18.

30 Glendinning (n 24), 66.

31 *Ibid.*, 67.

32 Sandholtz (n 14), 49.

> was tantamount to cutting it out of participation in the highest expression of culture and (in the language of the time) civilization. In the language of rights, so characteristic of the Enlightenment, people were entitled not just to their property but to their share of humanity's artistic patrimony.[33]

The subsequent debates, and the insistence among several of the victorious states on the return of plundered art 'crystallized the sense that such looting was illegitimate.'[34] The 1814 Congress of Vienna included provisions on the return of stolen art, invoking for the first time in this respect the notion of a 'common heritage of mankind.'[35] While consensus remained incomplete on the question of a prohibition on the looting of cultural objects, the debates engendered by the Napoleonic wars and their aftermath nevertheless laid the groundwork for an emerging norm prohibiting the plunder of art and cultural objects during war.[36]

During the early 19th century, the consolidating form of the nation-state further reinforced the social and political status of historic monuments and works of art as anchors for burgeoning notions of national identity and shared national past. This also prompted the establishment of numerous national bodies concerned with the preservation of historic monuments and works of art across Europe and more widely.[37] In this context, the idea of a national cultural heritage came to be increasingly significant 'in the definition of identities, belonging, and boundaries.'[38]

It is this normative environment, with its veneration of the arts, science, culture and heritage, that ultimately gave rise to the inclusion of specific legal protections for certain categories of cultural property during armed conflict in the first codification of rules governing the conduct of belligerents in war. Under the heading 'protection of persons, and especially of women, of religion,

---

33 *Ibid.*, 36.

34 *Ibid.*, 49, 71.

35 Dacia Viejo-Rose and Marie Louise Stig Sørensen, 'Cultural Heritage and Armed Conflict: New Questions for an Old Relationship' in Emma Waterton and Steve Watson (ed), *The Palgrave Handbook of Contemporary Heritage Research* (Palgrave Macmillan 2015), 283.

36 Sandholtz (n 14), 69.

37 O'Keefe (n 8), 16–17.

38 Marie Louise Stig Sørensen and Dacia Viejo-Rose, 'Introduction: The Impact of Conflict on Cultural Heritage: A Biographical Lens' in Marie Louise Stig Sørensen and Dacia Viejo-Rose (ed), *War and Cultural Heritage: Biographies of Place* (Cambridge University Press 2015), 4.

the arts and sciences',[39] the rules contained in the 1863 Lieber Code regulating the conduct of belligerent parties occupying enemy territory provided that 'the property belonging to churches, to hospitals, or other establishment of an exclusively charitable character, to establishments of education, or foundations for the promotion of knowledge, whether public schools, universities, academies of learning or observatories, museums of the fine arts, or of a scientific character is not to be considered public property',[40] and may not therefore be seized or appropriated.[41]

The Lieber Code further required that 'classical works of art, libraries, scientific collections, or precious instruments, such as astronomical telescopes, as well as hospitals, must be secured against all avoidable injury.'[42] While it was permitted for the occupying party to seize and remove such objects if this was possible without causing damage, the Code nevertheless required that 'the ultimate ownership [of these objects] is to be settled by the ensuing treaty of peace. In no case shall they be sold or given away, if captured by the armies of the United States, nor shall they ever be privately appropriated, or wantonly destroyed or injured.'[43]

Amidst the flurry of efforts to codify rules to regulate the conduct of war during the late 19th and early 20th centuries, the next significant developments in the codification of rules protecting forms of cultural property were the 1874 Draft International Regulations on the Laws and Customs of War ('the Brussels Declaration'), the first intergovernmental attempt to codify the laws of war, and the 1882 manual produced by the *Institut de droit international* ('the Oxford Manual'), which contained similar prohibitions to the Lieber Code on the unnecessary destruction of objects of cultural value.[44] In addition to provisions similar to those reflected in the Lieber Code, both also contained the new requirement that in sieges or bombardments 'all necessary steps must be taken to spare, as far as possible, buildings dedicated to art, science, or charitable

39 Section II, Instructions for the Government of Armies of the United States in the Field (Lieber Code), 24 April 1863.

40 *Ibid.*, Article 34.

41 *Ibid.*, Article 31.

42 *Ibid.*, Article 35.

43 *Ibid.*, Article 36.

44 While the Lieber Code permitted the seizure or removal of objects of cultural value by an occupying party on condition that were not sold or given away, the Brussels Declaration and Oxford Manual did not permit such seizure or removal. See O'Keefe (n 8), 22.

purposes, hospitals, and places where the sick and wounded are collected provided they are not being used at the time for military purposes.'[45]

The Brussels Declaration laid the basis for the subsequent codification of the 1899 and 1907 Hague Conventions concerning the laws and customs of war on land.[46] Along with a general prohibition on destruction or seizure of enemy property beyond the exigencies of military necessity,[47] these treaties codified the requirement originally articulated in the Brussels Declaration on sparing buildings dedicated to religion, art, science, or charitable purposes, historic monuments, hospitals, and places where the sick and wounded are collected during sieges and bombardments.'[48] They also prohibited seizing, destroying or wilfully damaging institutions dedicated to religion, charity and education, the arts and sciences, historic monuments and works of art and science during belligerent occupation.[49]

Reflecting its combined normative roots in the doctrine of necessity alongside the conception of cultural property as normatively particular and distinct, Francesco Francioni has highlighted how the legal framework governing the protection of cultural property during armed conflict at this stage in its development nevertheless remained somewhat normatively incoherent. He argues that protection was now afforded 'in a fragmented manner to certain property identified empirically [...] which [were] deemed worthy of protection as nonprotected sites, as private or public property, and bundle[d] with those destined to a humanitarian function, such as hospitals.'[50] In this way, while these provisions protected specifically enumerated forms of cultural property, these were nevertheless not treated as normatively distinct from the much broader humanitarian concerns of limiting unnecessary use of force or protecting the sick and wounded.[51] Francioni therefore suggests that, at this point, 'what is

45 Article 17, Project of an International Declaration concerning the Laws and Customs of War. Brussels, 27 August 1874. See O'Keefe (n 8), 19–20. See also John Henry Merryman, 'Two Ways of Thinking About Cultural Property', (1986) 80(4) *American Journal of International Law*, 834.

46 Francesco Francioni, 'The Evolving Framework for the Protection of Cultural Heritage in International Law' in Silvia Borelli and Federico Lenzerini (eds), *Cultural Heritage, Cultural Rights, Cultural Diversity New Developments in International Law* (Brill-Nijhoff 2012), 8.

47 Article 23(g), Convention (IV) respecting the Laws and Customs of War on Land and its annex: Regulations concerning the Laws and Customs of War on Land, The Hague, 18 October 1907.

48 *Ibid.*, Article 27.

49 *Ibid.*, Article 56.

50 Francioni (n 46), 8.

51 Frulli (n 2), 207.

still missing [...] is a normative definition of what can be considered cultural heritage.'[52]

Following this first codification of rules regulating the conduct of war, the subsequent experience of World War I, and the extensive destruction of cultural property that took place, catalysed greater engagement with the particular normative significance of cultural property in international law.[53] The damage inflicted during the course of the war to cities such as Louvain in Belgium and Kalisz in Poland, and the shelling of monuments such as Reims Cathedral,[54] provoked a heated public debate and propaganda campaigns on both sides, coming to serve a symbolic role as 'an instrument of national and international mobilization.'[55] This in turn contributed to a number of legal developments,[56] including the inclusion of the crime of 'wanton destruction of religious, charitable, educational and historic buildings and monuments' in a list of war crimes drafted by the Commission on Responsibilities of the 1919 Preliminary Peace Conference of Paris. While no trials ultimately took place, this represented the first attempt to codify a criminal prohibition at the international level applicable specifically to the destruction of objects and property of cultural significance.[57]

The interwar period saw a number of further developments in the codification of norms governing the protection of cultural property in armed conflict. In 1935, the Treaty on the Protection of Artistic and Scientific Institutions and Monuments ('the Roerich Pact') was signed by the United States and Latin American nations, representing the first international convention devoted specifically to the protection of cultural property.[58] The Pact is applicable to historic monuments, museums, scientific, artistic, educational and cultural institutions during times of peace as well as war.[59] It contains a number of protections for such buildings, including an affirmation of their neutrality, a general obligation to respect and protect them,[60] along with concomitant

52 Francioni (n 46), 8.

53 O'Keefe (n 8), 40.

54 Serge Brammertz et al., 'Attacks against Cultural Heritage as a Weapon of War: Prosecutions at the ICTY', (2016) 14 *Journal of International Criminal Justice*, 1147.

55 Dario Gamboni, *The Destruction of Art: Iconoclasm and Vandalism since the French Revolution* (Reaktion Books 1997), 42.

56 See O'Keefe (n 8), 40–43.

57 O'Keefe (n 8), 343.

58 Merryman (n 45), 835.

59 Article 1, Treaty on the Protection of Artistic and Scientific Institutions and Historic Monuments ('the Roerich Pact'), Washington, 15 April 1935.

60 *Ibid.*

specific obligations such as a system of flags for identifying protected buildings.[61] Importantly, Article 5 of the Pact states that monuments, musems and institutions only cease to enjoy protection if they are used for military purpose, in this way excluding a wider military necessity justification for the withdrawal of protection.[62]

From a normative perspective, perhaps the most significant development reflected in the Roerich Pact is the very fact that it was dedicated specifically and exclusively to the protection of buildings of historical, cultural and artistic significance.[63] Thus, while similar to the Hague Regulations and Convention of 1899 and 1907 in how it remained 'very general about the definition of the terms cultural property',[64] it also marked a departure from the provisions in these conventions, which grouped protection for different types of cultural property together with protection for buildings with purely humanitarian purposes. The creation of a specialised convention devoted exclusively to the protection of cultural property, along with its rejection of the exception of military necessity in the context of cultural property protection, in this way embodied an emerging articulation in legal terms of cultural property as something normatively distinct from property with purely humanitarian or civilian roles, and therefore worthy of protection 'for itself, because of its intrinsic value and importance to humanity.'[65]

Attempts by the League of Nations to codify a similar treaty were ultimately overtaken by the beginning of World War II.[66] The Second World War saw the deliberate and systematic destruction and plunder of galleries, museums, libraries and historic sites by the Nazis in Poland and the Soviet Union, the theft of private collections owned by Jews throughout Europe, and the destruction of thousands of libraries in China by Japanese forces.[67] At Nuremberg, attacks against cultural property were nevertheless not addressed directly but were captured through more general charges of plunder of public or private property, wanton destruction of cities, towns or villages, devastation not justified

61 *Ibid.*, Article 3.

62 O'Keefe (n 8), 52.

63 Sandholtz (n 14), 103.

64 Friedrich T. Schipper and Erich Frank, 'A Concise Legal History of the Protection of Cultural Property in the Event of Armed Conflict and a Comparative Analysis of the 1935 Roerich Pact and the 1954 Hague Convention in the Context of the Law of War', (2013) 9(1) *Archaeologies: Journal of the World Archaeological Congress*, 17.

65 Frulli (n 2), 205.

66 Merryman (n 45), 835.

67 Brammertz et al. (n 54), 1148.

by military necessity, or persecution.[68] For this reason, cultural property was addressed in a somewhat incoherent fashion in the Nuremberg judgment, and was 'squeezed in between other types of property, such as raw materials or agricultural stock including cows, pigs, poultry and agricultural machines of all kinds.'[69] In addition, the destruction of immovable forms of cultural property was strikingly absent from the Nuremberg judgment, with only some cursory references made to the burning and demolishing of synagogues, the destruction of museums and the plunder of art from museums, libraries and private collections.[70]

Despite the limited extent to which the destruction of cultural property as a normatively distinct act was addressed at Nuremberg, the events of the Second World War and the public condemnation they aroused are nevertheless seen to have played a significant role in bolstering political mobilisation around the need to protect cultural property as a category of property with specific status and value.[71] While the codification of the 1949 Geneva Conventions, which contain protections for civilian property as a general category,[72] did not yet reflect this evolution, following the establishment of UNESCO in 1946, work was resumed on codifying a specific multilateral convention devoted to ensuring protection for monuments and works of art during times of war.[73]

In 1954, the Hague Convention for the Protection of Cultural Property in the Event of Armed Conflict was adopted. The Convention contained a number of innovations from a legal perspective, including applicability to both movable and immovable property,[74] a system of identifying protected property

68 O'Keefe (n 8), 88.

69 Jadranka Petrovic, *The Old Bridge of Mostar and Increasing Respect for Cultural Property in Armed Conflict*, (Martinus Nijhoff 2012), 51–52.

70 *Ibid.*, 53. The plunder and looting of occupied states was addressed most explicitly in relation to the conviction of Alfred Rosenberg, who was found to have been 'responsible for a system of organised plunder of both public and private property throughout the invaded countries of Europe. […] he organised and directed the 'Einsatzstab Rosenberg', which plundered museums and libraries, confiscated art treasures and collections and pillaged private houses. […] As of July 14th, 1944, more than 21,903 art objects, including famous paintings and museum pieces, had been seized by the Einsatzstab in the West [alone].' – *The Trial of German Major War Criminals*, Proceedings of the International Military Tribunal sitting at Nuremberg, Germany, Part 22 (22 August 1946 to 1 October 1946), 496.

71 O'Keefe (n 8), 91.

72 Frulli (n 2), 207.

73 O'Keefe (n 8), 92.

74 Article 1, Convention for the Protection of Cultural Property in the Event of Armed Conflict with Regulations for the Execution of the Convention, 14 May 1954.

through the creation of an emblem,[75] as well as inclusion of individual criminal responsibility for breaches of the convention.[76] At a conceptual level, the adoption of the 1954 Convention represented a significant consolidation of the view that cultural property required specific and distinct protection 'for the intrinsic value of culture and not as an indirect consequence of the protection of property rights or State sovereignty',[77] that had emerged in legal form at a regional level with the adoption of the Roerich Pact.

In this respect, the 1954 Convention also constituted a development in terms of how the nature of this intrinsic value of culture was conceptualised. The 1954 Convention has been described as 'a charter for cultural internationalism'[78] by virtue of its preamble, which affirms that 'damage to cultural property belonging to any people whatsoever means damage to the cultural heritage of all mankind, since each people makes its contribution to the culture of the world.'[79] While a cultural 'nationalist' approach to cultural value identifies cultural property to be the exclusive property of its nation of origin, which 'gives nations a special interest, implies the attribution of national character to objects, independently of their location or ownership',[80] the 'internationalist' ethos invoked by the 1954 Convention approaches cultural objects and property instead as 'components of a common human culture, whatever their places of origin or present location, independent of property rights or national jurisdiction.'[81] Roger O'Keefe has noted that, while this type of internationalist cultural ethos was common by the mid-twentieth century, the preamble to the 1954 Convention constituted the first international convention to capture this conception of cultural property in legal terms.[82] In doing so, the Convention brought to legal life the cosmopolitan notion of a 'global interest' in protecting and conserving the cultural property of all peoples, which, in turn, is understood to constitute 'the civilization of the world.'[83]

75 *Ibid.*, Articles 6, 16 and 17.

76 *Ibid.*, Article 28.

77 Francioni (n 46), 9.

78 Merryman (n 45), 837.

79 Preamble, Convention for the Protection of Cultural Property in the Event of Armed Conflict with Regulations for the Execution of the Convention, 14 May 1954.

80 Merryman (n 45), 832. For a philosophical account of the claims involved in invoking international or national value see Erich Hatala Matthes, 'Impersonal Value, Universal Value, and the Scope of Cultural Heritage' (2015) 125(4) *Ethics*, 999–1027.

81 Merryman (n 45), 831.

82 O'Keefe (n 8), 94–95.

83 Francioni (n 46), 9.

In addition, the 1954 Convention offered the first definition of the term cultural property in an international convention, constituting a further development in how the nature of the cultural value of the property it seeks to protect was conceptualised. The 1954 Convention defines cultural property as 'movable or immovable property of great importance to the cultural heritage of every people', and goes on to provide a number of examples of such property.[84] This definition in this way incorporates an evaluative component, requiring that, in order for it to enjoy protection, the property must be considered of 'great importance to the cultural heritage of every people.'[85] In this sense, the category of immovable property protected by the 1954 Convention is narrower than that contained in the 1907 Hague Convention, which protects *all* 'buildings dedicated to religion, art, science, or charitable purposes, historic monuments',[86] regardless of whether they can be considered of particular significance or value. In doing so, the 1954 Convention invokes the idea that some forms of cultural property can be considered to be of higher value, and therefore of greater importance, than others.

Micaela Frulli has argued that this aspect of the 1954 Convention constitutes the moment at which two diverging approaches to the justification for protecting cultural property during armed conflict emerged in the international legal framework.[87] The approach reflected in the 1954 Convention, with its explicit invocation of a hierarchy among forms of cultural property, can be understood as a 'cultural value' approach, which Frulli describes as the idea that certain types of property are worthy of protection because of their 'intrinsic value and importance to humanity above and beyond [their] everyday use by civilians.'[88] By contrast, Frulli understands the 1907 Hague Convention to reflect the more traditional 'civilian use' approach to evaluating the normative significance of cultural property, which locates the need to protect it in relation to the broader need to protect civilians and their property during armed conflict.[89] This shift towards a more emphatically cultural value approach in the 1954 Convention is further reinforced through the reference to property of great importance to the cultural heritage every 'people', as opposed to the heritage of nations or

84 Article 1, Convention for the Protection of Cultural Property in the Event of Armed Conflict with Regulations for the Execution of the Convention, 14 May 1954.

85 *Ibid.*, Article 1(a).

86 Article 27, Convention (IV) respecting the Laws and Customs of War on Land and its annex: Regulations concerning the Laws and Customs of War on Land. The Hague, 18 October 1907.

87 Frulli (n 2), 204.

88 *Ibid.*, 205.

89 *Ibid.*

states. The term 'cultural heritage of peoples' instead invoked for the first time a conception of cultural value in social terms, understood to reflect the idea that 'as an anthropological matter, 'cultural' property [is 'cultural'] by virtue of social context – that is, by virtue of the meaning ascribed to it by a society.'[90]

While the adoption of the 1954 Hague Convention constituted perhaps the most significant evolution at a conceptual level in how the protection of cultural property during armed conflict was justified, the international legal regime governing the protection of cultural property during armed conflict has continued to develop over time. The adoption of the 1977 Additional Protocols to the Geneva Conventions consolidated the place of protections for cultural property in the general treaties of international humanitarian law, and broadly emulated the scope of protections contained in the 1954 Hague Convention.[91] Both Additional Protocols contain general protections for civilian property, with the explicit protections for cultural property contained in Article 53 of Additional Protocol I and Article 16 of Additional Protocol II considered *lex specialis* to these broader protections.[92] The language of the 1977 Additional Protocols refers to the prohibition on committing any acts of hostility directed against 'historic monuments, works of art or places of worship which constitute the cultural or spiritual heritage of peoples.'[93] Both articles are applicable 'without prejudice' to the 1954 Hague Convention, making clear that the nature of the property protected would be expected to equate to the evaluative threshold of 'cultural property' as defined in Article 1 of the 1954 Convention.[94]

This brief outline of the historical development of the legal regime governing the protection of cultural property during armed conflict has sought to trace its dual normative roots through early norms on military necessity combined with the fundamental social, political and cultural changes that took place in the 18th and 19th centuries, which resulted in art, culture, history and science coming to enjoy a particular venerated position in Western society. This dual rationale for the protection of cultural property during armed

90 O'Keefe (n 8), 95.

91 Roger O'Keefe, 'Protection of Cultural Property' in ed. Andrew Clapham and Paola Gaeta, *The Oxford Handbook of International Law in Armed Conflict* (Oxford University Press 2014), 496.

92 *Ibid.*, 497.

93 Article 53, Protocol Additional to the Geneva Conventions of 12 August 1949, and relating to the Protection of Victims of International Armed Conflicts (Protocol I), 8 June 1977; Article 16, Protocol Additional to the Geneva Conventions of 12 August 1949, and relating to the Protection of Victims of Non-International Armed Conflicts (Protocol II), 8 June 1977.

94 O'Keefe (n 8), 209, 211–214.

conflict continued to shape the development of the international legal regime during the 20th century, and underpins the contemporary criminalisation and prosecution of the targeting and destruction of cultural property under international criminal law.

2 Definitions of Attacks on Cultural Property in International Criminal Law

Following the development of rules providing for individual criminal responsibility for attacking or destroying cultural property during armed conflict in the specific treaty regimes and in international humanitarian law more widely, international prosecutions for such acts first materialised with the establishment of the ICTY. As part of the process of ethnic cleansing that took place during the conflict in Yugoslavia, religious and cultural property identified with particular ethnic and religious groups was systematically and deliberately attacked and destroyed. Secular monuments and institutions, most notoriously the Old Town of Dubrovnik, the National Library in Sarajevo, and the Old Bridge in the town of Mostar, were also targeted because of how they 'symbolized or contained material proofs of Bosnia's historic pluralist identity.'[95] The concerted attacks on cultural heritage that took place during the breakup of the former Yugoslavia provoked renewed attention to the destruction of cultural property in armed conflict, galvanising significant activity in the field of cultural property protection more broadly,[96] and resulting in the inclusion of the crime in the statute of the ICTY.

2.1 *ICTY Statute*

Article 3(d) of the ICTY Statute provided the Tribunal with the power to prosecute the war crime of 'seizure of, destruction or wilful damage done to institutions dedicated to religion, charity and education, the arts and sciences, historic monuments and works of art and science.' Despite the scope of Article 3(d) not being limited to immovable cultural property, the Tribunal has nevertheless

---

95 Helen Walasek, 'Destruction of the Cultural Heritage in Bosnia-Herzegovina: An Overview' in Helen Walasek (ed), *Bosnia and the Destruction of Cultural Heritage* (Ashgate 2015), 23. See also András Riedlmayer, 'From the Ashes: The Past and Future of Bosnia's Cultural Heritage' in ed. Maya Schatzmiller, *Islam & Bosnia: Conflict Resolution and Foreign Policy in Multi-Ethnic States* (McGill Queen's Press 2002), 99.

96 Helen Walasek, 'Introduction' in Helen Walasek (ed), *Bosnia and the Destruction of Cultural Heritage* (Ashgate 2015), 15–16.

focused on immovable property in its cases.[97] The language of Article 3(d) has its roots in Article 27 of the 1907 Hague Regulations.[98] In what Micaela Frulli has described as 'a little step forward'[99] in advancing the cultural value rationale for the protection of cultural property during armed conflict, Article 3(d) of the Statute nevertheless differs from the 1907 Regulations in that it is specific to certain forms of cultural property, recognising them as distinct from hospitals or places where the sick and wounded are collected.[100]

At the same time, Frulli also suggests that the extent to which Article 3(d) can be understood to invoke a cultural value approach is circumscribed by the absence of an evaluative element similar to that contained in the 1954 Hague Convention requiring that the property be of 'great importance to the cultural heritage of every people'[101] in order to enjoy protection. In her view, Article 3(d) 'reflects no differentiation among different elements of property'[102] meaning therefore that 'there is no graduation of gravity and, to give a concrete example, attacks against a small mosque have fallen under the very same provision (Art. 3(d)) as the shelling of the old town of Dubrovnik.'[103] While Frulli concludes that the ICTY Statute definition therefore 'only marginally takes into consideration the cultural value of the property to be protected',[104] the absence of an evaluative element can also be interpreted in another way; not as a dilution of the cultural value rationale for protecting cultural property but instead as an invocation of a more relativistic conception of cultural value than the hierarchical, universalist tone of the 1954 Convention, which 'condition[s] protection of these sites on a threshold of special significance or importance to humanity as a whole.'[105]

A relativist conception of cultural value, which is captured in some of the more recent conventions such as the UNESCO 2003 Convention for the Safeguarding of the Intangible Cultural Heritage and the 2005 Convention on the Protection and Promotion of the Diversity of Cultural Expressions, departs instead from the position that the importance of cultural heritage is established

97 Petrovic (n 69), 54.
98 Brammertz et al. (n 54), 1152.
99 Frulli (n 2), 207.
100 *Ibid.*
101 Article 1(a), Convention for the Protection of Cultural Property in the Event of Armed Conflict with Regulations for the Execution of the Convention 1954.
102 Frulli (n 2), 207.
103 *Ibid.*, 207, footnote 13.
104 *Ibid.*, 207.
105 Paige Casaly, 'Al Mahdi before the ICC: Cultural Property and World Heritage in International Criminal Law', (2016) 14 *Journal of International Criminal Justice*, 1205.

'relative to a certain community or population to whose the identity the cultural site is vital.'[106] In adopting a 'more localized, culturally based perspective'[107] to the value of cultural heritage, a relativist approach to cultural value reflects the notion that 'the scope of value can be highly variable depending on both the extent of individuals who have reason to value something and the kinds of reasons they have.'[108] On this view, while the small mosque in Frulli's example and the Old Town of Dubrovnik may be valuable in different ways to different people for different reasons, Article 3(d) has the scope to capture the cultural value that can be attached to both. In this sense, rather than watering down the extent to which Article 3(d) can be understood to reflect a cultural value rationale for the protection of cultural property and the criminalisation of its destruction, the absence of an evaluative dimension in the ICTY Statute instead invokes a different, wider, conception of what is understood to be culturally valuable.

2.2 *Rome Statute*

In a departure from the precedent set by the ICTY Statute, the Rome Statute's provisions on the war crime of destruction of cultural property more closely mirrors the language of the 1907 Hague Convention, with Articles 8(2)(b)(ix) and 8(2)(e)(iv) criminalising 'intentionally directing attacks against buildings dedicated to religion, education, art, science or charitable purposes, historic monuments, hospitals and places where the sick and wounded are collected, provided they are not military objectives' in both international and non-international armed conflict. While, similar to the ICTY Statute, the definition excludes an evaluative dimension to the nature of the property protected, the reversion to the formulation contained in the 1907 Hague Convention, to include protection for hospitals and places where the sick and wounded are collected alongside cultural property, has drawn criticism for 'equating cultural property with other types of protected civilian property [which] constitutes an unnecessary homologation of that which is distinct.'[109] From a normative perspective, hospitals and similar medical facilities are understood to be protected in this respect due to the presence of civilians and the

106 *Ibid.*, 1200.
107 *Ibid.*, 1201.
108 Matthes (n 80), 1003.
109 Andrea Carcano, 'The Criminalization and Prosecution of Attacks Against Cultural Property' in Fausto Pocar, Marco Pedrazzi and Micaela Frulli (eds), *War Crimes and the Conduct of Hostilities: Challenges to Adjudication and Investigation* (2013 Edward Elgar), 87.

humanitarian services that they offer, as opposed to the inherent value of the objects themselves.[110] By lumping them together with forms of cultural property, the Rome Statute's formulation of the crime draws it conceptually back in the direction of the more humanitarian-oriented, civilian-use-based rationale for the protection of cultural property reflected in the 1907 Convention.[111]

This is further reinforced by how the Rome Statute's definition of the crime is limited only to attacks on buildings or historic monuments.[112] In contrast to the ICTY Statute, which included 'works of art and science'[113] in the list of protected objects, the Rome Statute definition excludes movable objects from the scope of the crime. At a conceptual level, excluding movable cultural property from its scope has a similar effect to lumping together hospitals and medical facilities with forms of cultural property; it implies that the cultural value of the buildings protected is not the primary rationale for the criminalisation of their destruction. If the cultural value of the property or object to be protected were the primary normative basis for the crime, movable cultural property could also be expected to fall within its scope, as it did at the ICTY. In this sense, the exclusion of moveable objects of cultural value from the scope of protection in the Rome Statute invokes a normative conception of the crime that prioritises the humanitarian rather than the cultural dimensions of cultural property.

By the same token, the Rome Statute's criminalisation of 'directing attacks'[114] against protected buildings, as opposed to the ICTY Statute's criminalisation of 'seizure of, destruction or wilful damage done to'[115] protected buildings and objects, arguably also reduces the extent to which this formulation of the crime reflects a conception of the cultural dimensions of cultural property as worthy of protection in their own right. The term attack in the context of international humanitarian law has traditionally been interpreted by reference to Article 49(1) of Additional Protocol I[116] to refer to 'an act of violence against the

110 Yaron Gottlieb, 'Criminalizing Destruction of Cultural Property: A Proposal for Defining New Crimes under the Rome Statute of the ICC', (2005) 23(4) *Penn State International Law Review*, 865–866.

111 Frulli (n 2), 211. See also Gottlieb (n 110), 865.

112 Roberta Arnold and Stefan Wehrenberg, '9. Paragraph 2(b)(ix): Intentionally directing attacks against protected buildings' in Otto Triffterer and Kai Ambos (eds), *Rome Statute of the International Criminal Court: A Commentary* (Beck/Hart 2016), 419.

113 Article 3(d), ICTY Statute.

114 Knut Dörmann, 'Intentionally directing attacks against civilians not taking direct part in hostilities' in Otto Triffterer and Kai Ambos (eds), *Rome Statute of the International Criminal Court: A Commentary* (Beck/Hart 2016), 355.

115 Article 3(d), ICTY Statute.

116 Arnold and Wehrenberg (n 112), 419.

adversary, whether in offense or in defence [...] It refers to any *combat action*.'[117] The ICRC Commentary on the Rome Statute similarly notes with respect to Article 8(2)(b)(ix) that 'the concept of attack as defined in this provision refers to the use of armed force to carry out a military operation during the course of an armed conflict.'[118]

The criminalisation of 'attacks' on protected buildings is therefore more limited than the criminalisation of their seizure, destruction or damage, since attack relates to the conduct of military operations, while 'destruction or damage' does not specify the form through which the harm to the protected objects is required to take place. In the same way that excluding moveable cultural property from its scope dilutes the extent to which a cultural value rationale for the protection of cultural property can be understood to underlie this crime, restricting its scope to damage to cultural property inflicted specifically during the conduct of hostilities, as opposed to its seizure, destruction or damage during armed conflict through any means, similarly limits the extent to which the Rome Statute definition invokes a conception of the crime as centred upon the cultural value of these buildings. The requirement that an 'attack' take place, traditionally understood as the use of armed force during the conduct of hostilities, instead implies a rationale behind the criminalisation of this act as primarily normatively rooted in the protection of civilian objects, and therefore in reducing harm to civilians during the conduct of hostilities. Excluding destruction or damage to cultural property that does not take place in the context of an 'attack' implies that, without the risk of harm to civilians entailed by directing attacks at such buildings due to their civilian character, their cultural value does not enjoy protection in its own right.

In the *Al Mahdi* case, in which mausoleums in Timbuktu were demolished after having come under the control of the armed group Ansar Dine, the ICC has nevertheless rejected the traditional interpretation of 'attack' outlined here, precisely on the basis that doing so would fail to recognise that such buildings are protected at all times during armed conflict because of their important cultural value. The Trial Chamber argued that:

> the element of 'direct[ing] an attack' encompasses any acts of violence against protected objects and will not make a distinction as to whether it was carried out in the conduct of hostilities or after the object had fallen under the control of an armed group. The Statute makes no such

117 Dörmann (n 114), 355. Emphasis added.

118 Knut Dörmann, *Elements of War Crimes under the Rome Statute of the International Criminal Court: Sources and Commentary* (Cambridge University Press 2009), 216.

> distinction. This reflects the special status of religious, cultural, historical and similar objects, and the Chamber should not change this status by making distinctions not found in the language of the Statute. Indeed, international humanitarian law protects cultural objects as such from crimes committed both in battle and out of it.[119]

This indicates a shift to a more cultural-value oriented interpretation of the Rome Statute definition of the crime than the traditional approach to the interpretation of attack outlined here implies, and will be discussed in greater detail in the analysis of the case law below.

2.3 *ECCC*

Lastly, in contrast to the provisions contained in the ICTY and ICC Statutes, Article 7 of the Law on the Establishment of the Extraordinary Chambers in the Courts of Cambodia (ECCC) provides the court with 'the power to bring to trial all Suspects most responsible for the destruction of cultural property during armed conflict pursuant to the 1954 Hague Convention for Protection of Cultural Property in the Event of Armed Conflict', thereby incorporating the evaluative dimension of the 1954 Convention into its definition of the crime of destruction of cultural property. Problems have nevertheless been identified with this approach due to the 1954 Convention providing for sanctions for its violation without stipulating which breaches entail criminal responsibility, nor providing elements of a crime.[120] No charges for this crime have been pursued at the ECCC.[121]

3 Normative Themes in the Case Law

This section analyses the case law on destruction or damage to cultural property at the ICTY and the sole case involving such a charge at the ICC to date, focussing on how the different chambers articulated their understanding of the crime from a normative or conceptual perspective. The analysis identifies

119 *Prosecutor v. Ahmad Al Faqi Al Mahdi*, ICC-01/12-01/15, ICC, Judgment and Sentence, 27 September 2016, para 15 [hereafter Al Mahdi Judgment and Sentence].

120 Caroline Ehlert, *Prosecuting the Destruction of Cultural Property in International Criminal Law With a Case Study on the Khmer Rouge's Destruction of Cambodia's Heritage* (Martinus Nijhoff 2014), 200.

121 Nina H.B. Jørgensen, *The Elgar Companion to the Extraordinary Chambers in the Courts of Cambodia* (Edward Elgar 2018), 258.

four significant normative themes that emerged in the case law of the ICTY and were subsequently expanded on in the *Al Mahdi* case at the ICC. These four themes relate to constructing cultural property as a normatively distinct category; cultural internationalism; object-centrism; and functionalism or relationship to people. Taken as a whole, the case law invokes a multifaceted account of the normative dimensions of the criminalisation of destruction of cultural property, which combines elements of these various normative themes.

3.1 *Cultural Property as a Normatively Distinct Category*

The first notable theme that emerges in the case law is an emphasis on the distinction between general protection for civilian property and the protection enjoyed by cultural property as a distinct category, consolidating the shift away from a civilian use conception of the crime by making explicit its particular and culture-related normative foundations. For instance, in the *Jokić* case at the ICTY, the Trial Chamber noted that 'Miodrag Jokić is convicted of six war crimes, all of which have been found to be extremely serious in terms of the protected interests violated: life and integrity of the victims; protection of civilian objects; protection of cultural property.'[122] At a very basic level, by distinguishing between the protected interests underlying the criminalisation of the destruction of civilian objects and the destruction of cultural property, the Trial Chamber points to an understanding of the criminalisation of these acts as resting on distinct normative foundations.

In the context of its analysis of the element of 'direct[ing] an attack' at a protected object, discussed above, the Trial Chamber in the *Al Mahdi* case at the ICC reinforced this view, stating that the criminalisation of attacks on cultural property in the Rome Statute 'reflects the special status of religious, cultural, historical and similar objects.'[123] The Chamber went on to emphasise that 'cultural objects in non-international armed conflicts are protected as such, not generically as civilian objects.'[124] In doing so, the Trial Chambers in *Jokić* and *Al Mahdi* reinforced the developments in the conceptualisation of cultural property as a specific, normatively distinct category that initially emerged in international law with the adoption of the 1954 Hague Convention.

The Trial Chamber in *Kordić and Čerkez* expanded on this normative distinction between protection for civilian versus cultural property in its

122 *Prosecutor v. Miodrag Jokić*, IT-01-42/1-S, ICTY, Sentencing Judgment, 18 March 2004, para 113 [hereafter Jokić Sentencing Judgment].

123 Al Mahdi Judgment and Sentence (n 119), para 15.

124 *Ibid.*, para 16.

discussion of the conditions under which attacks on educational institutions would constitute a crime under Article 3(d) of the ICTY Statute. In its analysis of whether institutions dedicated to education enjoy special protection under international law, the Trial Chamber sought to reconcile the provisions of the statute with the protections afforded to 'movable or immovable property of great importance to the cultural heritage of every people' in the 1954 Hague Convention with those afforded to 'historic monuments, works of art or places of worship which constitute the cultural or spiritual heritage of peoples' in the Additional Protocols to the Geneva Conventions.[125] The Trial Chamber ultimately concluded that 'educational institutions are undoubtedly immovable property of great importance to the cultural heritage of peoples in that they are without exception centres of learning, arts, and sciences, with their valuable collections of books and works of arts and science.'[126] Based on this reasoning, the Trial Chamber went on to note that 'this offence overlaps to a certain extent with the offence of unlawful attacks on civilian objects except that the object of this offence is more specific: the cultural heritage of a certain population.'[127]

The Appeals Chamber ultimately overturned this reasoning as applied specifically to institutions dedicated to education by arguing that the protection accorded to a special category of objects by the 1954 Convention and the Additional Protocols is based on the principle of according protection to 'objects whose value transcends geographical boundaries, and which are unique in character and are intimately associated with the history and culture of a people',[128] concluding therefore that it 'cannot see how all educational buildings fulfil these criteria.'[129] Despite the reversal of the Trial Chamber's reasoning on the basis of this more hierarchical conception of cultural value, in identifying the object of the offence as the cultural *heritage* of a certain population, as opposed to the physical existence of a particular type of building, the Trial Chamber's initial decision nevertheless developed the normative

125 Article 53, Protocol Additional to the Geneva Conventions of 12 August 1949, and relating to the Protection of Victims of International Armed Conflicts (Protocol I), 8 June 1977; Article 16, Protocol Additional to the Geneva Conventions of 12 August 1949, and relating to the Protection of Victims of Non-International Armed Conflicts (Protocol II), 8 June 1977.

126 *Prosecutor v. Dario Kordić and Mario Čerkez*, IT-95-14/2-T, ICTY, Trial Judgment, 26 February 2001, para 360 [hereafter Kordić and Čerkez Trial Judgment].

127 *Ibid.*, para 361.

128 *Prosecutor v. Dario Kordić and Mario Čerkez*, IT-95-14/2-A, ICTY, Appeal Judgment, 17 December 2004, para 91.

129 *Ibid.*, para 92.

conception of the crime beyond its material dimensions and its nature as civilian property, to incorporate protection also for the broader concept of heritage. The concept of heritage has been understood to express a 'form of inheritance to be kept in safekeeping and handed down to future generations',[130] which is linked to 'group identity and [...] is both a symbol of the cultural identity of a self-identified group, be it a nation or a people, and an essential element in the construction of that group's identity.'[131] The notion of cultural heritage is understood in this sense as wider than the narrower category of cultural property in terms of how it refers to 'less of an objective, physical existence than the range of associations which accompany an object or monument and which provide the sense of being part of a group',[132] capturing in turn 'experience, identity, intangibility, memory and remembering, performance, place, and even dissonance.'[133]

The Trial Chamber in *Hadžihasanović and Kubura* at the ICTY offered a similar, more intangible conception of the value of religious property specifically. The charges in this case related to the vandalism of the interior of the Guča Gora monastery belonging to the Croatian community in Bosnia. The Trial Chamber quoted the testimony of witnesses who described the damage to the interior of the monastery in the following terms:

> Books had been thrown on the floor, there were inscriptions written in Arabic and part of the organ was broken. [...] The wooden confessional and a number of steles had been destroyed and everything else was covered in excrement. There were inscriptions on the walls and an attempt had been made to obliterate and hack away the frescoes. [...] Numerous objects had disappeared, several paintings had been damaged, benches had been smashed, and inscriptions and indecent photographs covered the walls and doors. [...] the organ and the statute of St Francis of Assisi in the monastery courtyard had been damaged.[134]

---

130 Janet Blake, 'On defining the cultural heritage', (2000) 49(1) *International and Comparative Law Quarterly*, 83–84.

131 *Ibid.*, 84.

132 *Ibid.*

133 Lucas Lixinski, *International Heritage Law for Communities: Exclusion and Re-Imagination* (Oxford University Press 2019), 56. On the distinction between the concepts of cultural property and cultural heritage see also Lyndel V. Prott and Patrick J. O'Keefe, ''Cultural Heritage' or 'Cultural Property'?', (1992) 1(2) *International Journal of Cultural Property*, 307–320; Malio Frigo, 'Cultural property v. cultural heritage: A "battle of concepts" in international law?', (2004) 86(854) *International Review of the Red Cross*, 367–378.

134 *Prosecutor v. Enver Hadžihasanović and Amir Kubura*, IT-01-47-T, ICTY, Trial Judgment, 15 March 2006, para 2003–2004.

In its analysis of the seriousness of this damage to the monastery for the purposes of determining the gravity threshold of Article 3(d) of the ICTY Statute, the Trial Chamber explicitly distinguished between the material and the intangible dimensions of religious buildings. It argued that 'while civilian property is afforded general protection under customary international law, special attention is paid to certain property, namely religious buildings, owing to their spiritual value. [...] The Chamber considers that the seriousness of the crime of destruction of or damage to institutions dedicated to religion must [...] take much greater account of the spiritual value of the damaged or destroyed property than the material extent of the damage or destruction.'[135] On this basis, the Trial Chamber concluded that the extent of the damage to the monastery, which it described as an act of 'desecration', while ultimately not found to be attributable to forces under the control of the defendant, was sufficient to constitute a crime under Article 3(d) of the ICTY Statute.[136]

This episode exposes precisely the significance of identifying the normative basis of the criminalisation of destruction of cultural property in its intangible qualities, since, in this case, it resulted in the chamber assessing the damage, and therefore the gravity threshold for the crime, from the perspective of its spiritual, as opposed to its material, impact. In other words, by adopting a spiritual value approach to assessing the damage to the monastery, and therefore to the threshold for finding that a crime had occurred, the chamber suggested that it is the spiritual, intangible quality to the building that is protected through criminalisation, rather than simply its physical, material existence.

3.2 *Cultural Internationalism*

The second thematic thread that runs through much of the case law involving charges of attacks on cultural property is an internationalist conception of the value of cultural property. The internationalist approach to cultural value, first captured in international legal form in the 1954 Hague Convention, approaches cultural objects and property from the cosmopolitan perspective of being 'components of a common human culture, whatever their places of origin or present location,'[137] which 'belong to all of us as a form of rightful inheritance.'[138] This normative conception of cultural property manifests itself primarily through formalist appeals to the internationally protected status of

135 *Ibid.*, para 63.
136 *Ibid.*, para 2005.
137 Merryman (n 45), 831.
138 Sarah K. Harding, 'Value, Obligation and Cultural Heritage', (1999) 31(2) *Arizona State Law Journal*, 302.

the property, or otherwise in language that closely mirrors that contained in the 1954 Hague Convention.

In the *Strugar* case at the ICTY, for instance, the Trial Chamber directly adopted the language of the 1954 Hague Convention in its analysis of the seriousness of the offence of damage to cultural property, asserting that 'such property is, by definition, of "great importance to the cultural heritage of every people".'[139] The Chamber went on to observe that that 'the Old Town of Dubrovnik in its entirety was entered onto the World Heritage List in 1979'[140] explaining that 'the properties inscribed on the World Heritage List include those which "because of their architecture, their homogeneity or their place in the landscape, are of outstanding universal value from the point of view of history, art or science."'[141]

In *Jokić*, the Trial Chamber further developed this internationalist account of the specific normative basis of the criminalisation of destruction of cultural property. The Trial Chamber described the Old Town of Dubrovnik as 'an especially important part of the world cultural heritage'[142] and asserted that the 'the shelling attack on the Old Town was an attack not only against the history and heritage of the region, but also against the cultural heritage of humankind.'[143] It went on to assert that this crime 'represents a violation of values especially protected by the international community',[144] referring to the preamble to the UNESCO World Heritage Convention, which provides that 'the deterioration or disappearance of any item of the cultural or natural heritage constitutes a harmful impoverishment of the heritage of all the nations of the world.'[145]

The same theme emerged in the context of acts of destruction of cultural property charged as the crime against humanity of persecution, which was often charged in conjunction with the war crime of destruction or damage to cultural property at the ICTY.[146] Persecution was defined in the jurisprudence of the ICTY as '[t]he gross or blatant denial, on discriminatory grounds, of a fundamental right, laid out in international customary or treaty law, reaching

139 *Prosecutor v. Pavle Strugar*, IT-01-42-T, ICTY, Trial Judgment, 31 January 2005, para 232 [hereafter Strugar Trial Judgment].
140 *Ibid.*, para 327.
141 *Ibid.*
142 Jokić Sentencing Judgment (n 122), para 51.
143 *Ibid.*
144 *Ibid.,* para 46.
145 *Ibid.,* para 49.
146 Brammertz et al. (n 54), 1157.

the same level of gravity as the other acts prohibited in Article 5'[147] of the ICTY Statute. On this basis, the Trial Chamber in *Kordić and Čerkez* argued that the destruction of religious buildings 'when perpetrated with the requisite discriminatory intent, amounts to an attack on the very religious identity of a people. As such, it manifests a nearly pure expression of the notion of "crimes against humanity", for all of humanity is indeed injured by the destruction of a unique religious culture and its concomitant cultural objects.'[148] This conception of how attacks on cultural property can be understood to cause injury to all of humanity departs from the more formalist emphasis on internationally protected status as a proxy for cultural value, to offer an account of cultural value as rooted in the cosmopolitan notion of the value of human diversity; injury is caused to humanity in terms of the loss of a unique religious culture and its cultural objects.

An internationalist conception of the value of cultural property was similarly emphasised in the *Al Mahdi* case at the ICC. The Trial Chamber noted 'the particular importance of international cultural heritage',[149] explaining in the Reparations Order that 'cultural heritage is considered internationally important regardless of its location and origin.'[150] It went on to stress that 'the destruction of cultural heritage erases part of the heritage of all mankind'[151] which 'carries a message of terror and helplessness; it destroyed part of humanity's shared memory and collective consciousness; and renders humanity unable to transmit its values and knowledge to future generations.'[152] The internationalist conception of cultural value was similarly reinforced through a formalist emphasis on the UNESCO status of the mausoleums destroyed by the armed group Ansar Dine, with the Trial Chamber reiterating that 'all these [attacked] buildings had the status of protected UNESCO World Heritage sites',[153] that 'UNESCO's designation of these buildings reflects their special importance to international cultural heritage'[154] since 'inscription on the World Heritage List

147 *Prosecutor v. Zoran Kupreškić et al.*, IT-95-16-T, ICTY, Trial Judgment, 14 January 2000, para 621.

148 Kordić and Čerkez Trial Judgment (n 126), para 207.

149 Al Mahdi Judgment and Sentence (n 119), para 17.

150 *Prosecutor v. Ahmad Al Faqi Al Mahdi*, ICC-01/12-01/15, ICC, Reparations Order, 17 August 2017, para 15 [hereafter Al Mahdi Reparations Order].

151 *Ibid.*, para 53.

152 *Ibid.*, para 22.

153 Al Mahdi Judgment and Sentence (n 119), para 39.

154 *Ibid.*, para 46.

requires [...] that the object or site at stake has an exceptional quality that transcends national borders.'[155]

The Trial Chamber in *Al Mahdi* also developed on the notion first expressed in the *Jokić* case at the ICTY, that destruction of cultural property 'represents a violation of values especially protected by the international community',[156] referring to the Constitution of UNESCO in this respect, which states that 'the wide diffusion of culture, and the education of humanity for justice and liberty and peace are indispensable to the dignity of man and constitute a sacred duty which all the nations must fulfil.'[157] The Trial Chamber declared that 'attacking these mausoleums and mosques was clearly an affront to these values',[158] underscoring this understanding of the destruction of the mausoleums as an attack specifically directed at international values by noting that the defendant himself stated as much during an attack on one of the mosques. The Trial Chamber quoted Al Mahdi as having said 'it's probably one of the oldest mosques here in town, and is considered a heritage site [...] a World Heritage Site. There are so many rumours relating to these shrines [...] Those UNESCO jackasses [...] they think that this is heritage. Does 'heritage' include worshipping cows and trees?'[159]

The Chamber went on to incorporate this internationalist conception of cultural value into its account of the gravity of the crime. It argued that the 'attack [on the mausoleums] appears to be of particular gravity as their destruction does not only affect the direct victims of the crimes, namely the faithful inhabitants of Timbuktu, but also people throughout Mali and the international community'[160] meaning that 'the entire international community, in the belief that heritage is part of cultural life, is suffering as a result of the destruction of the protected sites.'[161] The implication of a graduated degree of seriousness attaching to attacks on cultural property depending on whether they are understood to affect the international community, in addition to local and national communities, was made explicit in the Reparations Order in the *Al Mahdi* case, where the Chamber stressed that 'world cultural heritage is a most important category. Greater emphasis vested in an object

155 Al Mahdi Reparations Order (n 150), para 20.
156 Jokić Sentencing Judgment (n 122), para 46.
157 Al Mahdi Judgment and Sentence (n 119), para 46.
158 *Ibid.*
159 *Ibid.*
160 *Ibid.*, para 80.
161 *Ibid.*

by the international community reflects a higher cultural significance and a higher degree of international attention and concern.'[162]

The Chamber's analysis in this way constructs international status as a proxy for cultural value, with international recognition understood to be reflective of a higher degree of cultural significance, and therefore of greater gravity attributed to the crime. From a practical perspective, this invocation of international status as a proxy for cultural significance has been criticised as being inaccurate because of how the listing process for UNESCO world heritage sites is 'notoriously politicised and biased towards particular forms of heritage [and] by no means a perfect mirror of the most important cultural sites across the globe.'[163] In this respect, from a conceptual perspective, the notion that international recognition reflects a higher level of cultural value has been problematised precisely because of how the very concept of international value rests on Eurocentric underpinnings, which manifest in the forms of heritage that are therefore recognised as valuable. In this sense, appealing to international value as a marker of cultural significance has been problematised for how it 'may ultimately just be an appeal to another form of tribalism, where universal value is code for "important to Western civilization".'[164] The concepts of world cultural heritage, universal value or the common heritage of mankind have also been subjected to foundational critiques for having facilitated the looting and removal of cultural objects from colonies to museums in the West by emphasising universal over local or national value and ownership.[165] In this sense, internationalist approaches to cultural value, with the associated notion that anyone has the right to a cultural object, have not manifested in shared custody of such objects, but have instead created a one-sided dynamic, which, as noted by Prott:

> looks far more like cultural imperialism, based as it seems to be on the activities of those from wealthy countries with each other and with poorer states whose cultural resources are flowing in one direction, without an equal exchange. It is an observable fact that far more is flowing

162 Al Mahdi Reparations Order (n 150), para 17.

163 Sophie Starrenburg, 'Who is the victim of cultural heritage destruction? The Reparations Order in the case of the Prosecutor v Ahmad Al Faqi Al Mahdi', *EJIL: Talk!*, 25 August 2017 [available at: https://www.ejiltalk.org/who-is-the-victim-of-cultural-heritage-destruction-the-reparations-order-in-the-case-of-the-prosecutor-v-ahmad-al-faqi-al-mahdi/ – accessed 11 February 2022].

164 Erich Hatala Matthes, '"Saving Lives or Saving Stones?" The Ethics of Cultural Heritage Protection in War' (2018) 32(1), *Public Affairs Quarterly*, 77.

165 *Ibid.*

> in the direction of wealthy countries than the reverse; it is far from an exchange and, indeed, looks rather more like exploitation.[166]

In this sense, the Trial Chamber's invocation in the *Al Mahdi* case of internationally recognised status as reflective of a higher degree of cultural value reproduced and imported some of the partial and problematic dimensions of the notions of international or universal cultural value into its account of the gravity of this crime.

Beyond formalist appeals to world heritage status or purely abstract accounts of 'international' value, the *Al Mahdi* case nevertheless also pointed in the direction of a more tangible relationship between the local value of cultural heritage and its international or global value in highlighting its identity-constituting role for particular communities and groups. Emulating the cosmopolitan narrative of the value of human diversity that was constructed around acts of destruction of religious property charged as persecution in *Kordić and Čerkez* at the ICTY, the Trial Chamber in *Al Mahdi* emphasised that 'cultural property also allows a group to distinguish and identify itself before the world community.'[167] In emphasising its identity-constituting value for a particular group in the group's relationship to the world community, as opposed to a conception of an inherent universal value attached to cultural heritage that is distinct from and unconnected to its value for the community in which it exists, the *Al Mahdi* case at the same time invoked in a limited form a somewhat more granular and bottom-up perspective to the internationalist conception of the value of cultural heritage.[168]

The internationalist flavour of the narrative constructed around the crime of attacking religious and historic buildings in the *Al Mahdi* case ultimately manifested itself in material terms in how the Trial Chamber analysed the nature of victimhood for the purposes of awarding reparations. In the Reparations Order, the Chamber determined that the destruction of the mausoleums harmed the inhabitants of Timbuktu as direct victims of the crime, but also caused suffering to the wider population of Mali and the international community.[169] In addition to its decision to award both collective and individual reparations to the inhabitants of Timbuktu directly affected by the destruction

166 Lyndel V. Prott, 'The International Movement of Cultural Objects', (2005) 12(2) *International Journal of Cultural Property*, 228.

167 Al Mahdi Reparations Order (n 150), para 16.

168 For an analysis of different ways of understanding this relationship between personal and impersonal value in the context of cultural heritage see Matthes (n 80), 999–1027.

169 Al Mahdi Reparations Order (n 150), para 53.

of the mausoleums, in a 'symbolic gesture',[170] the Chamber also awarded one euro in reparations to the Malian State and a further euro to UNESCO as the representative of the international community in this case,[171] making material the internationalist conception of the value of cultural property that has characterised the history and the case law on this crime.

3.3 *Object-Centrism*

Elements of an object-centric approach to the value and significance of cultural property are also discernible in the case law of the ICTY and the ICC. An object-centric or intrinsic value approach derives the value of a cultural object or property from its 'immutable characteristics related to [its] fabric or history.'[172] For this reason, the more established object-centric approach to cultural heritage is often presented in a dichotomous relationship to the development a more functionalist approach, discussed in the next section.[173] In contrast to a functionalist approach, where the 'human element' of cultural property protection is central, object-centrism focuses on the primacy of the object, which is seen to 'have a value in [its] own right that exists independently of people.'[174] An object-centric approach therefore identifies the cultural value of an object in its own intrinsic significance, or in its artistic, aesthetic or historic importance.[175] Consequently, the principal concern for an object-centric approach is the integrity of the object.[176] From this perspective, the most important principles are preservation – 'protecting the object and its context from impairment'[177] – and knowledge – 'historical, scientific, cultural and aesthetic truth that the object and its context can provide.'[178] In this way, an object-centric approach 'prioritizes the cultural object and views its protection as a value in its own right.'[179]

170 *Ibid.*, para 106.

171 *Ibid.*, para 104–107.

172 Sophia Labadi, *UNESCO, Cultural Heritage, and Outstanding Universal Value: Value-Based Analyses of the World Heritage and Intangible Cultural Heritage Conventions* (Alta Mira Press 2013), 13.

173 See for instance Francesco Francioni, 'The Human Dimension of International Cultural Heritage Law: An Introduction', (2011) 22(1), *European Journal of International Law*, 17.

174 Markus M. Müller, 'Cultural Heritage Protection: Legitimacy, Property, and Functionalism', (1998) 7(2) *International Journal of Cultural Property*, 397.

175 Petrovic (n 69), 22.

176 Müller (n 174), 396.

177 Merryman (n 45), 64.

178 Merryman (n 45), 64.

179 Tolina Loulanski, 'Revising the Concept of Cultural Heritage: The Argument for a Functional Approach', (2006) 13 *International Journal of Cultural Property*, 215.

This approach to the intrinsic value of certain types of cultural property is apparent in the jurisprudence of the ICTY, often running in tandem with a more functional conception of the value of such property, addressed in the next section. For some of the less high-profile cultural and religious buildings, damage to which was charged in various cases, an object-centric conception of their inherent value emerges primarily through a particular emphasis on their significant age. For instance, in the *Karadžić* and *Mladić* cases, in addition to noting its status as a UNESCO protected site, the Trial Chambers stressed that the Aladža mosque, which was blown up, dated from 1555.[180] In its discussion of the destruction of 'over 100 mosques, 2 mektebs and 7 Catholic churches', the Trial Chamber in *Plavšić* stressed that 'some of these monuments […] dated from the Middle Ages. They were, quite obviously, culturally, historically and regionally significant sites.'[181] Similarly, in *Prlić et al.*, the Trial Chamber noted that the 'Ćejvan Ćehaja Mosque, dating from 1552, was razed to the ground by artillery projectiles, and the […] Roznamedžija Ibrahim Efendija Mosque, dating from 1620, was destroyed by artillery fire or shelling.'[182]

The inherent value of the more high-profile buildings and monuments that were damaged is addressed in more expansive terms, highlighting their age as well as their historical and artistic significance. For instance, the Trial Judgment in *Prlić et al.* emphasised the inherent value and historical significance of the Old Bridge in Mostar, noting the 'exceptional character of this monument – built by architect Hairudin and almost 500 years old.'[183] The Trial Chambers in *Jokić* and *Strugar* laid similar emphasis on the historical and architectural dimensions of the Old Town of Dubrovnik. In *Jokić*, the Trial Chamber noted that the Old Town was 'an outstanding architectural ensemble illustrating a significant stage in human history'[184] while in *Strugar*, the Trial Chamber described the Old Town in the following terms:

> The Old Town of Dubrovnik is endowed with an exceptional architectural heritage, including palaces, churches and public buildings. The city first rose to prominence as a significant trading centre in the 13th century,

---

180 *Prosecutor v. Radovan Karadžić*, IT-95-5/18-T, ICTY, Trial Judgment – Volume I, 24 March 2016, para 925; *Prosecutor v. Ratko Mladić*, IT-09-92-T, ICTY, Trial Judgment – Volume I, 22 November 2017, para 693.

181 *Prosecutor v. Biljana Plavšić*, IT-00-39&40/1-S, ICTY, Sentencing Judgment, 27 February 2003, para 44.

182 *Prosecutor v. Jadranko Prlić et al.*, IT-04-74-T, ICTY, Trial Judgment – Volume II, 29 May 2013, para 1373 [hereafter Prlić et al. Trial Judgment Volume II].

183 *Ibid.*, para 1282.

184 Jokić Sentencing Judgment (n 122), para 51.

> and the oldest buildings in the Old Town date from this period. The fortifications of the Old Town, begun in the 12th century and completed in the mid-17th century, are widely regarded as some of the finest examples of city fortifications in Europe.[185]

The *Jokić* decision reinforces this object-centric conception of the cultural value of Dubrovnik in its analysis of the possibility of restoring destroyed residential buildings located in the Old Town. The Trial Chamber noted that 'restoration of buildings of this kind, when possible, can never return the buildings to their state prior to the attack because a certain amount of original, historically authentic material will have been destroyed, thus affecting the inherent value of the buildings.'[186] In doing so, the Trial Chamber appealed to the notion of authenticity, in this case, the material authenticity of the Old Town, as central to its cultural value. The concept of authenticity is a key principle in the field of heritage conservation. In general terms it refers to the 'integrity or 'true' nature of objects defined in relation to their origins, fabric and the intentions of their makers. An authentic historical object or building is thus one that is true to its origins in terms of its date, material, form, authorship, workmanship and, in many cases, its primary context and use.'[187] Identification of value in the historically authentic material from which the buildings in the Old Town are constructed is in this sense paradigmatic of an object-centric conception of cultural value, which emphasises the integrity of the object itself and therefore its 'unique, irreplaceable character.'[188]

The object-centric conception of cultural value was significantly less prominent in the *Al Mahdi* case at the ICC, but nevertheless emerged in the Reparations Order in which the chamber endorsed the reasoning in *Jokić* with respect to this question of authenticity. Echoing this object-centric conception of uniqueness and irreplaceability, in the Reparations Order, the Chamber in *Al Mahdi* similarly stressed that the inherent value of cultural property is affected by the process of restoration, since the element of authenticity is lost, concluding that 'the inherently irreplaceable nature of historical buildings cannot be remedied by reconstruction.'[189]

185 Strugar Trial Judgment (n 139), para 21.

186 Jokić Sentencing Judgment (n 122), para 52.

187 Siân Jones, 'Negotiating Authentic Objects and Authentic Selves: Beyond the Deconstruction of Authenticity', (2010) 15(2) *Journal of Material Culture*, 184.

188 John Henry Merryman, Albert E. Elsen and Stephen K. Urice, *Law, Ethics, and the Visual Arts* (Kluwer Law International 2007), xxvii.

189 Al Mahdi Reparations Order (n 150), para 129.

3.4 *Functionalism*

The final, and perhaps most prominent, normative theme that appears in the case law of the ICTY and ICC relates to a more functionalist or anthropocentric approach to the value of cultural property, which captures what Janine Natalya Clark has termed the 'human element'[190] of cultural property destruction. This type of approach to understanding the significance and value of cultural property departs from the position that 'cultural heritage does not exist independently of humans; not only its substance but also its (assigned) meaning is made by people.'[191] A functionalist approach to the cultural significance of buildings or objects therefore emphasises their function in society; objects or property are seen to hold cultural significance or value to the extent that they are attributed with meaning by people, often in relation to identity-creation and communication.[192] On this view, 'buildings, sites and objects are not seen as having intrinsic qualities or values but these values are imposed on the fabric of sites by actors situated in time and space.'[193] The evaluation of the cultural value or significance of cultural property is therefore an extrinsic process in the sense that 'values are in our minds and not inherent to objects.'[194] This conception of value is fundamentally relativist; it recognises that the meaning and significance attached to cultural property is contingent upon the people, communities, and cultures that attribute value to it.[195]

From this perspective, Tolina Loulanski has argued that 'protection of cultural heritage becomes meaningless if it cares only for objects instead of human beings, because "preservation [of cultural property] is sought, not for the sake of the objects, but for the sake of the people for whom they have a meaningful life."'[196] In her analysis of the wider shift towards a more functionalist approach to heritage conservation, which better reflects this 'human element' of its value, she has therefore identified a shift in conceptual focus in three directions, including first, a shift in focus from monuments to people,

190 Janine Natalya Clark, 'The Destruction of Cultural Heritage in Armed Conflict: The 'Human Element' and the Jurisprudence of the ICTY', (2018) 18 *International Criminal Law Review*, 36–66.

191 Müller (n 174), 399.

192 Loulanski (n 179), 207–233; Petrovic (n 69), 21.

193 Johan Brosché, Mattias Legnér, Joakim Kreutz and Akram Ijla, 'Heritage under attack: motives for targeting cultural property during armed conflict', (2017) 23(3) *International Journal of Heritage Studies*, 250.

194 Labadi (n 172), 15.

195 *Ibid.*

196 Loulanski (n 179), 216.

second, a shift from objects to functions and third, a shift from preservation for its own sake to purposeful preservation, sustainable use, and development.[197]

This conception of cultural value, which centralises the connection between people and cultural property, the social functions it serves, and therefore the human impact of its destruction on individuals and communities, emerges as a prominent normative thread in three distinct forms in the case law of the ICTY and ICC. The first theme relates to the actual functions of cultural property in the sense of its everyday use by the people whose heritage it represents. The second relates to the social meaning attributed to cultural property because of its relationship to the community in which it exists, while the fourth highlights the affective, emotional relationship between individuals and objects of cultural property.

3.4.1 Functions

Consistent with Loulanski's identification of a shift in conceptual focus from objects to functions as characteristic of the more functional approach to the value of cultural heritage,[198] analysis of the attack on Dubrovnik in the *Jokić* and *Strugar* cases at the ICTY highlighted the continued everyday use of the protected Old Town as part of the city. Perhaps most emblematic of this approach is the *Jokić* Trial Chamber's description of the Old Town of Dubrovnik as 'a "living city"' noting that 'the existence of its population was intimately intertwined with its ancient heritage.'[199] In *Strugar*, the Trial Chamber similarly stressed that:

> One of the unique features of the Old Town is that it has remained a living city. In fact, in 1991, the Old Town had an estimated population of between 7,000 and 8,000 residents. Within its city walls, the Old Town is fairly densely populated. Its palaces, which would previously have housed not more than a single noble family, have been divided up into flats and line the narrow streets of the Old Town.[200]

In contrast to the more object-centric dimensions to the analysis of the Old Town outlined in the previous section, the *Jokić* and *Strugar* Trial Chamber's emphasis on the Old Town as a place where people continue to live suggests that its cultural value and significance as a heritage site is also tied up with the

---

197 *Ibid.*, 207.

198 *Ibid.*

199 Jokić Sentencing Judgment (n 122), para 51.

200 Strugar Trial Judgment (n 139), para 21.

presence of the population that makes its life there. In this sense, the description of Dubrovnik as a 'living city' embodies the idea that, when it comes to cultural property, 'what is to be protected is the relationship between these sites, objects, and artefacts and human beings.'[201]

This emphasis on functional and everyday use is particularly pronounced in the *Al Mahdi* case at the ICC. The Trial Chamber emphasised in detailed and concrete terms the uses of the sites for the communities in Timbuktu, noting that the mausoleums and mosques of Timbuktu 'are an integral part of the religious life of its inhabitants. […] These mausoleums are frequently visited by the residents – they are places of prayer and, for some, places of pilgrimage.'[202] The Chamber noted that the Alpha Moya Mausoleum is 'visited in order to pray and make offerings',[203] that the two mausoleums adjoining the Djingareyber Mosque are 'especially visited on Mondays and Fridays and for important religious celebrations'[204] and described the Sheikh Mouhamed El Mikki Mausoleum as 'a place of spiritual retreat and reflection.'[205] The Chamber also made note of how 'the people of Timbuktu were collectively ensuring the mausoleums remained in good condition in the course of symbolic maintenance events involving the entire community – women and elderly and young people.'[206] In this way, the Chamber pointed to the everyday uses of the sites by the community, their role in bringing the community together in shared practices and, in doing so, invoked a conception of their cultural value as rooted in how their functions and uses constituted 'their role in the cultural life in Timbuktu.'[207]

3.4.2 Social Meaning

Similarly in line with Loulanski's identification of a shift in focus from objects to people, the case law reflects a growing level of engagement with the social meaning attached to cultural property. This has partly emerged in general terms through an emphasis on the symbolic dimensions of cultural sites, speaking to a less tangible element of the relationship between cultural property and people that moves beyond the more utilitarian account of its actual

201 Lucas Lixinski, 'A Third Way of Thinking About Cultural Property', (2019) 44(2) *Brooklyn Journal of International Law*, 582.
202 Al Mahdi Judgment and Sentence (n 119), para 34.
203 *Ibid.*, para 38.
204 *Ibid.*
205 *Ibid.*
206 *Ibid.*, para 78.
207 *Ibid.*, para 46.

use in everyday life. At the ICTY, the emphasis on the symbolic dimensions of cultural property was most pronounced with respect to the destruction of the Old Bridge in Mostar. The Trial and Appeals Chambers in *Prlić et al.* went to significant lengths to highlight the symbolic value of the bridge, emphasising the 'importance of the bridge both for the inhabitants of the town of Mostar to which it gave its name and for the BiH and the Balkan region. The Old Bridge [...] symbolised the link between the communities, despite their religious differences.'[208] An emphasis on the symbolic nature of sites of cultural heritage is also pronounced in the *Al Mahdi* case. The Trial Chamber referred to the 'purpose and symbolism'[209] of cultural property and emphasised that the buildings 'were not only religious buildings but had also a symbolic and emotional value for the inhabitants of Timbuktu.'[210] The Chamber expanded on this by also noting that 'Timbuktu was an emblematic city with a mythical dimension [...] it played a crucial role in the expansion of Islam in the region. Timbuktu is at the heart of Mali's cultural heritage.'[211] In emphasising the symbolic dimensions of cultural property these decisions invoke a conception of their cultural value as not only inherent or intrinsic, but rather, through the emphasis on the social meaning attached to them, as rooted in a conception of cultural value as a 'human construction [...] not only because it is made by men and women but also because it is defined by them.'[212]

Linked to, and in some ways explanatory of, the symbolic role of cultural property in its relationship to a group or community, many decisions also invoke more complex conceptions of the social meaning and function of cultural property in terms of its role in constructing and representing the identities of communities and groups. Thus, at a basic level, the Trial Chamber in *Mladić* at the ICTY concluded that attacks on Muslim and Catholic sacred sites 'had a severe impact on the people who valued the property and amounted to an attack on the religious identity of Muslims and Roman Catholics',[213] while the Trial Chamber in *Kordić and Čerkez* famously argued with respect to charges of persecution that the destruction of religious buildings, 'when perpetrated with the requisite discriminatory intent, amounts to an attack on the very religious identity of a people.'[214]

208 Prlić et al. Trial Judgment Volume II (n 182), para 1282.
209 Al Mahdi Reparations Order (n 150), para 522.
210 *Ibid.*, para 78 – 79.
211 *Ibid.*, para 78.
212 Müller (n 174), 398.
213 *Prosecutor v. Ratko Mladić*, IT-09-92-T, ICTY, Trial Judgment – Volume III, 22 November 2017, para 3408.
214 Kordić and Čerkez Trial Judgment (n 126), para 207.

The Trial Chamber in *Stanišić and Župljanin* expanded on this account of the social meaning attached to cultural property, moving beyond the role of religious buildings as straightforwardly symbolising a particular religious identity, to allude briefly to the role of religious and cultural property in constituting a group's history and memory. The Chamber in *Stanišić and Župljanin* noted that 'wanton destruction and damage of religious and cultural property [was] carried out in a concerted effort to eliminate the historical moorings of the Bosnian Muslims and Bosnian Croats.'[215] Similarly, the Appeals Chamber in *Brđanin* quoted expert witness testimony on the motivation driving the systematic destruction of places of worship, which implicitly invoked a more complex account of how religious property may be tied up with a group's identity in terms of how it represents its system of beliefs as well as its history:

> When asked what he thought the reason was for why this campaign was pursued, Witness Kaiser speculated that it was to send a message: "one part of the message is 'we don't respect you, we don't respect your system of belief, we don't respect your culture or psychology.' Another one is 'we don't want you.' But there's the other message that is sort of towards society [...] which is annihilation, bulldozing a monument, it's like saying 'they weren't there' basically. Or even if you left a cemetery, 'well, they were there but you left nothing of value.'"[216]

The *Al Mahdi* case at the ICC significantly developed on some of the ideas alluded to here with respect to the social processes that give meaning to cultural heritage. Emphasising the historical significance of the attacked buildings in noting that they 'reflected part of Timbuktu's history and its role in the expansion of Islam,'[217] the Trial Chamber in *Al Mahdi* displayed a particular sensitivity to the constitutive relationship between cultural heritage and the history, memory and identity of communities. The Trial Chamber explained that 'cultural heritage is important not only in itself, but also in relation to its human dimension. Cultural property also allows a group to distinguish and identify itself before the world community.'[218] It therefore concluded that 'the attack against the Protected Buildings not only destroyed and damaged physical

215 *Prosecutor v. Mićo Stanišić and Stojan Župljanin*, IT-08-91-T, ICTY, Trial Judgment – Volume II, 27 March 2013, para 527.

216 *Prosecutor v. Radoslav Brđanin*, IT-99-36-A, ICTY, Appeal Judgment, 3 April 2007, para 338, footnote 693.

217 Al Mahdi Judgment and Sentence (n 119), para 78. See also para 60.

218 Al Mahdi Reparations Order (n 150), para 16.

structures. Its impact 'rippled out into the community and diminished the link and identity the local community had' with such valuable cultural heritage.'[219] Expanding on this account of the social processes that bind communities to their cultural heritage, the Trial Chamber went on to explain that:

> cultural heritage plays a central role in the way communities define themselves and bond together, and how they identify with their past and contemplate their future. UNESCO states that 'the loss of heritage during times of conflict can deprive a community of its identity and memory, as well as the physical testimony of the past. Those destroying cultural heritage seek to disrupt the social fabric of societies.' Cultural heritage is to be understood as encompassing the resources enabling cultural identification and development processes of individuals and groups, which they, implicitly or explicitly, wish to transmit to future generations.[220]

Explicitly adopting the view that cultural property is valuable for its human dimension and highlighting the social implications of its destruction as an attack on more than 'physical structures',[221] but on the social fabric of a community, this decision marks a pronounced shift towards a social, functionalist conception of cultural value. In doing so, it unambiguously invokes a normative conception of the crime of attacking cultural property as being rooted in the value of the social processes of identity formation, memory preservation and community definition and bonding, to which cultural heritage is understood to contribute.

This conception of the value and significance of the mausoleums in social terms is underscored by how the Trial Chamber went to lengths to explain the specific myths and beliefs that surround them and make them meaningful for the population of Timbuktu, exemplifying a social constructivist conception of cultural value that embodies the notion that 'our world is socially constructed, and so are the meanings and functions that are assigned to objects.'[222] The Trial Chamber explained that the mausoleums 'were of great importance to the people of Timbuktu [...] They reflected their commitment to Islam and played a psychological role to the extent of being perceived as protecting the people of Timbuktu.'[223] The Chamber further stressed that 'the

219 *Ibid.*, para 19.
220 *Ibid.*, para 14–15.
221 *Ibid.*, para 19.
222 Müller (n 174), 398.
223 Al Mahdi Judgment and Sentence (n 119), para 78.

Protected Buildings were widely perceived in Timbuktu as being the protectors of the community from outside harm. The attack on the Protected Buildings not only destroyed cherished monuments, but also shattered the community's collective faith that they were protected.'[224] This conception of the value of the sites as derived from how they are perceived by people and the role that they attributed to them is particularly pronounced in the discussion of the door of the Sidi Yahia Mosque. In its analysis of the destruction of the door, the Trial Chamber highlighted how 'legend had it that this door had not been opened for 500 years and that opening it would lead to the Last Judgment.'[225] The Chamber went on to recount statements made by the defendant while the destruction of the door was taking place, which similarly emphasise the significance of the myths attached to it. The Chamber quoted Al Mahdi as saying:

> We heard about a door in the ancient mosque of Sidi Yahya. If it is opened, the Day of Resurrection will begin. [...] Over time, a myth took hold, claiming that the Day of Resurrection would begin if the door were opened. We fear that these myths will invade the beliefs of people and the ignorant who, because of their ignorance and their distance from religion, will think that this is the truth. So we decided to open it.[226]

In highlighting how the destruction of the door was given a very specific meaning because of the myth attached to it, this analysis centralises the extrinsic, social meaning of the door in its account of its cultural value. In this sense, the Trial Chamber's emphasis on the community's belief in the protective role of the mausoleums, the particular myths attached to the door of the Sidi Yahia Mosque, and the impact of the destruction of these objects on the community, directly invokes a conception of the normative dimensions of the protection of cultural property and the criminalisation of its destruction as 'not for the sake of the objects, but for the sake of the people for whom they have a meaningful life.'[227]

3.4.3 Emotions

Some of the ICTY case law and the *Al Mahdi* case at the ICC does in this way construct an account of the value and significance of cultural property that makes some appeals to its social role, with the *Al Mahdi* case representing a

224 Al Mahdi Reparations Order (n 150), para 86.
225 Al Mahdi Judgment and Sentence (n 119), para 38(viii).
226 *Ibid.*
227 Loulanski (n 179), 216.

significant development in the extent to which the social, human dimensions of cultural property are given expression in a judgment. The final normative thread identified within this functionalist theme takes place at an individual, more granular level by articulating the emotional, affective dimensions of cultural property in its relationship to the feelings of the people 'that live in, with or around'[228] it, identified here not as abstract members of a community or group with a shared identity and culture, but as individuals whose relationship with a particular site of cultural heritage operates at the level of their personal thoughts and emotions.

The emotional dimension of the relationship between people and cultural heritage is developed primarily in the *Al Mahdi* case at the ICC. Noting that 'most cultural property and cultural heritage are unique and of sentimental value'[229] and that 'people feel strongly about their heritage',[230] the Trial Chamber emphasised in general terms that 'the mausoleums [...] were of great importance to the people of Timbuktu, who admired them and were attached to them. [...] The mausoleums were among the most cherished buildings of the city.'[231] It stressed that the sites were not only religious buildings but also had an 'emotional value for the inhabitants of Timbuktu.'[232] The Chamber went on to recount the testimony of a witness who had explained that 'destroying the mausoleums, to which the people of Timbuktu had an emotional attachment, was a war activity aimed at breaking the soul of the people of Timbuktu [...] the population of Mali [...] considered Timbuktu as a source of pride.'[233]

This recognition of the human value of cultural property from the perspective of feelings and emotions is further expanded in the Reparations Order through the Chamber's analysis of the harm inflicted on the population of Timbuktu by the destruction of the mausoleums.[234] In its analysis of the 'emotional distress and harm suffered across the Timbuktu community',[235] the Chamber quoted extensively from victim applicants' testimonies, selecting testimonies that speak directly to the individual emotional impact of the destruction of the sites:

---

228 Lixinski (n 201), 564.
229 Al Mahdi Reparations Order (n 150), para 22.
230 *Ibid.*, para 18.
231 Al Mahdi Judgment and Sentence (n 119), para 78.
232 *Ibid.*, para 79.
233 *Ibid.*, para 80.
234 Al Mahdi Reparations Order (n 150), para 85.
235 *Ibid.*, para 86.

> 'I was completely emotionally devastated by the destruction of the mausoleums.'
>
> 'I was a victim of the destruction of the mausoleum, upset and shaken in my body and to the depths of my being.'
>
> 'I have never suffered so deeply in my life [...] Mentally, I was devastated. I felt humiliated by the destruction. I am still suffering [...] I am still affected mentally.'
>
> 'I was so shocked and hurt on the day of the destruction that I could have died. [...] [M]y faith shattered and my belief unsettled. I lost everything with the destruction – my childhood, my belief and my attachment.' [...]
>
> 'The whole city suffered on the day the mausoleums were destroyed. I wept and many others wept, because we were in great pain. The saints are all important to us. They are ancestors of all of us.' [...]
>
> 'I cried a lot on the day of the destruction. My family, my friends and all the people of Timbuktu suffered. We will never forget. [...] When the mausoleums were destroyed, we were shattered as well. The pain is still there today.' [...]
>
> 'The destruction of the sacred shrines of my ancestors caused me suffering [...] I suffered, as did the other members of my family.'[236]

In emphasising the individual emotional suffering experienced by the residents of Timbuktu as a result of the destruction of the mausoleum, its impact on their memories of childhood, their spiritual beliefs and their connection to their ancestors, the Reparations Order humanised and personalised the social value of cultural property down to its most granular, individual dimensions. Doing so constructs an account of the social dimensions of the normative basis of the criminalisation of attacks on cultural property in somewhat more concrete, human terms, which moves beyond more abstract appeals to symbolism, identity, history and memory, to offer a bottom up perspective on the 'human element' of the crime.

Taken together, the decisions of the ICTY and the *Al Mahdi* case at the ICC in this way construct a multifaceted conception of the normative dimensions of the criminalisation of attacks on cultural property that builds significantly on the more basic conceptual distinction between a civilian use vs. cultural value approach seen to underlie the definitions of these crimes in the ICTY and Rome Statutes. The decisions invoke conceptions of the value of cultural

236 *Ibid.*, para 85.

property that draw on a number of different theoretical approaches that are complex and multidimensional, epitomising the notion that 'the scope of value can be highly variable depending on both the extent of individuals who have reason to value something and the kinds of reasons they have.'[237]

4 Narratives of Cultural Value During Trial Proceedings

The narratives constructed around attacks on cultural property during the course of trial proceedings provide the basis for the primary themes that are reflected in more limited form in the case law. Thus, the object-centric approach identified in the case law, with its emphasis on the intrinsic value of the material dimensions of cultural property, particularly with respect to the age of an object, also features heavily during trial proceedings.[238] For instance, the Aladža mosque in Foča was described as 'a pearl amongst the cultural heritage in this part of Europe. […] It is 450 years old'[239] while the 'value and the antiquity'[240] of a Dubrovnik palace was emphasised as a 'a priceless object, 200 years old.'[241] In *Blaskić*, a mosque was described as 'arguably the finest building in whole area. The reason is that this stonework here is extremely, extremely fine, a very carefully crafted building. There is almost no other building that you can actually see such stonework in the whole.'[242]

237 Matthes (n 80), 1003.

238 *Prosecutor v. Ratko Mladić and Radovan Karadžić*, IT-95-18-R61 & IT-95-5-R61, ICTY, Transcript 2 July 1996, 450–452, 441–443, Transcript 8 July 1996, 895 [hereafter Mladić and Karadžić Transcript Date]; *Prosecutor v. Pavle Strugar*, IT-01-42-T, ICTY, Transcript 16 December 2003, 277–285, Transcript 8 December 2004, 8634–8635 [hereafter Strugar Transcript Date]; *Prosecutor v. Jadranko Prlić et al.*, IT-04-74-T, ICTY, Transcript 4 December 2006, 11054, 11056, Transcript 22 May 2006, 2240, Transcript 24 May 2006, 2420 [hereafter Prlić et al. Transcript Date]; *Prosecutor v. Slobodan Milošević*, IT-02-54, ICTY, Transcript 15 February 2002, 373, Transcript 7 March 2002, 1661, Transcript 9 April 2002, 2674, Transcript 10 April 2002, 2699, Transcript 11 March 2003, 17687, Transcript 8 July 2003, 23801, 23803, Transcript 27 October 2005, 45916 [hereafter Milošević Transcript Date]; *Prosecutor v. Momčilo Krajišnik*, IT-00-39, ICTY, Transcript 4 February 2004, 380, Transcript 31 October 2005, 17949 [hereafter Krajišnik Transcript Date]; *Prosecutor v. Radovan Karadžić*, IT-95-5/18, ICTY, Transcript 9 December 2011, 22591 [hereafter Karadžić Transcript Date]; *Prosecutor v. Tihomir Blaškić*, IT-95-14, ICTY, Transcript 21 April 1998, 7558, Transcript 17 July 1998, 10613 [hereafter Blaškić Transcript Date]; *Prosecutor v. Enver Hadžihasanović and Amir Kubura*, IT-01-47, ICTY, Transcript 17 December 2003, 1125.

239 *Prosecutor v. Biljana Plavšić*, IT-00-39 & 40/1, ICTY, Transcript 16 December 2002, 400 [hereafter Plavšić Transcript Date].

240 Strugar Transcript 24 February 2004 (n 238), 3084.

241 *Ibid.*, 3100.

242 Blaškić Transcript 16 July 1998 (n 238), 10601.

The symbolic dimensions of cultural property are also repeatedly highlighted during proceedings, with the Stari Most being described as 'a symbol of Mostar',[243] 'a symbol more than anything else',[244] 'a symbol of the town [which] will remain a symbol forever'[245] and even as 'the soul of Mostar [...] which is a part and name of symbol [sic] of this town.'[246] The Old Town of Dubrovnik was characterised as 'the showcase of Croatia. [...] Croatian culture originates from that town. It is a jewel in the Republic of Croatia. And throughout the world, when you speak of Croatia, other cities are much less well known, but everybody knows of Dubrovnik.'[247] Symbolism also featured centrally in the trial discourse of the *Al Mahdi* case at the ICC, with the mausoleums in Timbuktu being described as 'the contemporary living symbol of the city',[248] a 'religious and symbolic [...] focal point [...] symbols of these men',[249] 'symbols that are the substrate of the identity and culture of a nation, namely Mali'[250] as well as 'a great symbol of the identity of a people [...] Timbuktu for Africa is like the tour Eiffel for France and the pyramids in Egypt.'[251]

The extent to which the OTP in the *Al Mahdi* case constructed an emphatically social constructivist account of the cultural value of the mausoleums in Timbuktu is also underscored by the record of proceedings, which reveal a detailed recounting of the legends and beliefs attached to the mausoleums. For instance, the OTP explained how:

> Timbuktu is an ancient city, a legendary city which has many mausoleums. And according to the local population, it is – it offers a protective bulwark to the city against dangers. The name of the city comes from a legend which is linked to the specific location of the city between the desert and the Niger river. According to oral tradition, a Touareg woman called Bouctou had the task of guarding over a well where caravans of traders would stop to water their animals, having crossed in the desert from the Maghreb and moving towards Yemen.[252]

243 Prlić et al. Transcript 17 May 2007 (n 238), 18725.
244 Prlić et al. Transcript 5 May 2009 (n 238), 39565.
245 Prlić et al. Transcript 4 May 2006 (n 238), 1281.
246 Prlić et al. Transcript 20 May 2009 (n 238), 4043.
247 Strugar Transcript 3 May 2004 (n 238), 5802.
248 *Prosecutor v. Ahmad al-Faqi al-Mahdi*, ICC-01/12-01/15, ICC, Transcript 22 August 2016, 19 [hereafter Al Mahdi Transcript Date].
249 Al Mahdi Transcript 23 August 2016 (n 248), 44.
250 Al Mahdi Transcript 24 August 2016 (n 248), 21.
251 *Ibid.*, 25. See similarly 16.
252 Al Mahdi Transcript 1 March 2016 (n 248), 23.

> Saint Bahaber Babadié was, according to oral tradition, a virtuous man, respected by all, who was notably famed for his talents as a conciliator. It is said that he took from the rich to give to the poorest and that is why his descendants carry on the tradition. They collect donations in particular during the celebration of Maouloud. According to local belief, the white sand of the mausoleum heals most illnesses.[253]

> Now, this mausoleum dates back to the 19th century and is dedicated to the saint of the same name, who was a renowned teacher, writer and law specialist. [...] According to oral tradition [...] this saint was known to carry out miracles and to predict the future. For this reason the local population go to this mausoleum when they face a dilemma or an important decision.[254]

The Trial Chamber ultimately reflected this approach in its analysis of the door of the Sidi Yahia mosque, which was described during proceedings as 'an ancient wooden door which was steeped in meaning for the people of Timbuktu. It was said that if the door was opened, crises would break out, war, droughts.'[255] This extrinsic, social constructivist approach to cultural value, which centralised the particular beliefs and cultural practices of the inhabitants of Timbuktu, was even made explicit during a presentation of photographs of the site during hearings, when the OTP called on the court to 'imagine the practices and the rights of the population carried out at those mausoleums. I'd ask you to view these buildings through the eyes of the people of Timbuktu.'[256]

While in this way the broad contours of the normative discourse on cultural value constructed during the proceedings of these cases was subsequently captured in decisions, some of the narratives that emerged during proceedings nevertheless also advance a thicker and more developed account of cultural value, in particular with respect to its social, human dimensions.

4.1 *International Public Opinion*

For instance, while the characteristic emphasis on internationalist conceptions of cultural value is present throughout the proceedings addressing the destruction of secular heritage,[257] usually in the form of references to the

253 *Ibid.*, 30.
254 *Ibid.*, 27.
255 *Ibid.*, 29.
256 *Ibid.*, 24.
257 Strugar Transcript 23 April 2008 (n 238), 171; Strugar Transcript 8 September 2004 (n 238), 8619; Strugar Transcript 20 January 2004 (n 238), 1001; Milošević Transcript 8 October 2002

UNESCO-protected status of some sites or appeals to the notion of the common heritage of humanity,[258] the internationalist narrative that emerged during proceedings at both the ICTY and the ICC also constructed a more tangible, human dimension to the internationalist character of cultural value in how it stressed the international renown of the cultural sites and the response to their destruction from the perspective of international public opinion. In *Milosević*, for example, Dubrovnik was described as 'one of the great cities, a pearl, and I suspect the best known, worldwide city from the former Yugoslavia'[259] while a witness explained that 'throughout the world, when you speak of Croatia [...] everybody knows of Dubrovnik. On the day when Dubrovnik was attacked [...] I got telephone calls from Italy, from London, protests were made from everywhere, from all over the world over that attack.'[260]

Similarly, in the *Al Mahdi* case, along with more general references to the international value of the destroyed mausoleums,[261] the OTP went to lengths to highlight the responses of other states in condemning the destruction, noting that 'the attack [...] rightfully raised a chorus of protests and outrage nationally, regionally and internationally.'[262] This was further reinforced through drawing parallels with other well-known instances of heritage destruction, such as the Buddhas of Bamyan and the ancient city of Palmyra, and emphasising their effect on international public opinion:

> For the public that are interested in world heritage [...] World Heritage sites are very, very well-known and people recognize them as part of modern culture. So when a site is destroyed [...] [it] raise[s] huge reactions from the public opinion, from institutions, cultural institutions around the world, the big museums and so on, when a site is destroyed deliberately, I think the entire community that believes that heritage is a

(n 238), 11201; Milošević Transcript 23 October 2003 (n 238), 28038; Prlić et al. Transcript 3 November 2009 (n 238), 46463.

258 See for instance Strugar Transcript 31 March 2004 (n 238), 4315; Strugar Transcript 25 October 2001 (n 238), 18; Strugar Transcript 28 January 2004 (n 238), 1461; Strugar Transcript 4 February 2004 (n 238), 1839–1840; Prlić et al. Transcript 20 May 2009 (n 238), 40432; Milošević Transcript 29 October 2001 (n 238), 31.

259 Milošević Transcript 16 September 2003 (n 238), 26720. See similarly Strugar Transcript 18 December 2003 (n 238), 363; Strugar Transcript 13 January 2004 (n 238), 573.

260 Strugar Transcript 3 May 2004 (n 238), 5802.

261 See for instance Al Mahdi Transcript 1 March 2016 (n 248), 16, 17, 21; Al Mahdi Transcript 23 August 2016 (n 248), 49–50; Al Mahdi Transcript 24 August 2016 (n 248), 9, 23, 28; Al Mahdi Transcript 17 August 2017 (n 248), 4–5.

262 Al Mahdi Transcript 1 March 2016 (n 248), 16.

> fundamental component of cultural, modern cultural life, it's suffering. So it is really a wound that is sometimes very hard to heal.[263]

These accounts of the international response to the destruction of cultural heritage imply a more tangible and sociological element to the notion of international cultural value, beyond the formalist emphasis on legal status or the abstract notion that 'humanity as a whole [is] affected by [the] loss'[264] of cultural heritage, by pointing to the effects of the destruction in provoking an actual response from actors outside the community or state directly affected. This narrative appears to seek to substantiate the more abstract account of the 'international' value of cultural property by suggesting that its value in these terms is evidenced by the responses and condemnation of actual people, outside of the state in which the object or site is situated, to its destruction.

4.2 *Remodelling the Landscape*

While the judgments that address the destruction of cultural property at the ICTY, in particular the destruction of houses of worship, reflect a recognition of its symbolic nature as tied up with the identity of religious and ethnic groups, the narratives that emerged during trial proceedings contribute an additional dimension to this theme, offering an expanded conception of their value and significance from a social and cultural perspective. These narratives highlight the communicative or meaningful dimensions of the targeting of such property by offering a conception of its role as a physical and visual anchor for a community's history and identity. This takes place through discussions of the motivations behind the targeting of religious property, which situate its destruction within the wider account of ethnic cleansing and intentional displacement. Firstly, the link between religious groups, their property and cultural or ethnic identity was highlighted, with one witness noting, for instance, that 'in Bosnia-Herzegovina cultural and ethnic identity historically has been tied up with the religious choices of one's ancestors and that, therefore, a religious monument tends to have an association with a particular cultural and ethnic group.'[265] Similarly, another witness observed that 'it's no secret that in those areas religious property is very important to preserving identity.'[266]

The motivations behind the destruction of religious property was then outlined in these terms. For instance, a witness described how 'there is a belief

263 Al Mahdi Transcript 23 August 2016 (n 248), 59–61.
264 Al Mahdi Transcript 1 March 2016 (n 248), 16.
265 Milošević Transcript 3 July 2003 (n 238), 23837.
266 Prlić et al. Transcript 21 July 2008 (n 238), 31100.

among the Serbs that if there are no mosques, there are no Muslims. And by destroying the mosques, the Muslims will lose a motive to return to their villages.'[267] Similarly, the police chief of Prijedor is recounted as having said that 'with their mosques it's not enough to break the minarets. You've got to shake the foundation. That way they [...] will leave and never come back. They cannot rebuild.'[268] Highlighting the communicative dimension of targeting religious buildings on this basis, witnesses explained that 'the fact that the church was targeted and why it was targeted [was] to send a message to the Croats living there that there was no reason to return'[269] and that 'destruction or damaging of a minaret is clearly a sign to a population. [...] This is a signal. Hitting a minaret is also one way of chasing, chasing the people.'[270]

Interwoven with this understanding of the motivation behind the targeting of houses of worship and the message this was intended to communicate is a sub-narrative that constructs the relationship between religious property and ethnic or religious identity not only in abstract, symbolic terms, but also more tangibly as a physical and visual anchor for a group's history and memory. It was, for instance, asserted by one witness that 'the targeting of a minaret, certainly does have a symbolic significance to it. It is trying to change this Bosnian town, to eliminate the memory.'[271] Another witness explained that 'Mosques were destroyed. Houses and buildings, which through their architecture reminded the people of the traditions – the architectural traditions of the area, they were destroyed completely. [...] Everything that in any way was reminiscent of the past, this was destroyed.'[272]

The visual dimensions of the existence of religious buildings featured particularly prominently in this understanding of the targeting of the physical traces of the presence of particular groups. The following expert witness testimony in *Mladić* is emblematic of this narrative, emphasising the importance of the visual for the symbolic role of religious buildings in signifying the presence of a particular community:

> Q. Based on your studies and your work, can you tell us about the role of houses of worship in Bosnian Muslim and Bosnian Croat cultures?

---

267 Krajišnik Transcript 29 June 2005 (n 238), 15431.

268 Karadžić Transcript 9 December 2011 (n 238), 22617.

269 *Prosecutor v. Milan Martić*, IT-95-11, ICTY, Transcript 26 June 2006, 5912 [hereafter Martić Transcript Date].

270 Mladić and Karadžić Transcript 2 July 1996 (n 238) 463.

271 *Ibid.* 481.

272 Plavšić Transcript 16 December 2002 (n 239), 399.

> A. Okay. Houses of worship in neighbourhoods and villages were often the centres of religious life and, to some extent, also of cultural and social life and they symbolised the visible presence of a community in a given place. So Mahala quarter of a city or a village would be immediately recognisable as a place where Muslims or Croats lived by the presence of a minaret or a church steeple. Many of these neighbourhoods and villages had a mixed population, and in that case you would see each groups' prominent religious monument visible in the landscape. In the late 20th century especially in urban areas the majority of the population was not particularly religiously observant. They might go to a mosque or a church mainly for the big transition of life events such as weddings or funerals. Nevertheless, the presence of these constituted the sign that this community to which they belonged had history in that place and belonged there.[273]

In similar terms, mosques were described as the 'clearest visual evidence of [the non-Serb community's] existence',[274] minarets as 'just like a church steeple in the landscape, it announces the presence of a community, in this case a Muslim community, in a particular location'[275] or as:

> a very characteristic sight in a Bosnian town. It is on the horizon. You can see the town sometimes for long ways away because of the minaret. The minaret means that this is a town which is inhabited by Muslims. It is a sign of the presence of Muslims.[276]

The motivation behind the targeting was therefore also framed in visual terms, with a witness in *Blaskić* explaining, for instance, that 'where there are no minarets, it seems to say that there are no Muslims. [...] this is remodelling the landscape to make it correspond to what the ethnic or national components of the landscape, in fact, are.'[277] A witness in *Blaskić* put together these elements of constituting a physical, visual anchor as a marker not only of a group's presence but also its history and memory, stating that:

273 *Prosecutor v. Ratko Mladić*, IT-09-92, ICTY, Transcript 16 October 2013, 17890 [hereafter Mladić Transcript Date].

274 Mladić Transcript 18 March 2014 (n 273), 20817.

275 Karadžić Transcript 8 December 2011 (n 238), 22535.

276 Mladić and Karadžić Transcript 2 July 1996 (n 238), 444.

277 Blaškić Transcript 16 July 1998 (n 238), 10632.

> If you destroy this mosque, you are doing several different things. One of them is that you are sort of removing the memory – it's been there since the end of the 16th century, you are removing the Muslims, not from just the present landscape or the future landscape, you are removing them from the past. In this case, you are even going back further. You are going to damage the perception of the past that everybody has had. If it goes far enough, you are taking the Muslims completely out of a chronology, not just out of space. You're saying that the Muslims were never there.[278]

The same idea was reflected in *Karadzić*, where a witness explained that '[t]he way of eliminating [a people] also involved a destruction of their heritage. In other words, you are eliminating a sacral building and in this way you are eliminating the memory of having lived together. [...] I mean, you have a kind of radical change in the physical environment in which people are living. This means that you are talking about the removal of the signposts of collective and individual life.'[279] In *Mladić*, this was described as '"memory-cide" [...] aiming at eradicating memory.'[280] This narrative of remodelling history and memory through eliminating the visual traces of a group in the landscape in this way implicitly consolidates the centrality of religious buildings for constituting group identity, history and memory in this context, implying a more developed and expansive account of the human, social value of such buildings, and the implications of their loss, than that offered by the case law of the ICTY.

4.3 *Individuals and Cultural Property*

The discourse around destruction of cultural property during trial proceedings at the ICTY also contributed an additional more personalised, individual conception of the human dimension of cultural value, which was later also captured in the Reparations Order in the *Al Mahdi* case, in highlighting the relationship between cultural property and the memories, identities and emotions of individuals. For instance, the testimonies of some witnesses at the ICTY reveal the human relationship between religious property and individuals by reference to their personal memories of buildings which were subsequently destroyed:

> Q. [...] you said that you were emotionally attached to the Catholic church in Dalj. Can you explain that?

278 *Ibid.*, 10633-10634.
279 Mladić and Karadžić Transcript 2 July 1996 (n 238), 457.
280 Mladić and Karadžić Transcript 11 July 1996 (n 238), 955.

A. I grew up in my childhood in that neighbourhood close to that church. That's where we played. And on some saint's day, we had the custom of going to the Catholic church, just like the Catholic church – Catholic people went to our church on some holidays, so I was emotionally attached to it because of my childhood memories.[281]

Q. Was there a mosque in your village? I'm sorry. Was there a mosque in your village?
A. The mosque was no longer standing. The minaret was destroyed. And I wanted to go up there because I remember as a little kid I used to go up there. And I wanted to go steps and my mom told me – somebody mentioned, "Don't go. Might be mines or something up there." So I didn't want to actually – I wanted to go, but I didn't want – they didn't let me to go. But minaret was totally destroyed.[282]

The same narrative is present with respect to secular heritage. Witness testimonies on the destruction of these buildings speak to an account of cultural value that also incorporates the role that buildings and monuments may play in individuals' lives at a personal, affective level. For instance, in *Blaskić* an expert witness provided the following testimony:

Q. Dr. Kaiser, why is this important? Why you as a representative of UNESCO, why is this issue concerning the sacral and cultural monuments and the safeguarding of those monuments an important issue?
A. It's important for reasons that are sort of second nature to people, but often sometimes harder to spell out. People are attached to their environment, first of all. Secondly, they are attached to specific objects in their own environment. If you take a building like Vijecnica, the national university library in Sarajevo, people are not attached to it because they know the name of the architect or they admire it aesthetically. They are attached to it because they had rendezvoused with their girlfriends in front of. Maybe they spent many good hours reading books in it. It's a landmark. It's something that is part of their lives. Maybe as time goes on, they start to know a little bit more about it and what it represents, what it signifies, in terms of the history of the town or the history of their district. So in an unconscious way, people

281 *Prosecutor v. Goran Hadžić*, IT-04-75-T, ICTY, Transcript 16 September 2014, 11563 [hereafter Hadžić Transcript Date].

282 Krajišnik Transcript 20 October 2004 (n 238), 7247–7248.

> are very attached to their environment and the buildings in their environment.[283]

This outline of the relationship between people and cultural property on an ordinary, everyday level was reinforced through testimonies that reflect how cultural property featured in particular in the inner lives and identities of some individuals. With respect to the destruction of the Old Bridge in Mostar, in *Prlić et al.* a witness argued that 'the Old Bridge in Mostar was a part of every man and woman in Mostar. It was a part of me.'[284] In *Strugar*, a witness testified directly to the role of the Old Town of Dubrovnik in constituting his personal identity:

> Q. Have you ever lived in the Old Town of Dubrovnik?
> A. Yes. That is my town. I'm actually a child of that town.
> Q. How would you describe your familiarity with the Old Town and the buildings and objects within it?
> A. I am very familiar with it. I had accumulated all of that from a material and spiritual point of view, and it actually formed my personality, living in the Old Town. I was always very proud of that. I am very proud of that. And I shall always be very proud of that.[285]

Lastly, resonating with the later attention to the emotional impact of the destruction of the mausoleums on individual inhabitants of Timbuktu in the Reparations Order in the *Al Mahdi* case, the affective dimensions of people's relationship to cultural property, in particular the emotional impact of its destruction at an individual level, while absent from the decisions of the ICTY, was nevertheless pronounced in the narratives of the trial proceedings on secular heritage. For instance, the burning down of the national library in Sarajevo was described as having caused a 'great shock'[286] to its citizens. The destruction of the Old Bridge in Mostar was often described in similar terms as having caused 'a great deal of shock, regret and shame',[287] as having affected the 'morale'[288] of the population of Mostar, with inhabitants of the town described as being 'very shocked and very upset.'[289] The bridge was also described as

283 Blaškić Transcript 17 July 1998 (n 238), 10585–10586.
284 Prlić et al. Transcript 13 January 2010 (n 238), 43317.
285 Strugar Transcript 4 May 2004 (n 238), 5818.
286 Mladić and Karadžić Transcript 1 July 1996 (n 238), 336.
287 Mladić Transcript 18 December 2002 (n 273), 14565.
288 Prlić et al. Transcript 3 November 2009 (n 238), 46463.
289 Prlić et al. Transcript 15 May 2006 (n 238), 2106.

being 'in the hearts and memories of the citizens'[290] and its destruction as having had a 'traumatic effect'[291] on them. Similarly, it was noted that 'the devastation of the bridge was matched by that of emotions with senior civil leaders reduced to tears. [...] this had a significant and deep emotional – it elicited a deep emotional reaction from many people.'[292]

The same type of sentimental narrative, emphasising the populations' affective relationship to the Old Town, is evident with respect to the attack on Dubrovnik. One witness rejected the defence's suggestion that inhabitants may have been drawing fire on to the city by stating that 'the people of Dubrovnik loved their town too much to allow themselves to fire a single shot at their own town. [...] for the men of Dubrovnik, the town of Dubrovnik is sacred.'[293] The impact of the attack on Dubrovnik on individuals was then described in these personal and emotional terms. With respect to the destruction of an historic palace, a witness noted his 'very deep feelings about this building'[294] stating that 'in a way my own soul is there, so this involved such hurt, such humiliation. I cannot understand until the present day why all of this happened.'[295] A witness testified that when they returned to the Old Town following the attack, 'I saw a lot of people coming into the downtown area, silent, mute with tears in their eyes. It's a sight that I will never forget.'[296] Another described the scene as 'a disaster to look at. There were people standing outside. An elderly man was crying, sitting there on the floor. He had perhaps devoted most of life to the reconstruction and preservation of that building, and the yet [sic] whole thing disappeared into thin air in a matter of minutes.'[297] These accounts of the place of sites of cultural heritage in the lives, identities and memories of individuals, and the emotional impact their destruction therefore had, contribute an additional personalised and granular dimension to the account of cultural value understood in more human terms, which is absent from the case law of the ICTY.

290 Prlić et al. Transcript 20 May 2009 (n 238), 40432.
291 Prlić et al. Transcript 22 February 2007 (n 238), 14606.
292 Prlić et al. Transcript 22 May 2007 (n 238), 18900. See similarly 18894.
293 Milošević Transcript 18 December 2002 (n 238), 14565.
294 Strugar Transcript 24 February 2004 (n 238), 3087.
295 *Ibid.*, 3102.
296 Strugar Transcript 4 May 2004 (n 238), 5826. See similarly Strugar Transcript 21 January 2004 (n 465), 1039.
297 Strugar Transcript 23 February 2003 (n 238), 2952.

4.4 *Social and Religious Practices*

This expanded account of the connection between people and religious buildings is further reinforced in the discourse of the proceedings at the ICTY through discussion of the concrete social and cultural practices that bind people to cultural and religious property at a social and community level. This was highlighted by a witness in *Mladić*, for example, who identified the symbolic role of religious buildings not only in terms of how they straightforwardly represent a particular set of religious practices, but also in terms of the wider social role that houses of worship played in communities. The witness explained that 'the message destroying mosques sent to Bosnian Muslim communities was that the people who worshipped there, who grew up there, who got married there, who celebrated their children there, who mourned their dead there, they and their communities were no longer welcome.'[298]

This witness's account points to a more mundane dimension to the value of religious property, as distinct from the 'spiritual' value identified by the Trial Chamber in the *Hadžihasanović and Kubura* case, in terms of its role in the everyday life of the community. This narrative captures a number of different aspects of the everyday-use-value of religious buildings and their place in the social and religious practices of the community. First, the obvious importance of a religious building for the purpose of holding religious services, and therefore the disruption caused to the community's religious customs and traditions by its destruction is highlighted. For instance, in *Prlić et al.* the damage caused by an attack on a Catholic church was described in the following terms:

> An explosive device was launched at the local Catholic church in Jablanic causing some material damage. However, the greater damage was the fact that it caused concern among people in Jablanica, especially the Catholics, especially when they found out that the Christmas mass would not be celebrated. For any Catholic the Christmas mass and Christmas itself is one of the most important religious festivities that they mark every year.[299]

The impact of the destruction of churches was articulated in similar terms in *Martić*, where a witness testified that 'churches were destroyed, which effectively deprived them of a place – to gather and pray, and indeed, I suppose to gather as a community. So it was literally breaking down the community.'[300]

298 Mladić Transcript 6 December 2016 (n 273), 44448.

299 Prlić et al. Transcript 13 October 2008 (n 238), 33025.

300 Martić Transcript 26 May 2006 (n 269), 4616.

Here, the role of a house of worship was identified both from the perspective of its role in religious practices, as a place to pray and worship, but also from the more prosaic perspective of how it functioned as a meeting place for the community. This social role of houses of worship as a place of meeting and socialising was particularly pronounced in the testimony of witnesses in the *Blaskić* and *Hadzić* cases in relation to mosques and churches respectively:

> to give you an example of how important a mosque is in the local life [...] people will go from a whole series of little villages around the town, they will go to the mosque which has the minaret. They will go do their devotions there; they will meet their friends there; they will exchange a lot of news there. So this is another way of pointing out how important the mosque is for the community's life on, sort of, a wider level.[301]

> Taking down the churches and the houses was [...] literally breaking down the sense of community. Church was a place where people went where there was very often social engagement by old folk who may not meet from one end of the week to the other, so there was – just apart from a religious element, there was a community side to it as well. So it was destabilising the whole community approach.[302]

The testimony of a witness in *Blaskić* tied together these social and spiritual dimensions to the value of religious buildings, invoking a particularly profound conception of the role of religious property and the implications of its destruction in this specific cultural context, which is worth quoting at length:

> We live in secularised societies. We don't always, immediately responsible [sic], to the simple messages that is in a lot of the sacral heritage. But there are societies and there are populations in any society which are extremely attached to certain types of buildings. They are a symbol of their past. A church contains often a cemetery. A cemetery contains the graves of our ancestors. A church also were most important parts of your life have gone through. You may have been married in the church. You may be buried in the church. The church points upwards. Religious buildings, sacral buildings are very, very important for the cycle of life. When you have the society groups in the society for whom those things are really

301 Blaškić Transcript 16 July 1998 (n 238), 10591.

302 Hadžić Transcript 20 June 2013 (n 281), 6133. See similarly Milošević Transcript 8 July 2003 (n 238), 23885–23886.

> important, then if you touch the church, if you touch the mosque, then you are touching something very, very important to those people. As we are talking here basically about sacral buildings, I think that's basically my answer. This is an intangible thing, but an extremely important thing.
>
> [...] I think the destruction of a mosque is different than the destruction of a Bosnian Muslim's house. The mosque or the church or whatever, it represents an order to the world. What happens to you, everybody knows that you're mortal. Your life is a series of accidents. But the mosque, the church, it represents an order. When you destroy that, you are sort of tempering, threatening the order of existence. I think that one reacts in that sense. It has often been said to me, during the war, and not just about churches, but about other major cultural buildings, that we get used to being killed. We know that human life is no more tangible or tougher than the life of a butterfly, but when we see these other buildings being destroyed, then the world starts to crumble around us. And I think it's more so, in the case of sacral buildings.[303]

In this way, the discourse around the destruction of religious property during the course of trial proceedings at the ICTY invokes a much more emphatically people-oriented account of the cultural value of religious buildings than the more generalised appeals to the concepts of symbolism and identity reflected in the ICTY case law. By addressing the role of houses of worship in this region in local, contextualised terms, the discourse of the trial proceedings constructed an account of the value of religious property as profoundly linked to the social fabric of the religious communities in question, with its destruction therefore constituting not only an attack on a symbol of a particular religious or ethnic identity, but also representing a threat to the 'order of existence'[304] for these communities.

While the themes identified in the decisions of the *Al Mahdi* case at the ICC reflect this type of social, human-oriented conception of cultural value much more strongly than the decisions of the ICTY, the narratives that emerged during the proceedings of this case nevertheless also offer a richer and more granular account of the nature of the social processes that contribute to the emphatically functionalist, anthropocentric conception of cultural value constructed in this case. Many of these narratives echo and expand upon some of the ideas reflected in the trial proceedings of the ICTY. For instance, the role of the mausoleums in the life of the community in Timbuktu was central to

303 Blaškić Transcript 16 July 1998 (n 238), 10586–10588.

304 *Ibid.*, 10588.

the discourse of the trial proceedings in the *Al Mahdi* case, with statements emphasising how the mausoleums were 'closely linked to the life of the inhabitants'[305] and 'occupied a place at the very heart of their lives.'[306] This notion was expanded upon through detailed descriptions of the important role of the buildings in the ongoing religious practices of the community. Thus, it was noted that:

> This shows you that the mausoleums and mosques are not only linked to the past of Timbuktu but are very much an important part of the life of the people of Timbuktu today. In fact, the people of Timbuktu travel or visit these mausoleums very regularly to pray, to read verses of the Quran, to make offerings or to have spiritual retreats.[307]

The importance of the religious practices attached to the mausoleums was also emphasised from a spiritual perspective, and linked to what was described as the 'most intimate part of a human being':[308]

> The mausoleums and saints of Timbuktu play an important role in the daily lives of the city's inhabitants. The mausoleums are frequently visited by the city's residents, usually on Fridays. They are places of worship. The act of going to the mausoleums is perceived as a sign of faith and religious piety. Some even travel to them on pilgrimages. […] It became impossible for the inhabitants of Timbuktu to devote themselves to their religious practices. These practices which were deeply rooted in their lives. These practices which signified the deepest and most intimate part of a human being: Faith. These practices were part of their shared life together.[309]

In addition to religious practices and their spiritual importance, the wider cultural practices attached to the maintenance of the mausoleums were recounted in detail and identified as playing a social role, contributing to strengthening the social fabric of the community in a similar manner to that identified with respect to houses of worship at the ICTY:

305 Al Mahdi Transcript 1 March 2016 (n 248), 14.
306 *Ibid.*, 12.
307 *Ibid.*, 25.
308 *Ibid.*, 14.
309 *Ibid.* See similarly 25–28.

> Additionally, the mausoleums played a key role in fostering the social cohesion that is so characteristic of Timbuktu. The mausoleums are related to families who take care of them and resort, when needed, to masons. These masons are considered to be living human treasures for their unique craftsmanship. And while they are the ones who maintain these buildings, the renovation of a mausoleum is a task in which the entire community joins and participates. Everyone helps the masons. At the level of neighbourhoods, materials are collected and meetings are held. It is an event that brings together and unites worshippers, different age groups and the community as a whole. These are not the only social functions linked to the mausoleums. The mausoleums which were destroyed also contributed greatly to what I would call "the workshop of peaceful coexistence."[310]

These elements of the narrative around the value of the mausoleums, which emphasise their religious and spiritual role as well as the importance of the social functions of the cultural practices attached to them in bringing the community together, contribute to a discourse in which the mausoleums were constructed as being central to the identity of the population of Timbuktu. An expert witness outlined in sociological terms the social processes through which cultural heritage can be understood to contribute to the construction of a community's identity in this way:

> If one were to talk about the social functions of Mali's cultural heritage, one would say that the cultural heritage, broadly speaking, is part of the education of the upcoming generations. It also contributes to providing social ethics and etiquette as well as educating the people on their history. Heritage, cultural heritage in one word is part of the socialisation of the people. So for each of the items of a people's cultural heritage you can always find a relation, a relationship to the community, a link to ethics with a link to cultural identity as it emerges from within a people.[311]

From this perspective, the attacks on the mausoleums were therefore depicted as having been undertaken 'with the intent to destroy monuments and the specific symbols that are the substrate of the identity and culture of a nation'[312]

310 Al Mahdi Transcript 22 August 2016 (n 248), 18.

311 Al Mahdi Transcript 23 August 2016 (n 248), 77.

312 Al Mahdi Transcript 24 August 2016 (n 248), 21.

as well as being an attack on 'what structures men and women and constitutes the[ir] roots',[313] which 'impacted on their very sense of self and of life.'[314]

4.5 *'Like Beings without Soul, History or Memory'*

In addition to the nature of the social processes that contribute to the place of a community's heritage in constituting its identity, in the *Al Mahdi* case the importance of the material dimensions of the mausoleums was also emphasised in this respect, in particular from the perspective of ensuring the continuity of the community's history and memory. For instance, cultural heritage in general was described as giving 'meaning as well as a sense of continuity and direction from the past to the future. Cultural heritage provides reference points.'[315] The mausoleums were therefore described as being 'an integral part of the memory of the country [...] they express part of the collective conscience of the people' because they 'are handed down generation to generation.'[316] From this perspective, the sites in Timbuktu were characterised as constituting a material anchor for the continuation of religious and cultural practices that have been passed down between generations, with their destruction therefore constituting a rupture in the continuity of the community's social memory:

> The destruction of such monuments constitutes the annihilation of structures that had survived the ravages of time and which stood as testimony to Timbuktu's glorious past and important place in history and to its people over generations. [...] More so, to destroy the mausoleums is to erase this element of collective identity that the people of Timbuktu built through the ages. It means the annihilation of a civilisation's landmark and crucible which constitutes necessary archetypes in the social memory and helps build and inspire future generations.[317]

The importance of the material connection between the people and the buildings for the temporal continuity of the community's religious and cultural practices was particularly pronounced in the representative for victims' explanation of the meaning attributed to the keys to the mausoleums by their guardians. The representative for victims explained that:

---

313 *Ibid.*, 54.
314 Al Mahdi Transcript 1 March 2016 (n 248), 32.
315 Al Mahdi Transcript 22 August 2016 (n 248), 21.
316 Al Mahdi Transcript 1 March 2016 (n 248), 31.
317 *Ibid.*, 51.

> The link between those who are alive and the saints is through the keys of the mausoleums who are handed over – which are handed over to their guardians, and that link is broken today. All the physical persons whom I today represent before you did indeed have a key, a symbolic key which is the link between the living and the spirits. This key is a relay, a link between one generation which leads on to another and all of that is linked to the existence of the mausoleums. Your Honours, we must understand that these keys represent a more or less palpable link between a physical person and the sacred monuments. A relationship with God may be represented symbolically by this key, the key whereby those who receive it have today become victims, so to speak, as they remain guardians of spiritual and ancestral values that have been handed down from generation to generation.[318]

This notion of the preservation of cultural identity and memory through the palpable materiality of a cultural site or object was captured most succinctly in the OTP's statement that 'if heritage is destroyed we are like a traveller without any belongings, like beings without soul, history or memory.'[319] The impact of the destruction of the mausoleums on the population of Timbuktu was therefore also framed from the perspective of this loss of history and memory in physical terms. The inhabitants Timbuktu were said to have 'watch[ed] their history being destroyed, their memories being destroyed, their roots being destroyed'[320] and 'the symbols of their identity, their history and their religious vision [...] reduced to dust.'[321]

Taken together, history, memory and identity form the constituent parts of an overarching narrative during the proceedings of the *Al Mahdi* case that unequivocally centralised the extrinsic, social and human value of cultural property, captured most emphatically in the following statement by the OTP:

> Last but certainly not least, the destroyed mausoleums played a crucial role in shaping the identity of the people of Timbuktu. [...] To destroy Timbuktu's mausoleums is therefore to erase an element of collective identity built through the ages. It is to eradicate a civilisation's landmark. It is the destruction of the roots of an entire people, which irremediably affects its social attitudes, practices and structures. [...] Your Honours,

318 *Al Mahdi* Transcript 24 August 2016 (n 248), 26.
319 *Ibid.*, 6. Al Mahdi Transcript 1 March 2016 (n 248), 24.
320 Al Mahdi Transcript 24 August 2016 (n 248), 7.
321 *Ibid.*, 16.

> culture is who we are. Our ancestors created paintings, sculptures, mosques, temples and other forms of cultural possessions all around us. They put their hearts and souls into the creation of such cultural heritage so that it represents the cultural identity of their times and is passed on for the benefit of future generations. Indeed, this cultural heritage shapes the spirit and identity of our own generation and of generations to come. With the passage of time, they become archetypes of social memory from which individuals shape their identity and grow. Make no mistake, for centuries, the mausoleums of Timbuktu have been an important foundational block on which the identity of the city's inhabitants has been built. That continues to be very much true today. To be born and raised in Timbuktu is to be inspired and shaped by the centuries-old mosques and mausoleums that personify this historic city's cultural foundation.[322]

In this way, the discourse of the trial proceedings in *Al Mahdi* constructs a normative account of this crime, and the justification for its prosecution in this case, as rooted in its impact on the identity and memory of the people living in Timbuktu, on their social and religious practices and therefore on the social fabric of the community. While the decisions in the *Al Mahi* case reflect a similar turn towards a more people-focussed, anthropocentric account of cultural value, and therefore of the justification for criminalising attacks on cultural property during armed conflict, the trial proceedings reveal the extent to which the OTP vigorously pursued this conception of cultural value in this case.

4.6 *Living Buildings*

This emphatically people-oriented conception of cultural value is given further force in a number of cases through the discursive construction of buildings and property as 'living' or 'alive'. While the *Al Mahdi* case reflects a pronounced shift towards emphasising this type of conception of cultural value, the metaphor of living cultural heritage also featured during proceedings at the ICTY. For instance, in the context of testimony addressing the functional uses houses of worship and their importance at the social heart of a community, a witness in *Blaskić* stated that 'there was no doubt about it that these mosques were alive and that they were important for the rural community. [...] There was a kind of vitality in the countryside, and this was proof of a kind of devotion, a devoutness, on the country population.'[323] Similarly, in *Mladić*, in response to

322 Al Mahdi Transcript 22 August 2016 (n 248), 19–20.

323 Blaškić Transcript 16 July 1998 (n 238), 10590.

the question of whether a newly built mosque could be understood to constitute cultural heritage, an expert witness responded by explaining 'yes. [...] What makes it cultural heritage is its cultural uses and the fact that it expresses artistry, belief, and it plays a cultural role. Obviously not every mosque is of the same cultural and historical value, but all religious monuments to one degree or another, mosques, churches, chapels, are part of cultural heritage. Culture is a living thing.'[324] This analysis provides a particularly clear example of an approach that identifies cultural value extrinsically, in its living connection with people, which characterised the discourse on the destruction in particular of religious property during the course of proceedings at the ICTY.

In addition, the 'living buildings' metaphor was particularly pronounced during proceedings at the ICTY in relation to the attack on the Old Town of Dubrovnik. The Old Town was frequently referred to as a 'live city'[325] or a 'living city, not a museum.'[326] This construction of the Old Town as a living city was stressed from a functional perspective, being described as 'quite unique in that as well as being a stunning ancient monument, it's lived in. It's a living structure as well.'[327] More poetically, in Strugar, Dubrovnik was described as 'never anything less than a finely balanced result of the work both men's hand and his irrepressible spirit',[328] while 'the streets with elegance and allure of Dubrovnik's Stradun, the city's main thoroughfare, are to be seldom seen anywhere. This mirror of stone lives on through humanity's touch through men's tread and its laughter.'[329] In *Strugar*, during questioning on the subject of the criteria used when listing the Old Town of Dubrovnik as a World Heritage Site, a witness made explicit the importance of this living relationship between the site and its inhabitants from the perspective of evaluating its value:

> Dubrovnik had to satisfy very high criteria and standards in the sense of being authentic and well-preserved in the sense of its artistic values and structural values, and I know, for example, that the fact that it was a living town, a live old town, was a very noteworthy factor, a point in its favour, and that throughout its existence it always catered to the needs of

---

324 Mladić Transcript 16 October 2013 (n 273), 17943. See similarly Milošević Transcript 9 April 2002 (n 238), 2680.

325 Milošević Transcript 11 March 2003 (n 238), 17690.

326 *Prosecutor v. Miodrag Jokić*, IT-01-42/1-S, ICTY, Transcript 4 December 2003, 194. See similarly Strugar Transcript 4 June 2004 (n 238), 6988.

327 Strugar Transcript 13 January 2004 (n 238), 574.

328 Strugar Transcript 16 December 2003 (n 238), 277.

329 *Ibid.*, 278.

> its inhabitants. And the relationship of those inhabitants and its citizens towards the cultural values was taken note of.[330]

While the narrative around the cultural value of the mausoleums in the *Al Mahdi* case did not use the same language to directly describe the structures as 'living' or 'alive', the OTP nevertheless constructed a normative discourse around the crime that embodied this notion. First, further elevating the emphasis on the human value of the mausoleums in social, cultural and religious terms, a frequent narrative motif that emerged during proceedings constructed the buildings as representing the 'soul' of the community and the city. The OTP asserted that 'what happened here [...] struck a blow to the very soul of Timbuktu and its inhabitants',[331] and went on to quote the Minister of Culture of Mali describing the attack as 'an attack on the lifeblood of our souls.'[332] An inhabitant of Timbuktu was similarly noted to have described the destruction as 'an attack on what drives our soul',[333] while the purpose of the attack was characterised as being intended 'to wipe out the people's soul and their roots.'[334] In a more developed account of the motivation behind the destruction, a witness testified that:

> when it came to the destruction of the Timbuktu mausoleums, this was indeed a matter of an activity of war to psychologically kill the people of Timbuktu [...] And from a cultural and religious perspective it is known that it is one of the means that's used during war, that is, to harm the other person in regards to the persons' deepest inner self. [...] It consists of killing the enemy in that person's soul through such type of activity.[335]

In a similar way to the notion of a living building or city, the construction of such a profound relationship between the mausoleums and a 'persons' deepest inner self',[336] 'the very core of their being',[337] such that the destruction of the buildings constituted an attack on the community's soul, invokes the idea of a living connection between people and buildings, supporting the idea

330 Strugar Transcript 5 February 2004 (n 238), 1880.
331 Al Mahdi Transcript 24 August 2016 (n 248), 7.
332 Al Mahdi Transcript 1 March 2016 (n 248), 15–16.
333 Al Mahdi Transcript 22 August 2016 (n 248), 42.
334 Al Mahdi Transcript 24 August 2016 (n 248), 27.
335 Al Mahdi Transcript 23 August 2016 (n 248), 89–90.
336 *Ibid.*, 90.
337 Al Mahdi Transcript 24 August 2016 (n 248), 8.

articulated by the Prosecutor that 'what is at stake here is not just walls and stones',[338] but rather the very soul of the community.

This was taken a step further in statements that personify the buildings themselves, investing them with living, human characteristics. For instance, the relationship between the inhabitants of Timbuktu and the mausoleums was described as involving 'a special link or tie, it's as if they can almost communicate or commune with the building',[339] attributing some form of consciousness or sentience to the buildings in people's ability to communicate with them. Similarly reflecting a conception of sentient buildings, the representative for victims declared that 'I am the voice of the monuments and mausoleums tolling here on behalf of these victims, tolling here that you may hear their cause.'[340]

The personification of the buildings not only as inextricably linked to the lives and souls of the inhabitants of Timbuktu, but as somehow living beings in their own right was particularly pronounced in the words of one inhabitant, which were quoted by the OTP. This witness stated that 'Timbuktu is on the verge of losing her soul. Timbuktu is threatened by outrageous acts of vandalism; Timbuktu is being held under a sharpened blade ready for use in cold-blooded murder.'[341] The mausoleums were in this way personified not only through their construction as being the soul of the city, but the attack on them was characterised as 'murder', reflecting an understanding of their destruction as the killing of something human and alive. Indeed, the mosques and mausoleums were said explicitly at one point to 'personify this historic city's cultural foundation.'[342] This motif moves beyond an anthropocentric account of the crime of attacking cultural property from the perspective of 'focus[sing] on the impact it has on persons'[343] to one that discursively constructs the mausoleums as living beings in themselves and their destruction as an act of killing, a destruction of life in itself. In doing so, this narrative seems to somehow seek to discursively and normatively root the destruction of the buildings within the core life and physical security norms typically understood to constitute the normative core of international criminal law.

338 Al Mahdi Transcript 1 March 2016 (n 248), 3.

339 Al Mahdi Transcript 23 August 2016 (n 248), 95.

340 Al Mahdi Transcript 24 August 2016 (n 248), 19.

341 Al Mahdi Transcript 22 August 2016 (n 248), 19.

342 *Ibid.*, 20.

343 Marina Lostal, 'The Misplaced Emphasis on the Intangible Dimension of Cultural Heritage in the Al Mahdi Case at the ICC', (2017) 1(2) *Inter Gentes – The McGill Journal of International Law & Legal Pluralism*, 46.

Building on this, the second dimension of this narrative takes on a more justificatory tone, where the OTP uses this anthropocentric conception of the mausoleums as representing the soul of the inhabitants of Timbuktu, being almost living things in their own right, as a means of situating the criminalisation of attacks on cultural property within the same normative framework as other international crimes. The more justificatory element of this narrative is captured in the following explanation by the Prosecutor during opening statements:

> the Rome Statute prohibits and punishes the most reprehensible criminal acts: Crimes of genocide, crimes against humanity and war crimes. These crimes can be perpetrated in various forms, but they all have one common denominator. They inflict irreparable damage to the human persons [sic] in his or her body, mind, soul and identity. The instant case concerns an international crime prohibited by the Rome Statute, a crime which affects the soul and spirit of a people.[344]

This statement, with its emphasis on the notion that what unites international crimes that take different forms is the damage they cause to the body, mind, soul and identity of the human person, reflects an intention to place attacks on cultural property on the same normative footing as other international crimes by constructing an account of their value that is ultimately situated in the mind, soul and identity of the people who value them. Indeed, the OTP made explicit this understanding of the crime in arguing that 'such an attack […] falls into the category of crimes that destroy the roots of an entire people and profoundly and irremediably affects its social practices and structures. This is precisely why such acts constitute a crime under Article 8(2)(iv) of the Rome Statute.'[345] In the context of a trial involving a sole charge of attacking buildings dedicated to religion and historic monuments, these statements in this way seem intended to employ an anthropocentric narrative of cultural value to elevate the crime from one that involves the destruction of material objects, to one that protects fundamental aspects of the human person in their mind, soul and identity.

344 Al Mahdi Transcript 1 March 2016 (n 248), 12.

345 *Ibid.*, 13.

5 Conclusion

Examining the changes in how the prohibition on the destruction of cultural property during armed conflict and its subsequent criminalisation have been conceptualised reveals that a significant degree of normative evolution has taken place both in how the fundamental justification for the protection of such property during armed conflict is conceptualised, but also in how the nature of a cultural value approach to this justification, i.e. what is considered to be culturally valuable about such property, is constructed. Much of this evolution reflects the dual normative roots of the prohibition in terms of its historical emergence as a result of a confluence of ideas about limiting the unnecessary use of force during war alongside the emergence of Renaissance and Enlightenment ideas that attached particular importance to art, history and culture. Prior to the emphatic turn towards an unambiguous cultural value approach to the criminalisation of the destruction of cultural property in the case law of the ICTY and in the *Al Mahdi* case at the ICC, the wider legal regime governing the protection of cultural property during armed conflict, the early criminal cases at the IMT Nuremberg and the definitions of the crime included in the statutes of the ICTY and the ICC reflect a degree of fluctuation between these two rationales. Some legal frameworks and cases addressed forms of cultural property generically alongside other types of property protected during armed conflict primarily for their civilian character or humanitarian functions while others, such as the 1954 Hague Convention and the *Strugar* and *Jokić* cases at the ICTY addressing the attack on the Old Town of Dubrovnik, invoked a conception of cultural property as normatively distinct, and worthy of protection for its distinctly cultural value.

As greater attention to the cultural value of attacked or destroyed property came to be incorporated into the narratives of cases involving the destruction of religious and cultural property at the ICTY, different dimensions to how this cultural value could be understood also began to coalesce. While the case law of the ICTY constructed a relatively conventional object-centric and internationalist approach to cultural value with respect to the secular monuments of the Old Town of Dubrovnik and the Old Mostar Bridge, the case law on the destruction of houses of worship, in particular when charged as persecution, began to appeal to elements of a more functionalist and people-oriented conception of cultural value in invoking, in a limited form, links between religious buildings and the notions of symbolism, identity and an ethnic group's history and memory.

While the shift towards an explicitly anthropocentric, human-value conception of the crime was consolidated in the *Al Mahdi* case at the ICC, the narratives during proceedings at the ICTY around the destruction of religious buildings in particular also constructed a more expansive and localised account of their human value than the dominant themes captured in the ICTY case law, emphasising in particular the everyday, social roles of houses of worship in sustaining the social fabric of religious communities. This approach to cultural value was expanded significantly in the *Al Mahdi* case, where the decisions and, in particular, the narratives constructed by the OTP during the course of proceedings invoked various elements of an emphatically extrinsic, anthropocentric conception of cultural value, recounting in detail the myths and beliefs attributed to the mausoleums by the inhabitants of Timbuktu, the social and religious practices that surrounded the structures and their constitutive place in the identity and social fabric of the community. In constructing an account of the harm inflicted by the destruction of the structures in these terms, the OTP added an emphatically justificatory dimension to this narrative, explaining the inclusion of this crime in the same normative framework as the forms of violence against persons criminalised under international criminal law on the basis of the profound living connection it invoked between people and sites of cultural heritage.

Overall, while the anthropocentric narratives reflected in the decisions and proceedings of the *Al Mahdi* case consolidated and significantly expanded on this social, human conception of the value of cultural property, the *Al Mahdi* case nevertheless also reflects a degree of continuity in terms of the narratives of cultural value that had initially emerged primarily in the context of the destruction of houses of worship charged as persecution at the ICTY. Taken as a whole, this continuity between the narratives highlighting the social value of religious buildings at the ICTY and the emphatically anthropocentric account of the cultural value of the more prominent UNESCO-listed site advanced by the OTP in the *Al Mahdi* case also invokes a less hierarchical conception of cultural value than more formalist appeals to internationally protected status or concepts such as the common heritage of mankind because of how it centralises 'the relationship between [...] sites, objects, and artefacts and human beings'[346] as the shared characteristic that is worthy of protection through criminalisation.

At the same time, while a civilian-use rationale for the protection of cultural property does not ultimately appear in these cases, having been displaced by an increasingly functionalist and anthropocentric conception of a cultural value rationale for the protection of cultural property during armed

346 Lixinski (n 201), 582.

conflict, the more traditional conceptions of cultural value have also not fallen away. The case law and proceedings of both the ICTY and the ICC ultimately construct a multifaceted account of their understanding of the normative dimensions of this crime, which incorporate elements of internationalism, object-centrism, and functionalism or anthropocentrism. In this sense, while the narratives surrounding the crime have shifted to engage more directly with the role of cultural heritage in the social fabric of communities, identities and the living, affective relationship between people and their heritage, these cases do not invoke a single, exclusive conception of the cultural value of the types of property protected by the criminalisation of attacks on cultural property during armed conflict. Rather, the complex patchwork of narratives constructed around the crime in these cases epitomises what Erich Hatala Matthes has termed 'the variable scope of value',[347] which captures 'the wide scope of reasons for valuing cultural heritage'[348] depending on an individal or actor's relationship to it.

347 Matthes (n 80), 1003.
348 *Ibid.*, 1027.

CHAPTER 3

Pillage

The war crime of pillage has received relatively limited scholarly attention in the field of international criminal law. This is despite having been addressed fairly extensively at Nuremberg and, more recently, having featured in ten cases at the ICTY, three of the four trials conducted by the SCSL, and in most of the cases that have proceeded to trial at the ICC to date.[1] The limited attention to pillage may result from its status as one of the most well-established prohibitions in international humanitarian law,[2] eliciting little controversy in legal terms, or from the lesser gravity understood to attach to crimes against property when compared to the acts of violence against persons criminalised under international law. This has been reinforced in how pillage has often featured as a somewhat peripheral charge in trials involving large-scale violence to life and person, with prosecutors having 'focused on discrete, often relatively small-scale episodes of theft.'[3] The limited existing scholarship on pillage in international criminal law has also focused almost exclusively on the question of how this crime could be employed to capture practices of natural resource exploitation during conflicts.[4] For these reasons, while international courts prosecute pillage as a matter of course, there has nevertheless been relatively limited interrogation of the normative basis of its criminalisation and therefore the justification for prosecuting such 'discrete, often relatively small-scale episodes of theft'[5] on their own terms.

1 Namely *Prosecutor v. Germain Katanga and Mathieu Ngudjolo Chui* (ICC-01/04-01/07), *Prosecutor v. Jean-Pierre Bemba Gombo* (ICC-01/05-01/08), *Prosecutor v. Bosco Ntaganda* (ICC-01/04-02/06) and *Prosecutor v. Dominic Ongwen* (ICC-02/04-01/15).

2 Eve La Haye, 'The Prohibition of Pillage in International Humanitarian Law' in Nina H. B. Jørgensen (ed), *The International Criminal Responsibility of War's Funders and Profiteers* (Cambridge University Press 2020), 190.

3 Patrick J. Keenan, 'Conflict Minerals and the Law of Pillage', (2014) 14(2) *Chicago Journal of International Law*, 527.

4 See Michael A Lundberg, 'The Plunder of Natural Resources During War: A War Crime', (2008) 39(3) *Georgetown Journal of International Law*, 495–525; James G. Stewart, *Corporate War Crimes: Prosecuting the Pillage of Natural Resources*, Open Society Institute, 2011; Larissa van den Herik and Daniëlla Dam-de Jong, 'Revitalizing the Antique War Crime of Pillage: The Potential and Pitfalls of Using International Criminal Law to Address Illegal Resource Exploitation during Armed Conflict', (2011) 22(3) *Criminal Law Forum*, 237–273; Keenan (n 3), 524–558.

5 Keenan (n 3), 527.

 | DOI:10.1163/9789004687844_005

This chapter first traces the historical roots of the prohibition on pillage in international humanitarian law, identifying its roots in self-interested needs to ensure military discipline and its later correlation with emerging liberal concerns with protecting rights to private property. The chapter goes on to argue that the definitions of pillage applied at the ICTY, SCSL and the ICC offer a normative conceptualisation of the crime as rooted in this liberal concern with protecting property rights during armed conflict. Next, the chapter traces the normative themes constructed around this crime in the case law of the courts and tribunals, outlining how the themes of scale, use value, and a dilution of the legal element of ownership contribute to a degree of evolution away from the centrality of property rights that underlies the definition, to contribute to a more harm-based and use value-oriented account of the crime. Lastly, the discourse analysis of the narratives that emerge around the crime of pillage during the course of proceedings further reveals a pronounced shift towards emphasising the nature of the harms inflicted on victims of pillage. This is reflected in a particular emphasis on the economic implications of pillage for those already living at a subsistence minimum, as well as in how certain aspects of the social dimensions of property, which attribute it with meaning and value in particular communities or for individuals, are highlighted.

1 Historical-Normative Roots in International Law

The prohibition on pillage has long historical roots in the laws of armed conflict.[6] In general terms, pillage is understood to align with most states' domestic laws on theft in how it involves, at a basic level, the unauthorised taking of public or private property.[7] In essence, pillage simply entails 'theft during war.'[8] The term pillage is also widely understood to be synonymous with looting, plunder, spoliation and sacking.[9] Historically, pillaging the enemy's property featured heavily in medieval feuding and became a typical part of European warfare by the 16th century.[10] During this period, pillage or looting

6 La Haye (n 2), 190.

7 Kerrin Geoffrey Buck, 'Displacement and dispossession: redefining forced displacement and identifying when forced displacement becomes pillage under international humanitarian law', (2017) 2(1) *Journal of International Humanitarian Action*, 12; Jean-Marie Henckaerts and Louise Doswald-Beck, *ICRC Customary International Humanitarian Law Volume I: Rules* (Cambridge University Press 2009), 185.

8 Stewart (n 4), 10.

9 van den Herik and Dam-de Jong (n 4), 251; Stewart (n 4), 10; La Haye (n 2), 190–191.

10 Fritz Redlich, *De Praeda Military: Looting and Booty 1500–1815* (Steiner 1956), 2–4.

was not viewed as deviant, but was instead seen as a legitimate method of causing injury to the enemy, an appropriate means of sustaining an army, a useful recruiting tool and therefore as a form of justified self-compensation for soldiers.[11] At this point, pillage was viewed as a 'bona fide "spoil of war" to which the victors were entitled'.[12] Writing in 1625, Hugo Grotius deemed pillage to be lawful, explaining that:

> Cicero, in the third of his Offices, declares, It is not against the Law of Nature to spoil or plunder him whom it is lawful to kill. No wonder then if the Law of Nations allows to spoil and waste an Enemy's Lands and Goods, since it permits him to be killed. [...] And we read in Livy, There are certain Rights of War, which, as we may do, so we may suffer, as the burning of Corn, the pulling down of Houses, the taking away of Men and Cattle. [...] And we may observe, these Things are lawful to be done, even to those that surrender themselves.[13]

Later developments towards condemning, and ultimately prohibiting, pillage initially emerged from armies' self-interested concern with maintaining discipline among their own troops.[14] As modern nation states emerged, with professional standing armies replacing mercenaries sustained through pillage, undisciplined armies came to constitute a hindrance to the ambitions of states and their monarchs in seeking total control over their territories. At the same time, pillage no longer benefitted the new states themselves as a recruiting incentive for mercenaries, whose soldiers instead received tax-funded salaries.[15] Maintenance of discipline among troops became a particular concern for professional armies when military tactics evolved to require unified formations on battlefields, meaning that the distraction of temptations such as pillage could break such unity and lead to defeat. From the perspective of military authorities, pillage therefore came to be seen as a practice that 'disrupts units and disturbs orderly procedure toward the essential end – the correct and efficient conduct of military operations.'[16] Early prohibitions on pillage in

11 H. Wayne Elliott, 'The Third Priority: The Battlefield Dead', (1996) 7 *Army Lawyer*, 14.

12 *Ibid.*, 14; Stuart Green, 'Looting, Law and Lawlessness', (2007) 81(4) *Tulane Law Review*, 1137.

13 Hugo Grotius, *The Rights of War and Peace Book III* (Liberty Fund 2005), 1303–1304.

14 La Haye (n 2), 189.

15 Tuba Inal, *Looting and Rape in Wartime: Law and Change in International Relations* (University of Pennsylvania Press 2013), 42.

16 Elbridge Colby, 'The Military Value of the Laws of War', (1926) 15 *Georgetown Law Journal*, 25.

the 16th and 17th centuries therefore emerged in response to the need to regulate the behaviour of one's own army, rather than as a result of a concern with the welfare of the enemy's population.[17] This underlying rationale for regulating pillage evolved over time, shifting by the early 18th century from a primary concern with the impact of the loss of discipline on the realisation of direct military objectives, to also reflect a desire not to embitter civilian populations towards invading armies, which was gradually also seen as counter-productive from the perspective of achieving overall military victory.[18] In this way, shifts in the cost-benefit structure around pillage, driven by wider changes in the structures of armies and the nature of belligerent parties, shaped the initial self-interested considerations behind early efforts to regulate pillage as a matter of military discipline.[19]

During the 17th and 18th centuries, the emergence and consolidation of the nation state engendered a shift in how wars were understood, with the earlier conception of feuding between kings or princes and their subjects replaced by an understanding of war as a relationship between states.[20] This shift, as the state came to develop its own identity, therefore resulted in a new understanding of war as taking place between the states themselves, rather than between their citizens, who ought for this reason to be 'left intact, except so far as they are disturbed by the necessities of war.'[21] This evolution underpinned the much wider change in contemporary theorisations of what was permissible during war, with jurists beginning to argue in favour of limiting permissible force solely to that which contributed to the attainment of military victory.[22] For this reason, the normative approach to pillage also began to shift to reflect the idea that:

> If it should prove true [...] that plundering would not harm the enemy as a whole nor the king, but instead innocent persons to such an extent that they would be plunged into the greatest misfortunes; and if such

17 Inal (n 15), 42.

18 Doris Appel Graber, *The Development of the Law of Belligerent Occupation 1863–1914: A Historical Survey* (Columbia University Press 1949), 198. See also Inal (n 15), 42.

19 Inal (n 15), 43.

20 Norman Bentwich, *The Law of Private Property in War, with a Chapter on Conquest* (Sweet and Maxwell 1907), 26.

21 *Ibid.*

22 Robert Kolb, 'The main epochs of modern international humanitarian law since 1864 and their related dominant legal constructions' in Kjetil Mujezinović Larsen, Camilla Guldahl Cooper and Gro Nystuen (eds), *Searching for a 'Principle of Humanity' in International Humanitarian Law* (Cambridge University Press 2012), 30; Redlich (n 10), 63.

> plundering would have no notable effect in ending the war or in weakening the public strength of the enemy, then the gain acquired ought to be considered unworthy of a just man and especially a Christian.[23]

Against the background of these military and normative developments, by the mid-18th century, pillage had come to be viewed as wrong and was often punished when it did take place.[24] At the same time, the 18th century saw major ideological changes in Europe as liberalism gained influence, reshaping European social, political, and economic structures. Tuba Inal has identified three key pillars of liberalism that came to form part of European states' self-image which, in turn, profoundly influenced the consolidation of norms against pillage in war and the shift in their normative justification. Inal highlights how the emergence of liberalism, with its valorisation of the notions progress, civilization and, in particular, the sanctity of private property, increasingly 'helped Europeans perceive pillage as an unpleasant practice.'[25]

The liberal concern with individual political and economic liberty gave rise to the extension of franchise and laid the foundations for the emergence of laissez-faire capitalism with its emphasis on free trade and private property. Underpinning the emergence of this economic system was the theory that unrestricted individual accumulation of property contributed to overall production and in turn ensured economic progress and the creation of wealth for all. While the notion of private property had pre-existed the emergence of liberalism, its normative roots were in theories of natural rights. As the liberal theory of economics emerged, the institution of private property came instead to be associated with wider ideals of political and civilizational progress.[26] Property laws came to feature as 'a central fixture in philosophical and political narratives of a developmental, teleological vision of modernization that [...] set the standard for what [could] be considered civilized.'[27] The colonial encounter and its modes of appropriation, in which property laws functioned as 'a crucial mechanism for the colonial accumulation of capital',[28] were also central to the emergence of modern property law and the justifications for private property ownership in Enlightenment thought.

---

23 Redlich (n 10), 63–64.

24 Inal (n 15), 47.

25 *Ibid.*, 44.

26 *Ibid.*, 44–45.

27 Brenna Bhandar, *Colonial Lives of Property: Law, Land and Racial Regimes of Ownership* (Duke University Press 2018), 4.

28 *Ibid.*, 2.

For these reasons, liberal standards of civilization came to include the moral factors of 'good government, religious toleration, and individual liberty, particularly freedom of expression and property ownership'[29] which, combined with the material factors of 'commerce, science, and advanced modes of production […] created the necessary conditions of individual autonomy and sociability.'[30] In this way, the institution of private property was a central pillar of liberal theories of progress and civilisation, which were in turn understood as being in some ways a 'side effect of the rise of property.'[31] These ideational factors in turn underpinned the shift towards understanding pillage as a wrong that ought to be prohibited not only for self-interested reasons, but also on more moralistic grounds, attached to European states' self-image.[32] In this respect, Inal suggests that it is 'no wonder […] that eighteenth-century Europe, in its euphoria over the progress of its civilization, would consider private property to be one of the main building blocks of its existence and treat it as such,'[33] resulting, therefore, in a consolidation of the view that pillage ought to be condemned as an 'uncivilised' practice.

By the mid-19th century, while not entirely uniform, the prohibition on pillage enjoyed widespread recognition and was included in the first codification of rules governing the conduct of belligerents in war.[34] Setting out its broad normative commitments, Article 22 of the 1863 Lieber Code asserted that 'the principle has been more and more acknowledged that the unarmed citizen is to be spared in person, property and honor as much as the exigencies of war will admit.' On the protection of private property, Article 38 stated that 'private property, unless forfeited by crimes or by offenses of the owner, can be seized only by way of military necessity, for the support or other benefit of the army or of the United States.' Article 44 then specifically prohibited 'all wanton violence committed against persons in the invaded country, all destruction of property not commanded by the authorized officer, all robbery, all pillage or sacking, even after taking a place by main force'. These provisions have been

29 Marco Duranti, *The Conservative Human Rights Revolution: European Identity, Transnational Politics, and the Origins of the European Convention* (Oxford University Press 2017), 53.

30 *Ibid.*

31 Inal (n 15), 44–45.

32 Stephen M. Miller and Jessica Miller, 'Moral and legal prohibitions against pillage in the context of the 1899 Hague Convention and the South African War', (2019) 26(2) *War in History*, 202.

33 Inal (n 15), 45–46.

34 Graber (n 18), 197–198.

understood to 'breathe a liberal spirit'[35] in how they reflect a 'stanch defence of property rights'[36] on the part of their author.

The Brussels Declaration of 1874 subsequently reinforced Lieber's initial codification of the prohibition on pillage in particularly emphatic terms. Article 18 stated that 'a town taken by assault should not be given over to pillage by the victorious troops.' Article 38 required that 'family honour and rights, and the lives and property of persons [...] must be respected. Private property cannot be confiscated', while Article 39 straightforwardly asserted that 'pillage is formally forbidden.' Lastly, Article 40, on taxes and requisitions, expounded on these general rules, explaining that 'as private property should be respected, the enemy will demand from communes or inhabitants only such payments and services as are connected with the generally recognised necessities of war'.

Inal attributes the particular centrality afforded to protections for property in the Brussels Declaration to the ideological convictions of its author, the Russian jurist Fyodor Fyodorovich Martens, whose dissertation addressed the law of private property during war.[37] Indeed, the moral significance of private property for Martens is reflected in the nature of the fundamental individual liberties he identified as being a 'yardstick of the degree of civilization of states and international relations'[38] in an 1883 treatise. Martens described 'the right to respect for [the] person, the inviolability of [...] family and of [...] property'[39] as rights that 'flow from the nature and conditions of humanity and therefore cannot be created by legislation. They exist by themselves.'[40] These early rules prohibiting pillage during war in this sense suggest an evolution in its underlying normative conception, from early roots in the self-interested concerns of military forces with the discipline of their own troops, to a more normative commitment to the notion of private property as a facet of individual liberty that emerged with the expansion of liberal ideas in the 18th and 19th centuries.

The Hague Conventions of 1899 and 1907 created the modern international prohibition regime on pillage, by and large reflecting those same rules infused with liberal ideas contained in the Brussels Declaration, and consolidating this

35 *Ibid.*, 193.

36 Frank Freidel, *Francis Lieber: Nineteenth-century Liberal* (Louisiana State University Press 1947), 335.

37 Inal (n 15), 33.

38 Vladimir Vasilievich Pustogarov, 'Fyodor Fyodorovich Martens (1845–1909) – A Humanist of Modern Times', (1996) 312 *International Review of the Red Cross*, 304.

39 Stephen C. Neff, *Justice Among Nations: A History of International Law* (Harvard University Press 2014), 274.

40 *Ibid.*

normative shift in legal terms.[41] Article 28 of the Regulations prohibits 'pillage of a town or place, even when taken by assault' during the conduct of hostilities. With respect to the rules applicable to occupied territory, Article 46 contains the same language as the Brussels Declaration, requiring that 'family honour and rights, the lives of persons, and private property [...] must be respected. Private property cannot be confiscated', while Article 47 similarly emphasises that 'pillage is formally prohibited.'

Highlighting how these rules codified the shift towards understanding pillage as normatively rooted in the principle of the sanctity of private property, Marco Duranti has interpreted the Hague Conventions as having given rise not only to new obligations on states to one another, but also to have 'safeguarded the fundamental freedoms of individuals as well. States party to them were bound by its terms to respect the liberties of combatants and noncombatants alike, enshrining their freedom of religion, property rights, and rights to a fair trial in international law.'[42] This interpretation of the Hague Conventions, and the rules they codified prohibiting pillage, underscores the significant shift that had taken place by the early 20th century from the historical condemnation of pillage as a matter related to efficient military operations and internal discipline, to its ultimate prohibition on normative grounds, as a violation of the freedoms of the individual in terms of property ownership, reflecting in this way a set of rules 'adopted in an atmosphere of nineteenth century liberalism, shaped by the basic philosophy of that era.'[43]

Pillage first appeared as a criminal offence among the list of war crimes produced by the 1919 Commission on Responsibility,[44] and was later included in the Nuremberg Charter under Article 6(b) as 'plunder of public or private property'. The International Military Tribunal at Nuremberg convicted Göring, Rosenberg, Seyss-Inquart and Schacht of plunder on the basis of evidence that 'the territories occupied by Germany were exploited for the German war effort in the most ruthless way, without consideration of the local economy, and in consequence of a deliberate design and policy.'[45] The tribunal outlined the systematic exploitation of raw materials, agricultural products, food, machines, transportation equipment, art, cultural treasures, furniture and textiles during

41 Ernst H. Feilchenfeld, *The International Economic Law of Belligerent Occupation* (Rumford Press 1942), 10–12.

42 Duranti (n 29), 27.

43 Feilchenfeld (n 41), 17.

44 La Haye (n 2), 197.

45 Trial of the Major War Criminals before the International Military Tribunal 14 November 1945–1 October 1946, Volume 1, 239.

German occupation,[46] noting that 'these resources were requisitioned in a manner out of all proportion to the economic resources of those countries, and resulted in famine, inflation, and an active black market.'[47]

Numerous trials involving charges of plunder also took place at the military tribunals established under Control Council Law No. 10, including the *Flick*, *I.G. Farben* and *Krupp* industrialist trials, which involved firms that acquired leases from the German authorities to operate factories in occupied territories, plundering raw materials, equipment and other goods in the process.[48] From a normative perspective, these post-war trials consolidated the construction of the crime of pillage as, at heart, about respect for the sanctity of private property. In this regard, the military tribunal in the *I.G. Farben* case, noting that the term 'spoliation' 'is used interchangeably with the words "plunder" and "exploitation"', considered the term to apply to 'the widespread and systematized acts of dispossession and acquisition of property in violation of the rights of the owners, which took place in territories under the belligerent occupation or control of Nazi Germany during World War II.'[49] Centralising the violation of ownership rights in its interpretation, the tribunal went on to state that it deemed it 'to be of the essence of the crime of pillage that the owner be deprived of his property involuntarily and against his will',[50] further adding that the 'essence of the offense is the use of the power resulting from the military occupation [...] as the means of acquiring private property in utter disregard of the rights and wishes of the owner.'[51]

Underscoring the centrality of the violation of individual property rights for its normative conception of the crime, the tribunal also rejected the prosecution's argument that 'the offenses of plunder and spoliation alleged in the indictment have a double aspect.'[52] The prosecution had argued that the crime of spoliation entailed both an offense 'against the rightful owner or owners by taking away their property without regard to their will, 'confiscation', or by obtaining their 'consent' by threats or pressure',[53] as well as being:

46 *Ibid.*, 239–242.

47 *Ibid.*, 240.

48 UN War Crimes Commission, Law Reports of Trial of War Criminals, Volume XV, Digest of Laws and Cases (1947), 126. For an exhaustive list of post-World War II trials involving charges of pillage or plunder see Stewart (n 4), 96–112.

49 *United States v. Krauch et al.* (*IG Farben Case*), Trials of War Criminals Before the Nuremberg Military Tribunals Under Control Council No. 10, Volume VIII, 1133 [hereafter Krauch et al. Judgment].

50 *Ibid.*, 1134.

51 *Ibid.*, 1150.

52 *Ibid.*, 1135.

53 *Ibid.*

> a crime against the country concerned in that it disrupts the economy, alienates its industry from its inherent purpose, makes it subservient to the interest of the occupying power, and interferes with the natural connection between the spoliated industry and the local economy. As far as this aspect is concerned, the consent of the owner or owners, or their representatives, even if genuine, does not affect the criminal character of the act.[54]

Rejecting the second, wider conceptualisation of the crime proposed by the prosecution on the grounds that the Hague Regulations contained no support for such an interpretation, the tribunal instead reasserted that the prohibition on plunder implies:

> action in relation to property committed against the will and without the consent of the owner. [...] If, in fact, there is no coercion present in an agreement relating to the purchase of industrial enterprises or interests equivalent thereto, even during time of military occupancy, and if, in fact, the owner's consent is voluntarily given, we do not find such action to be violation of the Hague Regulations.[55]

In this way, the tribunal's analysis, rejecting a wider account of the nature of plunder or pillage in its impact on the economy of the occupied territory, instead offered an interpretation that conceptualised the normative basis of the crime wholly in terms of the inviolability of private property; the offense is understood to hinge exclusively upon the violation of individual ownership rights through the presence or absence of the owner's consent to the appropriation of the property.

The tribunal in the *Krupp* case reached the opposite conclusion, arguing that 'spoliation of private property, then, is forbidden under two aspects; firstly, the individual private owner of property must not be deprived of it; secondly, the economic substance of the belligerently occupied territory must not be taken over by the occupant or put to the service of his war effort.'[56] This conclusion was reached by way of an analysis of the various rules protecting property in occupied territory in the Hague Regulations, rather than the specific prohibition on pillage or plunder, but nevertheless suggests a possible embrace

---

54 *Ibid.*

55 *Ibid.*

56 *United States v. Krupp et al.* (*The Krupp case*), Trials of War Criminals Before the Nuremberg Military Tribunals Under Control Council Law No. 10, Volume IX, 1343.

of a more expansive normative conception of the rule that also captures the potential impact of widespread pillage on the wider economy of an occupied territory.

In its subsequent discussion of the war crime of pillage, plunder or spoliation, the UN War Crimes Commission stressed that '[p]roperty offences recognised by modern international law are not [...] limited to offences against physical tangible possessions or to open robbery in the old sense of pillage, but include the acquisition of intangible property and the securing of ownership, use or control of all kinds of property by many ways other than by open violence',[57] describing forms of pillage involving the theft of personal property as 'war crimes of the more traditional type.'[58] The Commission went on to summarise the conflicting approaches to the crime adopted in the *I.G. Farben* and *Krupp* cases, in which it identified two possible aspects of the offence, which highlight the normative stakes at play in how the crime was interpreted in the post-World War II jurisprudence. These two aspects were, '(i) that private property rights were infringed' and '(ii) that the ultimate outcome of the alleged offences was that the economy of the occupied territory was injured and/or that of the occupying State benefitted.'[59] In its analysis, the Commission favoured the position adopted in the *I.G. Farben* case, concluding that:

> In so far as *private property* is concerned it seems sounder to base a definition of a war crime involved upon the first aspect, namely the infringement of the property rights of individual inhabitants of the occupied territory. [...] provided a sufficient infringement of private property rights has been proved to bring the offence within the terms of the Hague Regulation, the more public effects of the act are not necessary to constitute the crime. There is also *some* authority for saying that, conversely, if no illegal breach of private property rights has occurred no war crime can be said to have been committed, irrespective of the effects of the act upon the general economy of the occupied territory of the enemy State.[60]

Hannah Franzki has highlighted how centring rights to private property and the distinction between criminal and non-criminal conduct exclusively on the presence or absence of the owner's consent in this context effectively functioned to introduce a distinction between legitimate business transactions

57 UN War Crimes Commission (n 48), 129.
58 *Ibid.*, 130.
59 *Ibid.*, 126.
60 *Ibid.*

during occupation and seizure of property that constituted war crimes.[61] This centralisation of the violation of the owner's consent in this way constructed an operative distinction between 'free choice as criterion for the validity of business transactions and the presence of the occupying state forces ('coercion') as indicator for the lack of such freedom of choice.'[62] In Franzki's view, the industrialists' cases' interpretation of the crime of plunder in this way carried the implication that what was ultimately criminal about these offences was how they violated the logic of free choice central to economic liberalism and the free market economy.[63] From this perspective, the tribunal's and the UN War Crimes Commission's reasoning, rejecting a wider account of the nature of plunder or pillage in its impact on the economy of the occupied territory and instead offering a definition of the crime that hinged exclusively on the owner's exercise of free choice, suggests that, at this juncture, the crime was conceptualised primarily in terms of the inviolability of private property and the protection of individual property rights.

With the codification of the Geneva Conventions in 1949 this private property rights-based conception of the prohibition of pillage, while not abandoned in its entirety, nevertheless came to be somewhat diluted or tempered by the broader shift in the law of armed conflict from a concern primarily with military matters, to being increasingly understood as 'centred around the concept of humanitarian protection of the victims of war.'[64] In line with this shift, the prohibition on pillage, along with the wider protections for property contained in the Conventions, came to be conceptualised in more emphatically humanitarian terms. Article 16 of the Fourth Geneva Convention requires that 'each Party to the conflict shall facilitate the steps taken to search for the killed and wounded, to assist the shipwrecked and other persons exposed to grave danger, and to protect them against pillage and ill-treatment.' This article refers to the more archaic notion of pillage on the battlefield, explained in the ICRC commentary in terms of 'the presence of hordes of pillagers, formerly called the "hyenas of the battlefield" [which] may not be so common today but the possessions of the wounded and dead may well excite the greed of unscrupulous soldiers or civilians and incite them to pillage.'[65] Article 33 of the Convention IV states more straightforwardly that 'pillage is prohibited.'

61 Hannah Franzki, 'Criminal trials, economic dimensions of state crime, and the politics of time in international criminal law: a German-Argentine constellation' (PhD dissertation, Birkbeck University of London, 2018), 136.

62 *Ibid.*, 138.

63 *Ibid.*, 139–140.

64 Kolb (n 22), 2. See also 38–39, 45.

65 ICRC, *Commentary on the Geneva Conventions of 12 August 1949, Volume IV* (1958), 137.

While the Geneva Conventions did not in this way expand on the existing provisions with respect to pillage contained in the Hague Conventions, the wider regulatory framework on property within which they were embedded, and how this was interpreted, suggest a turn away from the concern with private property and ownership rights reflected in previous conventions, and made explicit in the jurisprudence following World War II, towards a normative account of the prohibition of pillage as relating instead to the 'use value' of property. In their analysis of the various dimensions of the legal framework protecting property in the Geneva Conventions, Lea Brilmayer and Geoffrey Chepiga argue that protections for property under international humanitarian law can be understood as distinct from protections for property contained in other areas of domestic and international law in how they centralise this 'use value' conception of property. In this respect, Brilmayer and Chepiga distinguish between domestic property regimes which 'privilege ownership and its corollary, the right to exclude [which] view property primarily as an end in itself'[66] from the protections for property contained in international humanitarian law, which, in their view, are 'driven by a conception of property that is more instrumental, and values property in direct proportion to its role in assuring the survival of civilians.'[67]

Revealing of this conceptual shift is the ICRC's 1958 Commentary on Article 33 of the Fourth Geneva Convention, prohibiting pillage, which begins its analysis by explaining that 'the purpose of this Convention is to protect human beings, but it also contains certain provisions concerning property, designed to spare people the suffering resulting from the destruction of their real and personal property (houses, deeds, bonds etc., furniture, clothing, provisions, tools, etc.).'[68] Hersch Lauterpacht's response to the developments contained in the Geneva Conventions reflects the same view, describing the 'true character' of the law of war as 'almost entirely humanitarian in the literal sense of the word, namely, to prevent or mitigate suffering.'[69] In relation to the protections for property contained in the Conventions, he similarly concluded that '[n]either is the humanitarian purpose absent from the rules relating to the treatment of private enemy property and to devastation. For property is not merely an economic asset; it may be a means of livelihood.'[70] In its discussion of Article 46

66 Lea Brilmayer and Geoffrey Chepiga, 'Ownership or Use – Civilian Property Interests in International Humanitarian Law', (2008) 49(2) *Harvard International Law Journal*, 417.

67 *Ibid.*

68 ICRC (n 65), 226.

69 Hersch Lauterpacht, 'The Problem of the Revision of the Law of War', (1952) 29 *British Year Book of International Law*, 363.

70 *Ibid.*

of the Fourth Convention, on the cancellation of restrictive measures relating to property after the close of hostilities, the ICRC commentary reinforced this sentiment in emphasising that:

> This provision, which is to be compared with those prohibiting pillage and reprisals, is nevertheless somewhat foreign to the real purpose of the Convention. The Diplomatic Conference emphasised on various occasions that its object was to protect people and not property. Consequently the question of the treatment of enemy private property in the territory of a belligerent is still, in general, governed by usage and by the Hague Regulations of 1907.[71]

These accounts of the intentions behind the prohibition on pillage in Article 33 and the protections for property during occupation under Article 46 of the Fourth Convention suggest that the prohibition on pillage had at this point evolved to be conceptualised primarily in terms of the 'use value' of property and its role in ensuring the survival of people.

In addition to the wider shift towards a more humanitarian understanding of the laws governing the conduct of belligerents during war, which partly informed this transformation in how the justification for prohibiting pillage was conceptualised, the move away from the previous emphasis on protections for private property and ownership rights also resulted from the place and nature of property in the different political-economic systems that had emerged by the time of the codification of the Geneva Conventions. While not involving the prohibition on pillage specifically, the debates during the drafting of Article 53 of the Fourth Geneva Convention, which prohibits the destruction of certain types of property during occupation, are illustrative of the significance of the ideological shift that had taken place by this point.

Initially, the prohibition on the destruction of particular types of property in occupied territory was contained in draft Article 30 of the Fourth Geneva Convention, which, along with prohibiting collective penalties, stated that 'measures of reprisal against protected persons or their property are prohibited. Any destruction of personal or real property which is not made absolutely necessary by military operations, is prohibited, as are likewise all measures of intimidation or terrorism.'[72] While the Hague Conventions and previous

---

71 ICRC (n 65), 271.

72 Final Record of the Diplomatic Conference Convened by the Swiss Federal Council for the Establishment of International Conventions for the Protection of War Victims and Held at Geneva from April 21st to August 12th 1949, Volume I, 118.

military codes prohibited the destruction and confiscation of private property in occupied territories except in cases of military necessity, property belonging to the state had not enjoyed such protection.[73]

For this reason, during the drafting of the Fourth Geneva Convention, the Soviet Union observed that the draft 'Article 30 as it stood did not take into account the changes that had supervened in the economic structure of many countries. In some countries, State property was the property of the people as a whole. Consequently, the destruction of such property affected not only the interests of the State but also those of individuals.'[74] China supported the Soviet Union's position, because 'it provided for the prohibition of destruction of all categories of property except in the case of military necessity',[75] stressing therefore that 'the Article should be worded in such a way as to ensure the alleviation of the sufferings of war victims.'[76] Following objections from the United States, Canada and the United Kingdom, a compromise proposed by Morocco which would protect property 'intended solely'[77] for use by individuals, and which the Norwegian delegate endorsed on the grounds that 'identical reasons prevailed for the protection of private and public property where the property was such as mainly served the needs of individuals',[78] the draft article was amended and became Article 53. This article ultimately states that 'any destruction by the Occupying Power of real or personal property belonging individually or collectively to private persons, or to the State, or to other public authorities, or to social or cooperative organizations, is prohibited, except where such destruction is rendered absolutely necessary by military operations.'

The debate during the drafting of Article 53 in this way illuminates how the ideological stakes in protections for private property contained in previous conventions, and deemed uncontroversial at the time,[79] had shifted with the emergence of socialist states and their abolition of the institution of private property. In addition, it underscores how a turn towards more humanitarian reasoning, and the increasing link being drawn between protecting property

73 Brilmayer and Chepiga (n 66), 425.

74 Final Record of the Diplomatic Conference Convened by the Swiss Federal Council for the Establishment of International Conventions for the Protection of War Victims and Held at Geneva from April 21st to August 12th 1949, Volume II A, 649.

75 *Ibid.*, 651.

76 *Ibid.*

77 *Ibid.*, 650.

78 *Ibid.*, 651.

79 Graber (n 18), 214.

and preventing suffering during war, allowed the compromise contained in Article 53 to therefore be achieved.

Most recently, the codification of Additional Protocols I and II to the Geneva Conventions in 1977 consolidated this conceptual shift in protections for property in international humanitarian law. Through the convergence of the rules contained in the Hague and Geneva Conventions, the language of private property came to be abandoned entirely, to be replaced by the more fundamental humanitarian distinction between military and civilian objects, and the prohibition on directing attacks against the latter in Additional Protocol I, regardless of ownership. In this respect, Brilmayer and Chepiga suggest that the rules governing the protection of property contained in the Additional Protocols, which 'discarded the concept of "ownership" altogether, substituting "civilian use" as the criterion for protection'[80] in this way 'exemplify and expand on the Fourth Geneva Convention's valuation of property according to its role in mitigating civilian suffering.'[81]

With respect to pillage specifically, Article 4(2)(g) of Additional Protocol II, based on Article 33 of the Fourth Geneva Convention, explicitly prohibits pillage in non-international armed conflict against persons who do not take a direct part or who have ceased to take part in hostilities. The ICRC commentary makes clear that, in line with the elision of the public-private distinction in favour of a civilian use approach as the criterion for protection in Additional Protocol I, the prohibition on pillage in Additional Protocol II 'applies to all categories of property, both State-owned and private.'[82] In this way, the codification of the Additional Protocols to the Geneva Conventions can be understood to have sealed the gradual evolution in how protections for property are conceptualised under international humanitarian law and, embedded within this wider change, how the prohibition on pillage was also understood. This conceptual evolution had its origins in armies' early self-interested concern with maintaining discipline among troops, which gradually evolved with the emergence of liberalism into a normative concern with the sanctity of private property as an indicator of 'civilised' societies, to be supplanted most recently by the more humanitarian commitment to protecting property to the extent that it ameliorates civilian suffering.

---

80 Brilmayer and Chepiga (n 66), 427.

81 *Ibid.*

82 ICRC, *Commentary on the Protocol Additional to the Geneva Conventions of 12 August 1949, and relating to the Protection of Victims of Non-International Armed Conflicts (Protocol II) 8 June 1977* (1987), 1376.

2 Definitions of Pillage in International Criminal Law

The war crime of pillage is contained in the statutes of each of the modern international criminal tribunals, but appears in different forms. Article 3(e) of the ICTY Statute criminalises 'plunder of public or private property' as a violation of the laws or customs of war. Article 4(f) of the ICTR Statute and Article 3(f) of the Statute of the SCSL criminalise 'pillage' as a serious violation of Common Article 3 to the Geneva Conventions, without further qualification. The Rome Statute refers to 'pillaging a town or place, even when taken by assault' in international and non-international armed conflict under Articles 8(2)(b)(xvi) and 8(2)(e)(v). The ICTY has confirmed that 'the unlawful appropriation of public and private property in armed conflict has varyingly been termed "pillage", "plunder," and "spoliation".'[83] The SCSL has similarly concluded that 'the prohibition of the unlawful appropriation of public and private property in armed conflict [...] has been variously referred to as 'pillage', 'plunder' and 'looting'',[84] similarly making clear that the provisions on plunder and pillage in each of these statutes refer to the same offence.

2.1 *Legal Elements*

At the ICTY, the crime of plunder or pillage was defined as 'the unlawful appropriation of public and private property in armed conflict.'[85] In the first case addressing pillage at the ICTY, the Trial Chamber in *Mucić et al.* raised the question of whether 'the concept of pillage in the traditional sense implied an element of violence not necessarily present in the offence of plunder.'[86] Determining that it was not necessary in this case to address the question of whether the terms pillage and plunder were entirely synonymous under international law, the Trial Chamber went on to conclude that the offence of plunder under the Statute of the ICTY 'should be understood to embrace all forms of unlawful appropriation of property in armed conflict for which individual criminal responsibility attaches under international law, including those acts traditionally described as "pillage".'[87] This understanding of pillage as a subcategory involving violence of a wider offence of plunder was nevertheless

83 *Prosecutor v. Zdravko Mucić et al.*, IT-96-21-T, ICTY, Trial Judgment, 16 November 1998, para 591 [hereafter Mucić et al. Trial Judgment].

84 *Prosecutor v. Alex Tamba Brima et al.* (*AFRC Case*), SCSL-04-16-T, SCSL, Trial Judgment, 20 June 2007, para 751 [hereafter Brima et al. Trial Judgment].

85 Mucić et al. Trial Judgment (n 83), para 591; Brima et al. Trial Judgment (n 84), para 751.

86 Mucić et al. Trial Judgment (n 83), para 591.

87 *Ibid.*

not adopted in subsequent case law.[88] 'Unlawful appropriation of public and private property in armed conflict'[89] has therefore remained an offence in its own right, without needing the addition of violence to constitute pillage under international law.

The elements of the crime of plunder at the ICTY were therefore identified as 'a) an act of appropriation of public or private property b) the appropriation was unlawful; and c) the act was committed with intent.'[90] Appropriation has been interpreted broadly to include 'all forms of seizure of public or private property'[91] while the requirement that the appropriation 'must be done without lawful basis or legal justification'[92] has been understood to refer to those circumstances in which appropriation of property is permitted during armed conflict, such as the seizure of military equipment as war booty or requisition for the needs of an occupying army.[93]

Beyond the elements of the crime, some of the reasoning as to the legal basis of the prohibition on pillage suggests that a property rights conceptualisation of the crime may have shaped how it was understood in normative terms at the ICTY. In its first case involving charges of plunder at the ICTY, the Trial Chamber in *Mucić et al.* explained that:

> In considering the elements of the offence of plunder, the Trial Chamber must take as its point of departure the basic fact that international

88 *Prosecutor v. Goran Jelisić*, IT-95-10-T, ICTY, Trial Judgment, 14 December 1999, para 48; *Prosecutor v. Tihomir Blaškić*, IT-95-14-T, ICTY, Trial Judgment, 3 March 2000, para 184; *Prosecutor v. Dario Kordić and Mario Čerkez*, IT-95-14/2-T, ICTY, Trial Judgment, 26 February 2001, para 352 [hereafter Kordić and Čerkez Trial Judgment]; *Prosecutor v. Mladen Naletilić and Vinko Martinović*, IT-98-34-T, ICTY, Trial Judgment, 31 March 2003, para 617 [hereafter Naletilić and Martinović Trial Judgment]; *Prosecutor v. Dario Kordić and Mario Čerkez*, IT-95-14/2-A, ICTY, Appeal Judgment, 17 December 2004, para 79 [hereafter Kordić and Čerkez Appeal Judgment]; *Prosecutor v. Emer Hadžihasanović and Amir Kubura*, IT-01-47-T, ICTY, Trial Judgment, 15 March 2006, para 49 [hereafter Hadžihasanović and Kubura Trial Judgment]; *Prosecutor v. Milan Martić*, IT-95-11-T, ICTY, Trial Judgment, 12 June 2007, para 101 [hereafter Martić Trial Judgment]; *Prosecutor v. Ante Gotovina et al.*, IT-06-90-T, ICTY, Trial Judgment – Volume 2, 15 April 2011, para 1777 [hereafter Gotovina et al. Trial Judgment – Volume 2]. See also the Trial Chamber in the *Bemba* case at the ICC emphasising that 'the Court's legal framework does not include any requirement of violence.' – *Prosecutor v. Jean-Pierre Bemba Gombo*, ICC-01/05-01/08, ICC, Judgment pursuant to Article 74 of the Statute, 21 March 2016, para 116 [hereafter Bemba Trial Judgment].

89 Mucić et al. Trial Judgment (n 83), para 591.

90 Gotovina et al. Trial Judgment – Volume 2 (n 88), para 1777.

91 *Ibid.*, para 1778.

92 Martić Trial Judgment (n 88), para 102.

93 *Ibid.*

> humanitarian law not only proscribes certain conduct harmful to the human person, but also contains rules aimed at protecting property rights in times of armed conflict. [...] The basic norms in this respect, which form part of customary international law, are contained in the Hague Regulations, article 46 to 56 which are broadly aimed at preserving the inviolability of public and private property during occupation. In relation to private property, the fundamental principle is contained in article 46, which provides that private property must be respected and cannot be confiscated. [...] this rule is reinforced by article 47, which unequivocally establishes that "[p]illage is formally forbidden." [...] The principle of respect for private property is further reflected in the four Geneva Conventions of 1949. [...] Likewise, article 33 of Convention IV categorically affirms that "[p]illage is prohibited." [...] The basic principle that violations of the rules protecting property rights in armed conflict can constitute war crimes, for which individual criminal liability may be imposed, has not been questioned in the present case.[94]

The Trial Chamber's analysis in *Mucić et al.* in this way invokes a normative conception of the crime of plunder as rooted explicitly and exclusively in the protection of property rights. Indeed, by explicitly distinguishing between those rules prohibiting conduct that is harmful to the human person and those that protect property rights in times of armed conflict,[95] the Chamber underscored this normative approach to the crime by implying that the two sets of rules rest on distinct normative foundations. This normative approach was echoed in *Kordić and Čerkez,* where the Trial Chamber identified the violation of ownership rights as central to its understanding of the crime. The Chamber concluded that 'acts of appropriation include both widespread and systematised acts of dispossession and acquisition of property in violation of the rights of the owners and isolated acts of theft or plunder by individuals for their private gain.'[96]

While the jurisprudence of the ICTY in this way contextualised its understanding of the definition of plunder in protections for property rights during armed conflict, the definitions of pillage adopted at the SCSL and the ICC capture this conceptualisation more clearly in legal terms. The elements of the crime of pillage at the ICC require that:

1) The perpetrator appropriated certain property.

94 Mucić et al. Trial Judgment (n 83), para 587–588.
95 *Ibid.*, para 587.
96 Kordić and Čerkez Trial Judgment (n 88), para 352.

2) The perpetrator intended to deprive the owner of the property and to appropriate it for private or personal use.
3) The appropriation was without the consent of the owner.
4) The conduct took place in the context of and was associated with an international armed conflict.
5) The perpetrator was aware of factual circumstances that established the existence of an armed conflict.[97]

At the SCSL, pillage was defined in essentially the same terms as 1) the perpetrator appropriated property 2) the appropriation was without the consent of the owner 3) the perpetrator intended to deprive the owner of the property.[98] In distinguishing between pillage and destruction of property, the Trial Chamber in the *CDF* case at the SCSL defined appropriation as 'the exercise of control over property; a taking or possession'[99] while in *Bemba* at the ICC, the Trial Chamber interpreted appropriation to imply that 'property has come under the control of the perpetrator.'[100]

A footnote to the ICC definition clarifies that 'as indicated by the use of the term "private or personal use", appropriations justified by military necessity cannot constitute the crime of pillaging.'[101] The Trial Chamber in *Bemba* similarly confirmed that 'the "special intent" requirement, i.e. the "private or personal use" element, allows it to better distinguish pillage from seizure or booty, or any other type of appropriation of property which may in certain circumstances be carried out lawfully.'[102] This suggests that the requirement that the appropriation took place for private or personal use does not significantly change the approach adopted at the ICTY of requiring that the appropriation be 'unlawful' in reference to those circumstances during armed conflict in which appropriation of property is lawful. At the SCSL, the Trial Chamber in the *AFRC* case nevertheless rejected the Rome Statute approach, noting that '[i]nclusion of the element of "private or personal use" in the definition

97 ICC Elements of Crimes, Article 8(2)(b)(xvi) War crime of pillaging. See Article 8(2)(e)(v) for non-international armed conflict.

98 Brima et al. Trial Judgment (n 84), para 755; *Prosecutor v. Moinina Fofana and Allieu Kondewa* (*CDF Case*), SCSL-04-14-T, SCSL, Trial Judgment, 2 August 2007, para 165 [hereafter Fofana and Kondewa Trial Judgment]; *Prosecutor v. Issa Hassan Sesay et al.* (*RUF Case*), SCSL-04-15-T, SCSL, Trial Judgment, 2 March 2009, para 207 [hereafter Sesay et al. Trial Judgment]; *Prosecutor v. Charles Ghankay Taylor*, SCSL-03-01-T, SCSL, Trial Judgment, 18 May 2012, para 452 [hereafter Taylor Trial Judgment].

99 Fofana and Kondewa Trial Judgment (n 98), para 166.

100 Bemba Trial Judgment (n 88), para 115.

101 ICC Elements of Crimes, Article 8(2)(b)(xvi) War crime of pillaging, footnote 47.

102 Bemba Trial Judgment (n 88), para 120.

appears to be at variance with *Čelebići*, since it may not include 'organized' and 'systematic' seizure of property. The Trial Chamber is therefore of the view that the requirement of "private or personal use" is unduly restrictive and ought not to be an element of the crime of pillage.'[103]

From a normative perspective, the most significant dimension of the definition of pillage applied at the ICC and the SCSL is how it centralises the perpetrator's intent to deprive the owner of their property, and the owner's lack of consent to the appropriation. This definition constitutes a change in legal terms from the definition identified by the ICTY, and echoes more strongly the dominant normative approach reflected in the post-World War II trials in terms of how it centralises the violation of ownership interests by making the owner's lack of consent to the appropriation the crux of the offence. The particular centrality of the violation of the owner's consent has been further reinforced in a number of decisions, which echo the reasoning in the *I.G. Farben* case. For instance, the Pre-Trial Chamber in *Katanga* emphasised that 'the Elements of Crimes expressly provide for the exculpation of the perpetrator's unlawful conduct where the perpetrator appropriated property with the owner's consent.'[104]

Similarly, the Trial Chamber in *Bemba* suggested that consent lies at the normative core of pillage in highlighting how 'the Court's legal framework does not include any requirement of violence as an element of the appropriation' but that 'in certain circumstances lack of consent can be inferred from the absence of the rightful owner from the place from where property was taken. Lack of consent may be further inferred by the existence of coercion.'[105] In a revealing footnote in the *CDF* case at the SCSL, during the Appeals Chamber's discussion of whether the burning of property could constitute the crime of pillage, the Chamber underscored this point in noting that 'acts of burning and destruction do not constitute acts of appropriation because no property interest is acquired or transferred by the perpetrator.'[106] In this sense, despite the similar nature of the harm experienced by a victim through the theft or destruction of their property, the Appeals Chamber implied that the decisive principle engaged by the definition of the crime of pillage, that distinguishes it

103 Brima et al. Trial Judgment (n 84), para 754.

104 *Prosecutor v. Germain Katanga and Mathieu Ngudjolo Chui*, ICC-01/04-01/07, ICC, Decision on the Confirmation of Charges, 30 September 2008, para 333.

105 Bemba Trial Judgment (n 88), para 116.

106 *Prosecutor v. Moinina Fofana and Allieu Kondewa* (*CDF Case*), SCSL-04-14-A, SCSL, Appeal Judgment, 28 May 2008, para 402 at footnote 780 [hereafter Fofana and Kondewa Appeal Judgment].

normatively from the war crime of destruction not justified by military necessity, relates to how it involves the acquisition or transfer of property interests from the owner to the perpetrator.

2.2 *Gravity*

While not strictly a definitional issue, from a normative perspective a significant dimension of the approach to pillage reflected in the case law of the international tribunals also relates to the question of the gravity of the conduct and its relationship to the court or tribunal's jurisdiction. In its first decision on plunder at the ICTY in the *Mucić et al.* case, the Trial Chamber dismissed charges involving the theft of money, watches and other valuables from detainees in a prison camp on jurisdictional grounds. The defence had argued with reference to the tribunal's jurisdiction over 'serious' violations of international humanitarian law under Article 1 of its Statute, that:

> [t]he Hague Regulations forbidding plunder were designed to prevent abuses such as those of the Nazis during the Second World War in taking valuable property such as artworks from occupied nations. They were not designed to punish under international law private soldiers who steal property of little value from civilians. [...] [s]tealing watches and coins is not what plunder is about. It is not a serious grave breach of the Geneva Conventions [...] Plunder is what Herman Goering did with the art of Eastern Europe. That's what grave breaches are. Or, for example, emptying entire houses of their quality furniture.[107]

The Trial Chamber rejected this argument, concluding that 'the prohibition against the unjustified appropriation of public and private enemy property is general in scope, and extends both to acts of looting committed by individual soldiers for their private gain and to the organized seizure of property undertaken within the framework of a systematic economic exploitation of occupied territory.'[108] It went on to note that '[c]onsistent with this view, isolated instances of theft of personal property of modest value were treated as war crimes in a number of trials before French Military Tribunals following the Second World War.'[109] The Trial Chamber in *Naletilić and Martinović* came to the same conclusion, noting that 'under international law, plunder does not require the appropriation to be extensive or to involve a large economic value.

107 Mucić et al. Trial Judgment (n 83), para 586.
108 *Ibid.*, para 590.
109 *Ibid.*

Dispossession of personal property, a common way individual soldiers gain illicit booty, is considered a war crime of the more traditional type.'[110]

However, in addressing the jurisdictional requirement of a 'serious' violation of international humanitarian law, the Chamber in *Mucić et al.* endorsed the defence's analysis that the conduct in this case failed to meet the conditions of seriousness laid out in the Tadić Jurisdiction Decision. In *Tadić,* the Appeals Chamber used precisely the example of appropriation of property to identify the conditions for an offence to be subject to the ICTY's jurisdiction under Article 3 of its Statute, namely that:

> the violation must be "serious", that is to say, it must constitute a breach of a rule protecting important values, and the breach must involve grave consequences for the victim. Thus, for instance, the fact of a combatant simply appropriating a loaf of bread in an occupied village would not amount to a "serious violation of international law" although it may be regarded as falling foul of the basic principle laid down in Article 46, paragraph 1, of the Hague Regulations (and the corresponding rule of customary international law) whereby "private property must be respected" by an army occupying an enemy territory.[111]

While the Trial Chamber in *Mucić et al.* emphasised that 'the prohibition against unjustified appropriation of private or public property constitutes a rule protecting important values',[112] it nevertheless concluded that 'the evidence before the Trial Chamber fails to demonstrate that any property taken from the detainees in the Čelebići prison-camp was of sufficient monetary value for its unlawful appropriation to involve grave consequences for the victims.'[113] For this reason, the Chamber concluded that the conduct charged as plunder in this case could not be considered to constitute a sufficiently serious violation of international humanitarian law to fall within the jurisdiction of the tribunal.[114] The Appeals Chamber in *Kordić and Čerkez* later made clear that 'the requirement of grave consequences [for victims] stems from the special jurisdictional provisions of the Statute. [The discussion of grave consequences] is therefore without prejudice to the general – less stringent – requirements for

110 Naletilić and Martinović Trial Judgment (n 88), para 612.

111 *Prosecutor v. Duško Tadić,* IT-94-1, ICTY, Decision on the Defence Motion for Interlocutory Appeal on Jurisdiction, 2 October 1995, para 94.

112 Mucić et al. Trial Judgment (n 83), para 1154.

113 *Ibid.*

114 *Ibid.*

the crime of plunder under international criminal law.'[115] While the question of the gravity of the conduct was therefore addressed as a jurisdictional, rather than a definitional issue, this finding went on to significantly shape the scope of the subsequent jurisprudence on plunder at the ICTY, and also informed its interpretation at the SCSL and the ICC.

Significant from a normative perspective is how the requirement that 'the breach must involve grave consequences for the victim' has been interpreted in different cases. In *Mucić et al.*, in which money, watches and other valuables were stolen from prisoners at the Čelebići camp, the Trial Chamber concluded that the property taken from detainees was not 'of sufficient monetary value for its unlawful appropriation to involve grave consequences for the victims'.[116] This reasoning, interpreting the jurisdictional requirement of grave consequences for victims from the perspective of the monetary value of the property appropriated, has been echoed in several cases at the ICTY.[117] Without doing so explicitly, this reasoning suggests something of a backwards shift in the conception of the prohibition on pillage, passing over the wider normative shift towards conceptualising international humanitarian law and its protections for property as rooted in the need to prevent civilian suffering that took place with the codification of the Geneva Conventions and the Additional Protocols, and instead harking back to the more property-rights based conception of protections for property that shaped the Hague Regulations and the post-World War II jurisprudence. Framing the analysis of the gravity of the consequences for victims in terms of monetary value raises the question of the nature of the 'consequences' that are evaluated for their gravity i.e. what *types* of consequences count towards a finding that appropriation of property caused grave consequences for victims.

In this respect, the reasoning in *Mucić et al.* and a number of other cases implied that the loss of property of sufficient monetary value may constitute a grave consequence for a victim, aside from whether or not such loss involved consequences in more obviously humanitarian terms, beyond the financial loss itself, such as in terms of the victim's fundamental needs or their economic security. From this perspective, the appropriation of property of high monetary value which nevertheless comprises only a small proportion of the property of a wealthy individual could constitute a sufficiently grave consequence to meet

115 Kordić and Čerkez Appeal Judgment (n 88), para 82, footnote 94.

116 Mucić et al. Trial Judgment (n 83), para 1154.

117 Kordić and Čerkez Trial Judgment (n 88), para 352; Naletilić and Martinović Trial Judgment (n 88), para 614; *Prosecutor v. Blagoje Simić et al.*, IT-95-9-T, ICTY, Trial Judgment, 17 October 2003, para 101.

the threshold of seriousness to have fallen within the subject matter jurisdiction of the ICTY, regardless of whether the loss of such property involved any type of consequence for the owner beyond the pure financial loss. On this normative reading, the approach to the gravity of pillage reflected in *Mucić et al.* invokes a normative conception of the crime that protects property as an end in itself, with its loss constituting a grave consequence for victims on a scale of value and harm measured only on its own terms. This contrasts with the notion that international humanitarian law, in which the crime of pillage has its conceptual and normative roots, 'is driven by a conception of property that is more instrumental, and values property in direct proportion to its role in assuring the survival of civilians.'[118]

While monetary value continued to be referred to as a relevant criterion in interpreting whether the appropriation of property constituted a serious violation of international humanitarian law under Article 1 of the ICTY Statute, the jurisprudence also evolved in this regard following the initial interpretation offered in *Mucić et al.*. In *Naletilić and Martinović*, the Trial Chamber broadened the analysis of grave consequences, noting the findings of the Trial Chamber in *Mucić et al.* with respect to monetary value, but going further to also assert that:

> the seriousness of the violation must be ascertained on a case by case basis, taking into consideration the specific circumstances of each instance. Plunder may be a serious violation not only when one victim suffers severe economic consequences because of the appropriation, but also, for example, when property is appropriated from a large number of people. In the latter case, the gravity of the crime stems from the reiteration of the acts and from their overall impact.[119]

In this respect, the Trial Chamber in *Naletilić and Martinović*, and the later jurisprudence that endorsed this interpretation,[120] tempered the exclusive focus on monetary value as the measure of the gravity of the consequences. These cases constructed a normative approach to the crime that, while not explicitly addressing more humanitarian notions of the use value of property in their analysis of the gravity of the conduct, provided greater scope to capture

118 Brilmayer and Chepiga (n 66), 417.

119 Naletilić and Martinović Trial Judgment (n 88), para 614.

120 Simić et al. Trial Judgment (n 117), para 101; Kordić and Čerkez Trial Judgment (n 88), para 82; Hadžihasanović and Kubura Trial Judgment (n 88), para 55–56; Martić Trial Judgment (n 88), 102–103.

these dimensions and the variety of consequences that may be experienced by victims of plunder, beyond simply the loss of the property as such. Indeed, the Trial Chamber in *Kordić and Čerkez* made explicit this shift to a marginally more humanitarian, civilian-protection conception of the crime in explaining that 'a serious violation could be assumed in circumstances where appropriations take place vis-à-vis a large number of people, even though there are no grave consequences for each individual. In this case it would be the overall effect on the civilian population and the multitude of offences committed that would make the violation serious.'[121] The SCSL endorsed the same reasoning, similarly finding that 'to determine the seriousness of the violation, reference may be made to the nature, scope, dimension, or the collective scale of the looting, for instance by considering the number of people from whom property is appropriated.'[122]

By contrast, the ICC's case law reflects a conflicting approach both to its interpretation of the elements of the crime of pillage with respect to the issue of scale, as well as to the matter of the 'seriousness' of the violation of international humanitarian law for the purposes of the court's jurisdiction. In this respect, in the Confirmation of Charges Decision in the *Bemba* case, the Pre-Trial Chamber interpreted the language contained in the Rome Statute referring to 'pillaging a town or place, even when taken by assault', which directly reflects Article 28 of the 1907 Hague Convention, to entail 'a somewhat large-scale appropriation of all types of property, such as public or private, movable or immovable property, which goes beyond mere sporadic acts of violation of property rights.'[123] On this interpretation, the language of pillaging 'a town or place, even when taken by assault' requires a certain scale-requirement to be met before appropriation of property falls within the definition of pillage. The Chamber went on to depart from the jurisprudence at the ICTY, noting that 'the Elements of Crimes do not require the property to be of a certain monetary value' but endorsed a similar understanding of its own jurisdiction with respect to pillage in stating that:

> bearing in mind the mandate of the Court as set out in article 1 of the Statute, the Chamber recalls that article 8(2)(e)(v) of the Statute is introduced as "[an]other *serious* [violation] of the laws and customs applicable

121 Kordić and Čerkez Trial Judgment (n 88), para 83.

122 Sesay et al. Trial Judgment (n 98), para 209–210, para 1027.

123 *Prosecutor v. Jean-Pierre Bemba Gombo*, ICC-01/05-01/08, ICC, Decision Pursuant to Article 61(7)(a) and (b) of the Rome Statute on the Charges of the Prosecutor Against Jean-Pierre Bemba Gombo, 15 June 2009, para 317 [hereafter Bemba Confirmation of Charges].

> in armed conflict not of an international character" [...]. In the opinion of the Chamber, this means that cases of petty property expropriation may not fall under the scope of article 8(2)(e)(v) of the Statute. A determination on the seriousness of the violation is made by the Chamber in light of the particular circumstances of the case.[124]

The Trial Chamber in *Katanga* endorsed this reasoning, echoing the language of the ICTY in stating that 'the gravity of the violation must be determined on a case-by-case basis, with due regard for the particular circumstances of the case. The Chamber will therefore determine the violation to be serious, where, for example, pillaging had significant consequences for the victims, even where such consequences are not of the same gravity for all the victims, or where a large number of persons were deprived of their property.'[125] This requirement of a certain level of gravity to the crime in its impact on victims, while still vague, somewhat tempers the extent to which the ICC and SCSL definitions of pillage offer a conception of the crime exclusively in terms of ownership interests by also taking into account, in addition to the normative question of the violation of the owner's consent, the impact of pillage in wider, harm-based terms for its jurisdictional analysis.

At the same time, the Trial Chamber in *Ntaganda* came to the opposite conclusion on the question of gravity, stating that the reference to other serious violations of the laws and customs applicable in armed conflicts not of an international character in Article 8(e) of the Statute 'refers to the seriousness of the nature of the crimes listed under (e), which by virtue of their inclusion in the Statute must all be considered 'serious violations'[126] and rejected the defence's submission that pillage must take place on a 'somewhat large-scale'.[127] The Trial Chamber in *Ongwen* similarly concluded that 'there is no requirement that appropriations must occur on a large scale basis before constituting the crime of pillaging.'[128] In this respect, the decisions of the ICC do not yet reflect a coherent approach to the gravity of the crime of pillage, with earlier decisions broadly echoing the approach adopted at the ICTY, but the

124 *Ibid.*

125 *Prosecutor v. Germain Katanga*, ICC-01/04-01/07, ICC, Judgment pursuant to article 74 of the Statute, 7 March 2014, para 909 [hereafter Katanga Trial Judgment]. The Trial Chamber in Bemba also endorsed this reasoning, see Bemba Trial Judgment (n 88), para 117.

126 *Prosecutor v. Bosco Ntaganda*, ICC-01/04-02/06, ICC, Trial Judgment, 8 July 2019, para 1044 [hereafter Ntaganda Trial Judgment].

127 *Ibid.*

128 *Prosecutor v. Dominic Ongwen*, ICC-02/04-01/15, ICC, Trial Judgment, 4 February 2021, para 2764 [hereafter Ongwen Trial Judgment].

more recent *Ntaganda* and *Ongwen* decisions suggesting a shift in the normative conception of the crime that instead treats pillage as 'serious' in its own right, regardless of the scale of the appropriation of property or the consequences for victims.

2.3 *Pillage as Persecution*

Some of the most explicit statements with respect to how the crime of pillage is normatively conceptualised have appeared in contexts where acts of pillage have been charged as the crime of persecution at both the ICTY and the ICC. While a property rights-based conception of pillage appears to have underpinned implicitly and explicitly the definitions adopted at the ICTY and ICC, in *Kordić and Čerkez* at the ICTY the Trial Chamber provided an analysis of acts of wanton destruction and plunder charged as the crime of persecution, which invoked traces of a more use value-oriented approach to this crime. The Trial Chamber argued that:

> If the ultimate aim of persecution is the "removal of those persons from the society in which they live alongside the perpetrators, or even from humanity itself", the widespread or systematic, discriminatory, destruction of individuals' homes and means of livelihood would surely result in such a removal from society. In the context of an overall campaign of persecution, rendering a people homeless and with no means of economic support may be the method used to "coerce, intimidate, terrorise and forcibly transfer … civilians from their homes and villages." Thus, when the cumulative effect of such property destruction is the removal of civilians from their homes on discriminatory grounds, the "wanton and extensive destruction and/or plundering of Bosnian Muslim civilian dwellings, buildings, businesses, and civilian personal property and livestock" may constitute the crime of persecution.[129]

Perhaps because the Trial Chamber was addressing the question of whether acts of plunder and wanton destruction of property may constitute persecution, it provided an analysis of both these crimes that points towards an understanding of their impact in more clearly humanitarian terms than when charged exclusively as a war crime. By embedding plunder within a wider account of the use value of property and the implications of its removal in

129 Kordić and Čerkez Trial Judgment (n 88), para 205. This analysis was endorsed by the Trial Chamber in *Simić et al.* See Simić et al. Trial Judgment (n 117), para 102.

terms of 'rendering a people homeless and with no means of economic support',[130] the analysis in *Kordić and Čerkez* highlighted for the first time in the case law of the ICTY how pillage may be conceptualised in broader terms than the more limited focus on ownership interests and property rights. The Trial Chamber in *Naletilić and Martinović* went on to make this approach explicit in relation to plunder in particular. It noted that 'plunder of personal belongings may rise to the level of persecution if the impact of such deprivation is serious enough. This is so if the property is indispensable and a vital asset to the owners.'[131] While plunder remains linked to the notion of ownership on this interpretation, the reference to property that is indispensable or a vital asset to the owner takes a clear step towards constructing a conceptualisation of pillage that addresses its consequences in more explicitly use-value and humanitarian terms.

The Trial Chamber in *Krajišnik* tempered the emphasis on ownership interests yet further in this respect. On the issue of the gravity of plunder or pillage when charged as persecution, the Trial Chamber in *Krajišnik* endorsed the finding in the post-World War II *Flick* case that 'the scale of the appropriation was not the critical issue when the act is considered as a crime against humanity. Rather, it was the impact of the appropriation on the victim. [...] A distinction should be made between industrial property and the dwellings, household furnishings, and food supplies of a persecuted people.'[132] On this basis, the Trial Chamber determined that 'appropriation or plunder as an underlying act of persecution is to be understood as any intentional appropriation of public or private property that has a severe impact on the owner or user of the property.'[133] Here, the impact on the *user* of the property was explicitly foregrounded for the first time. This contrasts with the exclusive focus on the owner and their rights invoked by the centrality of the violation of the owner's consent in the definition of pillage adopted at the SCSL and the ICC. In this way, the Trial Chamber in *Krajišnik* constructed a normative account of plunder more closely in line with the protections for property contained in the Additional Protocols to the Geneva Conventions in terms of how the civilian-use criterion for the protection of property in the Additional Protocols protects users' rather than owners' interests.

130 *Ibid.*

131 Naletilić and Martinović Trial Judgment (n 88), para 699.

132 *Prosecutor v. Momčilo Krajišnik*, IT-00-39-T, ICTY, Trial Judgment, 27 September 2006, para 767.

133 *Ibid.*, para 768. The Trial Chamber in *Gotovina et al.* endorsed this finding. See Gotovina et al. Trial Judgment – Volume 2 (n 88), para 1821.

At the ICC, by contrast, acts of pillage charged as the crime of persecution have instead been identified as being normatively rooted in a human right to property. In its analysis of the elements of persecution and the requirement that the perpetrator severely deprived, contrary to international law, one or more persons of fundamental rights, the Trial Chamber in the *Ongwen* case identified a number of human rights which it considered to constitute fundamental rights, including 'the right to life, the right to personal liberty, the right not to be held in slavery or servitude, the right not to be subjected to torture or cruel treatment, inhuman or degrading treatment, and the right to private property.'[134] On the basis of evidence of the looting of homes and shops at the Pajule IDP camp, where food items, household supplies and items such as a medicine, livestock and money were stolen,[135] the Trial Chamber found with respect to the charge of pillage as an underlying act of persecution, that 'LRA attackers severely deprived, contrary to international law, civilians of fundamental rights in the course of the attack on Pajule IDP camp. Specifically, the LRA attackers deprived civilians of [among others] the right to private property.'[136]

On this interpretation, and disctinct from the protections for property rights during armed conflict under international humanitarian law invoked by the ICTY, the Trial Chamber constructed a conceptualisation of pillage as engaging a fundamental human right to private property under international law. The notion of a human right to property, particularly a human right to *private* property is, however, not uncontroversial.[137] While the Universal Declaration of Human Rights contains a right to property, this was not repeated as a broadly formulated right in either the ICCPR or the ICESCR because of the 'absence of international agreement as to the exact content of property rights'[138] at the time the conventions were drafted. Underpinning this absence of consensus on the content of a human right to property was precisely the same ideological division, discussed in the previous section of this chapter, that gave rise to the exclusion of the reference to protections for 'private property' during the drafting of the Fourth Geneva Convention. This term was ultimately replaced

134 Ongwen Trial Judgment (n 128), para 2733.

135 Ongwen Trial Judgment (n 128), para 150. See paragraph 165 for a similar account of looting in Odek IDP camp.

136 Ongwen Trial Judgment (n 128), para 2846. See similarly paragraph 2906 with respect to the Odek IDP camp.

137 Catarina Krause and Guðmundur S. Alfreðsson, 'Article 17' in Guðmundur S. Alfreðsson and Asbjørn Eide (ed), *The Universal Declaration of Human Rights: A Common Standard of Achievement* (Martinus Nijhoff 1999), 359.

138 Theo R.G. van Banning, *The Human Right to Property* (Intersentia 2002), 5.

in the Convention with the language of 'real or personal property belonging individually or collectively to private persons, or to the State, or to other public authorities, or to social or cooperative organizations',[139] in order to reflect the differing position of property in the contemporary political and economic systems of different states. While a right to property was ultimately included in the UDHR, its drafting proved contentious, with some states having abolished property in private form, while others pursued national welfare programmes that subordinated absolute protections for private property to the public interest. The issue was ultimately solved by removing the term 'private' from the right to property enshrined in Article 17 of the UDHR.[140]

While the nature of the particular controversy over protections for private or collective forms of property have abated over time, other contours of the normative debate that took place during the drafting of Article 17 of the UDHR remain relevant to the continuing contestation over the content of a right to property under international human rights law in the present day,[141] and therefore remain relevant to a normative conception of the crime of pillage as rooted in this right. In broad terms, conflicts during the drafting of Article 17 of the UDHR centred upon the distinction between a conception of a right to property 'infused with the core liberal value of individualism and [...] the right to absolutely exclude others from one's property'[142] versus a right to property which would capture its social function.

A social function approach to a right to property understands this right as being 'determined by the relationship between the needs of the individual and the needs of society'[143] in relation to property, creating an obligation on states with respect to property to therefore 'act in a way which is compatible with social interests.'[144] In addition to the ideological East-West divide over the nature of the property system to be protected in terms of individual or collective property, during the drafting of Article 17 of the UDHR, several Latin American states also advocated in favour of a right to property that would more strongly reflect this social function. A right to property understood in

139 Article 53, Convention (IV) relative to the Protection of Civilian Persons in Time of War, Geneva, 12 August 1949.

140 Samuel Moyn, *Not Enough: Human Rights in an Unequal World* (Belknap Press 2018), 58.

141 For an overview see Laura Dehaibi, 'Liberal Property and Lived Property: A Critique of Abstract Universalism in the Human Right to Property' (PhD Dissertation, McGill University 2020); Corina Heri, 'The Human Right to Land, for Peasants and for All: Tracing the Social Function of Property to 1948', (2020) 20 *Human Rights Law Review*, 433–452.

142 Heri (n 141), 434.

143 van Banning (n 138), 148.

144 *Ibid.*

these terms entails a right to such property 'as is needed for a decent living and helps to maintain the dignity of the individual and the home.'[145] A right to property of this nature was included in the 1948 American Declaration of the Rights and Duties of Man, Article 23 of which states that 'every person has a right to own such private property as meet the essential needs of decent living and helps to maintain the dignity of the individual and of the home.' While the negative aspect of the social function of a right to property, in the sense that the State is entitled to limit property rights in the public interest,[146] was less controversial, this positive notion of a right to a subsistence minimum conflicted more strongly with the views of those states that advocated for the more liberal conception of a right to private property as an absolute right 'inherent to human dignity, necessary for individual independence.'[147]

Ultimately, the right to property contained in Article 17 of the UDHR, which protects 'the right to own property alone as well as in association with others' and the right not to be arbitrarily deprived of one's property, reflects protection for both individualist and collective forms of property, but ultimately excludes the social function conception of property and the idea that 'only a limited amount of property should enjoy human rights protection, or that every human has a right to a certain minimum of property necessary for survival in dignity.'[148] While subsequent consensus on the content of a right to property did not prove possible during the drafting of the ICCPR and the ICESCR, resulting in the absence of the right from the two principal international human rights treaties, the primary regional human rights conventions contain clauses referring to a right to property of some kind.[149] The particular nature of the right to property in these conventions, and how they have been applied by courts, nevertheless reflect different characteristics which 'reveal ideological preferences and sensitivity to location.'[150] This manifests in the differing degrees to which they reflect liberal conceptions of private property rights, how they balance individual and state interests, how they accommodate the social function of property and how they reflect the particular significance and implications of rights to property in postcolonial contexts.[151]

145 Krause and Alfreðsson (n 137), 370.

146 Heri (n 141), 438, 443.

147 van Banning (n 138), 42. See also Heri (n 141), 443.

148 Heri (n 141), 444–445.

149 See Article 21, American Convention on Human Rights; Article 1, Protocol I to the European Convention Human Rights; Article 14, African Charter on Human and Peoples' Rights; Article 31, Arab Charter on Human Rights.

150 Dehaibi (n 141), 149.

151 *Ibid.*, 134–149.

Understanding the right to property in international human rights law from this perspective reveals how the Trial Chamber's conclusion in the *Ongwen* case, that acts of pillage constitute the crime of persecution on the basis that they violate the right to private property, does not invoke a settled or unambiguous normative grounding for the crime of pillage in this context. This is particularly true with respect to the specific reference to 'private' property, which points explicitly to liberal ideas about individual and exclusionary rights to property, and does not represent the varying degrees to which different formulations of the right to property under international human rights law reflect this liberal premise.[152] In this way, the Trial Chamber's identification of the right to private property as the normative basis of the crime of pillage when charged as persecution situates the crime in the muddy and ambiguous realm of enduring debates over the nature and scope of a human right to property.

Taken together, these different definitions of the war crime of plunder or pillage, and those instances in which it has also been charged as persecution, construct a conceptualisation of the crime varyingly contextualised in a liberal commitment to the protection of property during armed conflict that emerged with the Hague Conventions, in the violation of ownership rights through the centralisation of the absence of the owner's consent as a legal element of the crime, and in a fundamental right to private property supposedly enshrined in international human rights law. By contrast, definitions of pillage that invoke a use value conception of property are much more limited, and only appear in the context of acts of pillage charged as persecution in a limited number of cases at the ICTY. This analysis suggests that, while not entirely coherent and with some exceptions, the dominant conception of the crime of pillage constructed by the definitions adopted in international criminal law draws primarily on the principle of protecting a liberal, individualised and exclusive notion of property rights for its normative basis.

3 Normative Themes in the Case Law

Beyond purely definitional and jurisdictional questions and the normative conceptualisation of plunder or pillage they invoke, decisions involving charges for these crimes reflect relatively limited concern with their normative dimensions. The ICTY, in particular, treated acts of plunder almost entirely in baldly factual terms, without the explicit engagement with normative questions

152 *Ibid.*

apparent in the discussion of some other crimes, such as attacks on cultural property or sexual violence. Certain dimensions of the factual accounts of pillage reflected in the decisions nevertheless contain implicit normative themes, with the decisions of the SCSL and the ICC also reflecting some evolution in this regard. The primary themes of relevance from a normative perspective in these decisions relate to the scale of the plunder or pillage, an emphasis on the use or social value of pillaged property, and a flexible interpretation of the issue of ownership, implying a widening of the conceptualisation of ownership rights invoked by the definitions of the crime.

3.1 *Scale*

In line with the identification of a gravity threshold as a jurisdictional requirement at each of the courts and tribunals that have addressed charges of pillage, the dominant normative theme around the crime, in particular at the ICTY and the SCSL, constructs the scale of the pillage that took place as the primary signifier of its gravity. The Trial Chamber's recounting of the plundering of the village of Erevnik in *Gotovina et al.* at the ICTY is paradigmatic of this type of factual account of the crime:

> [G]roups of persons in camouflage uniforms, referred to as Croatian soldiers, loaded furniture, electrical appliances, and other valuable household goods from houses in Ervenik onto civilian and military trucks and drove off. The evidence indicates that this happened on a daily basis. These persons also took cars, trucks, tractors, trailers, and farming vehicles, as well as parts from broken down vehicles, hay, and firewood on a large scale, and large numbers of livestock from farms. On one occasion a large number of goats were slaughtered, skinned, and taken away. A number of trucks left the town every day carrying property and livestock.[153]

In its analysis of the plundering of Mostar, the Trial Chamber in *Naletilić and Martinović* made clear its understanding of the relevance of the scale of the plunder for its reasoning as to the gravity of the crime, stressing that 'although single instances of plunder, taken in isolation, may not reach the threshold of seriousness set out above in order to vest the Tribunal with subject matter jurisdiction, collectively they show a clearly serious pattern of plunder against

153 *Prosecutor v. Ante Gotovina et al.*, IT-06-90-T, ICTY, Trial Judgment – Volume 1, 15 April 2011, para 656.

a large part of the BH Muslim population in Mostar.'[154] The same type of analysis is reflected in the *RUF* case at the SCSL, where the Trial Chamber found that 'AFRC/RUF fighters engaged in a systematic campaign of looting upon their arrival in Koidu, marking the continuation of Operation Pay Yourself. The evidence demonstrates that rebels appropriated many items of significant value, such as vehicles, but also that the appropriation of minor items such as foodstuffs occurred on a sufficiently large scale to cumulatively constitute a serious violation.'[155]

This reasoning with respect to the scale of plunder as the signifier of the gravity of the crime was further linked explicitly to the jurisdictional requirement that the crime involved grave consequences for victims in the *Martić* case at the ICTY. With respect to the theft of cars, tractors, tools, machinery, furniture and cattle from the village of Hrvatska Dubica, the Trial Chamber reasoned that, 'given the scale of the looting, the Trial Chamber finds that it resulted in grave consequences for the victims, having regard to the overall effect on the civilian population and the multitude of offences committed.'[156] The Trial Chamber in *Gotovina et al.* at the ICTY spelled out this harm-based approach to the link between the scale of pillage and the notion of grave consequences:

> certain incidents [of plunder] had in themselves grave consequences for the victims. Moreover, considering the overall effect of the various incidents of plunder on the civilian population, and the multitude of offences committed, the Trial Chamber finds that the plunder concerns property of a large number of people, and that the cumulative effect of the various incidents constitutes grave consequences. [...] Therefore, the Trial Chamber finds that the incidents referred to in the latter list above constitute plunder as violations of the laws or customs of war.[157]

While these decisions do not spell out explicitly what the precise effects of plunder on the civilian population were understood to be in terms of the grave consequences they identify, they nevertheless incorporated an evaluation of the nature of the harm to the civilian population, through the emphasis on scale, into the analysis of whether the crime fell within the jurisdiction of the

154 Naletilić and Martinović Trial Judgment (n 88), para 624–625. For similar accounts see Hadžihasanović and Kubura Trial Judgment (n 88), para 1873–1874 and Brima et al. Trial Judgment (n 84), para 238.

155 Sesay et al. Trial Judgment (n 98), para 1336–1337. See similarly para 1334.

156 Martić Trial Judgment (n 88), para 357. See similarly para 382.

157 Gotovina et al. Trial Judgment – Volume 2 (n 88), para 1787–1789.

court. On this account, the normative conception of pillage is shifted to some degree in the direction of a more humanitarian, harm-based approach to the crime than that suggested by the more abstract focus on property rights in the analysis of the crime's normative roots in the case law of the ICTY. To illustrate this point it is worth contrasting this reasoning with that of the tribunal in the post-Second World War *I.G. Farben* case, which explicitly rejected an approach to pillage that would capture both the violation of the owner's consent involved in the appropriation of property, but also incorporate the impact of the crime on the economy of the occupied territory.[158] The focus on scale in these cases, and the highlighting of the effects of plunder on such a scale on the civilian population in this way constructs a more instrumental account of the normative dimensions of the protections for property reflected in the criminalisation of pillage than the legal elements of the crime, and its historical roots, suggest.

3.2 *Use Value*

The Sentencing Decision in the *RUF* case at the SCSL fleshed out this more instrumental conception of the prohibition on pillage by beginning to provide a more concrete account of the nature of the harm that may be understood to underlie the references to 'the overall effect of [...] plunder on the civilian population'[159] in the case law:

> [T]he Chamber notes that many victims suffered emotional and psychological harm because they powerlessly had to watch their homes and livelihood arbitrarily taken from them or burned as a means of creating immeasurable fear amidst them. Many victims were deprived of property with no remedy for reclaiming it. The Chamber considers that in such impoverished communities, where victims lived on a subsistence basis, all forms of appropriation or destruction by fighters adversely impacted the victims.[160]

Highlighting the effects of large-scale pillage on livelihoods and subsistence, this analysis situates the protections for property underlying the crime of pillage clearly within a use value conception of its normative value. In constructing an account of the crime that explicitly values property 'in direct proportion

158 Krauch et al. Judgment (n 49), 1135.

159 Gotovina et al. Trial Judgment – Volume 2 (n 88), para 1787.

160 *Prosecutor v. Issa Hassan Sesay et al.* (*RUF Case*), SCSL-04-15-T, SCSL, Sentencing Judgment, 8 April 2009, para 172–176.

to its role in assuring the survival of civilians',[161] the Trial Chamber in the RUF case echoed the normative conceptualisation of protections for property reflected in the Additional Protocols to the Geneva Conventions and their 'civilian use' framework as the criterion of protection.

This turn to a theme that emphasises the use value of pillaged property is particularly pronounced in the approach adopted in the case law of the ICC, which contrasts with its absence from the narratives around plunder in cases at the ICTY, when not charged as persecution. The only other context in which this conception of pillage emerged in the decisions of the ICTY was implicitly, through the narrative around crimes of deportation or forcible transfer. For instance, in the context of its analysis of the deportation and forcible transfer of Serbs from the Krajina region, the Trial Chamber in *Gotovina et al.* noted that 'organised and systematic plunder and destruction of Serb owned or inhabited property was part and parcel of the campaign to drive out any remaining Serbs from the area and/or to prevent or discourage those who had fled from returning.'[162] The Chamber similarly made reference to testimony that 'when asking a number of HV soldiers why they participated in looting and destruction, they responded that [...] their superiors had specifically authorized them to "help themselves to the goods." They further stated that the destruction was intended to prevent the Serbs from returning.'[163] Underpinning this narrative is an implicit nod in the direction of a use value conception of property; it rests on a recognition that the appropriation of certain types of property may deprive people of their ability to subside in a place, thereby preventing their return.

In contrast to the ICTY case law, the decisions of the ICC reflect a narrative that endorses the use value approach in emphatic terms. In the first case involving a conviction for pillage at the ICC, the Trial Chamber in *Katanga* recounted the attack on the village of Bogoro, in which the attackers are described as having pillaged 'everything they found',[164] explaining that 'regarding the value of the property stolen, various witnesses underscored before the Chamber the qualitative and quantitative loss they had incurred as a result of the attack, whether roofing sheets, furniture from their homes or animals (cows, goats and fowl) – all considered essential to their daily life.'[165] The Chamber went on to stress the character of the plundered property as 'essential to daily life'

161 Brilmayer and Chepiga (n 66), 417.
162 Gotovina et al. Trial Judgment – Volume 2 (n 88), para 1510.
163 *Ibid.*, para 1717.
164 Katanga Trial Judgment (n 125), para 925.
165 *Ibid.*, para 928.

repeatedly throughout the judgment. It noted, for instance, how 'property belonging to the predominantly Hema civilian population of Bogoro, which was essential to its daily life, including roofing sheets, furniture and various other personal effects, food, and livestock and animals, was taken away by the attackers.'[166] The Chamber went on to explain the relevance of the notion of property 'essential for daily life' for its understanding of the value of the pillaged property:

> Whereas there is a great disparity in the value of the pillaged property – kitchen-ware and furniture but also livestock, goats and chickens, as the case may be – the property represented the bulk of the owners' possessions. To the extent that the civilians were deprived of their personal houseware and even their livestock, property essential to their daily life, the Chamber is of the view that the property was in fact of great value to them.[167]

On this account, the pillaged property is valued in direct proportion to its use value in the daily lives of the inhabitants of Bogoro. In its analysis of the plan to attack the village, the Trial Chamber went even further, to state that it 'considers that […] the Ngiti militia's objective was to drive the civilian population from Bogoro by killing it, destroying its homes and pillaging the property and the livestock essential to its survival.'[168] In doing so, the Chamber situated the crime of pillage at the apex of a use value approach to the protection of property, as 'essential to meet subsistence needs',[169] in stressing how the stolen property was essential to the very survival of the population. Lastly, the harm caused by the pillaging of property that is essential to survival was addressed in the sentencing order, where the Trial Chamber explained that:

> the property of the mainly Hema civilian population of Bogoro which was essential for daily life, such as roofing sheets, furniture and various other personal items, food and domestic animals, above all livestock, had been taken away by attackers […] The loss of this property had significant consequences for the daily lives of the victims, as was corroborated by the village chief, who, on 5 May 2014, testified before the Chamber that one of the most persistent consequences of the battle was poverty.

166 *Ibid.*, para 932. See similarly para 1660.
167 *Ibid.*, para 953.
168 *Ibid.*, para 1665.
169 van Banning (n 138), 184.

> Apparently, many locals have since been forced to start life afresh away from Bogoro, where they chose not to return as they would have had to start again from scratch or simply did not have the means.[170]

This centralising of a subsistence approach to property and the economic consequences of pillage is a feature of each of the cases that have addressed the crime at the ICC. In *Ntaganda*, the Trial Chamber echoed the language of *Katanga* in noting that:

> While there is some disparity in the value of the looted items and their likely significance and use for the victims, these items represented the bulk of the victims' possessions, played an important role in the victims' day-to-day lives and/or their businesses. [...] the Chamber is satisfied that the looted items – such as the harvest, the taking of which affected their livelihood and availability of food until new crops would had [sic] grown and could be harvested – also played an important role in their day-to-day lives.[171]

The Trial Chamber in *Bemba* similarly highlighted the economic consequences of pillage, explaining in relation to acts of pillage that occurred in various locations in the Central African Republic that 'the perpetrators took numerous items from the victims, including administrative documents, clothing, furniture, tools, radios, televisions, items of personal value, money, livestock, food, vehicles, and fuel. In [a witness's] words, they took "everything" and some victims were left with nothing. The consequences on victims were far-reaching, impacting various aspects of their personal and professional lives.'[172] In this respect, the Chamber highlighted how '[v]ictims of pillaging were often left with nothing. [....] P73 was unable to pay for medical treatment, V2's business has never recovered from the loss of necessary equipment, and many victims were left without, inter alia, their savings, foam mattresses, and clothes, which they had worked hard to obtain.'[173] In sentencing, the Chamber explained how '[t]he crimes impacted various aspects of the victims' lives, often leaving them without basic necessities. [...] MLC soldiers pillaged without concern for the

170 *Prosecutor v. Germain Katanga*, ICC-01/04-01/07, ICC, Decision on sentence pursuant to article 76 of the Statute, 23 May 2014, para 52.

171 Ntaganda Trial Judgment (n 126), para 1044.

172 Bemba Trial Judgment (n 88), para 646.

173 *Ibid.*, para 566.

victims' livelihood or well-being, such as the ability to seek treatment, arrange burial or funeral services, or even feed their families.'[174]

This emphasis on the significance of the economic consequences of pillage for the normative narrative constructed around the crime in the decisions of the ICC is underscored in how the Trial Chamber in *Katanga* approached its award of reparations. Referring to the analysis in the Trial Judgment that 'the keeping of grazing animals was a significant part of the Bogoro economy, especially amongst the Hema, who are herders by tradition',[175] the Chamber in the Reparations Order therefore explained that:

> in their applications for reparations, the Applicants allege that they suffered material harm as a result of the pillaging of their livestock or other animals, the destruction of their fields and harvests or the pillaging of their harvests. [...] keeping livestock was a significant activity in Bogoro and its population farmed the land. [...] the population of Bogoro's livelihood came in part from keeping livestock and farming the land. [...] Given the importance to the local society of agriculture and keeping livestock, the Chamber considers that it is reasonable to presume that the great majority of Bogoro's population owned livestock and/or fields to meet their daily needs.[176]

Offering a localised and contextualised account of the economic importance of the particular type of pillaged property in its analysis of the material harm resulting from these crimes, which constrasts with the montetary value approach to harm reflected in several decisions at the ICTY, the Trial Chamber in *Katanga* further reinforced the normative narrative constructed around pillage in these cases as relating primarily to the use value of property; this property was valuable because of its role in the livelihoods and economic security of the victims of pillage.

In the *Ongwen* case, the Trial Chamber went further, foregrounding in particular the importance of the stolen property for the very survival of the inhabitants of IDP camps that were pillaged. It argued that:

174 *Prosecutor v. Jean-Pierre Bemba Gombo*, ICC-01/05-01/08, ICC, Judgment pursuant to Article 76 of the Statute, 21 June 2016, para 51–53.

175 Bemba Trial Judgment (n 88), para 724.

176 *Prosecutor v. Germain Katanga*, ICC-01/04-01/07, ICC, Order for Reparations pursuant to Article 75 of the Statute, 24 March 2017, para 95–98.

> In relation to the war crime of pillaging, the Chamber notes that it is a crime against the right of property. As such, it is in principle of lesser gravity than the crimes against life, physical integrity, and personal liberty and dignity. However, the actual gravity of this crime is variable and depends also on the economic consequences for the victims who were deprived of their property. When such consequences are severe, like in the present case, the crime of pillaging reaches a considerable level of gravity. This is also the case if a large number of individuals were deprived of their property. Among the items looted by the LRA attackers were foodstuffs like beans, flour, salt, sugar, cooking oil, maize, sweets, biscuits, groundnuts, soda as well as household goods such as bedding, clothing, a radio set, saucepans and items such as medicine, livestock and money. These items represented the basic means of survival for the population living in Pajule IDP camp and the deprivation of the residents of these essential items, which cannot have been without knowledge on the part of Dominic Ongwen, represents a significant factor of gravity.[177]

In its description of attacks on other IDP camps the Chamber further recounted how 'when the people returned in the morning after the attack, there were no food items left, the rebels took the food items as well as cooking utensils that were newly distributed. This indicates the considerable impact of the crime of pillaging on the residents of Abok IDP camp.'[178] Similarly, in Odek IDP camp, '[t]he food aid which had been recently distributed to the camp was looted by the attackers. This meant that the impact on the residents was great. Indeed, Zakeo Odora, one of the camp's leaders, stated that the camp residents suffered a great deal as a result of the attackers having stolen the food. He stated that many people suffered from intense hunger, and that other nearby IDP camps in Awere, Acept and Aromo donated some of their food to assist the residents of Odek IDP camp.'[179]

These narratives in the ICC decisions, which construct an account of the value of the property stolen from victims of pillage from the perspective of its role in their day to day lives and livelihoods, in fulfilling their fundamental needs, ensuring their economic security and, in some instances, their very ability to survive, situates the normative conception of the crime emphatically within a use value approach to property. This is particularly striking given the

177 *Prosecutor v. Dominic Ongwen*, ICC-02/04-01/15, ICC, Sentence, 6 May 2021, para 169–170 [hereafter Ongwen Sentence].

178 *Ibid.*, para 273.

179 *Ibid.*, para 201.

nature of the definition of pillage in the ICC Elements of Crimes, which invokes an ownership rights-based conception of the crime through its centralisation of the legal element of the absence of the owner's consent.

3.3 *Ownership*

In this respect, how the case law of the ICC addresses the question of ownership, for the purposes of determining the legal element of the absence of the owner's consent to the appropriation of the property, further underscores the extent to which the narrative constructed around pillage at the ICC has moved away from the conceptual roots invoked by the definition of the crime. Some decisions do make statements that gesture in the direction of a more property rights-based conception of pillage in how they discuss the crime, such as, for instance, the Pre-Trial Chamber's statement in the *Bemba* case that, following the pillaging of property, 'the rightful owners were no longer in a position to rightfully dispose of their goods.'[180] The Trial Chamber in *Ongwen* similarly made an explicit gesture in this direction, describing pillage as 'a crime against the right of property'[181] and identifying the interest protected by the crime of pillage as 'the right to personal property.'[182]

These limited appeals to a conception of pillage as normatively rooted in the protection of property rights, that partly aligns with the conception of the crime invoked when pillage has been charged as persecution at the ICC, are nevertheless diluted by the more dominant use value approach constructed through the factual narrative around the crime. This is further reinforced in how the issue of ownership in relation to the legal element of the absence of the owner's consent to the appropriation of the property has been treated in these decisions. Often, the question of ownership has enjoyed relatively cursory analysis. For instance, in the *RUF* case at the SCSL, the Trial Chamber concluded, on the basis of general evidence of a systematic campaign of looting, that it 'is satisfied that a significant proportion of the items appropriated belonged to civilians, and that the only reasonable inference to be drawn from the evidence is that the owners did not consent to the appropriation by the rebels.'[183] In a similar manner, in the *Katanga* case at the ICC, the Trial Chamber explained with respect to the pillaging of livestock that, while it was 'unable to determine the owner of the cows and goats, it finds that Ngiti combatants stole cows and goats belonging to inhabitants of Bogoro and forced them to herd

180 Bemba Confirmation of Charges (n 123), para 331.

181 Ongwen Sentence (n 177), para 169.

182 *Ibid.*, para 393.

183 Sesay et al. Trial Judgment (n 98), para 1337.

them to a Ngiti camp',[184] concluding that, given the circumstances, the appropriation took place with the owners' consent.[185]

Despite the centrality of ownership for the elements of the crime of pillage at the ICC, which require that the perpetrator intended to deprive the owner of the property and that this took place without the owner's consent, both of these accounts to some extent brush aside the question of ownership, concluding instead that the circumstances in which the appropriation took place prove the owner's lack of consent, whoever they might be. The Trial Chamber in *Ntaganda* made explicit this approach in legal terms, stating that:

> For the purpose of pillage, the Chamber will consider the person who had the property under him or her as the 'owner'. Whether or not this person was the owner in the legal sense is not relevant for the Chamber's assessment. Moreover, in case it is not clear who the owner of a property was, for example, because at the time of the alleged appropriation the item found itself in a house whose residents had fled, or were not otherwise present, it suffices that the perpetrator was aware that the property belonged to someone else than him- or herself, and that as such any appropriation must be assumed to have [sic] without the owner's consent.[186]

It is unclear precisely what relationship to property the chamber intended to articulate with the phrase 'the person who had the property *under* him or her.'[187] It is nevertheless apparent, given the subsequent rejection of an interpretation of ownership in a purely legal sense, that the Chamber intended to capture a wider relationship to property than legal ownership, presumably also incorporating those who may have used certain property, without being its legal owners. In this respect, the Trial Chamber's approach departs from the traditionally liberal conception of property rights in their protection of the ownership right to exclude, to also capture injury to individuals whose relationship to the pillaged property may not fall into the category of 'ownership' in this narrowly defined sense.

This shift away from a conception of pillage as centring on the violation of individualised ownership rights was taken a step further in the Trial Chamber's interpretation of the very nature of property rights themselves in the *Ongwen*

184 Katanga Trial Judgment (n 125), para 938.
185 *Ibid.*, para 954.
186 Ntaganda Trial Judgment (n 126), para 1034.
187 *Ibid.* Emphasis added.

case. In the first direct engagement with the question of the nature of a right to property under international law in the case law on pillage, the Trial Chamber in *Ongwen* explained with respect to the element of the absence of the owner's consent that:

> When the property owner has fled, such appropriations must be assumed to have been without the owner's consent absent any contrary indication. This could occur, for example, when items are appropriated from an empty house whose residents have fled. The concept of private property and the right to property must be understood as encompassing not only the property of individuals, but also the communal property of the communities. It must also take into consideration the customary law of the community (i.e. practices on possession, titles and registration).[188]

In interpreting the right to property in this way, the Trial Chamber referred to the decisions of the African Commission on Human and Peoples' Rights (ACHPR) and the Inter-American Court of Human Rights (IACHR) on rights to property in the context of indigenous communities specifically. The Trial Chamber relied on the ACHPR's finding in the *Ogiek* case that, 'although addressed in the part of the Charter which enshrines the rights recognised for individuals, the right to property as guaranteed by Article 14 may also apply to groups or communities; in effect, the right can be individual or collective.'[189] The Trial Chamber also invoked the *Mayagna (Sumo) Awas Tingni Community v. Nicaragua* case at the IACHR, which similarly concluded that the right to property under international human rights law includes the rights of indigenous communities to communal property.[190] In this case, the Court explained that:

> Among indigenous peoples there is a communitarian tradition regarding a communal form of collective property of the land, in the sense that ownership of the land is not centered on an individual but rather on the group and its community. Indigenous groups, by the fact of their very

188 Ongwen Trial Judgment (n 128), para 2766.

189 *African Commission on Human and Peoples' Rights v. Republic of Kenya*, Application No. 006/2012, African Commission on Human and Peoples' Rights, Judgment, 26 May 2017, para 123 [hereafter African Commission on Human and Peoples' Rights v. Republic of Kenya Judgment].

190 *Case of the Mayagna (Sumo) Awas Tingni Community v. Nicaragua*, Series C No. 79, Inter-American Court of Human Rights, Judgment, 31 August 2001, para 148.

> existence, have the right to live freely in their own territory; the close ties of indigenous people with the land must be recognized and understood as the fundamental basis of their cultures, their spiritual life, their integrity, and their economic survival. For indigenous communities, relations to the land are not merely a matter of possession and production but a material and spiritual element which they must fully enjoy, even to preserve their cultural legacy and transmit it to future generations.[191]

The Trial Chamber's invocation of a communal or collective right to property by reference to the decisions of these human rights courts is conceptually significant because of how some of the characteristics of communal property directly challenge the liberal premises of property rights, specifically in terms of how communitarian traditions often regard property as inalienable or non-transferable.[192] Indeed, the ACHPR highlighted this point, in explaining that the 'classical' characteristics of property rights, namely 'the right to use the thing that is the subject of the right (usus), the right to enjoy the fruit thereof (fructus) and the right to dispose of the thing, that is, the right to transfer it (abusus)',[193] do not apply in the same way to the ancestral lands of indigenous peoples. The Commission went on to note that such ancestral rights to land 'do not necessarily entail the right of ownership in its classical meaning, including the right to dispose thereof', but instead place greater emphasis on 'the rights of possession, occupation, use/utilization of land.'[194]

From this perspective, while the invocation of a communal or collective right to property was not directly relevant to the particular acts of pillage charged in the *Ongwen* case, the Trial Chamber's normative statements on this issue further expand the conception of the crime beyond its roots in the liberal notion of the violation of an individual's ownership rights. In this way, the Trial Chamber in *Ongwen*, while continuing to make some limited appeals to the notion of 'private' property, also outlined a conception of the crime of pillage as normatively rooted in a more expansive interpretation of the right to property than the definition of pillage at the ICC, with its centring of ownership and consent, implies.

Taken together, the themes that have emerged in the case law of the ICC on the crime of pillage reflect a degree of development in terms of how the

---

191 *Ibid.*, para 149.

192 Dehaibi (n 141), 218.

193 African Commission on Human and Peoples' Rights v. Republic of Kenya Judgment (n 189), para 124.

194 *Ibid.*, para 124–127.

crime is normatively constructed. The normative themes of centring the use value of property and the harm its appropriation inflicts on victims in terms of their means of subsistence and survival, of interpreting ownership in broad terms, and of conceptualising the very nature of the property rights identified to underlie the crime in terms that implicitly challenge liberal notions of individualised ownership rights, contribute to a normative picture of the crime that reflects a significant shift away from its historical roots and the conceptual nature of the definition contained in the ICC Elements of Crimes. While these different normative themes do not provide a coherent or settled conception of pillage at the ICC, taken together, they begin to build an account of the crime that incorporates a more harm-based perspective alongside a more expansive approach to the nature of the property rights protected by its criminalisation.

4 Narratives During Proceedings

The narratives that have emerged around charges of plunder or pillage during the course of proceedings at the ICTY, SCSL and ICC broadly mirror those that are taken up and reflected in the case law in more limited forms. While the decisions of the ICTY and SCSL reflect relatively limited engagement with the normative dimensions of pillage, the narratives that emerged around the crime during the course of proceedings at these courts more strongly resemble the turn to an emphatically use value conception of the crime at the ICC. Proceedings at the ICC are further characterised by a focus on the nature of the harms inflicted on victims of pillage, with a particular emphasis on its implications for those already living at a subsistence minimum, while also offering elements of a localised and contextualised account of some of the more social dimensions of property, which attribute it with meaning and value in particular communities beyond its instrumental role in ensuring their survival.

4.1 *Subsistence and Survival*

Despite the limited emphasis on a use value approach to property in the context of charges of pillage in the decisions of the ICTY, some of the testimonies in these cases nevertheless highlight the impact of such crimes in these terms. For instance, in *Kordić and Čerkez,* the following exchange highlighted the subsistence impact of plunder in terms of victims' ability to fulfil their fundamental needs:

Q. You describe the two or three thousand Croat civilians who stayed behind in Bugojno following the Muslim attacks, sir. What was life like for the people that stayed behind?

A. Impossible. They plundered everything. […] People were frightened and we had nothing, and we didn't even have anything to eat. Because even what we had, there was this tremendous pressure, because they would come and loot our houses time and again.[195]

Testimony in the *Blaškić* case reflects a similar experience, with a witness explaining that 'I went back home on the next morning and I realised that my house had been vandalised and demolished […] During the first robbery they took all my food, so I did not have any food at home. For several days I remained without food, so people from the village brought me some food.'[196] The impact of pillage on livelihoods and subsistence also emerged in testimony which speaks to the intentional displacement of populations through the destruction and pillage of property. In *Gotovina et al.*, the Prosecution recounted the testimony of a witness who had explained that 'you understood exactly what they were saying because he comes from a farming background and to destroy the infrastructure and to destroy the means of a villager's livelihood would ensure that no one could return and live in that particular region.'[197] In this respect, a witness further explained how the economic context in the part of Croatia in which the destruction of property and pillage had occurred exacerbated the harm inflicted by pillage, ensuring that victims were unable to return:

> So once your house was burned and all possessions looted, your farm animals killed or stolen, there was nothing for you to return to. And this, incidentally, was a very marginal part of Croatia, and people had a very low income and suffered from four years of total isolation. People were living at the margin. So when you take away their house, you burn their house, you take away their property, you kill their farm animals, there is no way that anybody can return there and make a living.[198]

195 *Prosecutor v. Dario Kordić and Mario Čerkez*, IT-95-14/2, ICTY, Transcript 10 July 2000, 22427–22428.

196 *Prosecutor v. Tihomir Blaškić*, IT-95-14, ICTY, Transcript 29 April 1998, 8025.

197 *Prosecutor v. Ante Gotovina et al.*, IT-06-90, ICTY, Transcript 11 March 2008, 458 [hereafter Gotovina et al. Transcript Date].

198 Gotovina et al. Transcript 23 June 2008 (n 197), 4946.

The Prosecution advanced a similar argument around pillage in the *RUF* case at the SCSL, highlighting the relevance of the pre-existing economic circumstances of victims of pillage for understanding the harm inflicted by the appropriation of their property. The Prosecution argued that:

> The evidence that you have, for example, of Operation Pay Yourself, of the taking of rice, of taking of possessions of civilians was [...] clearly unlawful as it was not needed for the conduct or carrying out of any military operation and, indeed, the Prosecution would say that it was more serious as it deprived the already poor population, civilian population that is, of its means to survive.[199]

In the *AFRC* case, the Prosecution sought to make a normative argument in these terms on the question of whether the definition of pillage could include destruction or burning of property. The Prosecution's analysis highlights the contradiction between the harm-based, economic impact narrative it sought to advance around the crime during proceedings and the constraints of the ownership-rights model of the definition of the crime applied at the SCSL. With respect to the question of whether the destruction of property could fall within the definition of pillage, the Prosecution argued that:

> the most obvious answer is to say that it falls within the concept of pillage. The answer is obvious, we submit, if one looks at the value that the prohibition against pillage is intended to protect. International Humanitarian Law exists to protect those taking no part in the conflict, such as civilians. It includes rules to protect civilian life, civilian property and civilian human rights from the ravages of armed conflict, and the law against pillage is clearly one designed to protect civilian property. Obviously, the value is to protect the victim, and looking at it from the victim's point of view, it makes no difference to the victim whether the victim's property is destroyed or whether it is stolen. In fact, if it is stolen, that may be less bad, if I can put it that way; there may still be some hope of getting it back at some time. To suggest that pillage includes only theft is looking at matters from the perpetrators' point of view and not from the victims' point of view.[200]

---

199 *Prosecutor v. Issa Hassan Sesay et al.* (*RUF Case*), SCSL-2004-15-T, SCSL, Transcript 4 August 2008, 31.

200 *Prosecutor v. Alex Tamba Brima et al.* (*AFRC Case*), SCSL-2004-16-T, SCSL, Transcript 7 December 2006, 67 [hereafter Brima et al. Transcript Date].

This submission by the Prosecution, which was rejected by the court on the grounds that the legal element of *appropriation* required by the definition of pillage is not satisfied when property is instead destroyed,[201] nevertheless illuminates precisely the disjunct between the ownership-interests model of pillage contained in the definition applied at the SCSL and the ICC and the attempts to advance a more humanitarian/civilian-suffering narrative of the crime in the cases at these courts. In this analysis, the attempt to conflate acts of pillage and of destruction of property because of the shared harms they inflict on victims, and the rejection of this argument because of the definitional requirement that pillage involve appropriation of property specifically, underscores how the very fact of distinguishing between appropriation and destruction of property carries the implication that the crime of pillage does not ultimately prioritise the use value of the property protected, and therefore the harm its loss inflicts on victims. Rather, what is centralised through the requirement of appropriation, as articulated explicitly in the Appeals Chamber's decision in the *CDF* case, and discussed in section 2(a) of this chapter, is the transfer of a property interest in violation of the owner's consent.[202]

This disconnect between the conceptual nature of the definition of pillage and the narratives that emerge and are highlighted during the course of proceedings is most pronounced in the cases at the ICC. At the ICC, the central theme that dominates the discourse on pillage during proceedings relates to its impact on the livelihoods and survival of individuals already living in economically precarious circumstances, and the long-term economic consequences of the loss of property for victims and their communities. For instance, in *Katanga*, the legal representative for victims explained that '[m]y clients lost their means of living which was made up chiefly of cattle, goats, property, materials linked or attached to their houses, and harvests from the fields.'[203] In *Bemba*, the OTP recounted the experiences of a witness who explained that 'MLC soldiers stole in particular the bed, the mattresses, and car, as well as agricultural machinery of her husband. Previously her husband had used the agricultural machinery to earn a living, but the MLC soldiers had stolen everything that he had and that he needed for his work. The witness describes himself today as the poorest of peasants.'[204] The OTP similarly stressed how

201 Brima et al. Trial Judgment (n 200), para 757.

202 Fofana and Kondewa Appeal Judgment (n 106), 130 at footnote 780.

203 *Prosecutor v. Germain Katanga and Mathieu Ngudjolo Chui*, ICC-01/04-01/0736, ICC, Transcript 7 July 2008, 36.

204 *Prosecutor v. Jean-Pierre Bemba Gombo*, ICC-01/05-01/08, ICC, Transcript 14 January 2009, 31 [hereafter Bemba Transcript Date].

'[t]he victims of pillaging, heads of households, widows, traders, farmers have been reduced to being beggars. They have been stripped of their savings, their savings accumulated over the years. They're unable to provide for their families and to rebuild what they once had.'[205] It went on to explain that 'the looting [...] has left so many victims with no hope and no possessions, living a life in very difficult circumstances today having lost everything they had acquired over many long years of hard work.'[206] In *Ongwen*, the OTP explained that 'the LRA took everything [victims] owned, including all goods necessary to sustain life in the difficult conditions in northern Uganda; pans, cups, clothes, as well as livestock, constituting the key source of income of families.'[207]

This narrative is reinforced through a particular emphasis on the impact of pillage on the ability of victims to survive in such circumstances. In *Katanga*, the Prosecution emphasised with respect to the pillage of the village of Bogoro that 'the purpose of the attack was to eliminate the civilian population by looting their possessions, by destroying their possessions'[208] and that 'the destruction and the pillaging of goods was part of a common plan aiming to eliminate the Hema civilian population because it excluded any possibility of survival or possible return to Bogoro for those who managed to escape.'[209] In *Ntaganda*, the Prosecution similarly explained that '[b]y looting mattresses, roofs, crops, or medical equipment, by torching houses and destroying hospitals, but also schools and orphanages, the UPC was effectively depriving the population of all social support structures and means of survival.'[210] In *Bemba,* the Prosecution argued that 'Jean-Pierre Bemba [sic] troops stole from the poor people of one of the poorest countries in the world',[211] stressing with respect to the charge of pillage that:

> [W]e need to understand what it means to be left with nothing in a socio-economic context where things cannot be replaced. If they slaughter your livestock, your goats, your animals, you are probably left with no

205 Bemba Transcript 15 January 2009 (n 204), 99.
206 Bemba Transcript 18 May 2016 (n 204), 31.
207 *Prosecutor v. Dominic Ongwen*, ICC-02/04-01/15, ICC, Transcript 11 March 2020, 29 [hereafter Ongwen Transcript Date].
208 *Prosecutor v. Germain Katanga*, ICC-01/04-01/07, ICC, Transcript 6 May 2014, 6–7 [hereafter Katanga Transcript Date].
209 Katanga Transcript 5 May 2014 (n 208), 59.
210 *Prosecutor v. Bosco Ntaganda*, ICC-01/04-02/06, ICC, Transcript 28 August 2018, 46 [hereafter Ntaganda Transcript Date]. See similarly Ntaganda Transcript 20 September 2019 (n 210), 7.
211 Bemba Transcript 22 November 2010 (n 204), 10.

> food for you and your kids. If they steal your mattress, you have no place to sleep with you or your family. If they take your shutters, windows and doors, you and your family will be living in a house with no shutters, no windows and no doors. Persons were deprived of their essential means for sustaining their life and livelihood.[212]

The implications of pillage for residents of IDP camps living in economically precarious circumstances is particularly pronounced in the *Ongwen* case, where the Prosecution emphasised that '[u]nable to cultivate, the displaced civilians of Odek [IDP camp] were dependent on food aid. In stealing their food, the LRA robbed them of their basic means of survival'[213] and that '[e]ven at its least violent [...] collecting food for the LRA meant breaking into civilian homes and shops, stealing their food, their clothes, drinks, money, even livestock. At Abok [IDP camp] and elsewhere, it meant leaving those camp residents who weren't killed or abducted to face potential starvation and certain deprivation.'[214]

The centrality of this narrative, emphasising the importance of the pillaged property for the survival of individuals in precarious circumstances was particularly pronounced during the confirmation of charges hearings in the *Ongwen* case. In this respect, it is worth quoting the submissions of the Legal Representative for Victims at length for how they illustrate the centrality of survival and subsistence for the normative narrative that emerged around pillage in this case.

> Your Honours, the accounts you have heard over these three days include many gruesome and appalling crimes of physical violence against people. The brutal nature of those crimes is such that we are sometimes inclined to treat the destruction and pillage of property as unimportant by comparison. But we should know – we should not do so. The victims of the LRA attacks at Odek, Lukodi and Abok consistently describe the extreme consequences of the attacks on their livelihoods.
>
> Your Honours, from where we sit today in this modern courtroom in The Hague, the importance of a goat or cow might not be obvious. But for those living or formerly living in IDP camps in northern Uganda, these animals were prized possessions, which offered meat and resources for tilling and cultivating land or for trade. Victims who lost their goats, oxen

212 Bemba Transcript 11 January 2018 (n 204), 27.
213 Ongwen Transcript 22 January 2016 (n 207), 8.
214 Ongwen Transcript 10 March 2020 (n 207), 84.

and cows in LRA attacks are still today worse off economically than at the time of pillage. They cannot trade or exchange the animals and are without livestock for farming. Most have been unable to rebuild their herds, and the majority indulge in the markets to sell or buy a small basket of tomatoes or roast maize. And it was not only animals which were destroyed or stolen by the LRA. Most of the victims from Odek, Lukodi and Abok describe returning to their homes after the attacks to discover that their huts were burned, their livestock burned or stolen, and all their household items, including money, cooking utensils and even clothes, had been pillaged. Victims were left with quite literally nothing left.

Your Honours, the following are some accounts from victims which exemplify this situation, and I quote: "On that day, the LRA looted my goats, chicken, ducks, cooking utensils, mattresses, food, simsim, sorghum ... Now I am poor. I don't have any domestic animals ... I cannot support my children in school. Feeding has become a problem."

Another victim says, and I quote: "Starting a new life after losing all the things which I had gathered like my hut, clothes, among others has not been easy since then because also my goats and hens, which I used to sell and eat sometimes, were killed and others burned.

And another victim says, and I quote: "Our hut was burnt and all our livestock were burnt too. During the attack, I lost all my personal belongings in my hut; for example, clothes, utensils to mention only a few. In addition, my goats, which were next to the house, were also burnt. Up to this day, I have not been able to recover from the loss. Today I am in financial hardship."

Yet another witness account says that "My only pregnant cow was shot dead by a stray bullet, and all its meat was looted. In the morning, I came back and found only the head and the legs were left for me where I had tied the cow. My bicycle and chicken got burnt in the hut since all the huts in the camp were burnt that day. All my goats were looted too. I was left with nothing at all because even my clothes got burnt in my hut since my hut was burnt. From my hiding place, I saw the fire consume the entire camp. By now, my cow would have made me very wealthy. All my goats and property makes me worry a lot for all my wasted efforts and years."[215]

Lastly, the proceedings at the ICC centralise not only the harm inflicted by pillage in terms of the survival and subsistence of individuals, they also highlight

215 Ongwen Transcript 25 January 2016 (n 207), 27–29.

some of the more structural and long-term economic effects on the communities subjected to pillage. In *Katanga*, the chief of the village of Bogoro testified to the harm inflicted by pillage and destruction of property in these terms:

> Q. [...] Now, let us take the case of a civilian who lost everything. Would such a person be living the same kind of life as beforehand, before the attack?
> A. No.
> Q. Why?
> A. Well, I can give you an example. Before the attack, there was a person who had a number of cattle. Everything was looted and this person has to begin all over again by cultivating the fields. [...]
> Q. If you had to describe the main consequence of the Bogoro attack that is still seen today, what would that be? What is the most distinctive consequence that the community is still experiencing today in Bogoro?
> A. The main consequence is poverty.[216]

The same experience is reflected in *Ntaganda*, where a witness testified that '[t]he Lendus in this area are farmers, but they no longer had any way to make a living because they were terrorised, they feared returning to the fields and being attacked. The population had lost their houses, but also their livestock, the goats, the pigs, the hens. They had lost all their belongings, the Hema militia had taken everything. There was tremendous poverty and this poverty continued.'[217] The much wider, structural impact of pillage and the destruction of property, beyond the loss of personal belongings, is also highlighted in *Ongwen*. For instance, the Legal Representative for Victims recounted how 'the conflict had impacts on the economic structures of the communities. Our clients inform this Court that there was loss or they suffered loss of household and other family properties, including livestock, which impacts on community livelihoods and the local economy. [...] the livestock offered avenues for transactions and of course sustaining agriculture in the communities. The attacks rendered people destitute.'[218]

In addition to testimony that addresses the continuing, structural impact of pillage and destruction of property on livelihoods and economic security in general terms, the particular implications of the resulting economic precarity on access to education was highlighted in a number of testimonies. For

216 Katanga Transcript 5 May 2014, (n 208), 14.
217 Ntaganda Transcript 20 September 2019 (n 210), 7.
218 Ongwen Transcript 7 December 2016 (n 207), 62.

instance, a witness in *Ongwen* testified to the impact of the poor economic conditions on the community's children:

> Q. Mr Gipson, you've said a few things now about the economic impact and the livelihoods. What is the economic state of the community today?
>
> A. Our people are poor these days, because of the variable situation that people live in. In the past people had livestock. People had cattle. People had goats, chicken and other things. But all these things have been taken away and it's not easy to gain back. For me, as an example, I had cattle, I had goats because I had worked hard. But now I'm not able to farm enough resources, to farm and raise enough resources to buy more livestock. For that matter, people are economically poor. [...] it is not easy to create wealth among the community. People are desperate, desperately in a poor, living in a poor condition. People are not able to farm and get enough money to pay for the school fees, and for that matter children who should be in school are not going to school because they can't afford school fees. Some of the children who are living in the community try to go and look for money in the town areas and they come back with infections and end up dying. People are getting sick. And you are not able to go and get medical treatment. For that matter, the life, general life condition is very poor, not like it was in the past.[219]

Reflecting similar experiences, a witness in *Ntaganda* testified with respect to the harm he had suffered from looting that, 'we have difficulties, for instance, the child is chased out of school because of the inability to pay school fees, we suffer from that. I mean, we used to live better. But what happened happened, we can't do anything else.'[220] Similarly, in *Ongwen*, when asked about his ability to continue running his business after having been subjected to looting, a witness testified that he was unable to do so, meaning that '[b]ecause now there are many children and there are also grown-up and how to meet their education needs is difficult. But when I do some little farming, that's when I can earn some money to try and pay for their fees. But I am not doing any business.'[221] The more direct impact of pillage on children's education also emerged in testimony that speaks simply to the loss of materials necessary for

219 Ongwen Transcript 3 May 2018 (n 207), 25–26.
220 Ntaganda Transcript 18 November 2015 (n 210), 7.
221 Ongwen Transcript 7 November 2017, (n 207), 56.

their schooling. In *Bemba,* a witness who was asked what the impact of the situation was on their children explained that 'my first concern was for my school-going children. I lost all their school books. After the events, I was no longer able to buy other text-books in order to enable my children to continue with their studies.'[222] Similarly, in *Ntaganda,* a witness testified to how during the pillaging of the town of Bambu the 'primary, secondary school [was] looted, so there is no teaching available, no education.'[223]

Overall, the normative discourse around pillage in the proceedings of the ICC is in this way very much dominated by a use value approach to the nature of the property protected through its criminalisation, with a particular emphasis on the role of property in ensuring the livelihoods and survival of individuals already experiencing economic precarity. In addition, the discourse during proceedings at times also reflects some of the more structural implications of crimes of pillage, in inflicting greater poverty on communities and in moving somewhat beyond a subsistence and survival framework by highlighting the impact of the poverty inflicted by pillage on wider issues such as access to education.

At the same time, numerous acts of pillage involving items that would not necessarily fit as straightforwardly within this subsistence or survival narrative were also charged in many of these cases. For instance, the theft of, among many other types of items, vehicles, televisions and radios form part of the charges of pillage in the *Bemba* and *Ntaganda* cases[224] while the theft of similar items as well as, often, watches, featured heavily in the charges of pillage brought in various cases at the SCSL.[225] The pillage of such items nevertheless gives rise to little normative discussion during proceedings, leaving open the question of how they fit into the dominant subsistence and survival narrative that has emerged around these crimes at the ICC and the SCSL.

4.2 *Culture and Emotion*

While the dominant normative narrative that has emerged around pillage during proceedings at the ICC relates in this way to the use value of property, with

222 Bemba Transcript 26 June 2012 (n 204), 6.

223 Ntaganda Transcript 3 February 2017 (n 210), 54.

224 See Bemba Trial Judgment (n 88), para 502, 509, 547, 646; Ntaganda Trial Judgment (n 126), para 514, 1035, 1042; *Prosecutor v. Bosco Ntaganda*, ICC-01/04-02/06, ICC, Sentencing Judgment, 7 November 2019, para 139.

225 Brima et al. Trial Judgment (n 84), para 1426; Fofana and Kondewa Trial Judgment (n 98), para 460; Sesay et al. Trial Judgment (n 98), para 1535, 1594; Taylor Trial Judgment (n 98), para 1939.

an emphasis on the role of the pillaged property in meeting the fundamental needs of victims, traces of other dimensions of the value of pillaged property nevertheless appear in a small number of instances. Most prominently, the discourse on pillage in the *Katanga* and *Ongwen* cases at the ICC also captures some of the particularised social role of some of the pillaged property, highlighting in contextualised, local terms the cultural role of livestock in the communities that were subjected to pillaging. For example, in *Katanga* the Prosecution recounted how during the attack on Bogoro 'there was looting of chickens, of goats, cattle, and in the Hema tradition this is of great importance. Cattle is in actual fact a local way of saving money. It is – cattle are used as a form of savings so that one can pay a dowry, so that one can school one's children or buy possessions.'[226] Further highlighting the centrality of livestock in cultural-economic practices, a witness explained:

> A. Before the war, there were stock breeders in this groupement. You had people who were raising cattle, raising goats, and raising poultry. These individuals were carrying out the activities very well, and it was only after the war that these people were scattered, and several of them had their livestock pillaged, and so they scattered and went to live in other places.
>
> Q. Thank you. In your answer you talked about stock breeders. My question to you is the following: Were all inhabitants of Bogoro or all the families in Bogoro involved in stock breeding activities, or was this an activity that was reserved for a particular group of people?
>
> A. I think that this was an activity that was carried out by (Expunged) involved in this. You know, when a Hema dies, his son takes over his stock breeding activities. And when the girls reached the age of marriage, the girl's family would receive cattle as dowry from her husband's family, and so people who do not have cattle could agree with the girl's family that they will pay the dowry in cash instead of giving cattle. However, the money paid should be equivalent to the value of the cattle requested. The raising of cattle is something which is of capital importance to the Hemas.[227]

Similarly, in *Ongwen* the Prosecution explained how 'the LRA took everything [the victims] owned, including all goods necessary to sustain life in the difficult

226 Katanga Transcript 6 May 2014 (n 208), 5.

227 Katanga Transcript 30 November 2010 (n 208), 62–63.

conditions in northern Uganda [...] and other properties carrying a specific meaning for the affected communities, notably [...] for the accomplishment of traditional rituals.'[228] It went on to emphasise that, '[c]ommunities' livestock, one of the primary sources of wealth, was looted. As you heard from many witnesses, livestock plays a key role in the lives of family and community. As well as being a source of food and/or a means of farming, these animals are used for traditional rituals, marriage and economic transactions.'[229] The testimony of one witness in the *Ongwen* case illustrated the social value of the pillaged livestock in this respect, explaining the particular cultural practices attached to certain animals in Acholi communities:

Q. [...] You've spoken about the impact of people losing their livestock. If you look around you in the courtroom you'll see a lot of people who are lawyers and city people. Can you help us understand what the value of livestock was in your community before the conflict? What did people use the livestock for?

A. Livestock, especially cattle, was very useful in the community. It was used for paying bride wealth. It is used for ploughing. It is used as a source of beef. You also use the cattle to pay school fees because you sell and pay with this. When you are sick, you sell your livestock to get treatment. Things like goats, for example, help also in the same way. Goats are used for helping treat people in so many ways. There are some conditions like madness, they use goats in a traditional way to heal it. And for rituals that are culturally important to the community, they use goats to carry outside rituals. When there are funerals that are taking place in the community, the guests are fed on goats and cattle, and for that matter, this was an important element in the culture of Acholi, economically and socially. If you don't have, you are considered poor then, and they were very important. You are not able to do farming with the hand hoe, but if you have ox ploughs you are able to farm a larger land and get enough food to feed your family. That is the importance of livestock in the community where I live.

Q. Thank you. That's extremely helpful. You've said that the livestock is very important for Acholi cultural practices. What's been the impact now then when people don't have access to livestock on their ability to live in a traditional Acholi way?

228 Ongwen Transcript 11 March 2020 (n 207), 28.
229 *Ibid.*, 18.

> A. Cultural practices require that you should find these animals to use for the rituals. For example, if someone was raped in the bush and there is a need to use a goat to carry out a ritual to cleanse the person, because if you don't cleanse it, the person may get mad or may not bear children or may actually die. You have to look for a goat so that a ritual is conducted and the person is cleansed. You have to look for a goat in all ways possible to find a goat. They are some of the things which are listed as the challenges that people are facing in this condition as a result of the war. It results from the lack of resources such as livestock which has affected the cultural practices to be carried out.[230]

While not prominent in these cases, these accounts of the role of livestock in the cultural practices of the communities, and therefore of the disruption caused by pillage to the communities' ability to maintain their cultural practices, invoke an additional cultural dimension to the value of property that is not captured by the more economically-oriented subsistence/survival account of the crime that dominates the discourse during proceedings as well as the narratives that are ultimately constructed around pillage in the decisions.

In a similar, although much more limited manner, a small number of cases also reflect elements of an emotional relationship between people and certain items of pillaged property. For example, during questioning on the possible theft of an individual's wedding ring in the *Mucić et al.* case at the ICTY, the Prosecution asked a witness '[s]ir, do you have any possessions anywhere in the world that have what we would call a sentimental value, where the value to you is much more than the cash value of the item?', to which the witness responded '[y]es, those are personal items such as rings, watches.'[231] In the *Martić* case, a witness made reference to the loss of family photographs during the looting of their property[232] while in *Brđanin*, a witness described a watch that was appropriated as a 'memento'.[233] In *Bemba* at the ICC, a witness similarly explained with respect to the looting of his home, that 'they had even taken the tombstone that I had prepared, a granite slab that I had bought in Paris, and this was intended for the grave of my father who had passed away in 2001. They even stole that, and from an emotional point of view that was a very important item to me.'[234]

---

230 Ongwen Transcript 3 May 2018 (n 207), 26–27.

231 *Prosecutor v. Zdravko Mucić et al.*, IT-96-21, ICTY, Transcript 4 September 1997, 6819–6820.

232 *Prosecutor v. Milan Martić*, IT-95-11, ICTY, Transcript 31 March 2006, 3004.

233 *Prosecutor v. Radoslav Brđanin*, IT-99-36, ICTY, Transcript 28 March 2002, 6184.

234 Bemba Transcript 14 September 2012 (n 204), 50.

Discussion of this more emotional dimension of the value of certain items of pillaged property is very limited in these cases. However, in a similar way to the recognition of the specific cultural significance of certain types of property for particular communities, these few examples also imply a thicker possible normative account of the value of the property protected through the criminalisation of pillage than both the use value narrative, with its centralisation of the value of property in ensuring the survival of civilians, as well as the more abstract conception of pillage as a violation of ownership rights, embodied in the legal definition of the crime at the ICC, capture. These examples suggest a conception of people's relationships to material objects that is not exclusively economic. They invoke an approach to the value of property that captures how affective connections may exist between people and their possessions, in how people may develop 'emotional attachment to a specific material object [...] based on an ongoing personal history between the person and the possession',[235] which goes beyond owning, possessing or valuing the object in economic terms.

The recognition of the particular cultural role of certain types of property and the sentimental significance of some of the objects appropriated, while only incipient in these cases, nevertheless begins to invoke a conception of the criminalisation of pillage that may also capture the human relationships to the property that it protects in terms that construct property in more complex terms than simply a commodity over which individuals exercise ownership rights.

5 Conclusion

Tracing the development of the prohibition on pillage from its historical roots in concerns with military discipline, through its codification in international humanitarian law, to its prosecution as a war crime under international criminal law, reveals a significant degree of normative evolution in how the protections for property that underlie the crime, and the justification for its criminalisation and prosecution, have been conceptualised. This conceptual evolution has nevertheless not taken place in a linear fashion. The early self-interested concern with ensuring military discipline on the battlefield evolved into a more normative commitment to the sanctity of private property

235 Heather Conway and John Stannard, 'Property and Emotions', (2015) 8(1) *Emotion Review*, 39.

informed by the emergence of liberalism in Europe in the 17th and 18th centuries, which in turn shaped the initial international codifications of the prohibition on pillage in the law of armed conflict. This liberal spirit continued to dominate the approach to pillage adopted in the post-Second World War industrialists trials, which distilled the normative core of the crime down to the violation of ownership interests, explicitly excluding a more harm-based conception of the crime that would also have captured its impact on the economies of occupied territories.

While the subsequent codification of the Geneva Conventions contributed little to the development of the prohibition on pillage in legal terms, the wider shift towards a conception of the laws of war as increasingly concerned with the humanitarian protection of victims of war that the Conventions have been understood to represent, alongside the abolition of the institution of private property among socialist states, initiated a dilution of the centrality of this principle in the understanding of the protections accorded to property during armed conflict. This change was consolidated in legal terms with the codification of the Additional Protocols to the Geneva Conventions, which turned to an explicitly 'civilian-use' framework for the protection of property during armed conflict, centralising the use value of protected property in mitigating civilian suffering.

The definitions of pillage adopted at the ICTY, SCSL and ICC, the nature of the normative themes that are constructed in the case law and the narratives that emerge around the crime during the course of proceedings to some extent embody this inconsistent normative history. While the conceptual account of the crime invoked by the definitions adopted, particularly at the SCSL and ICC, appear to hark back to the normative approach of the Hague Conventions and the post-war industrialists trials, to capture an individual ownership rights-based conception of the crime, the dominant narrative that emerges from the case law and during proceedings tells an entirely different story.

Various dimensions of the approach adopted to the crime, in terms of the gravity of its consequences for victims as a jurisdictional threshold, an emphasis on the role of the pillaged property in the daily lives of victims as well as a more expansive interpretation of the element of ownership, significantly moderate the extent to which the conceptual model underpinning the definition is reproduced in the normative narratives of the cases, in particular at the ICC. Instead, while the case law of the ICTY and SCSL reflect more limited engagement with the normative dimensions of the crime, the decisions of the ICC construct an emphatically use value conception of the property protected through the criminalisation of pillage, rooting this in its role in ensuring the subsistence and survival of victims, in particular those already living at a subsistence minimum.

While normative appeals to rights to private property do take place in the decisions of the ICC, the most recent case involving charges of pillage offers an interpretation of the right to property under human rights law that conceptually distances itself from the classical property rights paradigm. This decision reflects developments at human rights courts that capture a broader relationship between people and the material world than is allowed for by the liberal conception of individual ownership rights. Indications of some other dimensions to the value of pillaged property, such as certain elements of their role in cultural practices and traces of an affective relationship between individuals and particular objects, also underscore the move away from the individual property-rights conception of the crime, although these remain minimal at present.

The normative narratives around pillage in these cases are in this way not unified or fully coherent. The dominant 'use value' narrative constructed around the value of the property protected by pillage nevertheless ultimately reveals a degree of tension between the conceptual underpinnings of the legal elements of the crime, and the emphatically humanitarian, harm-based narrative used to justify its prosecution. In this respect, the fact that several of the cases at the SCSL and the ICC, where the use value narrative around the crime is most prominent, involve charges of pillage based on the appropriation of items such as televisions, radios or watches, that do not fit as straightforwardly into the subsistence-survival framework as items such as livestock, food, cooking equipment or medicine, underscores a degree of incoherence between the definition of the crime, and what it can therefore capture, and the normative narrative constructed around it. Indeed, the normative justification for pursuing charges for the former types of objects is left largely unaddressed in these cases.

Seen from this perspective, the normative account of the criminalisation and prosecution of pillage invoked in these cases appears in some ways to seek to blur the lines between the notions of 'crimes against persons' and 'crimes against property' by constructing a narrative that centralises those instances of crimes against property that have a concrete and direct impact on the lives and physical security of persons. This ultimately suggests an attempt to distance the crime from its roots in the protection of property rights, to anchor it unequivocally within the basic security rights framework typically understood to underlie international criminal law.

CHAPTER 4

Sexual Violence

Crimes of sexual violence have come to occupy a particularly prominent position in international criminal law. Described by Karen Engle as a 'near-singular attention to sexual violence in the context of women and armed conflict',[1] this contemporary focus on conflict-related sexual violence emerged as a response to historical failures to recognise or address harms inflicted on women during times of war.[2] Over the past two decades, efforts by feminist legal actors to ensure recognition and redress for these harms produced significant developments in the degree of recognition accorded to crimes of sexual and gender-based violence in the emerging field of international criminal law. The inclusion of rape in the statutes of the ICTY and ICTR, and the resulting case law on rape and other forms of sexual violence are seen to have contributed to tackling attitudes to sexual violence as being an accepted and inevitable 'by product' of war.[3] The codification of a broader range of crimes of sexual and gender-based violence in the Rome Statute was similarly welcomed as a 'major advance'[4] in the gender-sensitivity of international criminal law and its ability to capture the experiences of men and women victims of sexual and gender-based violence during periods of conflict and large-scale violence.

At the same time, the codification of crimes of sexual violence in international criminal law has engendered significant debate in terms of their appropriate definitions, as characterised by the absence of consent or by the presence of violence or coercion, and the normative implications invoked by defining them in these terms. These debates partly mirror feminist law reform efforts at the domestic level, but have also evolved to respond to the specific environments addressed by international criminal law, considering the implications of different definitions of crimes of sexual violence for how women's agency is constructed and understood in such environments. In addition, the particular focus on sexual violence in addressing violence against women has

1 Karen Engle, *The Grip of Sexual Violence in Conflict: Feminist Interventions in International Law* (Stanford University Press 2020), 39.

2 Katherine M Franke, 'Gendered Subjects of Transitional Justice,' (2006) 15(3) *Columbia Journal of Gender and Law*, 823.

3 Doris Buss, "Rethinking 'Rape as a Weapon of War'", (2009) 17(2) *Feminist Legal Studies*, 146.

4 Cate Steains, "Gender Issues" in Roy Lee (ed), *The International Criminal Court: The Making of the Rome Statute* (Kluwer Law International 1999), 364.

 | DOI:10.1163/9789004687844_006

been subject to a number of more theoretical critiques in the feminist scholarship on international law.[5] Some of these critiques relate directly to the question of how sexual violence is normatively understood, with the dominant conception of this form of violence as a violation of women's bodily integrity coming under criticism for reinforcing constructions of women's bodies as inherently violable and female sexuality as submissive.[6] This focus on the physical dimensions of harm resulting from sexual violence has equally been criticised for overlooking the autonomy and discrimination harms inherent in such acts, with the result that they fail to problematise, and therefore naturalise, the gendered social structures that enable and give meaning to acts of sexual violence.[7]

In recent years, the wider scholarship on conflict-related sexual violence has developed beyond its initial focus on violence inflicted on women and girls. This scholarship also captures the sexual victimisation of men and boys during conflict, examines the experiences of LBGTI victims and survivors and challenges some of the gendered and heteronormative binaries that have underpinned the dominant explanatory frameworks for conflict-related sexual violence to date.[8] It has also scrutinised the distinctions between strategic

5 See for example Doris Buss, 'Performing Legal Order: Some Feminist Thoughts on International Criminal Law', (2011) 11 *International Criminal Law Review*, 416; Nicola Henry, 'The Fixation on Wartime Rape: Feminist Critique and International Criminal Law', (2014) 23(1) *Social and Legal Studies*, 97; Sara Brown, 'Female Perpetrators of the Rwandan Genocide' (2014) 16(3) *International Feminist Journal of Politics*, 448–469; Kiran Grewal, 'International Criminal Law as a Site for Enhancing Women's Rights? Challenges, Possibilities, Strategies', (2015) 23(2) *Feminist Legal Studies*, 151.

6 Grewal (n 5), 157–158.

7 Chiseche Salome Mibenge, *Sex and International Tribunals: The Erasure of Gender from the War Narrative* (University of Pennsylvania Press, 2013); Fionnuala Ni Aoláin, 'The Gender Politics of Fact-Finding in the Context of the Women, Peace and Security Agenda', University of Ulster Transitional Justice Institute Research Paper No. 14-08 (2014), 1–3; Vasuki Nesiah, 'Missionary Zeal for a Secular Mission: Bringing Gender to Transitional Justice and Redemption to Feminism,' in Sari Kouvo and Zoe Pearson (eds), *Feminist Perspectives on Contemporary International Law: Between Resistance and Compliance?* (Oxford: Hart 2014), 143; Engle (n 1), 151.

8 Heleen Touquet and Ellen Gorris, 'Out of the shadows? The inclusion of men and boys in conceptualisations of wartime sexual violence', (2016) 24(47) *Reproductive Health Matters*, 36–46; Chris Dolan, 'Victims who are men', in Fionnuala Ní Aoláin et al. (eds), *The Oxford Handbook of Gender and Conflict* (Oxford University Press 2018), 86–102; Ellen Anna Philo Gorris, 'Invisible victims? Where are male victims of conflict-related sexual violence in international law and policy?', (2015) 22(4) *European Journal of Women's Studies*, 412–427; Philipp Schulz and Heleen Touquet, 'Queering explanatory frameworks for wartime sexual violence against men', (2020) 96(5) *International Affairs*, 1169–1187.

and opportunistic accounts of conflict-related sexual violence as well as the fundamental underlying distinction drawn between sexual violence perpetrated during war and peace.[9] The history and social context that preceded the inclusion of rape and sexual violence as crimes under international law, the debates over the definitions of such crimes and how they ought to be normatively conceptualised, and the way in which the scholarship in this field continues to evolve to capture the complexity and diversity of lived experiences of sexual violence highlight in this sense how understandings of rape and sexual violence are not 'static and universal, insensitive to historical, cultural and spatial specificities.'[10] Rather, these crimes, perhaps more obviously than any other, are 'entangled in a complex, historically entrenched network of social relations, practices and beliefs',[11] which evolve over time and contribute to the high normative stakes that continue to attach to the criminalisation of acts of sexual violence in international law.

For this reason, this chapter traces the historical evolution of prohibitions on rape and sexual violence under international law, their subsequent criminalisation as acts constituting international crimes and the normative conception of such crimes invoked by their contemporary prosecution.[12] The chapter first outlines the historical conceptualisation of rape as a crime against property, which emerged from a social context in which women were widely denied subjectivity and were legally understood as the property of their fathers or husbands. This manifested in international humanitarian law in how prohibitions on rape were formulated as violations of honour, positioning sexual violence as distinct from and less serious than other physical assaults during war. Widely interpreted as a repudiation of the honour-based conception of sexual violence reflected in international humanitarian law, the chapter goes on to consider the definitions of the crimes of rape and sexual violence developed at the ad hoc tribunals and the ICC and examines the different normative conceptions of such crimes, as acts of violence and aggression, as assaults on human dignity, or as violations of sexual autonomy, that these definitions invoke.

9 Schulz and Touquet (n 8); Aisling Swaine, 'Beyond Strategic Rape and Between the Public and Private: Violence Against Women in Armed Conflict', (2015) 37(3) *Human Rights Quarterly*, 755–786.

10 Joanne Conaghan, 'The Essence of Rape', (2019) 39(1) *Oxford Journal of Legal Studies*, 156.

11 *Ibid.*, 181.

12 Some of the research contained in this chapter has previously been published in Ciara Laverty, 'What is Sexual about Sexual Violence? Narratives from International Criminal Law', (2023) 21(2) *Journal of International Criminal Justice*, 383–404.

The chapter subsequently turns to the normative themes constructed around crimes of sexual violence in the case law. It finds that, while sexual autonomy and integrity are explicitly identified in a small number of cases as principles protected by the criminalisation of sexual violence, the dominant normative theme that emerges around these crimes relates to their conception as violations of physical integrity that inflict bodily harm on victims. In this respect, the analysis reveals how, in the case law, crimes of sexual violence are constructed as distinct from other crimes of physical violence primarily in terms of how they act upon the social and cultural norms around sex and sexuality in a given society, causing harm to a group or community through violating the structures of its conjugal order and inflicting shame and stigma on victims. This contributes to constructing a conception of the sexual dimensions of crimes of sexual violence primarily in social terms, omitting the individual victim's perspective on the sexualised dimensions of sexual violence in its impact on their sexual subjectivity. Lastly, the chapter demonstrates how, while many of the narratives during proceedings have subsequently been reproduced in decisions, some testimonies undermine the dominant theme of shame and stigma in the case law, while others offer a perspective that is absent from the decisions in reflecting the harm inflicted on victims' sexuality and their sexual lives. In this way, the discourse during proceedings offers a less uniform account of the nature of crimes of sexual violence and the harms they inflict than the account constructed through the case law.

It is important to note that, as a result of the particular focus of this research project, the contents of this chapter reproduces the tendency in international criminal law to focus on crimes of sexual violence inflicted primarily on women and girls, which have featured significantly more prominently in international criminal trials to date.[13] Due to the methodological focus of this research on the normative discourses that have emerged around the criminalisation and prosecution of specific criminal acts, the data set of judgments and trial transcripts analysed with respect to crimes of sexual violence focusses on cases involving charges specifically for crimes of sexual violence, namely the crimes of rape, sexual assault, sexual slavery or any other form of sexual violence. As such, this data set was not exhaustive of all conduct addressed in international criminal trials that could be understood to constitute sexual violence but has been charged under other categories of crimes such as torture, outrages upon personal dignity or humiliating or degrading treatment.

13 Rosemary Grey, *Prosecuting Sexual and Gender-Based Crimes at the International Criminal Court: Practice, Progress and Potential* (Cambridge University Press 2019), 89.

In this respect, while a small number of international criminal trials have involved charges for acts of sexual violence inflicted on male victims, such acts have often been charged under these other 'non-sexual' categories of crimes.[14] Reflecting a wider tendency to conflate sexual violence with violence against women due to gendered and heteronormative norms that dichotomise masculinity and victimhood, and in particular sexual vulnerability and victimisation,[15] only a small number of cases at international criminal courts have involved charges specifically for crimes of sexual violence inflicted on men and boys to date.[16] As such, while examples are included in this chapter from the more recent practice of the ICC, where sexual violence inflicted on men has been charged explicitly as rape or other crimes of sexual violence, the analysis offered ultimately suffers from the same deficiencies as much of the practice in international criminal law to date, to the extent that it reflects in only limited form men and boys' experiences of sexual victimisation.

1 Historical-Normative Roots in International Law

In an analysis of the ICTY's record in prosecuting conflict-related sexual violence Michelle Jarvis, former Deputy to the Prosecutor at the ICTY, described the establishment of that tribunal as the moment when 'the international community expressed its determination that sexual violence crimes would be prosecuted along with all of the other crimes committed during the conflicts. For the first time in history, the rhetoric of accountability for sexual violence flowed readily around the globe.'[17] While the conflict in the former Yugoslavia

14 A small number of cases at the ICTY involved charges for acts of sexual violence inflicted on men and boys. The majority of these acts were not charged as crimes specifically of sexual violence, or were not included in the data set because they did not result in a trial, sentencing or appeal judgment. For discussion of these cases see Grey (n 13), 90–91. For further discussion of the tendency to charge sexual violence inflicted on male victims under 'non-sexual' crime categories see Ingrid Elliott, Coleen Kivlahan and Yahya Rahhal, 'Bridging the Gap Between the Reality of Male Sexual Violence and Access to Justice and Accountability', (2020) 18(2) *Journal of International Criminal Justice*, 469–498; Valerie Oosterveld, 'Sexual Violence Directed Against Men and Boys in Armed Conflict or Mass Atrocity: Addressing a Gendered Harm in International Criminal Tribunals', (2014) 10 *Journal of International Law and International Relations*, 107–128.

15 Gorris (n 8), 415, 418.

16 Grey (n 13), 89.

17 Michelle Jarvis, 'Overview: The Challenge of Accountability for Conflict-related Sexual Violence Crimes' in Serge Brammertz and Michelle Jarvis (ed), *Prosecuting Conflict-Related Sexual Violence at the ICTY* (Oxford University Press 2016), 1–2.

is recognised as having played a central role in catalysing international consensus around the issue of conflict-related sexual violence,[18] norms discouraging or prohibiting rape have a longer history in frameworks governing the conduct of soldiers during war.[19]

From a normative perspective, what is significant about these historical frameworks, and is most revealing of the normative shift constituted by the international legal developments of the 1990s, is how earlier norms proscribing rape were understood in terms of the rationale behind them and what they were intended to protect. In other words, the question of why rape was prohibited. Eithne Dowds highlights the ongoing relevance of this question in the present day, explaining that 'while there may be agreement that rape is wrong, significant controversy remains in relation to why it is wrong.'[20] The question of why rape was seen to be wrong in the past illuminates the particular normative significance of the developments in international criminal law and why the normative stakes attached to the criminalisation and prosecution of sexual violence under international law are seen to be particularly high.

Historically, rape has widely been understood as a property crime.[21] The etymology of the term in English is linked to notions of snatching or dragging away, with rape in this way understood to be comparable to theft or stealing.[22] With women's subject-hood not recognised in many societies until relatively recently, rape was, in general terms, framed 'wholly within a context of male ownership of female sexuality.'[23] Rape was in this way not conceived as a wrong inflicted on women as subjects, but rather as a crime against the property of the male subject; 'the taking from a father or husband of the potentially valuable commodity of a woman of reproductive age.'[24]

In the specific context of battle, informal codes governing the conduct of knights and soldiers prohibited rape, while early scholars of the laws of war argued that rape was legally prohibited in many circumstances.[25] In her

---

18 Engle (n 1), 20.

19 *Ibid.*, 8.

20 Eithne Dowds, *Feminist Engagement with International Criminal Law: Norm Transfer, Complementarity, Rape and Consent* (Hart Publishing 2020), 15.

21 Andrea Dworkin, *Life and Death: Unapologetic Writings on the Continuing War Against Women* (The Free Press 1997), 197; Louise du Toit, *A Philosophical Investigation of Rape: The Making and Unmaking of the Feminine Self* (Routledge 2009), 35–43; Anne Phillips, *Our Bodies, Whose Property?* (Princeton University Press 2013), 34–37.

22 du Toit (n 20), 35.

23 *Ibid.*

24 Phillips (n 21), 42.

25 For an overview of this history see Kelly Dawn Askin, *War Crimes Against Women: Prosecution in International War Crimes Tribunals* (Martinus Nijhoff 1997), 21–35.

analysis of the history of the distinction between combatant and civilian under the laws of war, Helen Kinsella reveals how early proscriptions on rape in the chivalric codes of the Middle Ages emerged from the general requirement to protect women, children and the aged because of their supposed weakness, ignorance and innocence.[26] Kinsella goes on to highlight how such norms were nevertheless not normatively rooted in a concern for the protection of these so-called 'vulnerable' groups, and therefore with the protection of women and children as subjects, but centred instead on the importance for the knight of manifesting his chivalric character. Kinsella explains in this respect that the values of 'knightly prowess, courage, and honour [were] fundamentally self-referential, having less to do with the actual value of those defended'[27] than with the performance of such values for fellow knights. Thus, medieval chivalric codes, which, like other contemporary legal codes where women were classed as the property of men, not only categorised rape as a crime against property, but were normatively rooted in a concern with the emasculation and dishonour of the offender, rather than in a concern for the protection of the victims of such acts.[28]

Kinsella goes on to trace a similar pattern in Hugo Grotius' writing on rape in the context of the laws of war. Highlighting how the contemporary social and legal order positioned women as 'both subject to and the property of men',[29] Kinsella outlines how Grotius' reasoning on the question of rape, which framed women as the property or possession of the enemy, was also rooted in the emerging doctrine of necessity, suggesting therefore that rape ought to be prohibited on the grounds that such acts do not contribute to furthering the military goals of a war.[30] Thus, on the basis of his view that enlightened nations act with restraint, moderation, judgment and reason, Grotius considered that such nations would punish rape in war on the grounds that 'transparent displays of sheer physicality, prurient excitement, and poor judgment indicate barbarity.'[31] In this way, and similar to the self-referential nature of prohibitions on rape in older chivalric codes, rape was considered impermissible partly because it was 'corrosive of the identity of Christian entities.'[32]

26 Helen Kinsella, *The Image before the Weapon: A Critical History of the Distinction between Combatant and Civilian* (Cambridge University Press 2011), 48.

27 *Ibid.*, 49.

28 *Ibid.*

29 *Ibid.*, 72.

30 *Ibid.*, 72–73.

31 *Ibid.*, 73.

32 *Ibid.*

Kinsella highlights how, in this way, Grotius' conclusion that rape in war was unlawful is ultimately 'not at all concerned with the fate of women.'[33] Rather, she explains, in Grotius' view:

> It is not that rape qua rape is wrong – impermissible, unlawful, or unjust. Instead, it is the characteristic and the intent of the act that render it unlawful – it is an aberration of appetite and it is not an efficient or rational strategy of war (or of conjugal sex). Moreover, rape is also to be punished and prohibited because it injures not only those against whom it is committed but those who commit it. Most significantly, it denatures and dehumanizes men, preventing their ascension into progressively more civilized relations.[34]

The laws and customs of war in Europe continued to develop during the 18th and 19th centuries, mandating increasing restrains on the waging of war. In this respect, the Lieber Code of 1863 represented the first codification of an explicit rule prohibiting rape in war.[35] The Code straightforwardly prohibited 'all wanton violence committed against persons in the invaded country [...] all rape, wounding, maiming, or killing of such inhabitants [...] under the penalty of death.'[36] Despite this initial explicit codification of a prohibition on rape, subsequent developments in international humanitarian law either did not refer to sexual violence, as in the case of the 1864 Geneva Convention, or turned to more oblique language in prohibiting rape, codifying instead an indirect, honour-based conception of sexual violence. Thus, without explicitly prohibiting rape, Article 46 of the 1899 and 1907 Hague Conventions required that parties to armed conflicts respect 'family honour and rights, the lives of persons, and private property, as well as religious convictions and practice,' with 'family honour' having been understood as a 'euphemistic prohibition on rape.'[37]

Framing sexual violence as a question of family honour and rights in this way embodied the crime against property conception of rape because of how the notion of female honour, or in more direct terms, female chastity, is inherently configured in terms of familial male ownership over women's sexuality

33 *Ibid.*

34 *Ibid.*, 74.

35 Askin (n 25), 36. For developments in the intervening period see Askin (n 25), 29–35.

36 Article 44, Instructions for the Government of Armies of the United States in the Field (Lieber Code), 24 April 1863.

37 Grey (n 13), 71.

and reproductive role.[38] The nature of the prohibition on rape in the Hague Conventions in this way invoked a normative conception of the wrong of rape as resting on the injury to the victim's family and its ownership over her sexual purity, reflecting the contemporary status of women as the property or possessions of the men in their families or communities. This early formulation of a prohibition on rape under international law in this way epitomised the historical conception of the crime as 'principally that of stealing or abducting a woman from her rightful proprietors, normally her father or husband. Moreover, in the case of a maiden, rape destroyed her property value on the marriage market, and because defloration polluted, heaped shame on her family.'[39] In this way, the honour-based conception of rape captured in the Hague Conventions, which centralised the injury to the male relatives to which the victim was understood to belong, reflected the contemporary social order from which these rules emerged, in which recognition or acceptance of women as subjects remained limited.

Despite significant wider developments in the law of armed conflict and international criminal law following the two world wars, including the recognition of rape and enforced prostitution as war crimes by the international commission established by the Allies after World War I and the 1943 UN War Crimes Commission, sexual violence was nevertheless omitted from the Charters of the Nuremberg and Tokyo Tribunals.[40] Rape was subsequently enumerated as a crime against humanity, although not a war crime, in Control Council Law 10.[41] The next significant legal development, which reinforced the emphatically honour-based conception of sexual violence reflected in international law, took place in the form of the codification of the Geneva Conventions of 1949. Article 27 of the Fourth Convention on the protection of civilians requires that 'women shall be especially protected against any attack on their honour, in particular against rape, enforced prostitution, or any form of indecent assault.' While less euphemistic than the language of the 1899 and 1907 Hague Conventions by listing the acts of rape and enforced prostitution, these acts were nevertheless explicitly framed as attacks on women's honour. The formulation contained in the 1949 Conventions nevertheless represented a degree of evolution in how it identified the woman victim, as opposed to her

38 Hilary Charlesworth, 'Feminist Methods in International Law', (1999) 93(2) *American Journal of International Law*, 386; Phillips (n 19), 34.

39 Roy Porter, 'Rape – Does It Have Historical Meaning?' in Sylvana Tomaselli and Roy Porter (ed), *Rape: An Historical and Cultural Enquiry* (Basil Blackwell 1989), 217.

40 For an overview see Askin (n 25); Grey (n 13), 71–74.

41 Grey (n 13), 72.

family, as the subject who is injured by sexual violence. This shift from framing sexual violence as a question of family honour and rights, to framing it as an attack on the woman's honour in this way 'correlate[d] with the modern turn in the understanding of rape, namely when the ownership of the female sexual body property shifted from the male owner to the woman herself.'[42]

At the same time, while the woman subject was identified for the first time as the site of the injury caused by rape, the nature of the injury inflicted on her continued to be identified as an attack on her honour. Thus, in this formulation, while the possessor of the honour had shifted to the woman victim, rape remained a crime essentially of 'sexual ravishment, which in turn was viewed as the theft of chastity and virtue, rather than of body and chattels.'[43] While the prohibition on rape and enforced prostitution in the Geneva Conventions in this way reflected contemporary changes in the position of women in society in terms of how it identified the woman victim as the subject injured by rape, this formulation nevertheless reproduced the conception of rape as, fundamentally, a violation of sexual purity. The Geneva Conventions in this way continued to point indirectly to property-based conceptions of the injury caused by rape, in the sense that notions of honour or chastity rely on their inherent configuration as belonging to the man who has a right to them.[44] The normative framing of rape as injury to honour in the Geneva Conventions also carried legal implications in ensuring that, while rape was prohibited, it was not included within the category of grave breaches of the Conventions, meaning that sexual violence was only subject to domestic jurisdiction at the discretion of national prosecutors.[45]

The language of honour was ultimately abandoned in the 1977 Additional Protocols, reflecting the continuing advancement in the position of women in many societies, with corresponding shifts in attitudes to sexual morality and increased sexual freedoms for women becoming more widespread, evidently to varying degrees depending on social and cultural context. Article 76 of Protocol I instead requires that 'women shall be the object of special respect and shall be protected in particular against rape, forced prostitution and any other form of indecent assault.' Article 4(2)(e) of Protocol II similarly prohibits 'outrages upon personal dignity, in particular humiliating and degrading treatment, rape, enforced prostitution and any form of indecent assault.'

42 du Toit (n 21), 36.
43 Porter (n 39), 217.
44 Phillips (n 21), 34; Charlesworth (n 38), 386.
45 Mibenge (n 7), 43.

While the explicit framing of sexual violence as an attack on honour was dropped in the Additional Protocols, turning instead to the language of indecency and dignity, these formulations nevertheless continued to distinguish sexual violence from other forms of physical violence prohibited by the Protocols. In this respect, while not denying that sexual violence also constitutes a violation of dignity, Catherine Niarchos has noted that 'the Protocols *distinguish* sexual assaults from crimes of violence'[46] in that they prohibit violence to the life, health, or physical or mental well-being of persons including murder, torture, corporal punishment and mutilation, while outrages upon personal dignity, including rape, are discussed separately.[47] Thus, although narratives of honour were no longer appearing in new codifications of international humanitarian law by the 1970s, the Additional Protocols nevertheless centralise indecency and personal dignity, as distinct from violence to persons, in their normative framing of rape and forced prostitution and, in doing so, invoke an account of such acts that implies that they may be understood as in some way normatively distinct from other forms of violent assault.

Against this entrenched historical and cultural legacy, the evolution represented by developments in international criminal law on rape and sexual violence in the 1990s, triggered by considerable feminist mobilisation, took on a particular significance, not only in terms of new opportunities for pursuing accountability, but also in terms of the normative understanding of sexual violence that they invoked. The following section provides a brief outline of the doctrinal developments in the definitions of rape and sexual violence in international criminal law, focussing on how the debate over non-consent or coercive circumstances as constituent elements of rape illuminates the shift in how the normative core of this crime came to be constructed. On this basis, the section goes on to provide a normative typology of the different definitions of rape identified in the case law of the courts and tribunals.

2 Definitions of Rape and Sexual Violence in International Criminal Law

The statutes of the ICTY and ICTR both included rape as an act constituting crimes against humanity, while the ICTR statute also included rape as a war

46 Catherine N. Niarchos, 'Women, War, and Rape: Challenges Facing the International Tribunal for the Former Yugoslavia', (1995) 17(4) *Human Rights Quarterly*, 675–676.

47 *Ibid.*, 675.

crime.[48] Without an existing international legal definition of rape, the tribunals were required to identify the elements of rape as a crime under international law. Reflecting contemporary developments in domestic laws on rape, the case law of the ad hoc tribunals is characterised by a degree of change and fluctuation centred primarily on the relevance of non-consent as a constituent element of the crime. Domestic feminist law reform efforts on the relevance of force and consent with respect to rape, and the issues that underpinned these debates, illuminate the normative implications of the varying definitions adopted at the ad hoc tribunals. It is therefore worth briefly outlining the content of the debates over the place of consent in defining rape and sexual violence, and how their relevance has been addressed in the context of international crimes.

2.1 *Consent vs. Coercive Circumstances*

In general terms, rape is commonly defined as non-consensual sexual behaviour.[49] A key controversy that has animated domestic law reform efforts on rape and sexual assault relates to the issue of how to understand the concept of consent and its proper place in the criminalisation of rape and sexual assault. Louise du Toit outlines how, against the historical property-model of sexual violation, which identified women as objects of male control, the principle of consent came to figure as an affirmation of women's sexual freedom and autonomy for the feminist law reform efforts of the 1970s. The feminist commitment to consent as central to understanding sexual assault in this way correlated with the increasing recognition of women as legal and political subjects with voices in the public sphere. Now, the woman's 'individual will was [...] the determining factor in the court's decision whether rape had occurred, since the harm of rape came to be seen as the violation of a woman's individual right to personal autonomy and sexual self-determination.'[50]

At the same time, more critical approaches to the place of consent in relation to sexual assault laws highlighted how the centrality of consent as the boundary between the lawful and the unlawful assumes 'an abstract, rational

48 Article 5(g) ICTY Statute and Articles 3(g) and 4(e) ICTR Statute.

49 Charlene L. Muehlenhard, Sharon Danoff-Burg and Irene G. Powch, 'Is Rape Sex or Violence? Conceptual Issues and Implications' in David Buss and Neil Malamuth (ed), *Sex, Power, Conflict: Evolutionary and Feminist Perspectives* (Oxford University Press 1996), 124.

50 Louise du Toit, 'From Consent to Coercive Circumstances: Rape Law Reform on Trial', (2012) 28(3), *South African Journal on Human Rights*, 388.

and self-serving framework for the operation of agency',[51] constructing an artificial 'image of unfettered self-determinism'.[52] Placing consent as central to the definition of rape as a crime in this way is understood to overlook how 'entrenched power disparities, material inequalities, relational dynamics, and socio-sexual norms'[53] function to construct and constrain women's ability to exercise free and unrestricted agency in this way. Ann Cahill explains the practical implications of this in applying the law:

> consent theory falters on locating the ethical wrong of rape in the absence of the victim's consent. To approach the wrong of rape as embedded in the non-consensual nature of the act is inevitably to place the ethical burden on the victim. The ethical question that courts must pursue becomes whether the victim sufficiently communicated her nonconsent, or whether that nonconsent was likely given the history of the victim. [...] and because gender relations are structured such that the consent of women is called for in remarkably different situations than that of men and hence evaluated in substantially different ways, consent theory does not provide a stable basis for an understanding of the ethical wrongs of rape. It too easily dismisses the structural inequalities that are inherent in most gender relations, and in its attempt at gender neutrality it ignores the political and bodily significances of sexual difference.[54]

The centrality of consent has for this reason been subject to critique for perpetuating myths around what counts as 'real' rape,[55] identified as situations where nonconsent is demonstrated in the use of force, usually amounting to physical violence, on the part of the perpetrator or evidenced through physical resistance on the part of the victim.[56] Catharine MacKinnon has explained how 'the deeper problem [with consent] is that women are socialized to passive receptivity; may have or perceive no alternative to acquiescence; may

51 Vanessa E. Munro, 'Constructing Consent: Legislating Freedom and Legitimating Constraint in the Expression of Sexual Autonomy', (2008) 41(1) *Akron Law Review*, 928.
52 *Ibid.*, 929.
53 *Ibid.*, 925.
54 Ann Cahill, *Rethinking Rape* (Cornell University Press 2011), 174–175.
55 Dowds (n 20), 112.
56 Stephen J. Schulhofer, 'Reforming the Law of Rape', (2017) 35(2) *Law and Inequality*, 336–342; Eithne Dowds, 'Towards a Contextual Definition of Rape: Consent, Coercion and Constructive Force', (2020) 83(1) *Modern Law Review*, 36.

prefer it to the escalated risk of injury [...] submit to survive',[57] highlighting in this way that the 'absence of force does not ensure the presence of that control'[58] assumed in the concept of consent. Louise du Toit takes this point a step further, also problematising consent as the boundary between lawful and unlawful sex at a conceptual level for the way that it constructs 'normal' sex through a framework of masculine agency, where male subjects have intercourse with female objects, who simply consent to the advances of the active male subject.[59] Within this symbolic order, 'women are implicitly stripped of their sexual agency and subjectivity, their sexual will and desire, to the point where it is limited to consenting or not consenting to intercourse.'[60]

Domestic feminist law reform efforts on rape and sexual assault have for these reasons sought to broaden the concept of consent beyond notions of force, coercion or duress to recognise the role of other kinds of inequalities, and their impact on victims' agency and their capacity to consent to sexual relations.[61] These efforts have sought to move away from a purely consent-based conception of rape, which requires evidence of the victim's state of mind or often their resistance to force, and has frequently resulted in extensive cross-examination of victims and intrusive inquiry into their personal lives. In domestic law, the move has instead been towards a conception of rape as protecting against all forms of nonviolent coercion, which may be demonstrated through contextual factors other than the victim's articulation of non-consent.[62]

The debate on the place of consent as a constitutive element of rape under international criminal law reflects the contours of this wider question, but focussed in particular on the relevance of a conventional consent-based model of rape given the nature of the environments in which international crimes are committed. Critics of adopting a consent-based model in international law have highlighted that, in order for acts of rape to fall within the scope of international criminal law, they would necessarily have to fulfil the contextual requirements for these crimes, namely that they occurred within an armed

57 Catharine MacKinnon, *Toward a Feminist Theory of the State* (Harvard University Press 1989), 177.

58 *Ibid.*, 178.

59 du Toit (n 21), 37–38.

60 du Toit (n 21), 38.

61 Stephen Schulhofer, *Unwanted Sex: The Culture of Intimidation and the Failure of the Law* (Harvard University Press 2000), 98.

62 Alison Cole, 'International Criminal Law and Sexual Violence: An Overview' in Clare McGlynn and Vanessa Munro (eds), *Rethinking Rape Law: International and Comparative Perspectives* (Routledge 2010), 54.

conflict, as part of a widespread or systematic attack on a civilian population or as part of a campaign aimed at destroying a national, ethnic, racial or religious group.[63] They therefore argue that, given the inherently and overwhelmingly coercive nature of such situations, consent is necessarily vitiated, making inquiry into the question of whether the victim consented unnecessary and irrelevant.[64]

Recognising the coercion inherent in the circumstances in which international crimes are committed is instead seen to approach rape 'fundamentally as a crime of inequality, whether of physical or other force, status, or relation';[65] coercion-based definitions see in rape 'power – domination and violence.'[66] In the context of international criminal law, focussing on coercive circumstances as constitutive of rape is in this way seen to place the acts of the perpetrator in intentionally taking advantage of circumstances of duress, captivity or violence at the centre of the crime, and precludes the necessity of examining whether the victim was in a position to exercise agency by giving meaningful consent.[67]

While approaches that recognise the role of coercive circumstances have for this reason been welcomed in terms of the more contextual understanding of agency and autonomy they provide, it has nevertheless also been argued that 'coercive circumstances can go too far – some concept of consent is necessary to allow people to act and be respected as moral agents who police the boundaries of their own personal intimacy.'[68] From this perspective, an overemphasis on coercive circumstances as the constitutive element of rape may have negative implications for understanding how women exercise agency during conflict and violence, and may for this reason reinforce gendered 'images of women as powerless victims of war.'[69] Some scholars have gone so far as to

---

63 Wolfgang Schomburg and Ines Peterson, 'Genuine Consent to Sexual Violence under International Criminal Law', (2007) 101(1) *The American Journal of International Law*, 121, 123.

64 *Ibid.*, 139; Alison Cole, 'Prosecutor v. Gacumbitsi: The New Definition for Prosecuting Rape under International Law', (2008) 8 *International Criminal Law Review*, 75.

65 Catharine MacKinnon, 'Defining Rape Internationally: A Comment on Akayesu', (2006) 44(3) *Columbia Journal of Transnational Law*, 941.

66 *Ibid.*

67 Niamh Hayes, 'Creating a Definition of Rape in International Law: The Contribution of the International Criminal Tribunals' in Shane Darcy and Joseph Powderly (eds), *Judicial Creativity at the International Criminal Tribunals* (Oxford University Press 2011), 152.

68 Vanessa E Munro, 'From consent to coercion: Evaluating international and domestic frameworks for the criminalization of rape', in Clare McGlynn and Vanessa Munro (eds), *Rethinking Rape Law: International and Comparative Perspectives* (Routledge 2010), 21.

69 Karen Engle, 'Feminism and its (Dis)Contents: Criminalizing Wartime Rape in Bosnia and Herzegovina', (2005) 99(4) *The American Journal of International Law*, 812.

suggest that an approach to coercion that recognises some circumstances as so inherently coercive as to preclude any possibility of consent implies that in certain circumstances, consensual sexual relationships are legally impossible.[70] This leads them to conclude that, while the women's human rights movement has sought to increase women's ability to have decision-making control over their lives and bodies, the debate as to the irrelevance of consent as a constitutive element of rape in international criminal law has 'required the removal of just such claims of autonomy and agency.'[71]

The debate over the relevance of consent for definitions of rape and, more importantly, the conceptual positions that underpin it, provide the wider normative framework within which the definitions identified by the various chambers of the ad hoc tribunals emerged. Eithne Dowds has offered a useful normative typology of these different definitions, which captures how these broader feminist philosophical currents on rape and sexual assault were given expression in the case law of the tribunals in three different forms, namely in conceptualisations of rape as an act of aggression, as a violation of human dignity and as a violation of sexual autonomy.[72] The following section draws on and expands Dowds' typology of the definitions of rape developed through the case law of the ad hoc tribunals and in the definition codified in the ICC Elements of Crimes to identify the normative conceptualisations of sexual violence that they invoke.

2.2 *Violence and Aggression*

The initial *Akayesu* definition of rape reflects its conceptualisation as an act of aggression. In *Akayesu*, the Trial Chamber described rape explicitly as 'a form of aggression'[73] and, comparing it to torture, noted that it 'is used for such purposes as intimidation, degradation, humiliation, discrimination, punishment, control or destruction of a person.'[74] The Chamber went on to define the crime of rape as 'a physical invasion of a sexual nature, committed on a person under circumstances which are coercive,'[75] explaining that coercive circumstances 'need not be evidenced by a show of physical force. Threats, intimidation,

70 *Ibid.*, 804.

71 Kiran Grewal, 'Rape in Conflict, Rape in Peace: Questioning the Revolutionary Potential of International Criminal Justice for Women's Human Rights', (2010) 33 *Australian Feminist Law Journal*, 79.

72 Dowds (n 20), 138–142.

73 *Prosecutor v. Jean-Paul Akayesu*, ICTR-96-4-T, ICTR, Trial Judgment, 2 September 1998, para 687 [hereafter Akayesu Trial Judgment].

74 *Ibid.*

75 *Ibid.*, para 688.

extortion and other forms of duress which prey on fear or desperation may constitute coercion, and coercion may be inherent in certain circumstances, such as armed conflict or the military presence of Interahamwe among refugee Tutsi women at the bureau communal.'[76] While noting that rape in domestic law is usually defined as 'non-consensual intercourse',[77] the Trial Chamber made no reference to non-consent as an element in its definition of the crime.

Dowds links the conceptualisation of rape as a crime of aggression contained in *Akayesu* to the second wave feminist debate on whether rape should be conceptualised as sex or as violence.[78] This long-running debate emerged partly in response to the historical understanding of rape as a crime against morality, with feminists seeking to instead situate rape within the framework of physical violence in order to ensure it was taken more seriously as a harm.[79] In addition, feminist arguments in favour of conceptualising rape exclusively as a form of physical violence, i.e. as violence and *not* sex, sought to oppose entrenched ideas about rape being a sexual experience that was unconsciously desired by the victim or was invited through provocative dressing or behaviour. In other words, the feminist effort to reframe rape as violence and not sex was intended to counter narratives of rape and sexual violence that centralised questions of sexual morality and blamed victims for inviting rape, consciously or unconsciously, by emphasising that rape was an inherently physically violent act that had little to do with sex from the victim's perspective.[80]

On the other side of the debate, some feminists have argued against 'taking the sex out of rape'[81] on the grounds that doing so promotes an understanding of rape that is divorced from the structural conditions of gender inequality of which rape is seen to be a paradigmatic expression. From this perspective, framing rape as violence and not sex is seen to obscure 'its social and cultural significance as an institutionalised expression of male violence.'[82] Instead, feminists that have advocated for an understanding of rape as sex have emphasised how social constructions of heterosexual sex eroticise male dominance and female submission, in this way collapsing the distinction between sex and violence.[83] Catharine MacKinnon, for instance, has argued that:

---

76 *Ibid.*

77 *Ibid.*, para 596.

78 For an overview of these debates see Muehlenhard, Danoff-Burg and Powch (n 49).

79 Conaghan (n 10), 165.

80 Muehlenhard, Danoff-Burg and Powch (n 49), 121, 130.

81 Conaghan (n 10), 165.

82 *Ibid.*

83 Muehlenhard, Danoff-Burg and Powch (n 49), 130–131.

> The more feminist view to me, one which derives from victims' experiences, sees sexuality as a social sphere of male power of which forced sex is paradigmatic. Rape is not less sexual for being violent; to the extent that coercion has become integral to male sexuality, rape may be sexual to the degree that, and because, it is violent.[84]

For these feminists, insisting on a rape-as-sex rather than a rape-as-violence paradigm in this way functioned to highlight how many socially acceptable forms of sex involve coercion in different forms than direct physical violence. This approach also problematises the rape-as-violence paradigm in practical legal terms, for how an understanding of rape as violence rather than sex runs the risk that legal systems fail to recognise forms of coercive sex as rape if they do not involve significant levels of extrinsic violence.[85]

While these wider conceptual undercurrents have underpinned legal and other international discourses on conflict-related sexual violence, the rape-as-violence conception of sexual violence has overwhelmingly dominated in this field, taking the form of the common narrative of rape 'as a weapon of war.'[86] Reflecting the wider rape-as-violence paradigm, this narrative is particularly emphatic in its exclusion of the relevance of sex for an understanding of the drivers of conflict-related sexual violence. On this account, conflict-related sexual violence has also been framed as 'decidedly not about sex, sexual desire, pleasure, or sexuality'[87] in order to refute socio-biological explanations for rape as rooted in male heterosexuality, and therefore as a natural and inevitable by-product of war. The *Akayesu* definition of rape 'as a crime of aggression and hostility, not a form of sexual release'[88] in this way captured the rape as a weapon of war conception of sexual violence and the wider rape-as-violence paradigm that underpins it. In emphasising physical violence and aggression in its account of the crime, the definition of rape offered by the Trial Chamber in *Akayesu* has similarly been understood to refute those myths that trivialised sexual violence as a less serious crime against sexual morality or as an opportunistic act peripheral to the main forms of physical violence utilised during war.[89]

---

84 Catharine MacKinnon, 'Feminism, Marxism, Method, and the State: Toward Feminist Jurisprudence', (1983) 8(4) *Signs*, 646.

85 Muehlenhard, Danoff-Burg and Powch (n 49), 130–131.

86 Maria Eriksson Baaz and Maria Stern, 'Curious erasures: the sexual in wartime sexual violence', (2018) 20(3) *International Feminist Journal of Politics*, 296.

87 *Ibid.*, 295.

88 Dowds (n 20), 140.

89 *Ibid.*

In addition, by centralising the context of coercion in which rape takes place as constitutive of the crime and determining that coercion may be inherent in certain circumstances, the *Akayesu* decision made clear that, in the context in which these acts took place, 'inquiry into individual consent was not even worth discussion.'[90] According to the critical analyses of the coercive circumstances approach to rape, outlined above, by defining the crime purely in terms of the context in which it occurred, the *Akayesu* definition of rape in this way invoked a normative account of the crime that excluded the relevance of agency or autonomy, and its violation, on the part of the victim.

In terms of the criminal wrong of rape, the *Akayesu* conception of rape as a crime of aggression, with its emphasis on the degree of extrinsic coercion or physical violence inflicted on victims, along with its exclusion of the relevance of consent, has been subject to the same criticism as the wider rape-as-violence paradigm, for suggesting that it is ultimately the physical violence rather than the unwanted sexual act, and therefore the violation of the victim's personal and sexual autonomy, that is the real crime.[91] By in this way identifying the wrong of rape to lie in its physical violence, similar to other acts of violence like torture, the *Akayesu* definition of rape has been problematised for ultimately obscuring what may be considered distinct about rape and sexual violence at a normative or experiential level.[92]

2.3 *Human Dignity*

The next significant development in the definition of rape at the ad hoc tribunals was contained in the *Furundžija* case, in which the Trial Chamber departed from the definition adopted in *Akayesu,* instead identifying the objective elements of rape as '(i) the sexual penetration, however slight: (a) of the vagina or anus of the victim by the penis of the perpetrator or any other object used by the perpetrator; or (b) of the mouth of the victim by the penis of the perpetrator; (ii) by coercion or force or threat of force against the victim or a third person.'[93] In defining rape in these terms, while reflecting the same contextual approach to the crime as the *Akayesu* case by making no evidential requirement of non-consent, the analysis of the crime in *Furundžija* placed less emphasis on an understanding of rape as an act of physical violence and aggression. Rather, the Trial Chamber in *Furundžija* rooted its conclusion that

90 MacKinnon (n 65), 943.

91 Grewal (n 71), 72–73.

92 Dowds (n 20), 141.

93 *Prosecutor v. Anton Furundžija*, IT-95-17/1-T, ICTY, Trial Judgment, 10 December 1998, para 185 [hereafter Furundžija Trial Judgment].

forced oral sex fell within the definition of rape in the principle of human dignity. This principle, or the similar notions of personal or inherent dignity, was also identified in several other cases at the ICTY, ICTR and ECCC in relation to rape and other forms of sexual violence.[94] Holding that 'the forced penetration of the mouth by the male sexual organ constitutes a most humiliating and degrading attack upon human dignity',[95] the Trial Chamber in *Furundžija* identified the protection of human dignity as the basic principle underlying international humanitarian and human rights law, which also permeates the whole body of international law.[96] On this basis, the Chamber went on to conclude that:

> This principle is intended to shield human beings from outrages upon their personal dignity, whether such outrages are carried out by unlawfully attacking the body or by humiliating and debasing the honour, the self-respect or the mental well being of a person. It is consonant with this principle that such an extremely serious sexual outrage as forced oral penetration should be classified as rape.[97]

94 Referring to human, personal, or inherent dignity see for instance Akayesu Trial Judgment (n 73), para 597; *Prosecutor v. Mikaeli Muhimana*, ICTR-95-1B-T, ICTR, Judgment and Sentence, 28 April 2005, para 539 [hereafter Muhimana Judgment and Sentence]; *Prosecutor v. Théoneste Bagosora et al.*, ICTR-98-41-A, ICTR, Appeal Judgment, 14 December 2011, para 723 [hereafter Bagosora et al. Appeal Judgment]; *Prosecutor v. Vlastimir Đorđević*, IT-05-87/1-A, ICTY, Appeal Judgment, 27 January 2014, para 850, 868 [hereafter Đorđević Appeal Judgment]; *Prosecutor v. Ramush Haradinaj et al.*, IT-04-84-T, ICTY, Trial Judgment, 3 April 2008, para 466; *Prosecutor v. Radovan Karadžić*, IT-95-5/18-T, ICTY, Trial Judgment – Volume I, 24 March 2016, para 512–513, 2505 [hereafter Karadžić Trial Judgment Volume I]; *Prosecutor v. Nikola Šainović et al.*, IT-05-87-T, ICTY, Trial Judgment – Volume 1, 26 February 2009, para 195, 201 [hereafter Šainović et al. Trial Judgment Volume 1]; *Prosecutor v. Nikola Šainović et al.*, IT-05-87-T, ICTY, Trial Judgment – Volume 2, 26 February 2009, para 1187, 1224 [hereafter Šainović et al. Trial Judgment Volume 2]; *Prosecutor v. Radoslav Brđanin*, IT-99-36-T, ICTY, Trial Judgment, 1 September 2004, para 485, 1012 [hereafter Brđanin Trial Judgment]; *Prosecutor v. Milomir Stakić*, IT-97-24-T, ICTY, Trial Judgment, 13 July 2003, para 756 [hereafter Stakić Trial Judgment]; *Prosecutor v. Zdravko Mucić et al.*, IT-96-21-T, ICTY, Trial Judgment, 16 November 1998, para 490, 495, 1066 [hereafter Mucić et al. Trial Judgment]; *Prosecutor v. Dragoljub Kunarac et al.*, IT-96-23-T & IT-96-23/1-T, ICTY, Trial Judgment, 22 February 2001, para 756 [hereafter Kunarac et al. Trial Judgment]; *Prosecutor v. Jadranko Prlić et al.*, IT-04-74-T, ICTY, Trial Judgment – Volume III, 29 May 2013, para 772 [hereafter Prlić et al. Trial Judgment Volume III]; *Prosecutor v. Nuon Chea and Khieu Samphan* (*Case 002/02*), 002/19-09-2007/ECCC/TC, ECCC, Trial Judgment, 16 November 2018, para 3687, 3701 [hereafter Nuon Chea and Khieu Samphan Trial Judgment].

95 Furundžija Trial Judgment (n 93), para 183.

96 *Ibid.*

97 *Ibid.*

In international law, in particular in the field of human rights, references to the concept to human dignity are 'as pervasive as they are difficult to pin down.'[98] While the concept's roots have been traced to Christian religious thought, the modern, secularised notion is frequently invoked in international legal and constitutional documents.[99] Human dignity has been defined in various ways, but in broad terms can be understood to signify 'a kind of intrinsic worth that belongs equally to all human beings as such, constituted by certain intrinsically valuable aspects of being human. [It] is a necessary, not a contingent, feature of all humans; it is permanent and unchanging, not transitory or changeable; and […] it sets certain limits to how humans may justifiably be treated.'[100] The concept of human dignity features centrally in the history and normative conception of human rights, in that human rights are understood to be 'based upon or derivative from human dignity. It is because humans have dignity that they have human rights.'[101] While some accounts of human dignity appeal to ideas about individual autonomy, empowerment and liberty for their substantive content, the concept has also been described as empty, elusive and without concrete meaning because of its vagueness and generality.[102]

While therefore somewhat vague and ambiguous, by rooting its conclusion that forced oral sex constituted the crime of rape in the principle of human dignity, the Trial Chamber in *Furundžija* invoked a distinct normative conception of the crime to that offered in *Akayesu,* which centred instead on physical violence and aggression. Without being specific, invoking the notion of human dignity in this way can nevertheless be understood to suggest certain normative dimensions to the crime that go beyond the tangible and the physical implied by the rape as violence and aggression conception of the crime. The *Furundžija* decision has for this reason been interpreted as having constructed an understanding of sexual violence that instead centralised 'the perpetrator's invasion into the private space of the victim and destruction of [their] personhood.'[103] At the same time, the generality of the principle of human dignity, which the chamber itself referred to as the basic principle underlying the whole body of international law, speaks little to what may be considered

---

98 Ginevra Le Moli, 'Three Circles of Dignity', (2019) 11 *Journal of Human Rights Practice*, 258.

99 *Ibid.*, 261.

100 Alan Gewirth, 'Human Dignity as the Basis of Rights' in Michael J. Meyer and William A. Parent (eds), *The Constitution of Rights: Human Dignity and American Values* (Cornell University Press 1992), 12.

101 *Ibid.*, 10.

102 Le Moli (n 98), 262–264.

103 Dowds (n 20), 142.

normatively specific and distinct about the criminalisation of sexualised forms of violence in particular.

2.4 *Sexual Autonomy*

Finally, the most significant shift in the definition of rape, and the clearest articulation of the relationship between the elements of consent and coercive circumstances from a conceptual perspective, took place in the Trial and Appeals Chamber decisions in the *Kunarac et al.* case at the ICTY. In *Kunarac et al.*, the Trial Chamber undertook a review of domestic laws on rape in order to clarify the element of coercion identified in *Furundžija*, which, it determined, had been 'stated more narrowly than is required by international law.'[104] Significantly, from this overview the Trial Chamber concluded that 'the basic principle which is truly common to these legal systems is that serious violations of sexual autonomy are to be penalized. Sexual autonomy is violated wherever the person subjected to the act has not freely agreed to it or is otherwise not a voluntary participant.'[105] Tying the principle of sexual autonomy in this way to the question of consent, the Trial Chamber in *Kunarac et al.* therefore defined rape as 'the sexual penetration, however slight: (a) of the vagina or anus of the victim by the penis of the perpetrator or any other object used by the perpetrator; or (b) of the mouth of the victim by the penis of the perpetrator; where such sexual penetration occurs without the consent of the victim.'[106]

In placing lack of consent at the centre of the crime and explicitly framing rape as a violation of sexual autonomy, the *Kunarac et al.* Trial Chamber responded precisely to those critiques of the *Akayesu* definition for failing to sufficiently address questions of individual agency and the distinctly sexualised dimensions of rape as a form of violence. For this reason, Eithne Dowds has described the conceptualisation of the crime invoked in *Kunarac et al.* as 'significant as it moves away from rape as a crime against male property to a crime against the woman and her right to sexual self-determination.'[107] In this way, the *Kunarac et al.* definition's inclusion of consent as an element of rape can be understood to invoke an account of the crime that reflects the broader societal shift towards recognising women's subjectivity by 'marking and proclaiming in law women's full humanity [...] as fully human creatures who could express their own sexual will.'[108]

---

104 Kunarac et al. Trial Judgment (n 94), para 438.

105 *Ibid.*, para 457.

106 *Ibid.*, para 460.

107 Dowds (n 20), 144.

108 du Toit (n 21), 388–389.

At the same time, the *Kunarac et al.* decision did not discard the *Akayesu* definition's recognition of external factors that may condition individual agency, but rather drew on the notion of coercive circumstances identified in *Akayesu* to offer a contextualised account of consent in the following terms; 'consent for this purpose must be consent given voluntarily, as a result of the victim's free will, assessed in the context of the surrounding circumstances.'[109] In articulating its understanding of the relationship between consent and these contextual factors, the *Kunarac et al.* Trial Chamber interpreted the *Furundžija* requirements of coercion, force or threat of force broadly, to make clear that 'coercion in particular would encompass most conduct which negates consent.'[110] Reinforcing this conclusion, the Appeals Chamber in the same case went on to note that 'the circumstances [...] that prevail in most cases charged as either war crimes or crimes against humanity will be almost universally coercive' and that in these circumstances 'true consent will not be possible.'[111]

In seeking to further harmonise the *Akayesu* and *Kunarac et al.* definitions of rape, the Trial Chambers in the *Muhimana* and *Gacumbitsi* cases further elaborated on this relationship by making explicit that 'coercion is an element that may obviate the relevance of consent as an evidentiary factor in the crime of rape',[112] emphasising that 'the Prosecution can prove non-consent beyond reasonable doubt by proving the existence of coercive circumstances under which meaningful consent is not possible.'[113] In *Muvunyi*, the Trial Chamber made this harmonisation between the two approaches explicit, noting emphatically that 'the underlying objective of the prohibition of rape in international law is to penalise serious violations of sexual autonomy [...] both the Akayesu and Kunarac definitions of rape reflect this objective of protecting individual sexual autonomy and are not therefore incompatible.'[114] This approach to rape, requiring lack of consent as constitutive of the crime while recognising that coercive circumstances negate the possibility of genuine consent, became the settled definition, variations on which were adopted by the rest of the ad hoc tribunals' cases involving charges of rape.[115]

109 Kunarac et al. Trial Judgment (n 94), para 460.

110 *Ibid.*, para 459.

111 *Ibid.*, para 130.

112 Muhimana Judgment and Sentence (n 94), para 550.

113 *Prosecutor v. Sylvestre Gacumbitsi*, ICTR-2001-64-A, ICTR, Appeal Judgment, 7 July 2006, para 155.

114 *Prosecutor v. Tharcisse Muvunyi*, ICTR-2000-55A-T, ICTR, Judgment and Sentence, 12 September 2006, para 521–522 [hereafter Muvunyi Judgment and Sentence].

115 See for example *Prosecutor v. Laurent Semanza*, ICTR-97-20-T, ICTR, Trial Judgment, 15 May 2003; *Prosecutor v. Juvénal Kajelijeli*, ICTR-98-44A-T, ICTR, Judgment and Sentence,

From an evidential perspective, the *Kunarac et al.* definition of rape may not therefore represent a dramatic shift from the *Akayesu* definition, since it 'both requires and presumes lack of consent.'[116] From a conceptual perspective, however, this blended approach to consent and coercive circumstances, with its roots in the *Kunarac et al.* decision's explicit identification of sexual autonomy as the principle underlying the prohibition on rape, constructed a definition of the crime which ultimately centred on the violation of the negative dimensions of a right to sexual autonomy and agency. In doing so, it invoked and endorsed the principle that individuals have 'the right to safeguard and exclude, the freedom to refuse to have sex with any person at any time, for any reason or for no reason at all.'[117]

The debate on consent or coercive circumstances as constitutive of rape also played out among different actors during the drafting of the Rome Statute, the Elements of Crimes and the Rules of Procedure and Evidence.[118] The definition ultimately set out by the Preparatory Commission on the Elements of Crimes in 2000 drew on the those developed in the *Akayesu* and *Furundžija* cases from 1998, at which point the 2001 *Kunarac et al.* definition had not yet entered international criminal jurisprudence.[119] Through its emphasis on coercive circumstances and its almost complete exclusion of consent as a relevant element, the definition of rape adopted in the ICC Elements of Crimes most closely resembles its conceptualisation as a crime of violence and aggression in the *Akayesu* case. The ICC's Elements of Crimes requires that:

1. The perpetrator invaded the body of a person by conduct resulting in penetration, however slight, of any part of the body of the victim or of the perpetrator with a sexual organ, or of the anal or genital opening of the victim with any object or any other part of the body.
2. The invasion was committed by force, or by threat of force or coercion, such as that caused by fear of violence, duress, detention, psychological oppression or abuse of power, against such person or another person, or by taking advantage of a coercive environment, or the invasion was committed against a person incapable of giving genuine consent.[120]

1 December 2003 [hereafter Kajelijeli Judgment and Sentence]; *Prosecutor v. Théoneste Bagosora et al.*, ICTR-98-41-T, ICTR, Trial Judgment, 18 December 2008; *Prosecutor v. Augustin Ndindiliyimana et al.*, ICTR-00-56-T, ICTR, Trial Judgment, 17 May 2011.

116 Engle (n 69), 804.

117 Schulhofer (n 56), 99.

118 Dowds (n 20), 100.

119 *Ibid.*

120 ICC Elements of Crimes, Article 7 (1) (g)-1 Crime against humanity of rape.

With the exception of the reference to persons incapable of giving genuine consent, which are identified in a footnote as individuals affected by natural, induced or age-related incapacity, the ICC Elements of Crimes definition of rape does not in this way include lack of consent as a constitutive element of the crime. In doing so, the ICC definition distinguishes clearly between the elements of coercive circumstances and consent, with the emphasis emphatically on the former. This differentiates it from the more blended approach reflected in the *Kunarac et al.* definition, which came to dominate the case law of the ad hoc tribunals, since in the ICC formulation, the coercive environment is what is central to the crime; it is not simply relevant to the extent that it vitiates consent.[121] The ICC definition of the crime therefore excludes consent, and its association with questions of agency and autonomy, more emphatically as a normatively relevant element of rape, with the exception of specific situations where the victim is an individual deemed to be incapable of giving genuine consent.

The ICC case law on rape has not developed significantly on the definition contained in the Elements of Crimes. In the Court's first analysis of the definition of rape, the Trial Chamber in *Katanga* sought to emphasise the irrelevance of consent for the Rome Statute definition, noting that 'save the very specific situation of a person whose "incapacity" was "tak[en] advantage of", the Elements of Crimes do not refer to the victim's lack of consent, and therefore this need not be proven.'[122] Reiterating that the establishment of coercive circumstances or any of the other conditions contained in the second element is therefore alone sufficient for penetration to constitute rape, the Chamber went on to reinforce this point by noting that 'in terms of procedure, the Rules of Procedure and Evidence confirm this interpretation by stipulating the principles applicable to evidence in matters of sexual violence. Rule 70 of the said Rules stipulates, inter alia, that consent cannot be inferred by reason of any words or conduct of a victim where force or coercion was used or advantage was taken of a coercive environment.'[123]

In its next case, the Trial Chamber in *Bemba* drew on and expanded the notion of coercive circumstances as articulated in *Akayesu*, providing a number of examples that would create such an environment, such as 'the number of people involved in the commission of the crime, [...] whether the rape is

121 Janine Natalya Clark, 'The First Rape Conviction at the ICC: An Analysis of the Bemba Judgment', (2016) 14(3) *Journal of International Criminal Justice*, 677.

122 *Prosecutor v. Germain Katanga*, ICC-01/04-01/07, ICC, Judgment pursuant to article 74 of the Statute, 7 March 2014, para 965 [hereafter Katanga Trial Judgment].

123 *Ibid.*, para 966.

committed during or immediately following a combat situation, or is committed together with other crimes.'[124] Similar to *Katanga*, the Trial Chambers in *Bemba* as well as *Ntaganda* were also at pains to stress that 'the victim's lack of consent is not a legal element of the crime of rape under the Statute.'[125] To date, the ICC's interpretations of the definition of rape contained in the Elements of Crimes in this way double down on a conception of the crime of rape as an act of violence and aggression in their explicit exclusion of the relevance of consent. From a normative perspective, doing so also explicitly excludes notions of sexual agency or autonomy from how the wrong of rape is constructed, situating the ICC's interpretation of the crime firmly within the rape-as-violence paradigm and opening it to those same criticisms directed at the *Akayesu* definition for constructing an account of the crime that discounts 'the violation of sexual agency but also that the victim has sexual agency to exercise and is not merely a harmed body.'[126]

3 Normative Themes in the Case Law

Beyond the normative implications of the evolving definitions of rape employed at the ad hoc tribunals and the ICC in their approaches to consent versus coercive circumstances, the case law on rape and other forms of sexual violence also engage directly with the normative dimensions of these crimes in the form of explicit normative statements that associate particular principles or values with these crimes. In addition, the case law also reflects a number of more general normative themes in terms of how the motivations behind and the harms inflicted by sexual violence are constructed in these decisions.

3.1 *Normative Statements*

First, a number of cases, most often at the ICTY, explicitly invoke specific values or principles that are violated through forms of sexual violence, to which their criminalisation may therefore be understood to be normatively linked.

---

124 *Prosecutor v. Jean-Pierre Bemba Gombo*, ICC-01/05-01/08, ICC, Judgment pursuant to Article 74 of the Statute, 21 March 2016, para 103–104 [hereafter Bemba Trial Judgment].

125 *Ibid.*, para 105. See similarly *Ntaganda* stating that 'save for the very specific situation of a person whose 'incapacity' was 'tak[en] advantage of', the Elements of Crimes do not refer to the victim's lack of consent, and therefore this need not be proven.' – *Prosecutor v. Bosco Ntaganda*, ICC-01/04-02/06, ICC, Trial Judgment, 8 July 2019, para 934 [hereafter Ntaganda Trial Judgment].

126 Olivera Simić and Jean Collings, 'Defining Rape in War: Challenges and Dilemmas', (2018) 6(1) *Griffith Journal of Law and Human Dignity*, 203.

3.1.1 Physical and Moral Integrity

In *Furundžija*, the Trial Chamber identified several different normative principles attaching to the criminalisation of rape and sexual assault. In addition to its invocation of the principle of human dignity to justify the expansion of the definition of rape to include forced oral sex, discussed in the previous section, the Trial Chamber also invoked the notions of physical and moral integrity in its account of the normative basis of the criminalisation of sexual assault. It noted that 'no international human rights instrument specifically prohibits rape or other serious sexual assaults. Nevertheless, these offences are implicitly prohibited by the provisions safeguarding physical integrity, which are contained in all of the relevant international treaties. The right to physical integrity is a fundamental one, and is undeniably part of customary international law.'[127] The Trial Chamber then went on to state that:

> international criminal rules punish not only rape but also any serious sexual assault falling short of actual penetration. It would seem that the prohibition embraces all serious abuses of a sexual nature inflicted upon the physical and moral integrity of a person by means of coercion, threat of force or intimidation in a way that is degrading and humiliating for the victim's dignity.[128]

In addition to the impact on the victim's dignity, the *Furundžija* decision in this way also articulated a conception of rape and sexual assault as involving violations of the physical and moral integrity of the victim. This emphasis on physical integrity as a central principle with respect to the criminalisation of sexual assault is particularly pronounced in the case law of the ICTY.[129] For instance, in *Mucić et al.*, the Trial Chamber asserted that rape and other forms of sexual assault constitute a violation of 'the inherent dignity and the right to physical integrity of the human being.'[130] In its analysis of sexual assaults charged as underlying acts constituting the crime of persecution, which requires the identification of a fundamental right that is denied or infringed by the act charged as persecution, the Trial Chamber in *Šainović et al.* similarly noted that 'the right not to be sexually assaulted has […] been subsumed under more general fundamental rights relating to physical integrity.'[131] In a wider account of

127 Furundžija Trial Judgment (n 93), para 170.

128 *Ibid.*, para 186.

129 In fact, the cases involving charges of sexual violence at the ICTR contain no references to principles of physical or bodily integrity.

130 Mucić et al. Trial Judgment (n 94), para 491.

131 Šainović et al. Trial Judgment Volume 1 (n 94), para 188.

acts of sexual violence that may not fall within the definition of rape, the Trial Chamber in *Karadžić* similarly invoked the notion of physical integrity, noting that 'sexual violence is found when (i) the perpetrator commits an act of a sexual nature on another or requires the victim to perform such an act, (ii) that act infringes on the victim's physical integrity or amounts to an outrage to the victim's personal dignity, and (iii) the victim does not consent to the act.'[132] In interpreting the residual category of other forms of sexual violence as a crime against humanity under Article 2(g) of its statute, the Trial Chamber in the AFRC case at the Special Court for Sierra Leone also endorsed the conclusion in *Furundžija* that the prohibition on sexual violence 'embraces all serious abuses of a sexual nature upon the physical and moral integrity of a person by means of coercion.'[133]

In the context of human rights law, the right to physical or bodily integrity does not enjoy a settled definition.[134] It appears in different forms – as a free-standing enumerated right, as a delegated right within rights to liberty and security of person, and as an interpreted right inherent to other rights such as the right to freedom from torture and cruel, inhuman and degrading treatment, the right to privacy and the right to the highest attainable standard of health.[135] In the human rights context, the right to bodily integrity specifically is often understood in terms of 'a right to be free from physical interference. [It] covers negative liberties: freedom from physical assaults, torture, medical or other experimentation, immunization and compelled eugenic or social sterilization, and cruel or degrading treatment or punishment. It also encompasses some positive duties on the state to protect people against interference

132 Karadžić Trial Judgment Volume I (n 94), para 513. A number of other cases frame the wrong of rape and sexual assault in terms of the right to physical integrity – see Stakić Trial Judgment (n 94), para 757; *Prosecutor v. Ranko Češić*, IT-95-10/1-S, ICTY, Sentencing Judgment, 11 March 2004, para 35, 53; Brđanin Trial Judgment (n 94), para 1012; *Prosecutor v. Dragan Zelenović*, IT-96-23/2-S, ICTY, Sentencing Judgment, 4 April 2007, para 36 [hereafter Zelenović Sentencing Judgment]; Šainović et al. Trial Judgment Volume 1 (n 94), para 201; Šainović et al. Trial Judgment Volume 2 (n 94), para 1187, 1224, 1244; *Prosecutor v. Vlastimir Đorđević*, IT-05-87/1-T, ICTY, Trial Judgment, 23 February 2011, para 1766–1769, 1791; *Prosecutor v. Jadranko Prlić et al.*, IT-04-74-T, ICTY, Trial Judgment – Volume I, 29 May 2013, para 116; Đorđević Appeal Judgment (n 94), para 850–852, 868.

133 *Prosecutor v. Alex Tamba Brima et al.* (*AFRC Case*), SCSL-04-16-T, SCSL, Trial Judgment, 20 June 2007, para 720 [hereafter Brima et al. Trial Judgment].

134 A.M. Viens, 'The Right to Bodily Integrity: Cutting Away Rhetoric in Favour of Substance' in Andreas von Arnauld, Kerstin von der Decken and Mart Susi (eds), *The Cambridge Handbook of New Human Rights: Recognition, Novelty, Rhetoric* (Cambridge University Press 2020), 365.

135 *Ibid.*, 364–365.

by others.'[136] In more general terms, bodily integrity has been described in terms of '[e]very human being's right to life [which] carries with it, as an intrinsic part of it, rights of bodily integrity and autonomy – the right to have one's own body whole and intact and (on reaching an age of understanding) to take decisions about one's own body.'[137]

At a more conceptual level, bodily integrity is linked to philosophical ideas around 'ownership of one's body',[138] and has therefore also been explained as being 'bound up with a claim to exclude others from one's physical space.'[139] In this way, the conception of rape and sexual assault as a violation of physical integrity speaks to and reinforces the normative account of crimes of sexual violence as acts of physical violence and aggression embodied in the definition of rape identified in the *Akayesu* case, with the emphasis therefore being on the physically violent and invasive dimensions of the crime on the body of the victim.

This construction of sexual violence as a form of violence constituting a violation of physical integrity was reinforced by the Appeals Chamber in *Šainović et al.*, which explicitly excluded a conception of sexual violence as normatively distinct from other violations of physical integrity. In the context of its analysis of 'whether the violations of physical integrity stemming from the sexual assaults fits in with the overall pattern of violations of physical integrity in the violent campaign',[140] the Appeals Chamber in *Šainović et al.* noted the Prosecution's argument that 'sexual assaults are not qualitatively different than other violent acts.'[141] This approach to sexual assault not only reinforces its conception as being a crime primarily of physical violence and bodily harm, embodying the conception of rape as a crime of aggression and violence, but goes so far as to explicitly exclude a conception of sexualised violence as in some way 'qualitatively' distinct from other forms of physical violence.

This understanding of conflict-related sexual violence, with its emphasis not only on physical violence and harm, but also its insistence on sexual violence as being 'about' violence and explicitly not about 'sex', in this way embodies

136 David Feldman, *Civil Liberties and Human Rights in England and Wales*, (Oxford University Press 2002), 241.

137 Jonathan Herring and Jesse Wall, 'The Nature and Significance of the Right to Bodily Integrity', (2017) 76(3) *Cambridge Law Journal*, 568.

138 Jill Marshall, *Personal Freedom Through Human Rights Law? Autonomy, Identity and Integrity Under the European Convention on Human Rights* (Martinus Nijhoff 2008), 170.

139 *Ibid.*, 165.

140 *Prosecutor v. Nikola Šainović et al.*, IT-05-87-A, ICTY, Appeal Judgment, 23 January 2014, para 1562.

141 *Ibid.*

the second wave feminist conception of rape-as-violence and its manifestation in international discourses on conflict-related violence in the form of the 'rape as a weapon of war' narrative. This narrative has nevertheless more recently been subject to critical scrutiny precisely for how it excludes any notion of 'the sexual' from its understanding of sexual violence, insisting instead on an account of sexual violence that sees it as comparable, and indistinguishable, from other forms of physical violence.

Maria Eriksson Baaz and Maria Stern have highlighted how this framing of conflict-related sexual violence in particular emerged partly as a refutation of socio-biological explanations for the occurrence of rape and sexual violence during war. These types of explanations construct sexual violence as a natural and inevitable by-product of male heterosexuality during times of war, which therefore belongs in the 'private' sphere, separate from the politically motivated forms of physical violence understood to constitute the 'real' means of waging war. The 'rape as a weapon of war' conception of conflict-related sexual violence has sought instead to counter this relegation of sexual violence to the private sphere, bringing it into the public by emphasising its strategic use for the pursuit of political and military goals, comparable to any other form of politically motivated physical violence, with the important accompanying attitude that sexual violence is therefore preventable.[142]

Dolan, Eriksson Baaz and Stern have nevertheless problematised this narrative from an experiential perspective, for how it functions to reduce the multi-layered experiences of victims and perpetrators of sexual violence into 'the palatably desexualized narratives of [conflict-related sexual violence] and its harms that prevail in humanitarian, juridical and policy spaces.'[143] Instead, they argue that survivor accounts of sexual violence 'unravel simplistic notions of [conflict-related sexual violence] serving only as a strategically deployed tool for humiliation and destruction.'[144] Their research has revealed in this respect how survivor accounts of conflict-related sexual violence reflect a much more complex relation between 'the erotic, sexual desire, pleasure, violence, aggression and domination'[145] to the dominant framing of conflict-related sexual violence as violence, not sex.

---

142 Eriksson Baaz and Stern (n 86), 295–296.

143 Chris Dolan, Maria Eriksson Baaz and Maria Stern, 'What is sexual about conflict-related sexual violence? Stories from men and women survivors', (2020) 96(5) *International Affairs*, 1168.

144 *Ibid.*

145 *Ibid.*

Agger and Buss Jensen have similarly highlighted the sexual dimensions of sexualised forms of torture from the victims' perspective, explaining that while sexual violence may also be motivated by power, aggression and violence, at the same time:

> the victim's as well as the torturer's sexual structures are involved in the psychodynamics of this interaction, and the victim experiences the torture as directed against his or her sexual body image and identity. Thus, the essential part of sexual torture's traumatic and identity-damaging effect is the feeling of being an accomplice in an ambiguous situation which contains both aggressive and libidinal elements of a confusing nature.[146]

In the context of conflict-related sexual violence, Gaby Zipfel has for this reason argued not only that sexuality cannot be discounted as a factor in understanding the experiences of perpetrators of sexual violence but also that 'the act, for its part, inflicts upon the victim something that is much more than an offence against physical integrity – s/he is potentially robbed of an expression of fundamental life, which is generally supposed to be positive.'[147]

Seen from this perspective, the framing of sexual assaults as not qualitatively different to other violent acts in *Šainović et al.* not only reinforces the centrality of physical or bodily integrity as the primary principle invoked with respect to crimes of rape and sexual violence, but goes further, to exclude the relevance of a notion of 'the sexual' from its normative conception of sexual violence. This embodies the disregard for sexuality as a relevant factor for understanding conflict-related sexual violence that characterises wider political and policy discourses, and results in the discounting of what may therefore be specific about this form of violence.[148]

Invoking physical integrity as the primary normative principle justifying the criminalisation of sexual violence in this way constructs a discourse around the crime that omits its sexual dimensions from both an experiential but also from a normative perspective, in terms of what it ultimately means to label a crime or form of violence 'sexual'. In other words, by declining to identify

---

146 Inger Agger and Søren Buus Jensen, 'The Psychosexual Trauma of Torture' in John P. Wilson and Beverly Raphael (eds), *International Handbook of Traumatic Stress Syndromes* (Plenum Press 1993), 687.

147 Gaby Zipfel, "Let Us Have a Little Fun": The Relationship between Gender, Violence and Sexuality in Armed Conflict Situations', (2013) 5 *RCCS Annual Review*, 34.

148 *Ibid.*

normative principles linked in some way to sex or sexuality as being of normative relevance to these crimes, this conception of crimes of sexual violence constructs a normative discourse in which the notion that individuals may enjoy rights or entitlements to be free from interference in their sexual lives in particular, as opposed to interference with their body in general, is absent, and not relevant for the purposes of criminal protection. Put simply, this account of sexual violence implies that such acts are criminalised to the extent that they amount to a violation of an individual's physical integrity, but not because individuals may also be entitled to be free from interference in their sexual lives specifically.

Alongside its identification of physical integrity as a central principle violated by rape and sexual assault, the *Furundžija* decision also appeals to the notion of moral integrity in this context.[149] While appeals to physical integrity feature more prominently, this formulation, in which physical and moral integrity are invoked alongside one another as normative principles attached to the crimes of rape and sexual violence, is reflected in several other decisions of the ICTY and also in the *AFRC* case at the SCSL.[150] The meaning of the term moral integrity is somewhat more ambiguous than that of physical integrity. In international law it frequently appears alongside references to physical integrity in the context of prohibitions on torture or inhuman and degrading treatment. For instance, Article 5 on the right to humane treatment of the American Convention on Human Rights requires that '1. Every person has the right to have his physical, mental, and moral integrity respected. 2. No one shall be subjected to torture or to cruel, inhuman, or degrading punishment or treatment.' The European Court of Human Rights has utilised the language of a right to physical and moral integrity in the context of its interpretation of Article 8 on the right to privacy,[151] nevertheless noting an overlap with the prohibition on torture to the extent that 'where a measure falls short of [constituting torture], it may, however fall foul of Article 8 of the Convention, which, inter alia, provides protection of physical and moral integrity under the respect for private life.'[152]

149 Furundžija Trial Judgment (n 93), para 186.

150 Brima et al. Trial Judgment (n 133), para 720.

151 See for instance *X and Y v. the Netherlands*, Application no. 8978/80, European Court of Human Rights, Judgment, 26 March 1985, para 22; *Wainwright v. the UK*, Application no. 12350/04, European Court of Human Rights, 26 September 2006, para 43. See also Marshall (n 138),1677-–168.

152 *Wainwright v. the UK*, Application no. 12350/04, European Court of Human Rights, 26 September 2006, para 43.

While explicit definitions of the concept of moral integrity independently of the notion of physical or bodily integrity appear limited in the international legal context, the International Committee of the Red Cross's 2020 Commentary on Article 14 of Geneva Convention III has offered some guidance, noting that 'there are two distinct aspects of the notion of respect for the person: physical integrity and moral integrity.'[153] The Commentary goes on to explain that respect for moral integrity entails 'respect for all the essential attributes of the human person, including their religious, political, intellectual and social convictions, gender and sexual orientation.[154] More widely, moral integrity has been recognised to constitute a more complex and difficult to pin down concept than that of bodily integrity.[155] It has been described as 'each person's psychic and moral space in which each individual is allowed to evaluate and represent who they are',[156] which might be engaged 'by serious interference with a person's ability to pursue a chosen life-style or plan for life.'[157] From this perspective, moral integrity as a legal principle could therefore be understood to constitute 'legal recognition of [an individual's] being and existence, and of non-intrusion into [...] their psychological constitution and moral framework.'[158]

Without a more precise elucidation of the meaning of moral integrity in the context of sexual violence, references to moral integrity may nevertheless invoke in general terms the relevance of certain intangible attributes of personhood that are not captured in an individual's physical being. These statements in the case law in this way go some way towards constructing a normative account of crimes of sexual violence that incorporates some dimensions of injury to selfhood beyond the physical. At the same time, and in a similar fashion to the invocation of the principle of human dignity, through their generality and their roots in prohibitions on torture and inhuman and degrading treatment, appeals to both physical and moral integrity construct a generalised, as opposed to a normatively specific, account of crimes of sexual violence that makes no links between sex or sexuality and the injury to physical or moral selfhood that they invoke.

---

153 ICRC, *Commentary on Convention (III) relative to the Treatment of Prisoners of War 1949* (2020), para 1665.

154 *Ibid.*, para 1665.

155 Marshall (n 138), 167.

156 *Ibid.*

157 *Ibid.*, 167–168.

158 *Ibid.*, 165.

3.1.2 Sexual Autonomy and Integrity

Against this normative backdrop, the inclusion of consent as an element of the crime of rape in *Kunarac et al.* carried significant implications not only as a legal and evidential matter but also in normative terms, in its explicit identification of sexual autonomy as 'the basic principle'[159] underlying its consent-based definition of the crime. While echoed in the *Kvočka et al.* case at the ICTY and in *Muvunyi* at the ICTR,[160] this normative language on rape and sexual violence did not become commonplace in the case law of the ad hoc tribunals and has only been invoked once at the ICC to date with respect to the crime of sexual slavery, which was described by the Trial Chamber in *Ongwen* as 'a specific form of the crime of 'enslavement', penalising the perpetrator's restriction or control of the victim's sexual autonomy while held in the state of enslavement.'[161] Alongside these appeals to sexual autonomy as a principle protected by the prohibition on rape and sexual violence, the case law of the ICTY and ICTR also contain a number of references to the principle of 'sexual integrity.'

For instance, in the context of its analysis of a separate set of factual circumstances to those involving forced oral sex found to have constituted rape in *Furundžija*, the Trial Chamber also found that a victim of rape 'suffered severe physical and mental pain [...] in what amounted to outrages upon her personal dignity and sexual integrity.'[162] The Trial Chamber in *Kunarac et al.* also described rape and other forms of sexual violence inflicted on victims of enslavement as 'violations of the victim's sexual integrity.'[163] Reference to the notion of sexual integrity further appeared in *Bagosora et al.* at the ICTR in a summary of the appellant's arguments in relation to a conviction for sexual assault inflicted on a victim who was already deceased. The Appeals Chamber noted that:

> Bagosora submits that the Trial Chamber erred in law by finding him guilty of the sexual assault of the Prime Minister because the conviction was based on actions taken after her death and sexual assault can be perpetrated only against a living person. He contends that the prohibition

159 Kunarac et al. Trial Judgment (n 94), para 457.

160 *Prosecutor v. Miroslav Kvočka et al.*, IT-98-30/1-T, ICTY, Trial Judgment, 2 November 2001, para 176–177 [hereafter Kvočka et al. Trial Judgment]; Muvunyi Judgment and Sentence (n 114), para 521–522.

161 *Prosecutor v. Dominic Ongwen*, ICC-02/04-01/15, ICC, Trial Judgment, 4 February 2021, para 2715 [hereafter Ongwen Trial Judgment].

162 Furundžija Trial Judgment (n 93), para 272, 279.

163 Kunarac et al. Trial Judgment (n 94), para 554.

> on sexual assault is meant to protect the sexual integrity of a person and there is no sexual integrity after death.[164]

No elaboration of the meaning understood to attach to the concept of sexual integrity was provided in these cases. From a historical perspective, Arlie Loughnan has linked the notion of sexual integrity to 'the rise of the individual as a social and legal subject, the development of a discourse of human rights and freedoms, as well as changing social mores'[165] in relation to sex and sexuality. In Loughnan's view, the concept of sexual integrity involves both positive and negative dimensions. The negative aspect of sexual integrity relates to freedom from harmful acts. Loughnan describes the positive dimension of sexual integrity in the context of criminal law in the following terms:

> The positive dimension of sexual integrity posits crime as a demarcation of proscribed sexual activity, thereby sanctioning and legitimating those sexual activities that fall into the category of the non-criminal. This dimension may be labelled positive because it connotes a freedom *to* engage in certain conduct.[166]

Elaine Craig similarly defines the concept of sexual integrity as 'both the freedom from unwanted, or not chosen, bodily violation and the conditions for sexual fulfilment, sexual diversity, and sexual literacy. [...] law ought to recognize sexual integrity as a social good, like language, that individuals require in order to be autonomous.'[167] The notions of sexual integrity and sexual autonomy appear to have been used interchangeably in the case law, and the concept of sexual autonomy has been interpreted in similar terms. For instance, Stephen Schulhofer has also defined sexual autonomy in such dualist terms:

> sexual autonomy, like other rights, has two facets. The first is active – the right to decide on the kind of life one wishes to live and kinds of activities one wishes to pursue, including activities with others who are willing. The other facet of sexual autonomy is the reverse – the right to safeguard

164 Bagosora et al. Appeal Judgment (n 94), para 723.

165 Arlie Loughnan, 'crime and sexual integrity' in Peter Crane and Joanne Conaghan (eds), *The New Oxford Companion to Law* (Oxford University Press 2009).

166 *Ibid.*

167 Elaine Craig, *Troubling Sex: Towards a Legal Theory of Sexual Integrity* (UBC Press 2012), 7–8.

> and exclude, the freedom to refuse to have sex with any person at any time, for any reason or for no reason at all.[168]

The invocation of the concepts of sexual autonomy and sexual integrity in some of the case law of the ICTY and ICTR in this way alludes to a thicker account of the normative principles attached to the criminalisation of rape and sexual violence than the more dominant physical integrity approach. At a fundamental level, appealing to the principles of sexual autonomy or sexual integrity invokes a normative account of these crimes as distinctly sexual forms of violation, distinct in this way from other forms of physical violence that violate physical integrity, because of how they are inflicted on 'one of the most intimate parts of one's identity',[169] functioning for this reason partly as 'a destruction and partly a denial of [a victim's] sexual subjectivity.'[170] While limited and under-elaborated, the appeals to sexual autonomy and sexual integrity in these cases in this way contribute to some limited discursive surfacing of the relevance of sex and sexuality for the normative understanding of these crimes, constructing an account of the wrong of rape that points in general terms to the principle that individuals are entitled to exercise agency, and therefore to be free from interference, whether through physical violence or other forms of coercion, in their sexual lives specifically, and that this principle is worthy of criminal protection.

3.2 *Normative Themes*

In addition to explicit normative statements identifying principles, interests or values protected by or justifying the criminalisation of rape and other forms of sexual violence, the case law also reflects a number of more general normative themes in terms of how accounts of sexual violence are constructed factually, how the harms inflicted on victims are described, and how perpetrators' motivations are recounted. These more factual accounts at times map on to and concretise the abstract normative principles invoked in the case law, but at other times reflect additional themes to construct a thicker and more complex account of the wrongs of crimes of sexual violence.

3.2.1 Rape as a Weapon of War

The factual narratives constructed around crimes of sexual violence in the case law build on and expand some of the elements of the rape as a weapon of

168 Schulhofer (n 61), 99.
169 Dowds (n 20), 145. See similarly du Toit (n 21), 80.
170 du Toit (n 21), 65.

war narrative that is reflected in the dominant normative conception of these crimes as forms of physical violence that violate bodily integrity. The characteristics of the rape as a weapon of war discourse that are also embodied in the factual narrative constructed around these crimes relate first to the centrality of physical harm experienced by victims, reinforcing the normative emphasis on the principle of physical integrity. In addition, the factual narratives on the motivations behind sexual violence construct a strategically driven, instrumental account of its commission, which at times also consciously dismisses sex or sexuality as a relevant factor in this context. These elements of the factual recounting of these crimes contribute to an overall theme that frames sexual violence as comparable to, and indistinguishable from, other forms of physical violence that occur during armed conflict.

In line with the emphasis on physical integrity as the main normative principle associated with rape and sexual violence, many of the factual narratives in the case law centre on the physical dimensions of the harm and injury to victims, which in turn feeds into the understanding of sexual violence as a strategic use of physical violence and aggression that is characteristic of the 'rape as a weapon of war' discourse.[171] In the case law of the ad hoc and hybrid tribunals, as well as at the ICC, this has manifested in a number of forms. The physical nature of the harm of sexual violence is commonly highlighted in analyses of its impact on victims' bodies, often in terms of an emphasis on physical pain experienced by victims and, in particular, the medical and psychological impact of such physical violence.

Various chambers highlight the direct physical pain and injury resulting from acts of sexual violence, noting, for instance that the witness 'suffered from physical wounds in several parts of her body',[172] that 'witness BP's knees were covered in blood and she had internal physical pain as a result of the assault'[173] or that a victim of multiple rapes 'suffered terrible pains and came to the clinic for treatment for haemorrhaging.'[174] The impact of sexual violence in physical terms is also stressed in the medical analysis of the injuries inflicted on victims, and the long-term health implications of such injuries. For instance, the Trial Chamber in *Hategekimana* at the ICTR made note of a victim's statement

171 Eriksson Baaz and Stern (n 86), 296.

172 *Prosecutor v. Ratko Mladić*, IT-09-92-T, ICTY, Trial Judgment - – Volume I, 22 November 2017, para 666 [hereafter Mladić Trial Judgment Volume I].

173 *Prosecutor v. Jadranko Prlić et al.*, IT-04-74-T, ICTY, Trial Judgment – Volume II, 29 May 2013, para 260.

174 *Prosecutor v. Duško Tadić*, IT-94-1-T, ICTY, Opinion and Judgment, 7 May 1997, para 175 [hereafter Tadić Trial Judgment].

that 'she suffered infections because of the rapes, and that some of her organs had been damaged, requiring surgery.'[175] In *Kajelijeli*, the Trial Chamber took note of the testimony of a victim of rape who 'has "little wounds everywhere", including on her sexual organ and breasts, stomach pains, and continues to bleed from her sexual organ.'[176] In the *RUF* case at the SCSL, the chamber specifically recalled 'Witness TF1-305, the victim of a violent gang rape, who, as a result of the rape, sustained injuries which left her genitally impaired and incontinent.'[177]

The case law of the ICC has also reflected a particular and methodical emphasis on the physical and medical consequences of sexual violence. In *Ntaganda*, the Trial Chamber recounted the impact of rape on a victim in the following terms:

> When the girl returned to her house, her clothes were soaked in blood, she had difficulty walking, and was unable to speak for a day. The wounds took several months to heal and required surgery years later.[178]

Similarly, in *Bemba* the Trial Chamber highlighted the medical consequences of injuries caused by sexual violence, emphasising the health problems faced by many victims, including injuries to the vagina,[179] back, pelvis, kidneys, and eyes,[180] abdominal pains, problems conceiving,[181] pain in the vagina and lungs,[182] skin disorders, and pelvic pain,[183] high blood pressure, gastric problems, and hypertension.[184]

---

175 *Prosecutor v. Ildephonse Hategekimana*, ICTR-00-55B-T, ICTR, Judgment and Sentence, 6 December 2010, para 155 [hereafter Hategekimana Judgment and Sentence].

176 Kajelijeli Judgment and Sentence (n 115), para 664.

177 *Prosecutor v. Issa Hassan Sesay et al.* (*RUF Case*), SCSL-04-15-T, SCSL, Sentencing Judgment, 8 April 2009, para 132 [hereafter Sesay et al. Sentencing Judgment].

178 Ntaganda Trial Judgment (n 125), para 520.

179 Bemba Trial Judgment (n 124), para 489.

180 *Ibid.*, para 488.

181 *Ibid.*, para 492.

182 *Ibid.*, para 551.

183 *Ibid.*, para 472. See also para 522.

184 *Ibid.*, para 510. For additional examples of where the physical and health consequences of sexual violence are highlighted see Tadić Trial Judgment (n 174), para 470; Mladić Trial Judgment Volume I (n 172), para 666; Kunarac et al. Trial Judgment (n 94), 299 at 1.8, 315 at 6.5; *Prosecutor v. Dragoljub Kunarac et al.*, IT-96-23&IT-96-23/1-A, ICTY, Appeal Judgment, 12 June 2002, para 139; Kvočka et al. Trial Judgment (n 160), para 103; Akayesu Trial Judgment (n 73), para 423; *Prosecutor v. Jean-Paul Akayesu*, ICTR-96-4-T, ICTR, Appeal Judgment, 1 June 2001, footnote 324; Kajelijeli Trial Judgment (n 115), para 655; *Prosecutor v. Issa Hassan Sesay et al.* (*RUF Case*), SCSL-04-15-T, SCSL, Trial Judgment,

While physical injuries and health problems feature most prominently in this discourse on the harms inflicted by sexual violence, the psychological impact of these crimes was also highlighted in a number of cases. The Trial Chamber in *Mucić et al.*, for instance, spelled out its view that:

> rape leaves deep psychological scars on the victim which do not respond to the passage of time as quickly as other forms of physical and mental violence. The applicant also experienced the acute physical pain of forced penetration, which must have left her feeling debased and violated both physically and emotionally.[185]

This recognition of the psychological injury caused by such violence is stressed in several other cases, with a number of chambers noting that victims subsequently experienced mental health problems including PTSD,[186] depression,[187] feeling suicidal or indifferent,[188] insomnia, weeping fits,[189] and nightmares.[190] The psychological injuries inflicted by sexual violence are particularly prominent in the victim testimonies highlighted and quoted directly by the chambers in some cases. For instance, in *Mucić et al.,* the Trial Chamber cited the testimony of a victim of rape, who had become suicidal as a result of her experiences, recounting her statement that 'psychologically and physically I was completely worn out. They kill you psychologically.'[191] In *Ntaganda*, the Trial Chamber also cited the words of a victim who had testified that her experience of rape made her feel 'as if [she] were dead.'[192]

---

2 March 2009, para 1185 [hereafter Sesay et al. Trial Judgment]; *Prosecutor v. Charles Ghankay Taylor*, SCSL-03-01-T, SCSL, Trial Judgment 18 May 2012, para 882 [hereafter Taylor Trial Judgment]; *Procureur c. Al Hassan Ag Abdoul Aziz Ag Mohamed Ag Mahmoud*, ICC-01/12-01/18, ICC, Rectificatif à la Décision relative à la confirmation des charges, 30 September 2019, para 593, 619 [hereafter Al Hassan Confirmation of Charges]; Katanga Trial Judgment (n 122), para 204, 989; Bemba Trial Judgment (n 124), para 498.

185 Mucić et al. Trial Judgment (n 94), para 488.

186 Furundžija Trial Judgment (n 93), para 94; Bemba Trial Judgment (n 124), para 508.

187 Mucić et al. Trial Judgment (n 94), para 964; Bemba Trial Judgment (n 124), para 472, 522.

188 Zelenović Sentencing Judgment (n 132), para 40; Bemba Trial Judgment (n 124), para 508.

189 Furundžija Trial Judgment (n 93), para 94.

190 Mladić Trial Judgment Volume I (n 172), para 663; Bemba Trial Judgment (n 124), para 510. For additional examples of where the psychological consequences of sexual violence are highlighted see *Prosecutor v. Radovan Karadžić*, Trial Judgment – Volume II, IT-95-5/18-T, 24 March 2016, para 1831; Mucić et al. Trial Judgment (n 94), para 495; Al Hassan Confirmation of Charges (n 184), para 597; Bemba Trial Judgment (n 124), para 551.

191 Mucić et al. Trial Judgment (n 94), para 938.

192 Ntaganda Trial Judgment (n 125), para 622.

This discourse around the harms inflicted by crimes of rape and sexual violence, which centralises primarily the physical injuries and medical consequences experienced by victims, alongside some of its destructive psychological effects, also partly feeds into the most characteristic element of the 'rape as a weapon of war' narrative of sexual violence; it contributes to the construction of an understanding of sexual violence as a form of physical violence, like any other, that is not incidental to the conduct of war but is instead driven by the pursuit of military and political goals.[193] As discussed in the previous section, the particular emphasis on the strategic, instrumental dimensions of sexual violence that characterises the broader discourse on conflict-related sexual violence has been underpinned by the wider feminist effort to reframe sexual violence as a public, political issue, rather than a matter of sex and sexuality consigned to the private sphere.[194] This has been achieved by 'establish[ing] the analytical and political connections between violent sexual politics and the processes of military strategy, economic interest and political domination more conventionally placed within the field of high politics.'[195]

In establishing these connections, the rape as a weapon of war discourse centralises an instrumentalist account of sexual violence, which invokes a narrative script of victims that are 'used as tools in a larger ploy to defeat the (collective) enemy [while perpetrators] serve as weapons in the wide arsenal of masculinized military violence.'[196] Identifying sexual violence in this way as rational and intentional, the rape as a weapon of war script in this way positions sexual violence 'as central, rather than tangential, in the practice of war'[197] and therefore as 'structural, persistent and functional.'[198] Importantly, in normative terms, a side effect of this emphasis on sexual violence as being rational and strategic, equivalent to any other form of physical violence in warfare, and emphatically not a form of private, incidental act motivated by sexual desire or pleasure, is to reinforce the normative construction of these crimes as acts primarily of physical violence and brutality through the rejection of that which may also make them distinct.

193 Eriksson Baaz and Stern (n 86), 296.

194 Dolan, Eriksson Baaz and Stern (n 143), 1153.

195 Paul Kirby, 'How is rape a weapon of war? Feminist International Relations, modes of critical explanation and the study of wartime sexual violence', (2012) 19(4) *European Journal of International Relations*, 807.

196 Eriksson Baaz and Stern (n 86), 296.

197 Kirby (n 195), 807.

198 *Ibid.*, 816.

This understanding of the motivations behind sexual violence and the form of its commission was particularly pronounced in the narrative forwarded around these crimes in a number of cases at the SCSL. In relation to crimes of sexual violence in the *RUF* case, the Trial Chamber first noted that 'the specific offences are designed to draw attention to serious crimes that have been historically overlooked and to recognise the particular nature of sexual violence that has been used, often with impunity, as a tactic of war to humiliate, dominate and instil fear in victims, their families and communities during armed conflict.'[199] The Chamber's subsequent analysis of sexual violence as the war crime of terror provides an archetypal example of an account of sexual violence which corresponds to the principal pillars of the dominant discourse on rape as a weapon of war:

> The Chamber observes that sexual violence was rampantly committed against the civilian population in an atmosphere in which violence, oppression and lawlessness prevailed. The Chamber finds that the nature and manner in which the female population was a target of the sexual violence portrays a calculated and concerted pattern on the part of the perpetrators to use sexual violence as a weapon of terror. These fighters employed perverse methods of sexual violence against women and men of all ages ranging from brutal gang rapes, the insertion of various objects into victims' genitalia, the raping of pregnant women and forced sexual intercourse between male and female civilian abductees. [...] The Chamber moreover finds that these acts were not intended merely for personal satisfaction or a means of sexual gratification for the fighter. We opine that the savage nature of such conduct against the most vulnerable members of the society demonstrates that these acts were committed with the specific intent of spreading fear amongst the civilian population as a whole, in order to break the will of the population and ensure their submission to AFRC/RUF control.[200]

In this example, the analysis of sexual violence placed particular emphasis on its instrumentalisation as a 'weapon' to terrorise the civilian population, highlighting particularly brutal acts involving significant extrinsic violence, which, it was emphasised, were committed for strategic reasons beyond personal satisfaction or sexual gratification. The Sentencing Judgment in the

199 Sesay et al. Trial Judgment (n 184), para 156.

200 *Ibid.*, para 1347–1348.

same case reinforced this emphasis on the brutality of the physical violence, using graphic language in recounting how '[g]ruesome acts of sexual violence were perpetrated with the specific intent to terrorise the civilian population, such as the slitting of the private parts of men and women with knifes, and the insertion of a pistol into the vagina of a woman.'[201] The Chamber went on to make clear the centrality of physical violence and aggression for its understanding of the crime by noting that 'that the gravamen of crimes of sexual violence involves physical aggression on the most private and intimate parts of an individual's body. The Chamber found ample evidence of gruesome crimes of sexual violence which were perpetrated exclusively and disproportionately against unknown number of the female population through the territory of Sierra Leone.'[202]

The Trial Chamber in *Ntaganda* at the ICC provided a similar analysis of sexual violence, stressing the strategic objective and aim behind the acts, as well as the 'particularly violent method used' in their commission:

> Regarding acts of sexual violence, the Chamber notes that the unfolding of the operations shows that these acts were, like the acts of killings and other acts of physical violence, a tool used by UPC/FPLC soldiers and commanders alike to achieve their objective to destroy the Lendu community in the localities under assault. The Chamber notes the words pronounced by a UPC/FPLC soldier during a rape and at a moment when many of the victims were raped: he compared the Lendu to non-human elements to be exterminated. It is significant that the UPC/FPLC soldiers killed or attempted to kill many of the civilians they subjected to sexual violence. A survivor compared her experience to dying. This aim of destruction is also evidenced by the particularly violent method used for the rapes committed during the course of the First and Second Operation including the use of sticks to wound victims during the rapes and the fact that UPC/FPLC soldiers forced detained victims to sexually assault each other.[203]

The *Bemba* case reflected a similar emphasis on the instrumental dimensions of sexual violence, stressing that 'the evidence also evinces certain specific motivations and objectives behind the commission of rape. Indeed, some MLC soldiers considered victims to be "war booty" and/or sought to destabilise,

201 Sesay et al. Sentencing Judgment (n 177), para 50.
202 *Ibid.*, para 118. See similarly Taylor Trial Judgment (n 184), para 872.
203 Ntaganda Trial Judgment (n 125), para 805–806.

humiliate, and punish suspected rebels and rebel sympathisers. Such objectives were often realised: rape victims experienced significant medical, psychiatric, psychological, and social consequences.'[204] The Trial Chamber further noted evidence 'that MLC perpetrators targeted their victims in order to self-compensate absent adequate payment and rations from the MLC organization, and/or to destabilise, humiliate, or punish suspected rebels, rebel sympathisers, or those who resisted pillaging and rape.'[205] In her dissenting opinion to the acquittal decision in the *Gbagbo and Blé Goudé* case, Judge Carbuccia not only articulated a similar instrumental understanding of the nature of sexual violence, but also made explicit how this narrative rests on an account of the motivations behind sexual violence that are either not sexual, or go beyond the sexual; Judge Carbuccia stressed that 'sexual violence is not only motivated by sexual desire. It is also a strategy for asserting social control and for humiliating, retaliating against or intimidating victims.'[206]

Taken together, the different dimensions of this normative theme, with its emphasis on physical violence, brutality and bodily harm that is motivated not by sexual gratification but is instead underpinned by the same rationalist, instrumental logic as any other such form of brutality and aggression during war, consolidates the dominant normative framing of sexual violence as a crime of violence and aggression and therefore, at a normative level, invokes a conception of the crime as fundamentally about protecting physical or bodily integrity. In addition, because this instrumental account of conflict-related sexual violence emerged precisely in order to counter its historical trivialisation as distinct from other forms of physical violence due to its association with sex, with the private sphere, and with opportunism, the instrumental or strategic account of sexual violence offered in these cases has come to rely on a logic that either rejects, or requires more than, a sexual motivation behind its commission.

---

204 Bemba Trial Judgment (n 124), para 567. See similarly ICC, *Prosecutor v. Jean-Pierre Bemba Gombo*, ICC-01/05-01/08, ICC, Decision Pursuant to Article 61(7)(a) and (b) of the Rome Statute on the Charges of the Prosecutor Against Jean-Pierre Bemba Gombo, 15 June 2009, para 109, 188.

205 Bemba Trial Judgment (n 124), para 664.

206 *Prosecutor v. Laurent Gbago and Charles Blé Goudé*, ICC-02/11-01/1, ICC, Dissenting Opinion Judge Herrera Carbuccia – Reasons for oral decision of 15 January 2019 on the Requête de la Défense de Laurent Gbagbo afin qu'un jugement d'acquittement portant sur toutes les charges soit prononcé en faveur de Laurent Gbagbo et que sa mise en liberté immédiate soit ordonnée, and on the Blé Goudé Defence no case to answer motion, 16 July 2019, para 438.

In this way, the rape as weapon of war narrative identified in these cases not only centralises physical violence, brutality and bodily harm in its normative construction of the criminalisation of sexual violence, but actively excludes elements from its account that could suggest that sexual violence may also be normatively particular and distinct to other forms of physical violence. The exception to this pattern of equating sexual violence to other forms of physical violence relates to how it is, at the same time, constructed as a unique form of injury in terms of how it impacts on communities and groups.

3.2.2 Harm to the Conjugal Order

In addition to the centrality of physical injury and harm, one of the most pronounced themes that emerges in the case law relates to the construction of sexual violence as a harm or injury directed at and experienced by communities or groups. This takes place most obviously in the context of charges of persecution and genocide, which necessarily require the privileging of group identity through the nature of the required intent, usually ethnicity, as the 'requisite condition of sexual victimization.'[207] Thus, reflecting a common form of reasoning in these contexts, in its analysis of rape as an act constituting persecution, the Appeals Chamber in *Đorđević* concluded that 'Witness K20 was targeted because of her ethnicity and that her rape was carried out with discriminatory intent. In this respect, the Appeals Chamber [...] considers that, even if it were to be assumed that the perpetrators also were motivated by sexual desire when they raped Witness K20, their decision to do so arose out of a will to discriminate against her on the basis of ethnic grounds.'[208]

However, the understanding of sexual violence as a harm or injury directed at and experienced by communities or groups is not exclusive to the intent element of charges of genocide and persecution. It also appears as a common theme in the narratives of harm constructed around crimes of sexual violence more widely, and is the primary narrative through which sexual violence is ultimately constructed as distinct from other forms of physical violence. Thus, in addition to the physical harms inflicted on individual victims of sexual violence discussed in the previous section, this narrative also highlights the impact and injury of sexual violence on the community or group of which the victim is a member.

For instance, the Trial Chamber in *Mucić et al.* considered that 'mass rape was employed during the conflicts in the former Yugoslavia in order to

207 Mibenge (n 7), 62.

208 Đorđević Appeal Judgment (n 94), para 892. See similarly with respect to charges of genocide Akayesu Trial Judgment (n 73), para 731–732.

punish the victims and/or intimidate them or their communities',[209] while in *Ntaganda* the Trial Chamber similarly concluded that victims 'suffered from serious injuries and required medical intervention; and they faced rejection and stigmatisation within their community. [...] by way of these acts, the UPC/FPLC intended at the same time to subject victims to these consequences that would go beyond the sexual violence itself.'[210] Making explicit this understanding of sexual violence as inflicting harm that goes beyond the direct injury to the individual victim, the Trial Chamber in *Karemera et al.* explained that 'these crimes did not only cause serious bodily and mental harm to the women themselves, but also, by extension, to their families and communities.'[211]

The Appeals Chamber in the *Taylor* case spelled this out further by identifying the actual processes through which sexual violence may function to harm victims' families and communities. The Chamber explained that 'sexual violence was deliberately aimed at destroying the traditional family nucleus, thus undermining the cultural values and relationships which held society together.'[212] The *RUF* case at the SCSL went further, providing a more concrete and elaborated account of the processes through which sexual violence may be understood to undermine family and community relationships in this way:

> We note that the physical and psychological pain and fear inflicted on the women not only abused, debased and isolated the individual victim, but deliberately destroyed the existing family nucleus, thus undermining the cultural values and relationships which held the societies together. Victims of sexual violence were ostracised, husbands left their wives, and daughters and young girls were unable to marry within their community. The Chamber finds that sexual violence was intentionally employed by the perpetrators to alienate victims and render apart communities, thus inflicting physical and psychological injury on the civilian population as a whole. [...] The Chamber recalls the testimony of TF1-029 describing the general perception among the rebels that "soldiers who captured

209 Mucić et al. Trial Judgment (n 94), para 448.

210 Ntaganda Trial Judgment (n 125), para 805–806. For similar accounts of sexual violence which emphasise its effects beyond harm to the individual victim, see Sesay et al. Trial Judgment (n 184), para 156, 1351; Sesay et al. Sentencing Judgment (n 177), para 51; Taylor Trial Judgment (n 184), para 873, 876, 2035; *Prosecutor v. Charles Ghankay Taylor*, SCSL-03-01-A, SCSL, Appeal Judgment, 26 September 2013, para 271 [hereafter Taylor Appeal Judgment].

211 *Prosecutor v. Édouard Karemera and Matthieu Ngirumpatse*, ICTR-98-44-T, ICTR, Judgment and Sentence, 2 February 2012, para 1667.

212 Taylor Appeal Judgment (n 210), para 265.

> civilians had a right to rape them and make them their wives." The Chamber considers this statement indicative of the atmosphere of terror and helplessness that the rebel forces created by systematically engaging in sexual violence in order to demonstrate that the communities were unable to protect their own wives, daughters, mothers, and sisters.[213]

These accounts begin to construct an explanation at a more granular level for why acts of sexual violence inflicted on individuals can be understood to harm or cause injury to a group or community. The Trial Chamber in the *RUF* case highlighted how victims of sexual violence were ostracised by their communities, their families, their relationships and marriage prospects destroyed, while the communities themselves experienced terror and helplessness as a result of their inability to protect their female members. Central to, but nevertheless implicit in, this explanation of how sexual violence inflicted on individuals expanded beyond individual harm to cause injury at the level of the community and its structures, is an indication of precisely why sexual violence functioned to produce these effects. In other words, why sexual violence in particular, as opposed to other forms of violence, impacted on social and community structures in this way, such that its infliction on a member of a community radiated outwards to cause harm to the community itself. The Trial Chamber's analysis in the Sentencing Judgment in the same case is illuminating in this respect:

> The Chamber further considers that the crimes of sexual violence were committed in a society where cultural values greatly dictate the sacred manner in which any form of sexual acts take place. Such violations in a society where the sexual lives of women and girls are strictly scrutinised would have an adverse impact on the family as a whole and the society at large. We therefore recall our finding that the brutal manner in which women and girls were debased and molested, in the naked view of their protectors, the fathers, husbands and brothers deliberately destroyed the existing family nucleus, and flagrantly undermined the cultural values and relationships which held the societies together. The Chamber observes that the shame and fear experienced by victims of sexual violence, alienated and tore apart communities, creating vacuums where bonds and relations were initially established. In the Chamber's view the AFRC/RUF inflicted physical and psychological pain and harm

---

213 Sesay et al. Trial Judgment (n 184), para 1349–1350.

> which transcended the individual victim and relatives to an entire society. These acts of sexual violence left several women and girls extremely traumatised and scarred for life, consequently destroying the bearers of future generations. The Chamber infers that crimes of sexual violence further erode the moral fibre of society.[214]

This explanation of why sexual violence caused harm to communities and groups centralised the social and cultural norms attached to sex in this context, emphasising that 'the sexual lives of women and girls are strictly scrutinised'[215] and that cultural values 'dictate the sacred manner in which any form of sexual acts take place.'[216] The Trial Chamber's account of the harm to the community caused by sexual violence in the *RUF* case in this way constructed a narrative of how these social and cultural norms underpinned and provided the conduit through which the sexual violence inflicted on the individual victim, by virtue of being sexualised, was rendered social and communal because of the role of her body and sexuality within that community.

This dimension of the narrative frames sexual violence as destructive because it is targeted at, and causes injury to, what Megan Mackenzie has termed 'the conjugal order', or the institutions and social norms associated with marriage and the family in a given society.[217] Mackenzie explains the logic of this group-based injury account of sexual violence in terms of patriarchal norms and institutions attached to marriage and the family, which position women, their bodies and their sexual lives under the authority of the men in their families and communities, which, in turn, gives meaning to acts of sexual violence not only as a violation of the victim's body, but also as a violation of the norms and structures of the community as a whole.[218] In Mackenzie's view, sexual violence is therefore understood as 'an effective strategy because it causes dis-order by desecrating the authority and property assured to males.'[219]

While not always invoked as directly as in the decisions of the SCSL, this logic underpins the common theme in the case law that constructs sexual violence as a form of violence that, in addition to violating the physical integrity of the individual victim, also harms the communities or groups to which the

---

214 Sesay et al. Sentencing Judgment (n 184), para 133–135.

215 *Ibid.*, para 133.

216 *Ibid.*

217 Megan Mackenzie, 'Securitizing Sex? Towards a Theory of the Utility of Wartime Sexual Violence', (2010) 12(2) *International Feminist Journal of Politics*, 205.

218 *Ibid.*, 203.

219 *Ibid.*, 206.

direct victims belong. This logic, and the understanding of sexual violence as effective 'because it causes dis-order by desecrating the authority and property assured to males'[220] that it relies on, is epitomised in the Trial Chamber's conclusion in the *RUF* case that rebel forces engaged in sexual violence 'in order to demonstrate that the communities were unable to protect their own wives, daughters, mothers, and sisters.'[221]

From a normative perspective, this theme contributes to one element of how crimes of sexual violence are constructed as being distinct from other crimes of physical violence, such as torture. In addition to causing physical harm to the victim, crimes of sexual violence are also understood to inflict harm on the community as a group, by violating its social structures around sex. In this way, this factual narrative suggests an additional dimension to the normative conception of crimes of sexual violence invoked by the explicit statements identifying principles or values attached to them in the case law. This factual narrative carries the implication that part of what is protected by the criminalisation of sexual violence is the conjugal order that gives sexual violence its meaning as an injury to a community or group. In other words, by constructing sexual violence as a crime that inflicts group-based harm that transcends the individual by violating a community's social structures around sex, this theme invokes a normative account of the criminalisation of such acts that positions these social structures as also worthy of criminal protection.

Ultimately, in doing so, this theme functions to reproduce some of the elements of the honour-based conception of the criminalisation of rape and sexual violence. It implies that the violation of social structures that place women's bodies and sexualities under the authority of their families and communities, with the result that the sexual violation of women also violates these structures and causes harm to the 'moral fibre'[222] of the community as a whole, form part of the wrong that underlies the criminalisation of sexual violence. In other words, instead of directly invoking an account of the criminalisation of sexual violence as rooted in the violation of a woman's honour, by stressing the violation of and harm to social structures that do valorise women's sexual purity in this way, this theme indirectly continues to invoke a normative account of the crime that rests partly on the same symbolic order, only in this case the effects of the violation of honour are constructed from the perspective of their impact on the social group, rather than the victim herself. The symbolic order on which this understanding of the harms inflicted by crimes of

220 *Ibid.*

221 Sesay et al. Trial Judgment (n 184), para 1349–1350.

222 Sesay et al. Sentencing Judgment (n 177), para 133–135.

sexual violence rests is further reinforced through an emphasis on how victims experience shame and stigma as a result of sexual violence.

3.2.3 Shame and Stigma

While the underlying logic of the group-based harm account of sexual violence is not articulated as explicitly in the case law of other courts and tribunals as in the *RUF* case at the SCSL, this narrative nevertheless features implicitly and underpins much of the analysis of the harms inflicted by sexual violence, even at the level of individual victims. This takes place through a significant emphasis on what Karen Engle has described as 'the socially corrosive operation of shame'[223] being invoked as an inherent effect of crimes of sexual violence.

Shame and stigma are emphasised in several different contexts in the case law addressing sexual violence. Numerous decisions highlight the testimony of victims who described the place of shame in their experience of sexual victimisation. For instance, in *Katanga* at the ICC, the Trial Chamber related the testimony of a victim who stated that 'out of shame she systematically avoided any conversation on the attack; she wished never to return to her village; her father had asked her never to bring up what had happened; and she put great effort into erasing these painful events from her memory.'[224] The Trial Chamber in *Bemba* similarly described how, following her rape, a victim 'was ashamed and had various medical problems.'[225] In *Mucić et al.,* the Trial Chamber recalled the words of a victim describing the effect of the rape she suffered: 'he trampled on my pride and I will never be able to be the woman that I was.'[226]

The operation of shame also emerges in how the responses to victims of sexual violence by families and communities are recounted, with a significant emphasis on the social stigmatisation and rejection experienced by victims of sexual violence in the case law of the ICC and SCSL in particular. The Trial Chamber in *Katanga* emphasised that victims of sexual violence 'were severely affected both physically and mentally by this experience and that they were rejected by their community.'[227] The Chamber expanded on this analysis in the Reparations Order, where it stated that it 'considers the physical pain from the act of rape to be compounded by psychological pain, which cannot be disregarded and which has repercussions on the life of the victim, but also on

---

223 Engle (n 1), 65.

224 Ntaganda Trial Judgment (n 125), para 338.

225 Bemba Trial Judgment (n 124), para 522.

226 Mucić et al. Trial Judgment (n 94), para 1262.

227 Katanga Trial Judgment (n 122), para 959.

the lives of the victim's nearest and dearest',[228] going on to recall that '"subsequently victims of sexual violence were often rejected by their community, which compounded the harm they suffered."'[229]

In *Bemba*, the Trial Chamber repeatedly noted that a victim was 'socially stigmatised, as people pointed and made fun of her',[230] another 'was socially excluded by other girls her age',[231] while another testified that 'she felt like she was no longer treated as a human being and was called "Banyamulengué wife"; such stigmatisation in her community left her unemployed and unable to provide for her children.'[232] While men and boys' experiences of sexual violence have not formed a prominent part of the discourse emerging from the practice of international criminal justice to date, the Chamber in *Bemba* identified how shame and social stigmatisation also emerge as distinct harms attached to sexual victimisation for male victims in recounting how, for a male victim, 'people in his community disrespected him. He considered himself a "dead man".'[233]

The case law of the SCSL reflects the same emphasis on stigma for victims of sexual violence, with the Trial Chamber in the *Taylor* case explaining that 'part of the terror experienced by victims included the fear of being stigmatised as victims of rape or other sexual violence, and the children conceived through such violence were often rejected by family and society.'[234] The Trial Chamber in the *RUF* case reflected a particular sensitivity to this social dimension of the harm inflicted by sexual violence, recalling:

> the demeanour and testimonies of various victims of sexual violence who expressed deep shame and stigma which they feel and face to date, several years after the abuse. [...] As we have found, the victims of sexual violence continue to live their lives in isolation, ostracised from their communities and families, unable to be reintegrated and reunited with their families and / or in their communities. Many of these victims of sexual

228 ICC, *Prosecutor v. Germain Katanga*, ICC-01/04-01/07, ICC, Order for Reparations pursuant to Article 75 of the Statute, 24 March 2017, para 146.

229 *Ibid.*

230 Bemba Trial Judgment (n 124), para 488.

231 *Ibid.*, para 489.

232 *Ibid.*, para 551.

233 *Ibid.*, para 494. For further examples of analysis of the impact of social stigma on victims of sexual violence in the case law see Bemba Trial Judgment (n 124), footnote 1761 at 281, para 492, 567; Katanga Trial Judgment (n 122), para 959; Ntaganda Trial Judgment (n 125), para 806; Al Hassan Confirmation of Charges (n 184), para 593, 701.

234 Taylor Trial Judgment (n 184), para 873.

> violence were ostracised or abandoned by their husbands, and daughters and young girls were unable to marry within their community.[235]

At times, the particular social structures underpinning this stigmatisation are foregrounded, making explicit how, similar to the group-based harm account of sexual violence, shame and stigmatisation resulting from sexual violence rests on a conjugal order that valorises female chastity, making sexual violation therefore shameful and deserving of stigmatisation. For instance, highlighting the relevance of the social and cultural conditions that give meaning to sexual violence in these terms, the Trial Chamber in *Mucić et al.* noted that 'the psychological suffering of persons upon whom rape is inflicted may be exacerbated by social and cultural conditions and can be particularly acute and long lasting.'[236] More explicitly identifying the relevance of the conjugal order in underpinning the socially destructive dimensions of sexual violence, the Trial Chamber in *Bemba* explained that 'revealing a Muslim girl's alleged rape would prevent her from being able to find a husband.'[237]

Eithne Dowds has explained how the shame and stigma associated with sexual violence are in this way again tied up with the notions of honour or virtue attached to female chastity, meaning therefore that in 'heavily patriarchal societies where women's bodies might carry symbolic meaning for a society or family, such as honour, [if] a woman in the community is raped she may feel the immediate violation as well as the additional layers of harm that derive from the societal conception of sex, sexuality and honour, which may induce shame and stigma.'[238] From this perspective, the shame and stigma attached to sexual victimisation is a logical result of and springs from the patriarchal understanding of sexual violence as an injury to the victim's and her community's honour, making sexual violation shameful and therefore worthy of stigmatisation. These same social structures underpin the nature of the shame and stigma experienced by male victims of sexual violence, where gendered norms linking masculinity with power and heteronormativity attribute meaning to the sexual violation of men therefore as an act of emasculation. Dubravka Žarkov

---

235 Sesay et al. Sentencing Judgment (n 177), para 132. See similarly Sesay et al. Trial Judgment (n 184), footnote 2514 at 404, para 1474; Sesay et al. Sentencing Judgment (n 177), para 51; *Prosecutor v. Alex Tamba Brima et al.* (*AFRC Case*), SCSL-04-16-T, SCSL, Sentencing Judgment, 19 July 2007, para 45; Taylor Trial Judgment (n 184), para 882; *Prosecutor v. Charles Ghankay Taylor*, SCSL-03-01-T, SCSL, Sentencing Judgment, 30 May 2012, para 41; Taylor Appeal Judgment (n 210), para 265, 698.

236 Mucić et al. Trial Judgment (n 94), para 495.

237 Bemba Trial Judgment (n 124), para 512.

238 Dowds (n 20), 145.

explains how, within this symbolic order, 'disempowered and homosexualized, the raped man loses the prerogatives of dominant modern masculinity, and consequently ceases to be a man.'[239] Recognising this underlying logic reveals how the emphasis on shame and stigma in framing the harms inflicted by sexual violence on victims of both genders 'thrives on narratives that make certain acts or experiences shameful.'[240]

While this underlying logic is implicit in the recounting of the shame experienced by victims and their rejection or stigmatisation by communities, in some decisions, the echoes of the crime against honour conception of sexual violence that the shame and stigma theme in this way invokes are particularly pronounced. For instance, the Trial Chamber in *Ntaganda* quoted the testimony of a witness who explained that '[y]ou may also want to understand that in our culture, and I'm telling you this, if my wife is raped, I no longer feel like a man and I can no longer stand tall in front of anybody because I am covered in shame.'[241] This testimony underscores how the logic of shame is deeply rooted in the patriarchal notion of honour. In this testimony, shame is inflicted not on the direct victim of sexual violence, but on her husband, whose masculinity is injured through the violation of his wife's honour, surfacing and making evident the nature of the social order from which the association of shame with sexual violence emerges.

This theme appears in perhaps its starkest form in the *Stakić* case at the ICTY, where the Trial Chamber asserted that '[f]or a woman, rape is by far the ultimate offense, sometimes even worse than death because it brings shame on her.'[242] This conception of rape was also later repeated and endorsed by the Trial Chamber in *Brđanin*.[243] By asserting that shame inherently attaches to sexual victimisation, the statement in *Stakić* not only reproduces the underlying logic of the honour-based conception of sexual violence, but goes further, to assert that, for women, such violation constitutes the ultimate offence, being at times worse than death, because it 'brings shame'[244] on them. The implication such a statement carries is that, for women, their honour may be more valuable than life itself.

239 Dubravka Žarkov, 'Sexual Violence Against Men in Contemporary Warfare' in Indira Rosenthal et al. (eds), *Gender and International Criminal Law* (Oxford University Press 2022), 114.

240 Engle (n 1), 171.

241 Ntaganda Trial Judgment (n 125), para 293.

242 Stakić Trial Judgment (n 94), para 803.

243 Brđanin Trial Judgment (n 94), para 1009.

244 Stakić Trial Judgment (n 94), para 803. This assertion was also endorsed by the Trial Chamber in *Brđanin*. See Brđanin Trial Judgment (n 94), para 1009.

In other words, the statement in *Stakić*, which was also reproduced in *Brđanin*, implies not only that the wrong of rape is rooted in the violation of the victim's honour, but that women's fundamental value ultimately rests in their honour i.e. in their chastity and their sexual behaviour, rather than in their personhood. In this way, the emphasis on shame in *Stakić*, and the framing of rape as the ultimate crime for women, worse than death, not only invokes a deeply patriarchal account of the criminalisation of sexual violence, but also one that ultimately negates female subjectivity by expressly positioning women's sexual purity above their lives and their personhood. In this way, while the Trial Chamber's analysis of rape in *Stakić* represents a particularly drastic example of this type of reasoning, the centrality of shame and stigma in the discourse constructed around the harms of sexual violence also invokes a normative account of its criminalisation that reproduces elements of the underlying logic of the historical conception of these crimes as worthy of shame and stigma because they constitute crimes against sexual purity.

3.2.4 Virginity

This implicit reproduction of an honour-based conception of the wrong of rape and sexual violence is given further prominence in the numerous references to the 'virginity' of victims of sexual violence, in particular in the case law of the ICTY, ICTR, and SCSL. For instance, the Trial Chamber in the *AFRC* case at the SCSL displayed a particular concern with the 'virgin' status of some victims prior to their sexual violation, noting with respect to two different victims that 'prior to this incident, the witness was a virgin'[245] or that 'prior to this incident, her daughter was a virgin.'[246] The Trial Chamber in the *Taylor* case used the same language in recounting that 'one woman later told Bull that the AFRC/RUF man who had selected her had taken her virginity and used her as a wife'[247] and that another witness had 'told the Court that she herself was a virgin and "had not yet begun her menses" at the time of capture.'[248]

At the ICTY, the Trial Chamber in *Prlić et al.* similarly noted that a victim of rape 'was a virgin and was bleeding during the intercourse',[249] later stressing that 'Witness DG, who was a virgin – which the perpetrators realised – was forced into successive sexual relations with three HVO members at her

245 Brima et al. Trial Judgment (n 133), para 1153.
246 *Ibid.*, para 1036.
247 Taylor Trial Judgment (n 184), para 1714.
248 *Ibid.*, para 837.
249 Prlić et al. Trial Judgment Volume III (n 94), para 402.

home.'[250] In *Kunarac et al.*, the Trial Chamber recounted an act of rape in the following terms:

> FWS-191 was assigned to Kunarac, he ordered her to undress and he tried to rape her while his bayonet was placed on the table. Kunarac did not entirely succeed penetrating FWS-191 because, as FWS-191 was still a virgin, she was rigid with fear. He succeeded in taking away her virginity the next day.[251]

The same approach is also evident at the ICTR, where the Trial Chamber in *Hategekimana* recounted that 'the soldiers took turns raping each of the girls, some of whom were virgins before that night'[252] while in *Nizeyimana* and *Muhimana* respectively, the Trial Chambers similarly stressed that a victim 'was a virgin prior to the rapes'[253] and recounted the evidence of a witness who testified that 'when the Accused raped her, she was fifteen years old and a virgin.'[254]

Stressing that a victim of sexual violence was a 'virgin' in recounting these crimes carries the implication that rape when inflicted on a virgin is somehow different, or worse, than rape inflicted on a person who is not considered to be a virgin. This was in fact made explicit in *Muvunyi*, where the indictment listed 'rape of virgin girls', alongside gang rape, multiple rape and rape in front of family members, as aggravating circumstances for sexual violence.[255] Highlighting the 'virgin' status of victims of sexual violence in this way unambiguously invokes a normative understanding of sexual violation that is tied to social structures that valorise female chastity because of how the institution of virginity is a patriarchal normative and social construct, which 'by any material reckoning, [...] does not exist.'[256]

The institution of virginity is rooted in the sexual morality of a number of religions and is deeply gendered to the extent that it has been termed 'a vehicle of misogyny'[257] and described explicitly as 'a social, cultural and religious

250 *Ibid.*, para 767.
251 Kunarac et al. n (94), para 724.
252 Hategekimana Judgment and Sentence (n 175), para 150.
253 *Prosecutor v. Ildéphonse Nizeyimana*, ICTR-2000-55C-T, ICTR, Judgment and Sentence, 19 June 2012, para 65.
254 Muhimana Judgment and Sentence (n 94), para 285.
255 Muvunyi Judgment and Sentence (n 114), para 378.
256 Hanne Blank, *Virgin: The Untouched History* (Bloomsbury 2008), 13.
257 Kathryn Schwarz, 'The Wrong Question: Thinking Through Virginity', (2002) 13(2) *Differences: A Journal of Feminist Cultural Studies*, 25.

construct – one that reflects gender discrimination against women and girls'[258] by the World Health Organisation. In patriarchal societies, virginity and its protection is tied to the object of controlling women's sexual-reproductive function in order to regulate lines of kinship.[259] On this view, female premarital virginity 'ensures that a woman's first child is of guaranteed paternity',[260] with the result that virginity therefore has a central role in determining a woman's marital market value.[261] Historically, virginity has for this reason been an exclusively, and tends to remain predominantly, a female attribute. As noted by Hanne Blank, 'virginity has never mattered in regard to the way men are valued, or whether they were considered fit to marry or, indeed, to be permitted to survive. […] virgins are, and always have been, almost uniformly female. […] Even today, "virgin" tends to mean female unless stated otherwise.'[262] The notion of virginity is in this way fundamentally and intrinsically rooted in structures intended to ensure control over women's sexuality as a means of regulating lines of descent and transfer and constitutes a core element of patriarchal restrictions on women, their bodies and their sexual lives.[263] It is through this role that virginity has come to be idealised as a symbol of a woman's virtue, moral purity and respectability i.e. to represent her 'honour' along with that of her husband, family and community.[264] From a normative perspective, the framing of crimes of rape in terms of the victims' virginity in this way explicitly constructs an account of the harm and injury inflicted on them as attaching precisely to the violation of their sexual purity, in other words, to the violation of their market value as as-yet-unused sexual-reproductive bodies.[265]

---

258 WHO, 'United Nations agencies call for ban on virginity testing', 17 October 2018 [available at https://www.who.int/news/item/17-10-2018-united-nations-agencies-call-for-ban-on-virginity-testing – accessed 11 February 2022]. See also WHO, OHCHR and UN Women, *Eliminating Virginity Testing: An Interagency Statement*, 2018 [available at https://apps.who.int/iris/bitstream/handle/10665/275451/WHO-RHR-18.15-eng.pdf?ua=1 – accessed 11 February 2022].

259 Harry T. Reis and Susan Sprecher, *Encyclopedia of Human Relationships* (SAGE 2009), 1673. See also Blank (n 253), 44–45.

260 Blank (n 256), 47.

261 Bonnie MacLachlan, 'Introduction' in Judith Fletcher and Bonnie MacLachlan (eds), *Virginity Revisited: Configurations of the Unpossessed Body* (University of Toronto Press 2007), 3.

262 Blank (n 256), 25.

263 Jean-Jacques Amy, 'Certificates of virginity and reconstruction of the hymen', (2008) 13(2) *European Journal of Contraception & Reproductive Health Care*, 111; Vimbai Sharon Matswetu and Deevia Bhana, 'Humhandara and hujaya: Virginity, Culture, and Gender Inequalities Among Adolescents in Zimbabwe', (2018) 8(2) *SAGE Open*, 2.

264 Matswetu and Bhana (n 263), 2.

265 Blank (n 256), 287.

It is important to note that this analysis of the normative implications of the invocation of virginity in the discourse on crimes of rape and sexual violence in the case law does not seek to imply that the notion of virginity ought to be entirely irrelevant to a court's analysis of sexual violence. Social and cultural understandings of sex and sexuality shape how individuals understand their own sexual identity which, in turn, affects how victims experience and understand such crimes and the harms that they cause.[266] As a result, in social contexts where virginity holds significant meaning, its 'loss' may be a significant factor in victims' experience of the harm and injury resulting from sexual violation. At the same time, by repeatedly noting the victims' 'loss of virginity', without contextualising the meaning attached to virginity for the victim in question, and the nature of the harm that individual therefore experienced as a result of the loss of this status, the discourse around crimes of rape and sexual violence function to construct this loss of sexual purity as a given and immutable harm for victims who have not previously experienced sex.

By contrast, a small number of cases address virginity in a way that does not carry these discursive implications because of how they provide a fuller contextualisation of the significance of virginity for the victims of sexual violence themselves. For example, in *Muvunyi,* testimony recounted by the Trial Chamber of a victim of rape who had been a nun underscores the significance of explaining why virginity may be understood to be relevant in an analysis of crimes of sexual violence. The Trial Chamber in *Muvunyi* noted that:

> AFV testified that at the time of the events she was a nun and a virgin and had never had sexual intercourse before. Witness AFV added that she was no longer a nun because she could not continue to be one after losing her virginity; she said that the soldiers had deprived her of that status.[267]

In this case, the Trial Chamber contextualised the issue of the victim's virginity, illustrating how the social, cultural and, in this case, religious norms governing the victim's occupation shaped her experience of sexual violence, giving specific meaning to the significance of virginity in her experience of sexual violation and the harm its 'loss' inflicted on her as a nun. While in this example the significance of virginity was tied very specifically to the victim's occupation, other cases invoke virginity in a way that also explains its wider relevance for the harms experienced by victims of sexual violence in particular social

266 Dowds (n 20), 145.

267 Muvunyi Judgment and Sentence (n 114), para 385.

and cultural contexts. For example, while addressed in general terms, the Trial Chamber in *Bemba* qualified its invocation of the relevance of virginity by explaining that 'some of the victims lost their virginity as a result of their rape, a harm that cannot be underestimated, particularly in the cultural context in which the crimes were committed.'[268] *Case 002/02* at the ECCC also provided a more expansive contextualisation of the meaning attached to virginity in its account of the harm inflicted on victims by its loss. In the context of its analysis of forced sexual intercourse inflicted on victims of forced marriages, the Trial Chamber in *Case 002/02* explained that:

> Forced sexual intercourse has serious and long-lasting traumatising effects on the victims. […] The loss of virginity featured prominently in the minds of many victims. In the Cambodian context, "daughters" are regarded as important property of the parents and women should be pure and keep their virginity until marriage. Considered in this cultural and social context, the loss of virginity in Cambodian women resulted in additional suffering to the victims, in some cases exacerbated by unwanted pregnancies.[269]

In articulating the relevance of virginity for the nature of the harm inflicted on victims of rape in the context of Cambodian culture, referring to victims' own interpretations of their experiences, the Chamber in *Case 002/02* framed the harm inflicted by sexual violation, and the relevance of the notion of virginity to this, in terms of its meaning for the victims as individuals, within the social and cultural context in which their sexual identities had been shaped. Without such contextualisation, the many other allusions to virginity contained in the case law of these tribunals,[270] which, as discussed above, results in a framing of crimes of sexual violence as violations of women's bodies as sexual-reproductive commodities, contributes to the construction of a normative discourse around such crimes which not only echoes, but loudly proclaims many of the most archaic dimensions of the normative conception of sexual violence as a crime against honour.

268 *Prosecutor v. Jean-Pierre Bemba Gombo*, ICC-01/05-01/08, ICC, Judgment pursuant to Article 76 of the Statute, 21 June 2016, para 38.

269 Nuon Chea and Khieu Samphan Trial Judgment (n 94), para 3684–3685.

270 With the notable exception of the ICC.

3.2.5 'The Sexual' is Private

Piecing together these different themes in the discourse around rape and sexual violence carries a number of implications for the normative conception of crimes of sexual violence constructed in the case law. At one level, the narrative constructed around sexual violence strongly reflects many of the characteristics of the rape as a weapon of war discourse, with its emphasis on rational, strategically driven physical violence and brutality, and its deliberate and explicit exclusion of a notion of 'the sexual' for understanding this form of violence.[271] Within this narrative, crimes of sexual violence are constructed primarily as violations of physical integrity, and the harm inflicted on victims is constructed in physical terms, through an emphasis on the degree of extrinsic physical brutality involved in the acts, the physical injuries inflicted on victims and the medical problems they later experienced as a result. From a normative perspective, crimes of sexual violence are on this account normatively similar to other crimes of physical violence causing bodily injury which are employed as a means of achieving political or military goals.

At the same time, the construction of crimes of sexual violence as causing harm or injury to communities or groups expands on this account, giving meaning to their categorisation as distinctly sexualised crimes by situating them within the framework of a group's conjugal order i.e. within the social, cultural and religious structures that govern sex and sexuality within a particular social group. This theme is further reinforced in how the non-physical harms inflicted on individual victims are recounted through narratives that similarly rely on a logic that constructs sexual violence as a violation of the conjugal order, in the form of an emphasis on the shame and stigma experienced by victims, and the loss of their virginity in some cases.

In this way, these themes not only implicitly invoke the honour-based conception of the criminalisation of sexual violence because of how they reproduce the underlying logic of social structures that valorise virginity and construct shame and stigma as inherent and immutable effects of sexual violation, they also serve to distinguish crimes of sexual violence from other crimes of physical violence on the same basis. In other words, according to the discourse constructed around these crimes in the case law, crimes of sexual violence are normatively distinct from other crimes of physical violence because they are directed at and violate a group's conjugal order, resulting in harm to the social fabric of the community itself as well as the social harms of shame and stigma experienced by the individual victim.

---

271 Dolan, Eriksson Baaz and Maria Stern (n 143), 1157–1158.

In this way, this discourse serves to magnify a wider and well-established structural feminist critique of international criminal law, which problematises the implications of the legal definitions of international crimes, in particular genocide and crimes against humanity, for reinforcing a gendered 'communal narrative of pain.'[272] On this view, acts of sexual violence inflicted on women are constructed inherently as crimes against a collectivity, since they require the targeting of a community through the commission of an individual act of sexual violence.[273] In her early analysis of the *Akayesu* case's treatment of rape as genocide, Hilary Charlesworth noted that this structural feature of international crimes, in this case genocide, carries the implication that 'rape is wrong, not because it is a crime of violence against women and a manifestation of male dominance, but because it is an assault on a community defined only by its racial, religious, national or ethnic composition. In this account, the violation of a woman's body is secondary to the humiliation of the group.'[274] This critique has highlighted how the focus on group-based harm inheres in the very legal structure of international crimes, with the result that the criminalisation of sexual violence under international law offers a 'far from individualized construction'[275] of the harm and injury of such acts.

The discourse on crimes of rape and sexual violence in the case law, in which sexual violence is constructed as distinct from other forms of physical violence because it targets and injures the social structures around sex and sexuality within a community, in this way serves to exacerbate this critique and exposes its relevance at a normative level, beyond the legal structure of crimes specifically involving the targeting of ethnic or racial groups. It does so by centralising 'the collective and its rules'[276] in how crimes of sexual violence are constructed as being distinct from other crimes of physical violence. In other words, in how these crimes are ultimately constructed as being 'sexual'. This reveals how the feminist critique of the definitions of the crimes of genocide and crimes against humanity for offering a 'far from individualized construction'[277] of sexual violence also holds true at a more fundamental level, in terms of how the narratives of harm in the case law construct an account of sexual violence in which this collective element inheres in the very nature of sexual violence as a distinctly sexualised form of violence.

272 Buss (n 3), 146.
273 *Ibid.*, 150.
274 Charlesworth (n 38), 387.
275 Mibenge (n 7), 70.
276 Kirby (n 195), 813.
277 Mibenge (n 7), 70.

In this way, according to the discourse around crimes of sexual violence in the case law, what is different about sexual violence as a specifically sexualised form of violence, distinct from other forms of physical violence causing bodily injury, is that it also affects the norms governing sex and sexuality within a particular community. On this account, this discourse distinguishes crimes of sexual violence from other crimes of physical violence almost exclusively in how they are understood to target and violate a group's conjugal order, in this way harming the social fabric of a community and inflicting shame and stigma on the victim. Put simply, this discourse centralises the injury to a group's social structures around sex and sexuality in how it constructs what is understood to be 'sexual' about crimes of sexual violence.

The normative implications of this relate to how the discourse therefore operates to construct an account of the sexual dimensions of sexual violence that is exclusively 'social.' On the one hand, sexual violence is constructed as being 'sexual' in how it causes harm directly to groups by acting upon their social structures around sex. On the other hand, at the level of the individual victim, sexual violence is constructed as being 'sexual', and therefore distinct from other forms of physical violence, in how the victim experiences shame, stigma and rejection, which similarly derives from the social structures that designate certain acts to be shameful or to elicit stigma from others. Thus, while the harms of shame and stigma are inflicted on and are experienced by the individual, they are nevertheless rooted in and emanate from the violation of the norms of the social group of which the victim is a member, and the group's own response to this. Precisely this dynamic has led Karen Engle to conclude that the treatment of sexual violence as genocide at the ICTR 'essentially placed the blame for the genocide (or at least for the role of rape and sexual violence in it) on the very group that was the target of it'[278] because the shame, stigma and ostracisation inflicted on victims of sexual violence derive from the community itself.

This reveals how the case law constructs an account of crimes of sexual violence in which the 'sexual' nature of those crimes is understood almost exclusively in terms of their social dimensions i.e. in terms of their impact on social and cultural norms governing sexuality, resulting in shame and stigma inflicted on victims by their own communities and harm to the social fabric of the community itself. In this way, the individualised analysis of harm resulting from crimes of sexual violence takes the form of an emphasis on the physical – on brutality, bodily injury and the long-term health implications of sexual

278 Engle (n 1), 112.

violation – while how these crimes are constructed as being sexual, and the implications in terms of the harm and injury inflicted by specifically sexualised crimes, emerges exclusively in terms of the violation of the community or group's social structures around sex and sexuality.[279]

From this perspective, beyond the violation of the group's norms around sex, and the shame and stigma resulting from this, the discourse around crimes of sexual violence is almost silent on whether and how such crimes may inflict harm on individual victims specifically as sexual, not just physical, violence. In other words, what remains almost entirely unaddressed in the case law is what it may mean for victims, as individuals, that the crimes inflicted on them were sexualised, beyond the secondary victimisation they may experience in how their community responds to their sexual violation.

The overwhelming absence of the victim's perspective on the sexualised dimensions of sexual violence at the individual level is significant for the normative conception of crimes of sexual violence invoked by the case law because of what it implies about which dimensions of sexual violence are understood to constitute a form of 'public' violence, and to therefore be of relevance to international criminal law. Problematising the liberal distinction between the public and private spheres to reveal how this dichotomy functions to structure the public sphere as a masculine political space, while the private sphere remains feminine and apolitical, has been central to feminist efforts to combat violence against women, and sexual violence in particular. Feminists have argued that one of the effects of distinguishing between public and private spheres has been to render violence against women as confined to this private, apolitical sphere, outside of the realm of political concern or state intervention.[280]

Precisely the feminist aim of overcoming this dichotomy and making sexual violence a matter of public concern is partly what has underpinned the shift towards centralising the 'rape as a weapon of war' narrative, which constructs sexual violence as a public form of physical violence and aggression used for

279 For more on this argument see Ciara Laverty, 'What is Sexual about Sexual Violence? Narratives from International Criminal Law', (2023) 21(2) *Journal of International Criminal Justice*, 383–404.

280 Harriet Gray, Maria Stern and Chris Dolan, 'Torture and sexual violence in war and conflict: The unmaking and remaking of subjects of violence', (2020) 46(2) *Review of International Studies*, 207; Diane Otto, 'Feminist Approaches to International Law' in Anne Orford and Florian Hoffman (eds), *The Oxford Handbook of the Theory of International Law* (2016 Oxford University Press), 494; Cecily Romay, 'Women as Aliens: A Feminist Critique of the Public/Private Distinction in International Human Rights Law', (1993) 6 *Harvard Human Rights Journal*, 87–125.

political and strategic ends during conflict, rather than an inevitable 'by product' of war.[281] As discussed in the previous section of this chapter, an important component of this shift has taken the form of a deliberate effort to 'move away from sexualised framings [because of] a concern that such framings associate the crime with sexual desire and lust.'[282] In this way, the element of the 'rape as a weapon of war' discourse that emphasises that 'rape is not about sex but about violence'[283] is partly intended to contribute to overturning its framing as 'an albeit terrible personalised, private sexual act'[284] and, in doing so, to situate it firmly in the public, political sphere.[285]

From this perspective, the construction of crimes of sexual violence as distinct from other crimes of physical violence exclusively in how they impact upon social and cultural norms around sex and sexuality, causing harm to the social group as a collectivity and shame and stigma for the victim, carries the implication that the sexual dimension of these crimes only matters when they are constructed as 'public' in some way, i.e. in these cases, that they engage and injure a group's social and cultural norms around sex and sexuality. This is in turn reinforced by how the harm to the individual victim is constructed primarily in physical, bodily terms, distinguished only from other forms of physical harm in how it attracts a particular type of socialised harm from the victim's own community, in the form of shame and stigmatisation. According to this discourse, 'the sexual' in sexual violence is located in the public sphere because the harm it inflicts as a distinctly sexualised form of violence is ultimately social, in its impact on groups and in the nature of how it impacts on individuals.

Ultimately, what this means is that the sexualised nature of these crimes, outside of their 'public' dimensions in how they operate through and impact on the norms of social groups, is overwhelmingly absent from this discourse. Importantly, the narratives contained in the case law are therefore almost entirely silent on what it might mean for a victim for violence inflicted on them to be sexualised in terms of their experience as an individual, not only in how their community subsequently responds to them, or in how sexual violence inflicts physical or mental injury in the same way as other forms of physical violence. Only two minor allusions to harms of this nature have taken

281 Kirby (n 195), 799–800.
282 Dowds (n 20), 144.
283 See Dowds (n 20), 144.
284 Maria Eriksson Baaz and Maria Stern, *Sexual Violence as a Weapon of War? Perceptions, Prescriptions, Problems in the Congo and Beyond* (2013 Zed Books), 56–57.
285 Kirby (n 195), 809.

place in the case law analysed, with the Trial Chamber in *Ntaganda* referring to an expert witness' testimony on reactions to experiencing sexual violence as including 'issues with sexuality, for example engaging in marital relations with a spouse',[286] while a victim in *Bemba* was described as being 'reluctant to engage in any sexual relationship'[287] after experiencing rape. Seen from this perspective, the discourse constructed in the case law, with these two minor exceptions, invokes a normative account of crimes of sexual violence in which the sexual dimension of the harm inflicted on individuals by sexual violation remains confined to the 'private' sphere, beyond the concern of international criminal law.

In this way, this discourse ultimately excludes the victim's own sense of sexual subjectivity, and the impact of sexual violence on it, from the normative account of crimes of sexual violence constructed in these decisions. In general terms, sexual subjectivity has been defined as 'a person's sense of herself as a sexual being, combined with a feeling of agency and the ability to identify one's own desires.'[288] Linda Martín Alcoff has developed this concept of sexual subjectivity in the context of her analysis of how to adequately capture the harm of sexual violation. She argues that sexual subjectivity encompasses the capacity for having sexual agency, which captures but also goes beyond notions of 'consent, desire, the capacity for pleasure, or will',[289] and forms part of individuals' 'self-making capacities.'[290] In Alcoff's view, sexual subjectivity in this sense involves 'more than our arousal patterns and our conduct or sexual choices. It also includes a complex constellation of beliefs, perceptions, and emotions that inform our intrapsychic sexual scripts and affect our very capacity for sexual agency.'[291]

This understanding of sexual subjectivity also draws on Ann Cahill's philosophical scholarship on rape. In responding to the wider feminist debate on whether rape ought to be approached conceptually as sex or as violence, she centralises the question of the victim's subjectivity in arguing that '[t]he act of rape is a distinctly sexual attack on the possibility of embodied subjectivity. It is an act that at least temporarily denies the (bodily, and sexually differentiated)

286 *Prosecutor v. Bosco Ntaganda*, ICC-01/04-02/06, ICC, Sentencing Judgment, 7 November 2019, para 106 [hereafter Ntaganda Sentencing Judgment].

287 Bemba Trial Judgment (n 124), para 508.

288 Rebecca F. Plante, 'In Search of Sexual Subjectivities: Exploring the Sociological Construction of Sexual Selves' in Michael Kimmel (ed), *The Sexual Self: The Construction of Sexual Scripts* (Vanderbilt University Press 2007), 32.

289 Linda Martín Alcoff, *Rape and Resistance* (Polity 2018), 111.

290 *Ibid.*

291 *Ibid.*

agency of the victim and that almost certainly involves a transformation of the victim's subjectivity.'[292] For this reason, Cahill characterises rape as an act of violence that is nevertheless 'indelibly marked by the presence of sexuality',[293] the nature of which is what distinguishes rape from other acts of violence. In more concrete terms, then, Linda Martín Alcoff articulates the relevance of this understanding of the violation of sexual subjectivity involved in sexual violence, and how this therefore distinguishes sexual from other forms of violence, in how she outlines the consequences of such violations for victims in 'the way it touches our sex lives, our capacity for pleasure, our ability to move about in the world and to trust others, our ability to trust our judgment and responses, and, thus, our relationship to our selves.'[294] It is ultimately this perspective, reflecting a recognition of the harm or injury caused by sexual violence as a distinctly sexualised form of violence to the individual victim and their sexual subjectivity, that is almost entirely absent from the discourse on crimes of rape and sexual violence in these decisions.

It is important to note that relatively little attention has been paid in general to how victims of conflict-related sexual violence themselves ultimately 'make sense of what may or may not be sexual about the violence inflicted upon them.'[295] Identifying this absence in the narrative around sexual violence contained in the case law is in this sense not intended to imply that some kind of universalised sense of sexual subjectivity or experience of sexual victimisation has been left out of the account of the crimes constructed in these decisions. In this respect, Ann Cahill stresses that an individual's subjectivity emerges in the interplay between the self as a subject and society, meaning that the nature of an individual's sexual subjectivity and how they experience its violation is necessarily shaped by and emerges through their social immersion in a given context.[296] From this perspective, the recounting of testimony by victims that reflects personal feelings of shame can in this sense be understood to reflect some limited level of recognition of the impact of sexual violence on a victim's sexual subjectivity in social contexts in which sexual violation is considered shameful, because of how 'an individual's conception of their sexual identity may be shaped by social and cultural understandings of sex and sexuality [which] will affect how victims experience rape and the different harms that ensue.'[297]

292 Cahill (n 54), 142.

293 *Ibid.*

294 Alcoff (n 289), 110.

295 Dolan, Eriksson Baaz and Maria Stern (n 143), 1152–1153.

296 Cahill (n 54), 143.

297 Dowds (n 20), 145.

Beyond the limited issue of shame and the two minor allusions to victims' reluctance to engage in sexual relationships in the *Ntaganda* and *Bemba* decisions,[298] the discourse constructed in the case law reflects no other dimension of the harm or injury caused by sexual violence as a distinctly sexualised form of violence at the individual level. Given the individually and socially contingent nature of the experience of sexual subjectivity, which will also be shaped by factors such as an individual's gender identity or sexual orientation, this absence is not one of a substantive nature, in the sense that specific types of harm are absent from the narrative constructed in these cases, but rather is a simpler one of a structural or perspectival nature. Aside from recognising the physical harms, and some types of psychological harms, inflicted on victims, in the construction of what crimes of sexual violence are 'about', the case law does not address the individual's perspective on the sexual dimensions of their victimisation and how they experience the violation of their sexual subjectivity, however that may be.

Rather than being an absence of substance, in the sense that particular types of harms experienced by victims of sexual violence have been overlooked, this absence is therefore a structural feature of how the harms and injuries caused by sexual violence are constructed in these cases, in which the very existence of a sense of sexual subjectivity on the part of the victim, and the possible impact of sexual violence on it, is rarely contemplated. This is not a characteristic unique to international criminal trials, but rather reflects Louise du Toit's broader analysis of rape in the dominant symbolic order as an act which relies for its meaning and for the harm that it causes on a symbolic framework which repudiates women's selfhood and subjectivity, particularly women's sexual subjectivity, because it dichotomises women's sexuality and agency in the first place.[299] This same framework can be understood to underpin the meanings attached to sexual violence inflicted on male victims, because, within this symbolic order 'to violate a man sexually is to enact his social denigration, which under patriarchy automatically means he is designated as female because sexually vulnerable.'[300] Du Toit argues that this symbolic order ultimately 'makes it difficult to see the damage of rape because for us to appreciate its damage, rape has to stand out as an anomaly against a background which in fact normalises rape.'[301] On this view, understanding rape as a violation of the victim's

298 Ntaganda Sentencing Judgment (n 286), para 106; Bemba Trial Judgment (n 124), para 508.

299 du Toit (n 21), 5, 65.

300 Louise du Toit and Elisabet le Roux, 'A feminist reflection on male victims of conflict-related sexual violence', (2021) 28(2), *European Journal of Women's Studies*, 123.

301 du Toit (n 21), 5.

sexual subjectivity 'cannot happen because it cannot feature or appear as what it truly is, within a patriarchal symbolic order which denies and undermines women's sexual subjectivity systematically.'[302]

In this sense, the narratives around rape and sexual violence in these decisions construct a normative conception of the criminalisation of sexual violence that exemplifies and reinforces these wider cultural discourses in how it overlooks the injury to individual sexual subjectivity inflicted by crimes of sexual violence and, in doing so, relegates this type of harm to the private sphere, outside of the concern of international criminal law. In this way, the explicit normative statements made by a number of chambers, discussed in the previous section of this chapter, conceptualising crimes of sexual violence as violations of sexual autonomy or sexual integrity, which go some limited way towards invoking this type of understanding of such crimes, are ultimately diluted by the factual narrative constructed around them in the case law.

4 Narratives During Proceedings

The main contours of the narratives constructed around crimes of sexual violence during the course of proceedings broadly reflect those reproduced in the case law. While the different conceptions of the relevance of consent, the centrality of physical violence and bodily injury, the rape as a weapon of war narrative, and the emphasis on the social harms inflicted on victims and their communities through the violation of their conjugal orders have been emulated in the decisions, the analysis of the proceedings nevertheless reveals an additional degree of complexity to the normative discourse around crimes of sexual violence. This discourse at times reinforces and deepens some of the dominant elements of the normative themes constructed in the case law. At other times, testimonies emerge that counter these themes, offering a more complex and nuanced account of crimes of sexual violence than the more synthesised themes constructed in the case law.

4.1 *The Suffering Body*

In the analysis of the case law, the bodily integrity and physical harm conception of rape and sexual violence was identified as providing the dominant normative framing of such crimes, which have been constructed primarily as strategic acts of physical violence and aggression, in line with the wider

302 *Ibid.*, 65.

discourse on rape as a weapon of war. The nature of the specific discourse around physical harm that has emerged during the course of proceedings reinforces this dominant theme in how it focuses in particular on bodily pain and suffering, revealing how the prosecution in particular has often placed graphic accounts of physical suffering at the centre of the narratives constructed around crimes of sexual violence in many cases.

As subsequently reflected in the case law, the physical harms of sexual violence have commonly been addressed during proceedings in questions to victims and medical expert witnesses on the nature of the physical injuries sustained through sexual violence, the physical condition of victims subsequent to experiencing sexual violence, and its effects on physical health.[303] To take a small number of examples, in *Kunarac*, a witness was asked how she 'suffered physically'[304] while in *Šainović et al.* a judge asked a witness 'did you suffer from any medical – any disease of your body, ever since then? Did you have any other disease you suffered from or – because of consequences and so on?', to which the witness responded '[i]llness? Well, my emotional state is not right.

303 *Prosecutor v. Radoslav Brđanin*, IT-99-36, ICTY, Transcript 21 November 2002, 11948; *Prosecutor v. Miroslav Kvočka et al.*, IT-98-30/1, ICTY, Transcript 5 September 2000, 4778–4779, 4782–4783 [hereafter Kvočka et al. Transcript Date]; *Prosecutor v. Dragoljub Kunarac et al.*, IT-96-23 & 23/1, ICTY, Transcript 3 April 2000, 1527–1528 and Transcript 11 September 2000, 5413–5414 [hereafter Kunarac et al. Transcript Date]; *Prosecutor v. Ratko Mladić and Radovan Karadžić*, IT-95-18-R61 & IT-95-5-R61, ICTY, Transcript 2 July 1996, 418; *Prosecutor v. Nikola Šainović et al.*, IT-05-87, ICTY, Transcript 23 August 2006, 2234 and Transcript 24 August 2006, 2287 [hereafter Šainović et al. Trascript Date]; *Prosecutor v. Duško Tadić*, IT-94-1, ICTY, Transcript 19 July 1996, 3753, 3763–3764 [hereafter Tadić Transcript Date]; *Prosecutor v. Jean Paul Akayesu*, ICTR-96-4-I, ICTR, Transcript 3 November 1997, 19, 68; *Prosecutor v. Sylvestre Gacumbitsi*, ICTR-01-64-T, ICTR, Transcript 6 August 2003, 11 [hereafter Gacumbitsi Transcript Date]; *Prosecutor v. Tharcisse Muvunyi*, ICTR-00-55-A.T, ICTR, Transcript 22 June 2005, 5; *Prosecutor v. Ildephonse Nizeyimana*, ICTR-00-55C-T, ICTR, Transcript 17 February 2011, 26 [hereafter Nizeyimana Transcript Date]; *Prosecutor v. Augustin Ndindiliyimana et al.*, ICTR-00-56-T, ICTR, Transcript 10 October, 2005, 70 and Transcript 20 June 2005, 30 [hereafter Ndindiliyimana et al. Transcript Date]; *Prosecutor v. Charles Ghankay Taylor*, SCSL-2003-01-T, SCSL, Transcript 7 October 2008, 18106–18107 and Transcript 29 January 2009, 23859; *Prosecutor v. Alex Tamba Brima et al.* (*AFRC Case*), SCSL-2004-16-T, SCSL, Transcript 27 July 2005, 29–30 [hereafter Brima et al. Transcript Date]; *Prosecutor v. Dominic Ongwen*, ICC-02/04-01/15, ICC, Transcript 8 November 2017, 66–67, Transcript 30 November 2017, 27 and Transcript 24 January 2018, 24 [hereafter Ongwen Transcript Date]; *Prosecutor v. Jean Pierre Bemba Gombo*, ICC-01/05-01/08, ICC, Transcript 1 March 2011, 12, Transcript 2 February 2011, 21, Transcript 29 November 2010, 24 and Transcript 8 February 2011, 25–26 [hereafter Bemba Transcript Date]; *Prosecutor v. Bosco Ntaganda*, ICC-01/04-02/06, ICC, Transcript 1 March 2017, 61 and Transcript 11 April 2017, 27 [hereafter Ntaganda Transcript Date].

304 Kunarac et al. Transcript 18 May 2000 (n 303), 3507.

That's the biggest illness I have.'[305] In *Ntaganda*, a witness was questioned as to whether '[f]ollowing the rapes that you suffered, did you have any physical injuries?',[306] while in *Ongwen* the question was posed 'were you injured; were you injured in any way during any of those acts?'.[307] The following exchanges in *Gacumbitsi* at the ICTR and *Bemba* at the ICC are emblematic of much of the questioning and testimony on physical harm that has occurred during the course of proceedings:

Q. What was your physical condition?
A. It was as if I had lost my head, I'd gone crazy.
Q. And physically, in terms of your body, what injuries had you sustained?
A. My vagina was bleeding profusely – was injured and bleeding profusely.[308]

Q. Were you injured as a result of the rape?
A. I had a lot of injuries in my vagina. I had serious injuries in my vagina, and my aunt and my grandfather tried to treat it with – by having me sit in a liquid.
Q. Thank you, Madam Witness. What caused these injuries in your vagina?
A. When they took me, they really assaulted me sexually very violently. They took me by force and they put my arms behind me, they bent me over and they did these horrific things to me and that's the reason why I ended up with these terrible injuries.[309]

At times, some of the questioning of victims has focussed in particular on the degree of extrinsic force involved in the act. For example, in *Tadić* a witness was asked '[w]hen you were raped were you also beaten?'[310] while in *Kunarac*, in the context of her rape, a witness was asked '[d]id they physically abuse you when they took you to the house?' to which she responded '[d]o you mean did they beat me? […] No, they did not.'[311] The anatomical detail elicited from

305 Šainović et al. Transcript 24 August 2006 (n 303), 2287.
306 Ntaganda Transcript 1 March 2017 (n 303), 61.
307 Ongwen Transcript 24 January 2018 (n 303), 24.
308 Gacumbitsi Transcript 6 August 2003 (n 303), 11.
309 Bemba Transcript 2 February 2011 (n 303), 21.
310 Tadić Transcript 19 July 1996 (n 303), 3753.
311 Kunarac et al. Transcript 3 April 2000 (n 303), 1527–1528.
See similarly Kvočka et al. Transcript 5 September 2000 (n 303), 4778–4779, 4782–4783.

witnesses in many cases, the descriptions of bodily pain and suffering that are provided in response to questions about injuries sustained and victims' physical condition subsequent to being raped[312] are underscored in a number of cases that reflect a particular concern with eliciting evidence on the degree of physical pain victims experienced during the act of rape itself, as well as on physical, material evidence of the injures they suffered. For example, in *Ongwen*, the OTP sought additional detail on the pain a witness had referred to in her testimony:

> Q. You mentioned that you were raped by the first husband you were given to and that it was very painful and that you could not walk the next day. For how long did you feel this pain?
> A. I took three days without being able to walk properly. I would walk with my legs apart.
> Q. What impact has this injury had on your life now?
> A. I feel a lot – I feel a lot of pain, even up to now as an older person. It has given me difficulty in my life that even giving birth is a problem, and so it has made me get contraceptives so that I don't give birth again.[313]

In *Milošević*, two exchanges reflect the OTP's particular concern with whether or not rape was painful.

> Q. And what did he do?
> A. Then he put out his genital organ and placed it inside my genitals.
> Q. Did you have pain?
> A. Yes.[314]

> Q. Then what happened?
> A. And he started raping me.
> Q. By "rape," you mean what?
> A. I don't know. He was penetrating me all the time. I was trying to push him off – correction – to fight him off, but I couldn't.
> Q. Did you have pain?

312 See for example Bemba Transcript 1 March 2011 (n 303), 12; Ongwen Transcript 16 September 2015 (n 303), 7; Ongwen Transcript 30 November 2017 (n 303), 27; Ongwen Transcript 18 September 2015 (n 303), 40.

313 Ongwen Transcript 21 February 2018 (n 303), 41.

314 *Prosecutor v. Slobodan Milošević*, IT-02-54, ICTY, Transcript 8 April 2000, 2530 [hereafter Milošević Transcript Date].

A. Yes, very much pain.[315]

At times, the nature of some of the questioning on the issue of pain appears perhaps superfluous in light of the factual circumstances under discussion.

Q. Where on your body did he shove the stick?
A. In my vagina.
Q. Was this painful for you, Madam Witness?
A. It pained me so much that over five years I'm now still in the pain.[316]

Q. The gang-rape you described, was it painful?
A. Yes.
Q. How did this make you feel?
A. I felt dead.[317]

Q. Witness TAP, as Sylvestre Gacumbitsi was putting the police truncheon into your vagina repeatedly, was it painful?
A. Yes.
Q. As this was happening, how did you feel?
Q. I'm not sure how I can explain this – or express this, rather. But I got to a point where I was hoping for death. I cannot explain it to you in any other way.[318]

In other cases, the OTP has appeared particularly concerned with eliciting material evidence of the bodily pain suffered by the victim, focusing in several instances on whether or not the victim bled as a result of the sexual violence inflicted on them. For example, in *Kunarac*, a witness who had just testified to the fact she was raped every day for around twenty days was asked '[d]id you have any bleeding at that time or any pains of any kind?', to which she replied 'I had bleeding one day when I came from I don't know where, and when I came, I bled for – to Pazar, I bled for two months.'[319] During closing arguments in *Kunarac*, the OTP also highlighted that, in the case of one witness, the perpetrator 'raped her so aggressively that the witness started to bleed.'[320] In *Kvočka*

315 *Ibid.*, 2583.
316 *Prosecutor v. Issa Sesay et al.* (*RUF Case*), SCSL-2004-15-T, SCSL, Transcript 1 February 2005, 26. [hereafter Sesay et al. Transcript Date].
317 Kunarac et al. Transcript 30 March 2000 (n 303), 1391.
318 Gacumbitsi Transcript 6 August 2003 (n 303), 25.
319 Kunarac et al. Transcript 25 April 2000 (n 303), 2294.
320 Kunarac et al. Transcript 20 November 2000 (n 303), 6238.

et al., a witness was asked if she 'experience[d] bleeding due to the multiple rapes that you endured at the Omarska camp?', to which she replied '[y]es, throughout I was there.'[321]

Taken together, the general emphasis on the physical harm resulting from sexual violence in the form of physical injuries and health problems, the particular concern with highlighting the physical pain experienced by victims while they were being raped, along with the material evidence of the injuries they sustained, constructs a discourse around crimes of sexual violence that places the materiality of the suffering body front and centre. These stories of violated, injured and suffering bodies, that emerge through how the testimonies of victims are elicited and shaped during proceedings has in this way contributed to a discourse in which, while mental, emotional and social harms are also addressed, bodily suffering nevertheless becomes in some ways 'hypervisible' in the sense of 'an insistence or "excess" of visibility, which overloads with signification the object that has been represented [...] privilege[ing] the "overexposed", the "all-too-visible".'[322] This excess of visibility of bodily pain and suffering in the discourse around crimes of sexual violence can be understood to carry implications for how victims are constructed as subjects, because of how the figure of the passive, suffering body produces a symbolic order in which victims are 'diminished to docile figures, stripped away from their wider social relations.'[323] This wider critique of how the suffering body has become a key currency in international politics, in the sense that the '"idea that we might have obligations to human beings beyond our borders" [...] is increasingly based on bodily suffering, on our imaginings of the terror and deprivation to which bodies elsewhere are subjected',[324] is particularly potent in the context of sexual violence in particular because of the gendered social relations within which such violence is embedded.

From this perspective, Kiran Grewal has highlighted how international criminal law, with its graphic accounts of sexual violence inflicted on the bodies of women and girls, '(re)produces a vision of female sexuality that associates it with vulnerability, violence, pain and degradation'[325] and in doing so fails 'to conceive of women as anything other than sexually violable/violated body.'[326]

---

321 Kvočka et al. Transcript 4 October 2000 (n 303), 6230.

322 Veronica Buffon and Christine Allison, 'The gendering of victimhood: Western media and the Sinjar genocide', (2016) 4(2) *Kurdish Studies*, 182.

323 Tobias Kelly, *This Side of Silence: Human Rights, Torture, and the Recognition of Cruelty* (University of Pennsylvania Press 2013), 170.

324 Carolyn Dean, 'Empathy, Pornography, and Suffering', (2003) 14(1) *Differences*, 900-–91.

325 Grewal (n 5), 157.

326 *Ibid.*

In terms of the normative narrative constructed around crimes of sexual violence during proceedings, the focus on graphic, detailed accounts of pain and suffering experienced by women's bodies in this way constructs a normative frame around such violence which zooms in so far on the body, on physical pain and suffering, that it produces what Buffon and Allison have described as a '"hypervision in close-up" of the object'[327] with the effect of erasing or obscuring that which surrounds it.

In this way, the detailed focus on physical injury, pain, suffering and body parts during proceedings reinforces the dominant normative theme invoked in the case law around rape and sexual violence as crimes of physical violence and bodily harm. The narratives during proceedings embody this rape-as-violence paradigm in how they construct a normative conception of the criminalisation of sexual violence that implies that the bodily injury, pain and physical suffering experienced by victims is the real wrong that underlies these crimes. In doing so, these narratives exacerbate how the dominant factual theme in the case law dilutes the more explicit normative statements articulated in some cases with respect to the notions of sexual autonomy and sexual integrity. By constructing a narrative around such crimes that is so focussed on bodily injury, pain and suffering, victims' subjectivity as more than just violated bodies, and the relevance of the impact of sexual violence on their sexual subjectivity, is further discounted from the normative conception of the criminalisation of sexual violence that this discourse invokes.

4.2 *'I Felt Dignified and Proud'*

The analysis of the narratives contained in the decisions also revealed how crimes of sexual violence are constructed as being specifically 'sexual' primarily in terms of how they violate the norms of the conjugal order, causing harm to communities and groups and inflicting shame and stigma on victims, who are in turn rejected by their families and communities. This narrative similarly dominates the discourse that emerges during the conduct of proceedings, but in this context reflects a less uniform account of the harms of shame, stigma and social rejection, to some extent undermining the conception of these harms as inherent and immutable effects of crimes of sexual violence invoked by the dominance of this narrative in the case law. Pointing out how the emphasis on shame and stigma in wider discourses on conflict-related sexual violence often reproduces racialised and colonial tropes that essentialise certain cultures by branding them as brutal and barbaric, Karen Engle has

327 Buffon and Allison (n 322), 182.

argued that the centrality of these types of narratives often fail 'to make room for the possibility that communities might respond differently from the ways suggested by the stereotypes about them and their cultures.'[328]

The analysis of the testimonies on the issue of shame, stigma and social rejection during proceedings exposes the relevance of Engle's argument for the narrative constructed around crimes of sexual violence in the case law, because some testimonies reveal that victims and their families and communities did not always respond to sexual violation in the same way. For instance, the testimony of some victims does not conform straightforwardly to the narrative of inherent and inevitable stigmatisation and social rejection by families and communities. Most straightforwardly, responding to the question '[c]an you describe your emotions, your state of mind, after the rapes? [...] What type of reaction, if any, have you received from your community after the events?', a witness in *Bemba* answered '[t]here were no problems with the community.'[329] At the SCSL, one witness's testimony strongly reflected the dominant narrative in expressing personal feelings of shame, but at the same time contradicts the notion that families always reject victims of sexual violation by explaining how a family member supported the victim to overcome her sense of shame:

> After the meeting they asked for those people who had suffered the problems in the war. At that time I was very, very much ashamed. I was unable to appear in public or even speak about what happened to me in public to anybody. My aunt told me not to be ashamed. She said, "This is an illness which you got not by your own will but through this war, so it is nice for you to go and explain to them, maybe they will be able to help you." And they called me and I explained to them what had happened to me.[330]

Other witness testimonies construct a similarly more complex and varied picture, with one witness in *Bemba* responding to the question '[h]ow did your return to Bossangoa go to the town, to the people?' by explaining that '[w]hen I arrived in Bossangoa, my family welcomed me. They were surprised to see that I was still alive and that I had a child with me. But what made me sad when I returned to Bossangoa is that the population turned its back on me. I was stigmatised. They said, "Oh, it's a wife of the Banyamulenge who is in town."'[331] Reflecting the same type of mixed experience of stigmatisation,

328 Engle (n 1), 66–67.
329 Bemba Transcript 17 January 2011 (n 303), 40–41.
330 Sesay et al. Transcript 27 July 2003 (n 316), 50.
331 Bemba Transcript 17 May 2016 (n 303), 51.

a male witness who experienced sexual violence responded to the question '[d]o they view you the same way as they viewed you before the rape or has it affected you in any way?' by explaining that '[y]es. Amongst the population, there are some people who respect me. There are others who make fun of me.'[332] Each of these accounts either directly contest the narrative of stigmatisation and rejection as an immutable and universal experience resulting from sexual violation, or contribute nuance and greater complexity to this narrative by illustrating how some families, and some members of a community did not respond in this way, while others did.

Similarly, some witness's responses to questions on this issue suggest that the social consequences of their sexual violation may have played a less central role in their own understanding of the harm inflicted on them, than the centrality of this type of harm in the narratives of many of these cases would imply. For example, in *Gacumbitsi* at the ICTR, a witness was asked 'are you able to tell this Court what it means to be a single Rwandan woman who was raped before she is married?', to which she responded 'I would use myself as an example, from the time of those events. I suffer a great deal as a consequence of those events. I have many side-effects. My periods – my monthly periods last three months normally – three days normally, but with me, they last a whole month.'[333] In this example, while evidently not reflecting a complete account of how the witness approached the harm she experienced, it is nevertheless striking that the OTP framed her experience from the perspective of her identity as 'a single Rwandan woman who was raped before she is married',[334] while her response was provided purely in physical, medical terms dissociated from questions of society or culture.

The individual experience of shame is also often framed in terms of its silencing effects, in the sense that many witnesses testified to having difficulty disclosing their experiences as a result of their feelings of shame and humiliation. For example, at the ICTR, witnesses explained their hesitancy in coming forward to testify to having been raped by stating that 'for me it was something very shameful and I did not have the courage to talk about it'[335] and 'we were ashamed to talk about it to other people. It is shameful and sad to talk about it, that is why I did not talk about it.'[336] In *Kunarac* at the ICTY a victim of rape explained with respect to her experience that '[i]t's very difficult to describe

332 Bemba Transcript 24 January 2011 (n 303), 35.

333 Gacumbitsi Transcript 6 August 2003 (n 303), 26.

334 *Ibid.*

335 *Prosecutor v. Mika Muhimana*, ICTR-95-1B-T, ICTR, Transcript 15 April 2004, 64.

336 Ndindiliyimana et al. Transcript 5 April 2005 (n 303), 14.

that. I know that I was terribly frightened, I felt ashamed in a way, and in a way I felt very, very dirty, soiled.'[337] In *Ntaganda* at the ICC, a witness explained her reason for not telling her husband that she had been raped was because she 'was frightened because it's a source of shame'[338] while a witness in *Bemba* explained that '[a]fter what I had suffered, I did not have the courage to tell the Mongoumba doctors about it because it was shameful and humiliating to tell anyone what had happened to me. So, frankly, I did not have that courage.'[339]

While the difficulty of disclosing having experienced sexual violence due to shame is in this way a prominent part of the testimony of many witnesses, and reinforces the narrative of shame and stigma that dominates the case law, at the same time, the silencing effect of shame does not emerge as universal even within the framework of the proceedings themselves. The testimony of some witnesses at times reflect experiences and attitudes that almost directly contradict this dominant discourse. Perhaps most powerfully, two exchanges during the testimony of a witness in the *Kunarac* case at the ICTY directly repudiate the assumption of inherent and inevitable feelings of shame and its silencing effects on victims of sexual violence:

> Q. Witness, I have noticed that sometimes when you answer my questions, you smile, or when you consider, you smile. Are you nervous?
> A. Yes. But there's something even more important. I'm proud to be here. Let the world know what they did.[340]

This exchange reflects an attitude on the part of this individual that contains almost a mirror image of the more common sentiment expressed by witnesses during proceedings of the silencing effects of shame and stigma. Centralising the actions of the perpetrators, this witness instead articulated a sense of pride in having the opportunity to speak and publicly expose what they had done. In a further exchange, the same witness expressed similar sentiments in describing her feelings while she was imprisoned and raped:

> Q. How did this make you feel while you were in Karaman's House?
> A. Awful, dreadful, helpless. But at the same time I felt dignified and proud.
> Q. Of what?
> A. I didn't understand the question.

337 Kunarac et al. Transcript 4 April 2000 (n 303), 1675.
338 Ntaganda Transcript 11 April 2007 (n 303), 40.
339 Bemba Transcript 15 March 2011 (n 303), 6.
340 Kunarac et al. Transcript 25 April 2000 (n 303), 2224.

Q. You said at the same time you felt dignified and proud, and what do you mean? What made you feel this way?
A. Yes. We girls, children, were hopeless. They were men under arms and they used force. But simply I did not want to be subdued. They would often describe us as slaves, but I wouldn't accept that, though I couldn't say it often. But intimately I would refuse to accept it, though it was the truth.[341]

This witness's account of feeling dignified and proud similarly undermines the totalising centrality of shame and silence in the discourse around crimes of sexual violence in the case law, demonstrating that, while for many victims this may have formed part of the harms they experienced, it may not always be an inherent, exclusive or immutable part of the experience for all victims of such violence. In less emphatic terms, another witness in *Kunarac* also articulated a more complex position on the silencing effects of shame and stigma in relation to the experience of testifying, suggesting that she regarded the process of speaking about her experiences in this context as a positive one:

Q. Can you describe why you finally decided to speak to the Tribunal?
A. Because of my future.
Q. Can you be more specific about what you mean?
A. To say what happened.
Q. And in what way is that related to your future?
A. It will make me feel better.[342]

These testimonies in some way chip away at the assumption that victims of sexual violence are always, inevitably stigmatised and rejected by their families and communities and feel shame as a result of their experience, which necessarily produces a silencing effect and a reluctance or inability to disclose what happened. While this is true for many of the witnesses who testified in these cases, the particular testimonies highlighted here nevertheless reveal how individual experiences recounted during the course of proceedings do not always conform to the dominant narrative of social harm constructed in the case law, even within the parameters of international criminal proceedings themselves. Recognising how the discourse that emerges during proceedings reflects a greater degree of diversity in individuals' experiences of the harms

341 Kunarac et al. Transcript 26 April 2000 (n 303), 2424.
342 Kunarac et al. Transcript 14 April 2000 (n 303), 2033.

of sexual violence than the dominant themes in the case law suggest in this way illuminates how the normative conception of crimes of sexual violence invoked by the discourse in the case law rests on a flattening and obscuring of experiences that do not conform directly to that dominant narrative. This filtering out of more complex dimensions of the narratives during proceedings plays a particularly significant role with the respect to the issue of the impact of sexual violence on the victims' sexual subjectivity, and its absence from the discourse constructed in the case law.

4.3 *Sexual Subjectivity*

As discussed in the previous section of this chapter, the narrative in the case law around what is 'sexual' about sexual violence constructs this almost exclusively as a social question, in how sexual violence violates the norms surrounding sexuality in a given society, with the effect that what it may mean for individuals that the violence inflicted on them is sexual, and the impact of such violence on their sexual subjectivity, is almost entirely unaddressed. The discourse that emerges from the trial proceedings suggests that this perspective, while not prominent, has nevertheless also not been entirely absent from how victims have articulated their experiences or how expert witnesses have described the impact of sexual violence on individuals.

Most notably, the testimony of a psychiatrist and psychotherapist with expertise in trauma, who testified as an expert witness for the defence in *Kunarac* at the ICTY, reflects a much broader sense of the impact of sexual violence on individuals' sexual lives in a way that captures the injury to sexual subjectivity, beyond the narrow focus on physical injury and social harm contained in the case law. The following testimony was elicited by the defence to support the argument that victims of sexual violence who had not received psychological support could not have re-adjusted effectively to life in the way the defence suggested some witnesses did. In other words, this testimony formed part of defence arguments that sought to cast doubt on the veracity of some witness' claims to have been victims of sexual violence on the grounds that they were too well able to adjust to life following trauma. While this testimony did not therefore form part of the prosecution's narrative of the harms inflicted by crimes of sexual violence, it is nevertheless revealing of precisely the perspective that has often not been present in the discourse around sexual violence in international criminal law.

The expert witness on trauma in *Kunarac* began by explaining that the effects of traumas suffered by women can be grouped into three categories;

minor consequences, medium consequences, and serious consequences.[343] She went on to explain that '[t]he minor consequences consist of social isolation, nightmares, insomnia, difficulties in establishing the so-called object relations, which is a professional term for love relations. Women find it very hard to establish such relations following these traumas, and psychotherapy helps in that.'[344] Going on to describe the process through which victims may re-adjust to 'normal life', the witness further explained that '[e]motional rehabilitation is a major problem, that is to say, to establish an object relationship, that is to say a relationship of confidence and trust with the opposite sex.'[345] Responding to the question of whether she had encountered women who were victims of rape who had gone on to marry, the witness provided the following testimony:

> I must say that I worked with women who were married and women who were unmarried and who were raped. Only one of the girls who were unmarried found a boyfriend, and it was now after the bombing, and she was raped in 1992. The others did not manage to establish a permanent relationship based on partnership. Many of them did not have any sexual intercourse after the rape. And women who were married have great difficulty in returning to the marital beds of their husbands, and there are two from my experience who have not even told their husbands what had happened to them. So they take tranquillisers in order to be able to have sex with their husbands. That is merely having sex. That is not enjoying sex. So practically in order to keep their marriages alive, that is what they resort to.[346]

In response to this answer, the witness was then asked '[a]re you saying, Doctor, that a person who has been raped will never, ever love again?', to which she responded '[n]o, I'm not saying that. I hope that that person will love again, but I'm sure that it will be very difficult for her to love with full confidence. It's a question of confidence. [...] These are among the consequences. So, you see, even such grave things that happen in one's life are classified as minor consequences.'[347]

---

343 Kunarac et al. Transcript 12 September 2000 (n 303), 5450.
344 *Ibid.*
345 *Ibid.*, 5468.
346 *Ibid.*, 5469.
347 *Ibid.*, 5469–5470.

This testimony reflects an understanding of the harms of sexual violence as partly acting upon the victim's sense of self as a sexual being.[348] It captures how Linda Martín Alcoff has articulated her understanding of sexual subjectivity and how it is violated by sexual violence, which she explains in terms of how sexual violence 'touches our sex lives, our capacity for pleasure, our ability to move about in the world and to trust others, our ability to trust our judgment and responses, and, thus, our relationship to our selves.'[349] In doing so, this testimony introduces a perspective on sexual violence which transcends the focus on bodily injury, the more generalised discussion of psychological harms, and the particular centrality of social harms, to incorporate recognition of the specifically sexualised nature of sexual violence at an individual level, in its possible impact on the victim's sexual and romantic relationships, their sexual lives and their capacity for sexual agency and pleasure.

Expert witnesses in the *Bemba* and *Ongwen* cases at the ICC pointed in somewhat less direct terms to harms of a similar nature. In *Bemba*, reflecting on the analysis of the psychological harms experienced by victims of rape, an expert witness outlined a similar understanding to the witness in *Kunarac* of the impact of sexual violence on victims' social and romantic relationships, describing how 'with rape victims, very often, you know, sort of every experience with a male will be perceived as something of a very dangerous nature. They cannot be involved in a trusting relationship. They're always under the perception that they are currently unsafe and under stress.'[350] The expert witness went on to identify other, wider harms that also speak to an understanding of sexual violence as harming the individual's sexual subjectivity in a way that may go beyond a clinical account of mental health problems experienced by victims:

> In a community where it's hard – where that many people have been affected by something like rape, and we're using an instrument which is specifically a mental health measurement instrument like post-traumatic stress disorder rating scale, what we're not picking up on is how many, you know, mothers lost interest in being mothers or became divorced because of the rape that happened? How many marriages were affected to the point where, you know, there is no happiness or divorce occurs? These are damages and sufferings that are had by the victim that aren't

348 See Plante (n 288), 32.

349 Alcoff (n 289), 10.

350 Bemba Transcript 17 May 2016 (n 303), 32.

> accounted by through, you know, a straightforward psychiatric measuring tool.[351]

In *Ongwen*, a Ugandan professor of psychiatry familiar with Acholi culture, who testified as an expert witness on the cultural challenges involved in communicating with victims about harms of this nature, addressed the impact of sexual violence on an individual's sexuality and sex life in direct terms, explaining that:

> To ask an Acholi girl from the rural area about her sexual intercourse with a man in public, she won't answer that. Those things are unmentionables. Those words don't pass through in the mouth, so the saying would go, you know.
> So she would, you know, say "Yes, there is difficulty."
> She said, next page: Well, I have pain.
> And then, quote, that is understood in the western way.
> But we know it's more than pain, you know. You're asking about somebody's sexuality now after rape and how they forge relationships and trusts and all of that and enjoyment. They're not going to talk about that. I can now, given this western hat of a psychiatrist, you know, I can say that you enjoy sex. You don't say those things in ordinary cultural, culture of African people in public, in front of elders. Sex is for the bedroom and the bedroom only. So there are these things that I think will pose difficulties in communication.[352]

This testimony highlights the psychiatrist's understanding of the nature of sexual violence as impacting on individual sexual subjectivity, on the victim's sexuality and their ability to experience trust in and enjoy sexual relationships, in a way that does not emerge in the dominant narrative of harm constructed in the case law. Importantly, this understanding of the harms inflicted by sexual violence, in terms of how it acts upon victims' sense of sexual subjectivity, emerges not only in the testimony of 'expert' witnesses speaking from a medical, psychiatric perspective, but also on rare occasions in how victims themselves articulate their experiences when testifying.

For example, a witness in *Bemba* made directly clear the impact of sexual violence on her sexuality and sexual life in testifying that 'when I remember

351 Bemba Transcript 16 May 2016 (n 303), 89–90.
352 Ongwen Transcript 28 May 2018 (n 303), 45.

the atrocities perpetrated upon me by the Banyamulengues I didn't have any wish to have any sexual relationship and, even when I thought about what (Redacted), I could not want to have any sexual relationship during that time.'[353] In less direct language, a witness in *Mucić et al.* at the ICTY also pointed towards this type of injury to her sense of self in the context of her romantic and sexual life, explaining that '[i]t was difficult for me. I was a woman who only lived for one man and I was his all my life, and I think that I was just getting separated from my body at this time.'[354]

At the SCSL, the testimony of a witness in the *AFRC* case articulated the impact of rape on her own life as well as that of her daughter, who had also experienced rape, in terms that similarly highlighted its effects on their trust in men, their romantic relationships and their sexual lives:

> Q. Madam Witness, at the time you were raped, how many children did you have?
> A. I have seven children.
> Q. So I take it you have had no children since the date you were raped?
> A. Not at all. They made me to be afraid of men. In fact, I cannot even think about having sex with a man.
> Q. Madam Witness, you told us that at the time your daughter [...] was also raped, she was a virgin. [...] It is your testimony that she was raped by two men?
> A. That is what she told me.
> Q. Did she give birth as a result of the incident?
> A. Not at all. Not at all. Not at all. That is not how it happened. Should I explain?
> Q. Please do.
> A. When this had happened, when this had happened to us, well, for sometime, you know, whenever a man spoke to her, she would even insult him. In fact, she did not marry quickly during that time. So if I should tell you that she was impregnated having been raped, that's not true.[355]

It is important to distinguish the perspective offered in this testimony from the more dominant emphasis on the social or cultural impact of sexual violence on women's place in a particular conjugal order, in terms of their marriage

353 Bemba Transcript 1 December 2010 (n 303), 42.
354 *Prosecutor v. Zdravko Mucić et al.*, IT-96-21-T, ICTY, Transcript 17 March 1997, 503.
355 Brima et al. Transcript 27 July 2005 (n 303), 27–29.

prospects or their rejection by existing partners. What is distinct about this testimony is how it reflects the impact of sexual violence on these dimensions of the witness and her daughter's lives from their own perspective as individuals, in this case resulting in a mistrust of men and an aversion to sex. In this way, this testimony shifts the focus from the group or community and the injury to its social and conjugal order, which results in the re-victimisation of victims of sexual violence, towards a perspective that also captures the injury to the victim's subjectivity through experiencing violence of a specifically sexual nature.

Taken together, these testimonies reflect experiences of sexual violence that surface the victim's sexual subjectivity, and the injury caused to it by sexual violence, in how they recount the harms inflicted on the victims' sense of their sexuality and their ability or desire to pursue sexual or romantic lives. In this way, in contrast to the dominant normative themes reflected in the case law, the narratives that emerge around crimes of sexual violence during the course of proceedings at times reflect a conception of crimes of sexual violence in which the violation of the individual's sexual subjectivity is invoked as relevant to the criminalisation of rape and sexual violence. The particular normative implications of the absence of this dimension of the harm inflicted by crimes of sexual violence from the normative account of such crimes constructed in the case law is underscored by contrasting it with those limited aspects of individual sexual subjectivity that have ultimately been incorporated into the normative narrative of sexual violence invoked in the case law, namely the issues of shame and virginity.

The themes of shame and loss of virginity in the case law can be understood to capture aspects of the impact of sexual violence on victims' sexual subjectivity because how an individual approaches their sexuality and sexual life will be partly shaped by the social and cultural norms within which they are immersed.[356] In this sense, in social contexts in which sexual violation is considered shameful and virginity is valorised, feeling shame and regretting the loss of virginity may form part of how crimes of sexual violence act upon victims' sense of their sexual selves and how they therefore experience the sexualised dimensions of the violence inflicted upon them. This is evident in how victim testimonies discussed in the previous section often express personal feelings of shame, while the loss of virginity is highlighted by others as a significant part of their experience of sexual violence. For example, at the ICTR, a witness explained that rape 'had a significant effect on me. I had health problems. I had to be operated on. I was no longer a virgin. I had lost my virginity.

356 See Cahill (n 54), 143.

When I think of all that I underwent without any prior preparation I feel very diminished.'[357] In *Lubanga* at the ICC a witness similarly emphasised that 'I used to be a virgin before I entered the UPC, but they took my virginity away I saw the blood; that destroyed my life completely.'[358]

From this perspective, the testimonies on shame and virginity that emerged during the course of proceedings can be understood to constitute the only elements of individual sexual subjectivity, and the injury to it caused by sexual violence, that have ultimately been incorporated into the normative narrative around crimes of sexual violence in the case law. In this sense, virtually the only articulations of sexual subjectivity that emerge in proceedings which are ultimately incorporated into the normative account of crimes of sexual violence constructed in the case law relate to those dimensions that are defined precisely by chastity, by the construction of sex as shameful and virginity as valuable, and therefore by the absence of sexual will, agency and the positive aspects of an individual's sexual life. The inclusion of these elements and the discounting of others that might affirm a more positive conception of sexual subjectivity as also worthy of criminal protection, that captures a person's sexuality, their capacity for pleasure, will and sexual agency, underscores the extent to which the dominant narrative in the case law ultimately struggles to move beyond an account of sexual violence that does not reproduce some of the underlying logic of the patriarchal notion of rape as a crime against honour.

5 Conclusion

Against the historical backdrop of entrenched property and honour-based conceptualisations of rape and sexual violence, the normative evolution reflected in the criminalisation of sexual violence under international law and the normative discourse that emerged around it remains remarkable. The doctrinal debate over consent versus coercive circumstances as constituent elements of rape, and the feminist debates which underpinned it, reveal much about the varied normative conceptions of these crimes invoked by the definitions identified in the case law – as acts primarily of violence and aggression, as

357 Nizeyimana Transcript 17 February 2011 (n 303), 61.

358 *Prosecutor v. Thomas Lubanga Dyilo*, ICC-01/04-01/06, ICC, Transcript 6 March 2009, 29. See also Milošević Transcript 16 July 2002 (n 314), 8162; Sesay et al. Transcript 2 March 2006 (n 316), 11.

violations of human dignity, or at times as violations of rights to personal and sexual agency and autonomy.

Beyond the prominence of the debate over consent and coercive circumstances, the case law also reflects a degree of variety in the nature of the principles invoked as providing a normative basis for the criminalisation of rape and sexual violence. While, in line with the conception of rape as an act of violence and aggression, the general principles of physical and moral integrity dominate, the invocation of sexual autonomy and integrity as principles protected by these crimes contribute to a degree of discursive surfacing of the relevance of sex and sexuality, and the notion of an individual right to be free from interference in one's sexual life in particular, for the normative conception of crimes of sexual violence invoked in the case law.

At the same time, in both the doctrinal developments in the Rome Statute as well as in the factual themes identified in the case law, the framing of sexual violence that comes to the fore is its physically violent, aggressive dimensions, causing bodily pain and suffering to victims, deployed strategically like any other form of physical violence in war. This framing responds directly to the feminist concern with ensuring that sexual violence became recognised as a violent assault on individual women's bodies, and in this sense reflects a significant transformation from historical notions of rape, in which the harm inflicted on women as subjects was recognised in passing, if at all. At the same time, the efforts to firmly situate sexual violence within the public sphere of political concern by framing it as 'violence not sex', have produced a narrative around such crimes in the case law that excludes the relevance of sex and sexuality for how they are normatively conceptualised.

In this respect, the distinctly sexualised dimensions of crimes of sexual violence ultimately only emerge in the case law in terms of how they are constructed as inflicting harm to groups through the violation of their conjugal order, which in turn results in the infliction of shame and stigma on victims. This implicitly reproduces some elements of the underlying logic of an honour-based conception of the criminalisation of sexual violence in how it suggests that the violation of social structures that position women, their bodies and their sexual lives under the authority of family or community form part of the underlying wrong of crimes of sexual violence. From this perspective, while some of the normative statements in the case law related to sexual autonomy and integrity point in a limited way to the relevance of individual rights to agency specifically in one's sexual life, the factual narrative constructed around the crimes in the case law to some extent dilutes these statements in constructing an account of the sexual dimensions of sexual violence that is instead tied almost exclusively to the social and cultural norms that govern sex within a community.

This framing is reinforced through the dynamics around what is included within and excluded from the construction of what is 'sexual' about crimes of sexual violence in the case law. Despite some testimonies during proceedings revealing the distinctly sexualised dimensions of the harms inflicted by sexual violence at the individual level, their absence from the discourse constructed in the case law reinforces a gendered binary in which these individualised, sexualised harms are ultimately relegated to the private sphere, outside of the concern of international criminal law. On this reading, the sexual dimensions of sexual violence only count when they are constructed as 'public' in some way; in these cases, when they are understood to engage and violate a community or group's social or conjugal order. Excluded from the narrative of what is sexual about sexual violence that is constructed in the case law is therefore an account of its impact on a victim's sexual subjectivity – of how sexual violence, by virtue of being violence that takes a sexualised form, may violate and cause harm to more than a person's body or social standing, but may touch upon how they understand their own sexuality, how they experience trust and relationships with others, and ultimately their capacity to exercise will and agency in their sexual lives.

In this way, the narratives that emerge in the case law and during the course of proceedings reveal how the case law functions to flatten the diversity of experiences of sexual violence, even among those articulated within the trial process itself, producing a synthesised narrative around such crimes that constructs certain harms as inevitable and immutable, while obscuring experiences that contradict or do not conform fully to the generalised narrative contained in the case law. In these cases, this takes the form of obscuring how some witness testimonies undermine the understanding of sexual violence as inflicting inherent and immutable shame and stigmatisation on victims, and overlooking testimonies that contain traces of harms experienced by victims that reflect injury to their wider sense of sexual subjectivity. Ultimately, this contributes to the construction of a normative conception of the criminalisation of sexual violence which reproduces some of the underlying logic of an honour-based conception of rape and has proved itself, to date, not to be receptive to embracing a thicker normative account of the harms of sexual violence that recognises and considers worthy of criminal protection victims' full subjectivity, including in their sexual lives.

CHAPTER 5

Reproductive Violence

While the issue of sexual violence has gained a degree of prominence in the field of international criminal law, reflected in the development of a significant body of case law and scholarship, an equivalent debate on the nature of reproductive violence, and the criminalisation of forced pregnancy and enforced sterilization, has only recently begun to emerge.[1] The relatively limited engagement with these crimes may be partly attributable to a wider tendency within discourses on conflict-related violence to group forced pregnancy and enforced sterilization into an umbrella category of 'sexual violence', with the result that these crimes have been addressed primarily through the lens of this wider category.[2] However, as this chapter illustrates, the normative history of crimes of reproductive violence, as well as how they have been interpreted more recently in the case law, suggests that these crimes may bear distinct normative features which are worth examining independently. This is particularly relevant given that reproductive matters directly engage normative questions that relate to 'sensitive issues of human sexuality, moral order, and gender relations and roles',[3] which continue to be controversial at the international level,

1 See for instance Dieneke de Vos, 'Can the ICC prosecute forced contraception?', *European University Institute Blog*, 14 March 2016 [available at https://me.eui.eu/dieneke-de-vos/blog/can-the-icc-prosecute-forced-contraception/ – accessed 11 February 2022]; Rosemary Grey, 'The ICC's First 'Forced Pregnancy' Case in Historical Perspective' (2017) 15 *Journal of International Criminal Justice*, 905–930; Christie J Edwards, 'Forced Contraception as a Means of Torture' in Center for Human Rights and Humanitarian Law, *Gender Perspectives on Torture: Law and Practice* (American University Washington College of Law, Washington, DC 2018), 139–160; Ciara Laverty and Dieneke de Vos, ''Ntaganda' in Colombia: Intra-Party Reproductive Violence at the Colombian Constitutional Court', Opinio Juris, 25 February 2020, [available at – http://opiniojuris.org/2020/02/25/ntaganda-in-colombia-intra-party-reproductive-violence-at-the-colombian-constitutional-court/ – accessed 11 February 2022]; Tanja Altunjan, *Reproductive Violence and International Criminal Law* (T.M.C. Asser Press, 2021); Ciara Laverty and Dieneke de Vos, 'Reproductive Violence as a Category of Analysis: Disentangling the Relationship between 'the Sexual' and 'the Reproductive' in Transitional Justice', (2021) 15 *International Journal of Transitional Justice*, 616–635.

2 Laverty and de Vos (n 1), 6–8.

3 Julia Gebhard and Diana Trimiño Mora, 'Reproductive Rights, International Regulation' in *Max Planck Encyclopaedia of Public International Law* (Oxford University Press 2013), para 39.

 DOI:10.1163/9789004687844_007

making forced pregnancy in particular the most contentious crime during the drafting of the Rome Statute.[4]

This chapter therefore examines the distinct normative roots of the crimes of forced pregnancy and enforced sterilization, outlining how reproductive matters initially emerged in international discourses through the population control paradigm, which addressed reproduction primarily through the lens of governmental control over fertility in order to limit population growth. With growing recognition of rights to sexual and reproductive health and a normative shift towards emphasising a human-rights centred approach to population growth, the chapter highlights how the reproductive sphere nevertheless gradually came to be understood as being governed by individual rights, which challenged some of the more coercive practices legitimated by the collective concerns of the population control paradigm. Along with the catalysing effects of the reports of forced pregnancies from the former Yugoslavia, this ultimately culminated in acts such as forced pregnancy and enforced sterilization being directly labelled as forms of violence against women at a number of significant multi-lateral conferences during the early 1990s, which laid the groundwork for the subsequent inclusion of these crimes in the Rome Statute. The chapter argues that, at this point, the nature of how and contexts in which forms of reproductive violence were recognised, including in a liminal way in the field of international criminal law, nevertheless reflected a continuing concern with the collective implications of reproductive issues, approaching reproductive violence as principally targeting, and harming, ethnic groups.

In its analysis of the codification of the crimes of forced pregnancy and enforced sterilization in the Rome Statute, the chapter goes on to highlight how their normative roots and the tension between the nascent individual rights-conception of reproductive issues versus the ongoing concern with exercising control over women's reproductive lives, continued to animate controversies during the drafting process. This ultimately shaped the nature of the legal definitions of these crimes and their conceptual implications. Lastly, the chapter examines the normative themes and narratives that were constructed around the crime of forced pregnancy in the *Ongwen* case at the ICC, which constituted the first case at an international criminal tribunal to include charges for crimes of reproductive violence. It finds that the dominant normative theme reflected in the legal decisions as well as in the narratives constructed during

4 Michael Cottier and Sabine Mzee, 'Article 8(e) War crime of forced pregnancy', in Otto Triffterer and Kai Ambos (eds), *Rome Statute of the International Criminal Court: A Commentary* (Beck/Hart 2016), 499. See also Lucía Berro Pizzarossa, 'Here to Stay: The Evolution of Sexual and Reproductive Health and Rights in International Human Rights Law', (2018) 7(3) *Laws*, 13–14.

proceedings constitutes a remarkable shift in the normative conception of the crime in terms of how it directly and unequivocally invokes reproductive rights, including an individual right to reproductive autonomy, as constituting its normative basis.

1 Historical-Normative Roots in International Law

In broad terms, the development of international norms around reproductive violence in many ways tracks the normative history of the recognition and prohibition of sexual violence under international law, in terms of how this has reflected historical changes in the social position of women, their recognition as subjects, and how violence against them has therefore been conceptualised. While the boundaries of what may constitute reproductive violence, as distinct from sexual violence, may not always be clear cut, emerging scholarship addressing acts such as forced pregnancy, sterilization, abortion or contraception under international law increasingly distinguishes between sexual and reproductive forms of violence, often on normative grounds.[5] The history of how reproductive forms of violence came to be recognised and addressed within wider international frameworks on violence against women is illustrative in this respect of the distinct normative dimensions of the contemporary criminalisation of forms of reproductive violence under international criminal law, namely the crimes of forced pregnancy and enforced sterilization.

Evidence suggests that during periods of conflict and repression throughout history acts of violence that target a person's reproductive capacity have taken place. Citing the example of the Athenian massacre of the Melians in 416BC, Charli Carpenter has argued, for instance, that the ancient wartime practice of killing all men and sexually enslaving women 'suggests the use of forced impregnation to eradicate the cultural unity of enslaved survivors.'[6] In more recent history, reproductive violence was inflicted on enslaved Black women in North America, where slaveowners sought to ensure, through sexual violence or coercion, that female slaves would bear children as often as biologically possible, often treating them as '"breeders" – animals, whose monetary value

5 See for instance Laverty and de Vos (n 1), 616–635; Rosemary Grey, 'Reproductive Crimes in International Criminal Law' in Indira Rosenthal, Valerie Oosterveld and Susana SáCouto (eds), *Gender & International Criminal Law* (Oxford University Press, forthcoming), 4–5; Altunjan (n 1), 98–99.

6 Robyn Charli Carpenter, 'Forced maternity, children's rights and the genocide convention: A theoretical analysis', (2000) 2(2) *Journal of Genocide Research*, 223, footnote 36.

could be precisely calculated in terms of their ability to multiply their numbers.'[7] The most commonly recognised historical example of large-scale reproductive violence is Nazi Germany's eugenics policy of 'racial hygiene', in which people deemed 'unworthy of life', such as those with cognitive and physical disabilities, those suffering from mental illness and LGBTI individuals, were forcibly sterilized.[8] Forced sterilizations also formed part of the Nazis campaign to exterminate the Jewish people and others groups in concentration camps, with evidence of forced sterilizations through surgical and medicinal means having been inflicted on male and female inmates of the Auschwitz and Ravensbrück camps.[9]

While the evidence from Nazi Germany cast into disrepute policies of coerced sterilization pursued much more widely against individuals with physical and mental disabilities in the United States, Canada and Europe, many of these programmes nevertheless continued until the 1970s,[10] and the ideas behind them, with their roots in eugenics, came to form part of the growing concern with population control by the middle of the century.[11] The international concern with controlling global population growth emerged as a response to a belief among Western states that rapid population growth, particularly in poorer states, would hinder poverty alleviation measures, hold back economic development and outstrip global resources.[12] At the international level, reproductive matters were therefore predominantly approached through the lens of population control from the mid-1960s until the 1994 International Conference on Population and Development.[13]

---

7 Angela Y. Davis, *Women, Race and Class* (First Vintage Books 1983), 14–16. See also Pamela D. Bridgewater, 'Ain't I A Slave: Slavery, Reproductive Abuse, and Reparations', (2005) 14(1) *UCLA Women's Law Journal*, 89–161.

8 See Randall Hansen and Desmond King, *Sterilized by the State Eugenics, Race, and the Population Scare in Twentieth-Century North America* (Cambridge University Press 2014), 141–162.

9 *The Trial of German Major War Criminals*, Proceedings of the International Military Tribunal sitting at Nuremberg, Germany, Part 22 (22nd August 1946 to 1st October 1946), 466 [hereafter Trial of German Major War Criminals]; William Schabas, *The International Criminal Court: A Commentary on the Rome Statute* (Oxford University Press 2016), 192.

10 Hansen and King (n 8), 6–7, 163–164.

11 *Ibid.*, 186–207.

12 George Zeidenstein, 'The Conundrum of Population and Reproductive Health Programs in the Early Twenty-First Century' in Laura Reichenbach and Mindy Jane Roseman (eds), *Reproductive Health and Human Rights: The Way Forward* (University of Pennsylvania Press 2009), 41–42.

13 Paige Whaley Eager, 'From Population Control to Reproductive Rights: Understanding Normative Change in Global Population Policy (1965–1994)', (2004) 18(2) *Global Society*, 146.

In this sense, the normative roots of the later recognition of forms of reproductive violence at the international level are somewhat distinct to those of sexual violence in terms of how they initially emerged within the framework of population growth and control. Reproductive matters were in this way not conceptualised in terms of individual rights but were instead understood as 'belonging to the domain of demographers.'[14] Indeed, population control policies resulted in numerous examples of coercive practices directed at impoverished populations in the Global South with the aim of limiting population growth, including offering material incentives for contraceptive use to those so poor they could not refuse, and imposing penalties on individuals who failed to use contraceptives.[15]

At the international level, reproductive matters were first linked with the notion of human rights in the 1968 Proclamation of Teheran adopted by the UN General Assembly as an outcome of the International Conference on Human Rights that took place that year. While the Proclamation states that 'parents have a basic human right to determine freely and responsibly the number and the spacing of their children',[16] identifying some form of reproductive choice as a human right for the first time, at this point, the relationship between rights discourse and reproductive matters nevertheless remained conceptualised in terms of the importance of population control for the realisation of other human rights. Resolution XVIII from the 1968 conference states, for instance, that '[t]he present rate of population growth in some areas of the world hampers the struggle against hunger and poverty [...] thereby impairing full realization of human rights.'[17] In this way, reproductive matters were linked somewhat indirectly to human rights in the sense that population growth was understood to represent 'a "problem" – an obstacle to the enjoyment of human rights',[18] which consequently justified coercive and discriminatory practices that undermined the embryonic commitment to some level of right to reproductive choice.

An initial shift from the dominant population control approach to reproductive matters took place at the 1974 Bucharest World Conference on Population, in which the World Population Plan of Action (WPPA) was adopted. At this

14 Pizzarossa (n 4), 2.

15 Zeidenstein (n 12), 45.

16 UN Population Division, Proclamation of Teheran, Final Act of the International Conference on Human Rights 22 April - – 13 May 1968, A/CONF. 32/41, Resolution XVIII [hereafter 1968 Proclamation of Teheran].

17 *Ibid.*

18 Pizzarossa (n 4), 3.

conference, a number of states in the Global South challenged the dominant approach to population and development, arguing that rapid population growth was 'a consequence and not a cause of underdevelopment and that the crux of the problem was not scarcity of resources but rather their distribution.'[19] The Plan of Action adopted at the conference also reflected this shift in approach in how it contained significantly greater emphasis on the individual-rights dimension of reproductive issues. The Plan of Action recommended that all countries '[r]espect and ensure, regardless of their over-all demographic goals, the right of persons to determine, in a free, informed and responsible manner, the number and spacing of their children.'[20] The addition of the language of 'regardless of their over-all demographic goals' highlighted the shift towards prioritising individual rights to reproductive choice over the interests of governments in population control.[21] This was reinforced in the explicit inclusion of the rights of individuals, as opposed to the language of 'parents' reflected in the Proclamation of Teheran, in the statement that 'all couples and individuals have the basic right to decide freely and responsibly the number and spacing of their children and to have the information, education and means to do so.'[22]

During the 1970s, feminist critiques of coercive reproductive practices resulting from population control policies continued to mature, with women's rights organisations, in particular from the Global South, increasingly calling for a right to reproductive choice rooted in the notion of bodily integrity and control.[23] The 1979 Convention on the Elimination of All Forms of Discrimination against Women reflected a significant legal development, codifying men and women's equal right 'to decide freely and responsibly on the number and spacing of their children and to have access to the information, education and means to enable them to exercise these rights.'[24] The 1984 International Conference on Population in Mexico further reflected some of these normative developments in an increasingly human rights centred approach to population control, with its Recommendations for the Further Implementation of the

---

19 *Ibid.*

20 UN Population Division, UN World Population Conference 19 to 30 August 1974, Bucharest, World Population Plan of Action (WPPA), E/CONF, 60/L. 55, para 29(a) [hereafter 1974 World Population Plan of Action].

21 Pizzarossa (n 4), 3.

22 1974 World Population Plan of Action (n 20), para 14(f).

23 Sonia Corrêa and Rebecca Lynn Reichmann, *Population and Reproductive Rights: Feminist Perspectives from the South* (Zed Books 1994), 57.

24 Article 16(e), Convention on the Elimination of All Forms of Discrimination against Women New York, 18 December 1979.

WPPA reiterating the 'basic human right of all couples and individuals to decide freely and responsibly on the number and spacing of their children.'[25] The recommendations further required that '[l]egislation and policies concerning the family and programmes of incentives and disincentives should be neither coercive nor discriminatory and should be consistent with internationally recognized human rights as well as with changing individual and cultural values.'[26]

Despite the increasing association of reproductive matters with the question of individual human rights, the conference in Mexico notoriously also reflected continuing controversies that surrounded the issue that captures the notion of individual reproductive choice in perhaps its clearest form – abortion. Reflecting the expansion of a transnational 'pro-life' movement that originated in the United States, at the Mexico conference the US announced what came to be labelled the 'global gag rule'. Namely, that the US would significantly reduce funding for international family planning organisations, and would no longer fund those that provided abortion services.[27] While women's rights organisations lobbied to include reference to access to legal and safe abortion in the text, only Sweden strongly contested the subsequent inclusion of the statement in the plan of action that called on governments 'to take appropriate steps to help women avoid abortion, which in no case should be promoted as a method of family planning.'[28]

The most significant consolidating development in the evolving international discourse on reproductive matters took place at the 1994 International Conference on Population and Development in Cairo. The Cairo Conference has been described as having 'transformed the conversation'[29] around population control in the extent to which it came to centre human rights. The dominant discourse and policy debate on population prior to the ICPD had been 'focused on the control of fertility, understood entirely as women's fertility.'[30] By contrast, the 1994 Programme of Action called for 'sustained economic

25 UN Population Division, Second Conference on Population 6 to 14 August 1984, Mexico, Recommendations for the Further Implementation of the World Population Plan of Action Adopted in the World Population Conference, E/CONF.76/19, Recommendation 30 [hereafter 1984 World Population Plan of Action].

26 *Ibid.*, Recommendation 31.

27 Jutta M. Joachim, *Agenda Setting, the UN, and NGOs: Gender Violence and Reproductive Rights* (Georgetown University Press 2007), 139.

28 1984 World Population Plan of Action (n 25), para 18(e). See also Joachim (n 27), 141.

29 Pizzarossa (n 4), 6.

30 Mindy Roseman and Laura Reichenbach, 'Global reproductive health and rights: reflecting on ICPD' in Laura Reichenbach and Mindy Roseman (eds), *Reproductive Health and Human Rights: The Way Forward* (University of Pennsylvania Press 2009), 4.

growth in the context of sustainable development; education, especially for girls; gender equity and equality; infant, child and maternal mortality reduction; and the provision of universal access to reproductive health services, including family planning and sexual health.'[31] The Programme of Action in this way represented a significant evolution in how reproductive matters were addressed within the population control paradigm; it stressed that population concerns were indivisible from the wider economic and social development agendas, in particular the need for women's empowerment.[32]

In addition, the Programme of Action adopted an explicit definition of reproductive rights and reproductive health. Stressing that 'reproductive rights embrace certain human rights that are already recognized in national laws, international human rights documents and other consensus documents', the Programme of Action defined reproductive rights as resting on 'the recognition of the basic right of all couples and individuals to decide freely and responsibly the number, spacing and timing of their children and to have the information and means to do so, and the right to attain the highest standard of sexual and reproductive health.'[33] Importantly, the Programme of Action went on to stress that reproductive rights also includes the right to 'make decisions concerning reproduction free of discrimination, coercion and violence, as expressed in human rights documents.'[34] The Programme of Action defined reproductive health as 'a state of complete physical, mental and social well-being and not merely the absence of disease or infirmity, in all matters relating to the reproductive system and to its functions and processes. Reproductive health therefore implies that people are able to have a satisfying and safe sex life and that they have the capability to reproduce and the freedom to decide if, when and how often to do so.'[35]

While remaining embedded within the field of population policy, the definitions of reproductive health and rights adopted in the 1994 Programme of Action, with their emphasis on individual freedom and choice, in this way nevertheless consolidated the normative shift in the international discourse on reproductive matters away from a top-down concern with regulating fertility

31 UNFPA, Programme of Action Adopted at the International Conference on Population and Development 5–13 September 1994, Cairo, A/CONF.171/13, para 1.12 [hereafter 1994 Programme of Action].

32 Roseman and Reichenbach (n 30), 4.

33 1994 Programme of Action (n 31), para 7.3.

34 *Ibid.*

35 *Ibid.*, para 7.2.

'toward the notion of reproductive health, predicated on the exercise of reproductive rights and women's empowerment.'[36]

The Cairo Conference was nevertheless not without controversy, with conservative states, led by the Holy See, and Catholic and Muslim-majority countries hotly contesting draft texts that referred to abortion, individual sexual and reproductive rights, sterilization and the use of condoms.[37] These debates continued to animate discussion during the 1995 Fourth World Conference on Women in Beijing, but did not succeed in altering the consensus achieved the previous year, with the Beijing Declaration and Platform for Action declaring emphatically that '[t]he right of all women to control all aspects of their health, in particular their fertility, is basic to their empowerment.'[38] In this way, the evolution of how reproductive matters were addressed on the international stage reflects a pronounced shift from a collective, governmental concern with limiting population growth through controlling women's fertility, towards an individual rights paradigm in which individual freedom and choice in matters of sexual and reproductive health came to be understood instead as being intrinsically linked to achieving women's equality and empowerment.

In addition to consolidating the turn towards a human rights-based approach to reproductive health, the Beijing Declaration and Programme for Action also expanded on the link between reproductive matters and violence and coercion, initially identified in the 1994 Programme of Action on population and development. The 1995 Beijing Declaration and Programme for Action reiterated that 'the human rights of women include their right to have control over and decide freely and responsibly on matters related to their sexuality, including sexual and reproductive health, free of coercion, discrimination and violence.'[39] It went on to include specific acts of reproductive violence in its identification of forms of violence inflicted on women, explaining that these 'include violation[s] of the human rights of women in situations of armed conflict, in particular murder, systematic rape, sexual slavery and forced pregnancy, [and] include forced sterilisation and forced abortion, coercive/forced use of contraceptives, female infanticide and prenatal sex selection.'[40] This recognition of certain acts targeting women's reproductive capacity as constituting forms of violence that violate international human rights and humanitarian

36 Roseman and Reichenbach (n 30), 4.

37 Pizzarossa (n 4), 7.

38 UN, Beijing Declaration and Platform for Action, Fourth World Conference on Women 4 to 15 September 1995, Beijing, A/CONF.177/20, para 92.

39 *Ibid.*, para 96.

40 *Ibid.*, para 114–115.

law underscores the extent of the normative shift that had taken place by this point, from a paradigm that prioritised control of women's fertility as a means of limiting population growth, and to some extent tolerated practices involving coercion in order to achieve these aims, to one which instead identified such acts explicitly as forms of violence against women.

Significant developments have continued in the legal arena on rights to sexual and reproductive health, with human rights courts and treaty bodies expanding on the nature and scope of these rights and how they interact with other human rights, such as the right to life, freedom from torture and cruel inhuman or degrading treatment, the right to equality and non-discrimination and the right to respect for private and family life.[41] At the same time, the international discourse on reproductive matters has remained primarily tied to the notions of rights to sexual and reproductive *health*, with the nature and scope of reproductive rights per se continuing to be disputed.[42] Only the 2003 Protocol to the African Charter on Human and Peoples' Rights on the Rights of Women in Africa (Maputo Protocol) explicitly affirms, as a legal instrument, that women's reproductive rights are human rights.[43] While the Maputo Protocol also codified in this respect an obligation on states parties to take measures to 'protect the reproductive rights of women by authorising medical abortion in cases of sexual assault, rape, incest, and where the continued pregnancy endangers the mental and physical health of the mother or the life of the mother or the foetus',[44] representing the first and only binding human rights instrument that guarantees access to abortion as a right in some circumstances,[45] the issue of abortion also continues to be heavily contested in international fora.[46]

Historically, the normative environment that existed prior to the criminalisation of forms of reproductive violence under international law was in this way characterised by the normalisation of female reproductive labour and

---

41 Carole J Petersen, 'Reproductive Justice, Public Policy, and Abortion on the Basis of Fetal Impairment: Lessons from International Human Rights Law and the Potential Impact of the Convention on the Rights of Persons with Disabilities', (2015) 28(1) *Journal of Law and Health*, 146.

42 Gebhard and Trimiño Mora (n 3), para 2.

43 Article 14, 2003 Protocol to the African Charter on Human and Peoples' Rights on the Rights of Women in Africa (Maputo Protocol).

44 *Ibid.*, Article 14(1)(c).

45 Christina Zampas and Jaime M. Gher, 'Abortion as a Human Right-International and Regional Standards', (2008) 8(2) *Human Rights Law Review*, 250.

46 Pizzarossa (n 4), 13.

limited reproductive agency for women in many societies.[47] Reflecting this wider social order, in international discourses, coercive practices targeting individuals' reproductive capacities ultimately enjoyed a degree of legitimacy on the grounds that they contributed to population control, which was in turn framed as necessary for the fulfilment of human rights, only later coming to be conceptualised as constituting forms of violence. It is therefore perhaps unsurprising that forms of reproductive violence, outside of the context of genocide, were not explicitly prohibited under international law until the codification of the Rome Statute in 1998.

Despite this pre-Rome Statute doctrinal omission of forms of violence targeted at a person's reproductive capacity, international criminal law has also addressed – often indirectly and never categorised explicitly as such – multiple different forms of reproductive violence that have taken place in the context of armed conflict or widespread human rights abuses. The contexts in which these acts of violence were recognised, and how they were conceptualised, nevertheless mirrors in many ways the collectivist concerns of the population control paradigm, in how they subordinated individual interests to the perceived need to control the growth of a population as a whole. The same conceptual pattern is apparent in how evidence of reproductive violence was dealt with in international criminal legal frameworks, in which those forms of reproductive violence that were addressed indirectly were conceptualised primarily as targeting and harming groups, with more limited attention to the individual on whom the reproductive violence was directly inflicted.

Violence targeted at a person's reproductive capacity was first addressed factually in international law at the Nuremberg trials, where evidence was heard of medical experiments involving forced sterilization inflicted on male and female inmates of concentration camps in Auschwitz, Dachau and Ravensbruck.[48] These experiments were the first instance of violence targeting reproductive capacity, while not labelled as such, to be recognised as constituting war crimes and crimes against humanity.[49] There is also some limited evidence in the records of the UN War Crimes Commission of experiments involving forced abortions having taken place in concentration camps.[50] The

47 Rosemary Elliot and Zubin Mistry, 'Introduction: Gender and Reproduction', (2020) 32(3) *Gender and History*, 515–516.

48 Trial of German Major War Criminals (n 9), 466; Schabas (n 9), 192.

49 Christopher K Hall, Joseph Powderly and Niamh Hayes, 'Article 7(1)(g) Rape ... or any other form of sexual violence of comparable gravity' in Otto Triffterer and Kai Ambos (eds), *Rome Statute of the International Criminal Court: A Commentary* (Beck/Hart 2016), 216.

50 Altunjan (n 1), 81.

experiments involving forced sterilizations were explicitly linked to the genocidal campaign at Nuremberg, described by the prosecution in one case as part of a strategy to develop 'a new branch of medical science which would give them the scientific tools for the planning and practice of genocide. The primary purpose was to discover an inexpensive, unobtrusive, and rapid method of sterilization which could be used to wipe out Russians, Poles, Jews, and other people.'[51]

Evidence of widespread reproductive violence inflicted on women who were sexually enslaved at so-called 'comfort stations' operated by the Imperial Japanese Army during the Second World War also emerged at the International War Crimes Tribunal on Japan's Military Sexual Slavery (Tokyo Women's Tribunal), a peoples' tribunal established by civil society in 2000. The findings of the Tokyo Women's Tribunal revealed that many of the victims of sexual slavery were also subjected to forced impregnation as a result of rape. In such cases, women had no choice over whether to continue with a pregnancy. Some were forced to undergo abortions while others were denied access.[52]

Following the Second World War, the codification of the Genocide Convention in 1948, with its criminalisation of '[i]mposing measures intended to prevent births within the group',[53] constituted the first direct engagement with reproductive violence under international law. It also captured the dominant contemporary conceptualisation of reproductive violence in how it reflected the goal of protecting the existence of a group, rather than being normatively concerned with interference with an individual's reproductive capacity in its own right.[54]

Violence targeting reproductive capacity during armed conflict next came to international attention during the Yugoslav war. The UN Commission of Experts, established to investigate violations of international humanitarian law in the former Yugoslavia, found evidence that in some instances women were being detained for the purpose of being forcibly impregnated. The Commission's Final Report provided accounts from victims of prison camps, who stated that they had been forcibly impregnated by their captors and kept in detention until it was too late for them to obtain an abortion.[55] This conduct

51 Transcripts of the *Medical Case* as cited in Altunjan (n 1), 81.

52 Grey (n 1), 914.

53 Article 2(d), Convention on the Prevention and Punishment of the Crime of Genocide (1948).

54 Grey (n 5), 1.

55 UN Security Council, Final Report of the Commission of Experts Established Pursuant to Security Council Resolution 780 (1992), 27 May 1994, S/1994/674, para 248.

was understood to form part of the broader policy of ethnic cleansing, with victims being forcibly impregnated in order that they would give birth to children of the perpetrator's ethnicity.[56]

The wider scholarly and civil society discourse around crimes against women taking place in Yugoslavia reflected the continuing normative conception of reproductive violence as primarily directed at and harming ethnic groups, or taking place as a consequence of or exacerbating factor in other crimes. Charli Carpenter has argued that those advocating for the legal recognition of forced impregnation in Yugoslavia relied on two types of arguments to support their advocacy. Firstly, forced impregnation was addressed in the context of advocacy around rape and sexual violence, as a factor exacerbating the seriousness of rape, becoming in this way 'an exclamation point to arguments that *rape* should be treated as a war crime and a crime against humanity.'[57] In addition, forced impregnation figured centrally in arguments advocating for the recognition of rape as an act of genocide. Secondly, forced impregnation was addressed in its own right as an act of genocide, or, in some instances, as a war crime or crime against humanity. This last group of arguments reflected an emerging normative shift in how they began to draw out more emphatically the individualised dimensions of the harms of forced impregnation, comparing the act to torture and arguing that it constituted a violation of a woman's self-determination and personal dignity on its own terms.[58]

Charges related to forced pregnancy were nevertheless not ultimately pursued at the ICTY. However, a number of cases dealt indirectly with evidence of women being forcibly impregnated in the context of the campaign of ethnic cleansing. In the *Kunarac* case, the defendant, who detained women and girls in the Foča camp and used them as sex slaves, told one of his victims that she would now bear a Serb baby.[59] Similar evidence was submitted in the initial indictment in the *Gagović* case.[60] Witnesses at the Trnoplije camp spoke of women at the camp seeking abortions for pregnancies resulting from rape[61] while in the *Brđanin* case, one of the direct perpetrators of rape was described as having 'made no secret that he wanted a Bosnian Muslim to "give birth to a

56 *Ibid.*, 250(b).

57 R. Charli Carpenter, 'Surfacing Children: Limitations of Genocidal Rape Discourse', (2000) 22(2), *Human Rights Quarterly*, 432. Emphasis in the original.

58 *Ibid.*

59 *Prosecutor v. Dragoljub Kunarac et al.*, IT-96-23-T & IT-96-23/1-T, ICTY, Trial Judgment, 22 February 2001, para 342, 583.

60 *Prosecutor v. Dragan Gagović et al.*, IT-96-23, ICTY, Indictment, 19 June 1996, para 9.13.

61 *Prosecutor v. Mićo Stanišić & Stojan Župljanin,* IT-08-91-T, ICTY, Trial Judgment, 23 March 2013, para 629.

little Serb'".[62] During the review of indictments against Karadžić and Mladić, the Trial Chamber noted that 'some camps were specially devoted to rape, with the aim of forcing the birth of Serbian offspring, the women often being interned until it was too late to undergo an abortion', adding that 'the aim of many rapes was enforced impregnation.'[63]

Despite evidence of widespread rape resulting in pregnancies having taken place during the genocide in Rwanda, with an estimated 2,000–5,000 women and girls having become pregnant as a result of rape,[64] no charges addressing reproductive violence directly were pursued at the ICTR either. The judgment in the *Akayesu* case nevertheless contained evidence of various forms of reproductive violence that took place in the context of the genocide. The Trial Chamber addressed evidence of pregnant women having suffered miscarriages as a result of being raped and beaten by Hutu militia[65] and also noted that 'even pregnant women, including those of Hutu origin, were killed on the grounds that the foetuses in their wombs were fathered by Tutsi men, for in a patrilineal society like Rwanda, the child belongs to the father's group of origin.'[66]

In its analysis of imposing measures intended to prevent births within the group as a constitutive act of genocide, the Trial Chamber in *Akayesu* also recognised that 'in patriarchal societies, where membership of a group is determined by the identity of the father, an example of a measure intended to prevent births within a group is the case where, during rape, a woman of the said group is deliberately impregnated by a man of another group, with the intent to have her give birth to a child who will consequently not belong to its mother's group.'[67]

While evidence relating to different forms of reproductive violence has in this way appeared throughout the history of international criminal law, it had

62 *Prosecutor v. Radoslav Brđanin*, IT-99-36-T, ICTY, Trial Judgment, 1 September 2004, para 1011.

63 *Prosecutor v. Radovan Karadžić and Ratko Mladić*, ICTY-95-5-R61 & ICTY-95-18-R61, ICTY, Oral Ruling on Review of the Indictments pursuant to Rule 61 of the Rules of Procedure and Evidence Transcript 11 July 1996, 959–960 [as cited in Saeeda Verrall, 'The Picture of Sexual Violence in the Former Yugoslavia Conflicts as Reflected in ICTY Judgments', in Serge Brammertz and Michelle Jarvis (ed), *Prosecuting Conflict-Related Sexual Violence at the ICTY* (Oxford University Press 2016), 328–329].

64 Binaifer Nowrojee, *Shattered Lives: Sexual Violence During the Rwandan Genocide and its Aftermath*, Human Rights Watch and FIDH, 1996, 3.

65 *Prosecutor v. Jean-Paul Akayesu*, ICTR-96-4-T, ICTY, Trial Judgment, 2 September 1998, para 428, 437.

66 *Ibid.*, para 121.

67 *Ibid.*, para 507.

been addressed only indirectly, and acts of reproductive violence had not been charged as crimes in their own right. In addition, evidence of reproductive violence had been addressed overwhelmingly in contexts of genocide or ethnic cleansing. In such contexts, and mirroring the normative orientation of the wider international discourse on reproductive matters through the population control paradigm, the focus therefore continued to be placed on 'the impact on the group to which the victim 'belongs'',[68] with the interests of the individual victim, and the harms inflicted on them, subordinated to this wider normative concern.

This group-based conception of reproductive violence has clear parallels with the evolution of the recognition of rape and sexual violence in international law. As discussed in the previous chapter, in their early iterations, prohibitions on rape and sexual violence were defined in terms of protecting women from 'any attack on their honour.'[69] Such definitions were criticised on the grounds that they 'assume that women should be protected from sexual crimes because they implicate a woman's honour',[70] reinforcing the idea that women are to be protected as the property of men or communities, rather than because such acts constitute violence inflicted on them as individuals.

The treatment of reproductive violence in international criminal law until this point, with its focus on situations involving violence directed at an individual's reproductive capacity as a result of their identity as a member of a group, has followed a similar trajectory. By acknowledging this type of violence only in such contexts, international criminal law repeated the tendency to focus on the violation of the rights of the group to which the victim belongs, as opposed to the violation of their rights as an individual. This framing of reproductive violence has been criticised for perpetuating the traditionally patriarchal view of women as 'little more than vessels for childbearing.'[71] The historical treatment of reproductive violence in international criminal law has for this reason attracted criticism similar to that directed at historical definitions of sexual violence in how it has 'drawn condemnation only when it reflects an intent to harm the victimized race',[72] and in doing so, failed to recognise the direct

68 Grey (n 1), 908.

69 Article 3(c), Convention (IV) relative to the Protection of Civilian Persons in Time of War, Geneva, 12 August 1949.

70 Hilary Charlesworth, 'Feminist Methods in International Law', (1999) 93(2) *American Journal of International Law*, 386.

71 Rhonda Copelon, 'Surfacing Gender: Re-Engraving Crimes Against Women in Humanitarian Law', (1994) 5(2) *Hastings Journal of International Law*, 263.

72 *Ibid.*

victims, most of whom have been female, as individual subjects outside of their role in ensuring the reproduction of a particular group.

2 Definitions of Reproductive Violence in the Rome Statute

The codification of the Rome Statute marked a normative turning point in this respect. It added forced pregnancy and enforced sterilization as crimes against humanity and war crimes to the forms of reproductive violence criminalised under international law, alongside the existing genocidal act of imposing measures intended to prevent births within a group.[73] Despite their prior recognition as violations of international human rights and humanitarian law in the 1993 Vienna Declaration and Program for Action and the 1995 Beijing Platform for Action,[74] the drafting of the crimes of reproductive violence, in particular forced pregnancy, proved to be some of the most contentious provisions negotiated at the Rome Conference, with lack of consensus on their definitions continuing until the very final days of the conference.[75] The particular nature of the debates that took place during the drafting of the crimes of forced pregnancy and enforced sterilization captured the continuing controversies over reproductive rights that had animated discussions during the Vienna and Beijing conferences between states that adopted more progressive positions and those that vigorously resisted developments in this area.

2.1 *Forced Pregnancy*

During the Preparatory Committee meetings in 1996, the proposed language on forced pregnancy referred to 'forced impregnation' as a crime against humanity. This language was not acceptable to certain delegations, including a number of women's rights NGOs, on the grounds that it could be understood to refer only to the act of making the victim pregnant, and excluded keeping her pregnant. These delegations preferred the language of 'enforced pregnancy', understood to also include keeping the victim pregnant.[76] By contrast, religious-conservative delegations, including the Holy See, certain Catholic

73 Article 7(1)(g) and Article 8(2)(b)(xxii), Rome Statute.

74 Cottier and Mzee (n 4), 498.

75 *Ibid.*, 499. For a comprehensive overview of the drafting of the crimes of forced pregnancy and enforced sterilization see Altunjan (n 1), 196–207, 273–274.

76 Cate Steains, 'Gender Issues' in Roy S. Lee (ed), *The International Criminal Court: The Making of the Rome Statute – Issues, Negotiations, Results* (Kluwer Law International 1999), 366.

and Islamic states and anti-abortion NGOs, opposed the language of 'enforced pregnancy' on the grounds that this could include situations in which women were denied access to abortions.[77] For instance, Iran objected to the criminalisation of forced pregnancy on the basis that doing so could 'be used as an argument against the prohibition of abortion and should therefore be dropped.'[78] Other states also expressed disagreement with the underlying principle of recognising reproductive violence as in some way distinct from sexual violence, taking the position that 'enforced pregnancy was the result of rape and it was the act itself that should constitute the crime.'[79] The Holy See was particularly concerned that the language of enforced pregnancy could be interpreted to reflect a recognition of a right to abortion, whether during armed conflict or as a more general precedent in international law.[80] In this sense, disagreement centred fundamentally around some delegations' concerns that criminalising violence of this nature might entrench a broader recognition of rights to reproductive choice in international law.[81]

As a result of this controversy, the term '*en*forced pregnancy' was replaced with that of 'forced pregnancy' during the Rome Conference, with the inclusion of a definition of the crime in the Statute.[82] The Rome Statute defines forced pregnancy as 'the unlawful confinement of a woman forcibly made pregnant, with the intent of affecting the ethnic composition of any population or carrying out other grave violations of international law.'[83] The restriction that the definition of forced pregnancy 'shall not in any way be interpreted as affecting national laws relating to pregnancy'[84] was also added in order to satisfy those states concerned that the crime could be used to undermine domestic anti-abortion laws or complicate the position of Catholic hospitals that do not permit women who have been victims of rape to access abortions.[85] The compromise achieved through this definition makes clear that the actus reus of

---

77 Altunjan (n 1), 201–202; Steains (n 76), 366–367. See also for instance United Nations Diplomatic Conference of Plenipotentiaries on the Establishment of an International Criminal Court 15–17 July 1998, Summary records of the plenary meetings and of the meetings of the Committee of the Whole – Volume II, 163 at para 21.

78 *Ibid.*, 166 at para 72.

79 *Ibid.*, 160 at para 63. See also Kuwait, 162 para 11; Egypt, 164 para 33.

80 Cottier and Mzee (n 4), 498.

81 Grey (n 1), 919; Kristen Boon, 'Rape and Forced Pregnancy under the ICC Statute: Human Dignity, Autonomy and Consent', (2000) *Columbia Human Rights Law Review*, 658.

82 Boon (n 81), 658.

83 Article 7(1)(g), Rome Statute.

84 Article 7(2)(f), Rome Statute.

85 Steains (n 76), 368.

forced pregnancy is the confinement of the victim to keep her pregnant, rather than the act of forcibly making her pregnant.[86] In this way, a number of situations where either of these requirements are not met, such as situations where a woman is forcibly made pregnant without being subsequently confined, but who may nevertheless be unable to terminate the pregnancy, would therefore not meet the definition of forced pregnancy.[87]

The second dimension of the definition of forced pregnancy requires that the perpetrator undertook the conduct with the intent of 'affecting the ethnic composition of any population or carrying out other grave violations of international law.'[88] The first type of intent was included as a direct response to the reports of forced pregnancies that emerged during the conflict in Yugoslavia.[89] It ties the definition back to situations in which reproductive violence is used as a tool of genocide or ethnic cleansing. At a conceptual level, this requirement perpetuates the previously discussed tendency to de-centralise the harms inflicted on the direct victims of crimes of reproductive violence by subordinating them to the purpose with which the crime is committed. By requiring this type of intent, the definition of forced pregnancy in this way partly prioritises the preservation of the 'ethnic composition' of a population over the normative significance of the violence directly experienced by the victim.[90]

The alternative intent of 'carrying out other grave violations of international law' is broader, with suggested interpretations drawing on the links between torture, cruel and inhumane treatment, and sexual assaults[91] or understanding grave violations of international law to refer to the crime categories of genocide, war crimes and crimes against humanity.[92] The interpretation of this intent element in the first trial to involve charges for forced pregnancy at the ICC is discussed in the next section of this chapter. This aspect of the definition has nevertheless been characterised as a 'qualified success'[93] for feminist

86 Kai Ambos, *Treatise on International Criminal Law: Volume II: The Crimes and Sentencing* (Oxford University Press 2014), 102.

87 Grey (n 1), 921.

88 Article 7(1)(g).

89 Grey (n 1), 918.

90 Alyson Drake, 'Aimed at Protecting Ethnic Groups or Women? A Look at Forced Pregnancy under the Rome Statute', (2012) 18(3) *William and Mary Journal of Women and the Law*, 596.

91 Boon (n 81), 665.

92 Ambos (n 86), 10.

93 Louise Chappell, 'Women's Rights and Religious Opposition: The Politics of Gender at the International Criminal Court' in Yasmeen Abu-Laban (ed), *Gendering the Nation State: Canadian and Comparative Perspectives* (UCB Press, 2008), 154.

actors, since it expands the possible scope of the crime beyond situations involving ethnic conflict and in this way also broadens its normative scope beyond the protection of ethnic groups. At the same time, by continuing to require evidence of an intent to carry out other violations of international law, the definition nevertheless continues to imply that forced pregnancy, in the absence of an intent to commit other violations of international law, would be insufficiently grave to justify criminalisation.

Ultimately, on a conceptual level, by requiring an additional level of intent of any kind, the definition of forced pregnancy arguably subordinates the normative significance of the wrong inflicted on the direct victim to the intent of the perpetrator in carrying out the crime. This evidently also has practical effects, since 'even if the prosecutor shows that the perpetrator did confine a victim forcibly made pregnant, that the perpetrator intended that act to be part of a widespread or systematic attack [...] the perpetrator will not be found guilty if the prosecutor is unable to show this further intent.'[94] From a normative perspective, these intent requirements therefore limit the extent to which the individual wrong experienced by the victim of forced pregnancy may be considered to underlie this definition of the crime. Arguably, the principle or value invoked by the criminalisation of forced pregnancy in these terms is ultimately the existence of an ethnic group or those principles or values understood to attach to the other provisions of international law that the perpetrator intended to violate. For this reason, the crime of forced pregnancy has been interpreted to be reflective of 'the continuing insistence [...] that control is maintained over women's reproductive capacity [which] has subjugated gender identity to ethnic identity or other international law imperatives.'[95]

2.2 *Enforced Sterilization*

Enforced sterilization is defined in the ICC Elements of Crimes as that the perpetrator deprived one or more persons of biological reproductive capacity, which was neither justified by the medical or hospital treatment of the person or persons concerned nor carried out with their genuine consent.[96] While less contentious than the drafting of the crime of forced pregnancy, enforced sterilization produced similar concerns among some states in terms of the potential impact of the definition of the crime on domestic legislation related

94 Drake (n 90), 616.

95 Christine Chinkin, 'Gender-related Violence and International Criminal Law and Justice', in Antonio Cassese, Dapo Akande and Guido Acquaviva (eds), *The Oxford Companion to International Criminal Justice* (Oxford University Press 2009), 77–78.

96 Article 7(1)(g)-5, ICC Elements of Crimes.

to reproductive rights.[97] Highlighting in this respect the continuing tension between some states' concern with controlling population growth and notions of individual reproductive self-determination, the Chinese delegation, for instance, proposed the inclusion of a footnote to the elements of the crime of enforced sterilization to state that '[t]he deprivation is not intended to include national birth-rate control measures aiming at controlling the growth rate of the nation's whole population.'[98]

While the Chinese proposal was not adopted, concerns of this kind ultimately resulted in the first element, that the perpetrator deprived one or more persons of biological reproductive capacity, being qualified by a footnote requiring that 'the deprivation is not intended to include birth-control measures which have a non-permanent effect in practice.'[99] In a similar way to the qualifications related to intent imposed on the definition of forced pregnancy, the requirement that the sterilization be permanent in order to constitute enforced sterilization necessarily limits the extent to which the crime can be considered to invoke a wrong related to the violation of reproductive self-determination in the absolute, since temporary violations of this principle would not in this way meet the definition of the crime.

Taken together, the shift away from the exclusive focus on identity-based motivations for reproductive violence in the Rome Statute reflected a development in the scope of application of such crimes and a moderate evolution in how they were therefore normatively conceptualised. However, the nature of their codification nevertheless reflected a continuing discomfort among some states over the relationship between the criminalisation of such acts and the recognition of reproductive rights or principles of reproductive self-determination more broadly. Both crimes were ultimately defined in a restrictive manner as a result of such concerns. In this sense, the normative underpinnings of forced pregnancy and enforced sterilization, i.e. precisely the principles or values they were (not) intended to protect, was central in how their definitions were ultimately formulated.

---

97 Altunjan (n 1), 273–274. See also Hall, Powderly and Hayes (n 49), 216.

98 Preparatory Commission for the International Criminal Court 1999h as cited in Altunjan (n 1), 274.

99 Article 7(1)(g)-5, ICC Elements of Crimes.

3 Normative Themes in the Case Law

Since their codification in the Rome Statute in 1998, the crimes of forced pregnancy and enforced sterilization have not featured prominently in the case law of the ICC or other international courts and tribunals. At the time of writing, the crime of enforced sterilization had not been charged in an international criminal trial. With the exception of the *Ongwen* trial at the ICC, which is discussed below, the crime of forced pregnancy has only been addressed by the Extraordinary Chambers in the Courts of Cambodia (ECCC) in *Case 004*.

3.1 *No Rights, No Crime*

In 2016, the Civil Party Lawyers in *Case 004* at the ECCC requested investigative action into forced pregnancy as a crime against humanity, to be charged under the residual category of 'other inhumane acts.'[100] The request for investigation related to pregnancies resulting from the Khmer Rouge's policy of forced marriage, in which couples were forced into marriage and coerced into having intercourse under threat of punishment, as a means of increasing the birth rate to support Cambodia's agricultural production.[101] While the request to investigate acts of forced pregnancy was ultimately rejected by the Chamber, its analysis of the nature of the category of other inhumane acts in relation to forced pregnancy for the period in question, namely the late 1970s, underscores some of the thorny normative questions attached to the criminalisation of this form of violence from a historical perspective.

The Chamber rejected the request to investigate forced pregnancy for a number of reasons, including on the grounds that 'there was no settled definition of the concept of forced pregnancy in Cambodian or international law between 1975 and 1979, and no clear human rights standard tied to conduct amounting to forced pregnancy, a violation of which could rise to the level of an "other inhumane act."'[102] In its analysis of the appropriate method for determining whether a certain act may be considered to fit within the category of 'other

100 *Prosecutor v. Ao An and Yim Tith* (*Case 004*), 004/07-09-2009-ECCC-OCIJ, ECCC, Consolidated Decision on the Requests for Investigative Action Concerning the Crime of Forced Pregnancy and Forced Impregnation, 13 June 2016, para 13 [hereafter Ao An and Yim Tith Decision on the Requests for Investigative Action].

101 Maria Lobato, 'Forced Pregnancy During the Khmer Rouge Regime: Acknowledging Forced Pregnancy as a Distinct Crime in the ECCC Proceedings', Cambodian Human Rights Action Coalition 2016, 12–19. See also *Prosecutor v. Nuon Chea and Samphan Khieu* (*Case 002/02*), 002/19-09-2007-ECCC/OCIJ, ECCC, Second Request for Investigative Actions Concerning Forced Marriages and Forced Sexual Relations, 15 July 2009, para 29.

102 Ao An and Yim Tith Decision on the Requests for Investigative Action (n 100), para 31.

inhumane acts', and therefore to have constituted customary international law at the relevant date, the Chamber explained that 'there must be a customarily accepted standard, tied to the appropriate human rights, by which the "inhumanity" of the act is judged.'[103] The subsequent analysis therefore consists of seeking to identify a possible normative standard to which the criminalisation of forced pregnancy as an other inhumane act could have been linked at the time. It is worth quoting at length:

> Pre-1975 international human rights instruments contained neither a definition of forced pregnancy, nor a clear human rights standard against which to assess forced pregnancy. Various international human rights instruments acknowledged the rights to physical integrity and freedom from interference with one's privacy and family life, which encompassed "the right to personal autonomy, personal development and to establish and develop relationships with other human beings and the outside world." [...] The linkage between reproductive choice and sexual violence in the context of armed conflict was not articulated until 1993 in the Vienna Declaration and Programme of Action, and the 1995 Beijing Declaration and Platform for Action. [...] Given that by 1975 in Cambodia, there was no law against forced pregnancy, and abortion was explicitly criminalised, and that even today there is no global consensus on abortion rights, even after rape, it cannot readily be said that the right to physical integrity, freedom from interference in family and private life and to determine the number and spacing of children were widely accepted as fundamental rights, the serious violation of which could amount to "other inhumane acts." [...] The gradual, but slow, acknowledgment of forced pregnancy as a crime in international criminal law highlights the divide between collectivist and individualistic legal traditions, where differences in norms have resulted in contrasting views on reproductive choice, sexual relations, abortion, and the expansion of women's rights. While the concept of personal and reproductive autonomy has gained prominence, there is insufficient evidence of state practice or *opinio juris* on which to assert that from 1975 to 1979, breaches of such autonomy were considered by the international community to be a serious violation of fundamental human rights.[104]

103 *Ibid.*, para 64.

104 *Ibid.*, para 70–74.

This decision brings into relief the relatively rapid normative development constituted by the criminalisation of forced pregnancy in the Rome Statute in 1998. This took place from a position only two decades earlier in which such acts were not only not explicitly criminalised under international law but also, as the Chamber argues, were not even widely considered wrongful or understood to constitute a violation of a victim's rights, since the relevant rights had not at that point emerged within international discourses.

Reflecting a significant shift in how this crime is normatively conceptualised compared to the historical analysis offered by the ECCC, the trial of Dominic Ongwen at the ICC was the first and, at time of writing, only case at an international criminal tribunal to have involved charges for forced pregnancy. In this case, the Trial and Appeals Chambers engaged extensively with the normative dimensions of the crime of forced pregnancy, marking a radical departure from the crime's normative history.

3.2 *Intent: Beyond Ethnic Groups*

Dominic Ongwen, a former commander in the Lord's Resistance Army (LRA) in northern Uganda, was convicted, among other crimes, of having abducted women and girls to serve as forced wives for members of the LRA. These women were used as sexual and domestic slaves and many became pregnant as a result of rape. Ongwen was convicted of three counts of forced pregnancy for having forcibly impregnated two women through rape, who he also confined during their pregnancies by using threats and coercion to prevent them from escaping.[105] During the confirmation of charges process, the Prosecution had argued that this conduct fulfilled the definition of forced pregnancy on the grounds that Ongwen confined women with the intention of carrying out 'other grave violations of international law', namely to continue to rape, torture and sexually enslave them.[106] The Trial and Appeals Chambers endorsed this interpretation of the necessary intent for forced pregnancy, concluding that Ongwen's conduct fulfilled the definition of the crime on the grounds that he confined the victims with the intent to sustain the continued commission

---

105 *Prosecutor v. Dominic Ongwen*, ICC-02/04-01/15, ICC, Trial Judgment, 4 February 2021, para 3056–3062 [hereafter Ongwen Trial Judgment].

106 *Prosecutor v. Dominic Ongwen*, Decision on the confirmation of charges against Dominic Ongwen, ICC-02/04-01/15, ICC, 23 March 2016, para 101 [hereafter Ongwen Confirmation of Charges].

of other crimes, namely those of forced marriage, torture, rape and sexual slavery.[107]

In doing so, this case marks a factual and conceptual departure from how reproductive violence has appeared fleetingly in international criminal law in the past. For the first time, it directly addressed forms of reproductive violence that take place outside of the context of ethnically motivated violence or genocide and, in doing so, also affirmed that the intent of carrying out other grave violations of international law can refer to the commission of other crimes under the Rome Statute that require no connection to ethnically motivated violence. At a conceptual level, this interpretation of the alternate intent requirement nevertheless continues to invoke a conception of the wrong that attaches to forced pregnancy which de-centralises the injury to the individual victim inflicted by forced pregnancy specifically, ultimately subordinating this to the wrongs caused by forced marriage, torture, rape and sexual slavery in this case.

At the same time, simply the nature of the facts dealt with in this case, with the intent requirement having been found to be fulfilled by the commission of crimes that also constituted the context in which the forced pregnancies were committed, have had the effect of beginning to construct a frame around forced pregnancy that extracts it from its association with harm to groups, and therefore from the construction of victims simply as vessels for childbearing, to one that invokes a normative account of the crime as a wrong in its own right.

3.3 *Reproductive Autonomy and Rights*

This conceptual shift is reinforced in a number of explicit normative statements in this case, in which the Pre-Trial, Trial and Appeals Chambers articulated a normative understanding of the crime as centring on the principle of reproductive autonomy and on protections for reproductive rights. In the Confirmation of Charges decision, the Pre-Trial Chamber asserted in this respect that 'the essence of the crime of forced pregnancy is in unlawfully placing the victim in a position in which she cannot choose whether to continue the pregnancy.'[108] In doing so, the Pre-Trial Chamber articulated a conception of the crime that invokes the principle of reproductive choice as its defining feature. This statement reflects a significant departure from the historical conceptualisation of forced pregnancy in terms of how it not only explicitly

107 Ongwen Trial Judgment (n 105), para 3061; *Prosecutor v. Dominic Ongwen*, ICC-02/04-01/15 A, ICC, Appeal Judgment, 15 December 2022, para 1101 [hereafter Ongwen Appeal Judgment].

108 Ongwen Confirmation of Charges (n 106), para 99.

centralises the direct victim as the subject that is harmed by the crime, as distinct from a group to which they belong, but also in how it constructs the nature of the wrong as emanating from the infringement on the individual's agency with respect to their reproductive life.

The Trial Chamber went even further in this respect. In its analysis of the crime, the Chamber framed the infringement on the victim's ability to make choices with respect to pregnancy explicitly as the violation of a right, concluding that 'the crime of forced pregnancy is grounded in the woman's right to personal and reproductive autonomy and the right to family.'[109] The Trial Chamber also went to lengths to emphasise the relevance of the principle of fair labelling in this respect, stressing the importance of distinguishing forced pregnancy from other crimes of sexual or gender-based violence on the basis of its distinct normative dimensions, namely 'the effect that the woman is deprived of reproductive autonomy.'[110]

On appeal, the defence engaged directly with the normative dimensions of the criminalisation of forced pregnancy, questioning the validity of the norms around reproductive autonomy and rights identified by the Trial Chamber. In its appeal brief, the defence challenged the Trial Chamber's interpretation of forced pregnancy, suggesting that the conclusion that the crime is grounded in the woman's right to personal and reproductive autonomy and the right to family 'brings forced pregnancy into the political and ideological debate on women's personal and reproductive autonomy and the right to family.'[111] Referring to the provision in the Rome Statute that the definition of forced pregnancy 'shall not in any way be interpreted as affecting national laws relating to pregnancy',[112] the defence went on to argue that the Trial Chamber:

> failed to make a reasoned enquiry about whether its interpretation [...] affects the national law of Uganda on abortion for it to satisfy the letter and spirit of the Statute. [...] The provision was added to provide guidance in the interpretation of the Statute and to avoid importing divisive contentious political, religious, cultural and ideological issues into the jurisprudence of the Court.[113]

109 Ongwen Trial Judgment (n 105), para 2717.

110 *Ibid.*, para 2722.

111 *Prosecutor v. Dominic Ongwen*, ICC-02/04-01/15, ICC, Defence Appeal Brief Against the Convictions in the Judgment of 4 February 2021, 19 October 2021, para 961 [hereafter Ongwen Defence Appeal Brief].

112 Article 7(2)(f), Rome Statute.

113 Ongwen Defence Appeal Brief (n 111), para 962.

The Appeals Chamber rejected the defence's arguments, ultimately consolidating and expanding on the Trial Chamber's interpretation of the normative basis of the criminalisation of forced pregnancy as rooted in protections for individual reproductive autonomy and rights. The Appeals Chamber endorsed the Trial Chamber's conclusion that Article 7(2)(f)'s reference to national laws relating to pregnancy does not add an additional element to the definition of the crime of forced pregnancy and stressed that Ugandan law on abortion was not therefore relevant to an assessment of the crime of forced pregnancy.[114]

In arriving at this conclusion, the Appeals Chamber outlined the observations of a number of *amici curiae,* who directly addressed the normative dimensions of the criminalisation of forced pregnancy and its legal basis in international law. The observations of the *amici curiae* highlighted by the Chamber centralised the normative conception of the crime as being rooted in protections for reproductive autonomy and rights. The Chamber recounted submissions which argued that 'the interests protected by the crime of forced pregnancy "are personal, sexual and reproductive autonomy, [which are] values central to the protection of physical integrity and human dignity"',[115] that '[t]he key distinctive component of the crime of forced pregnancy is the violation of a woman's reproductive health and autonomy'[116] and that forced pregnancy also violates 'rights to determine the way in which [an individual] may choose to be pregnant.'[117] The Appeals Chamber went on to recall the drafting history of the crime, noting that the criminalisation of forced pregnancy and enforced sterilization originated from a proposal by the Women's Caucus for Gender Justice to include what it described as 'attacks on reproductive integrity' within the list of sexual and gender-based crimes enumerated in the Statute.[118] On this basis, the Chamber concluded that the crime of forced pregnancy 'has been considered as an attack on reproductive integrity since its inception.'[119]

The Chamber went on to make its normative understanding of the crime unequivocal, stating emphatically that:

> this crime intends to protect a woman's reproductive rights, including the right to be pregnant and to autonomously determine the way

---

114 Ongwen Appeal Judgment (n 107), para 1065–1066.
115 *Ibid.*, para 1049.
116 *Ibid.*
117 *Ibid.*
118 *Ibid.*, para 1053.
119 *Ibid.*, para 1054.

> in which she carries out her pregnancy. The Appeals Chamber concurs with the Pre-Trial Chamber's finding in the Confirmation Decision that "the essence of the crime of forced pregnancy is in unlawfully placing the victim in a position in which she cannot choose whether to continue the pregnancy". The Appeals Chamber also considers that the unlawful confinement of women made pregnant can impact a number of their sexual and reproductive rights. Indeed, women in those circumstances are prevented from accessing healthcare services and information which may facilitate their decision-making on the pregnancy, including abortion. Therefore, the definition provided in article 7(2)(f) of the Statute indicates that the main focus of this crime is to protect a woman's reproductive autonomy.[120]

The Chamber rooted this understanding of the normative basis of the crime in a number of human rights conventions and instruments, enumerating in particular Article 16(1)(e) of CEDAW relating to the right to decide freely and responsibly on the number and spacing of children, Article 12(1) of CEDAW on women's equal access to healthcare, including in relation to family planning, and Article 12(1) of the ICESCR on the right to health.[121] It went on to highlight General Comment No. 22 of the UN Committee on Economic, Social and Cultural Rights on the right to sexual and reproductive health, which includes 'the right to make free and responsible decisions and choices, free of violence, coercion and discrimination, regarding matters concerning one's body and sexual and reproductive health.'[122] The Chamber further referred to the Declaration on Violence against Women, Girls and Adolescents by the Committee of Experts of the Follow-up Mechanism to the Inter-American Convention on the Prevention, Punishment and Eradication of Violence against Women, which states that 'sexual and reproductive rights are part of the catalogue of human rights that are protected and defended by the universal and inter-American human rights system; and that sexual and reproductive rights are grounded in other essential human rights.'[123] On the basis of this analysis, the Appeals Chamber confirmed that 'the crime of forced pregnancy seeks to protect, among others, the woman's reproductive health and autonomy and the right to family planning.'[124]

---

120 *Ibid.*, para 1055, 1063.
121 *Ibid.*, para 1056–1058.
122 *Ibid.*, para 1059.
123 *Ibid.*, para 1060.
124 *Ibid.*, para 1063.

The varied nature of the rights invoked by the Appeals Chamber in this context reflects how, in human rights discourses more widely, the category of 'reproductive rights' do not enjoy a settled definition and have instead been advanced by building on 'previously enshrined and widely accepted human rights, articulating [...] reproductive rights as already existing human rights that are now specifically applied to experiences related to reproduction.'[125] In the human rights context, 'reproductive rights' are therefore understood to refer either to a collection of rights that touch upon reproductive issues, such as the right to family, to decide on the number and spacing of children, to access family planning and education, or, on a wider understanding, to also capture other more well-established rights, such as the right to health or the right to equality and non-discrimination, when applied to experiences related to reproduction.[126]

Taken against a wider normative context in which the category of reproductive rights remains unsettled, and where the 'question of to what extent reproductive choice is given to the individual is very much disputed within societies [...] there exists a wide divergence of views within the international community',[127] the Trial Chamber's explicit invocation of a right specifically to reproductive autonomy, with its implication of individual reproductive agency, choice and control,[128] as a normative basis for the criminalisation of forced pregnancy, reflects a significant development. Together with the Appeals Chamber's expansive account of the nature and universality of the reproductive rights protected by the criminalisation of forced pregnancy, with individual autonomous decision-making over pregnancy and reproductive healthcare central to its analysis of these rights, these decisions constitute a significant degree of normative evolution in how forms of reproductive violence, and the wrongs that attach to them, are conceptualised and constructed in international criminal law.

4 Narratives During Proceedings

The significant emphasis in the Trial and Appeal Judgments on the principle of reproductive autonomy as central to a normative understanding of the crime of forced pregnancy mirrors the narrative that was forwarded by the

125 Pizzarossa (n 4), 8.
126 Gebhard and Trimiño Mora (n 3), para 3–5.
127 *Ibid.*, para 6.
128 Boon (n 81), 642; Laverty and de Vos (n 1), 616–635.

OTP during the course of proceedings. During opening statements, the OTP began its discussion of forced pregnancy by similarly stating that 'the value protected by the criminalisation of forced pregnancy [...] is primarily reproductive autonomy.'[129] This normative conception of the crime also emerged through the factual narrative advanced by the OTP, which followed a pattern of highlighting the question of whether or not the victim had a choice over whether to bear children.

4.1 *Did You Have a Choice?*

During opening statements the OTP described the situation of the women and girls abducted and used as forced wives by Dominic Ongwen in terms that centralised the violation of their agency and choice, stating that 'many of them became pregnant without any choice in the matter, and some gave birth to numerous children who were themselves then ingested into the ranks of the LRA.'[130] The OTP described the experience of one witness in similar terms; 'as a result of her rape by Dominic Ongwen, the witness gave birth to a son. This was not her choice. She felt that she was not ready to bear children.'[131] In its closing brief, the OTP similarly reiterated that 'these women and girls had no reproductive autonomy', emphasising that 'Mr Ongwen's forced wives were confined and monitored such that they could not refuse to become pregnant, or determine when to get pregnant, as they had no control over their bodies, no contraceptives, and no family planning was practised.'[132]

The emphasis on the centrality of choice is also apparent in the nature of the OTP's questioning of witnesses in relation to forced pregnancy, where each witness was asked directly whether she felt she had a choice in whether or not she became pregnant:

> Q. Did you have any choice or option about becoming pregnant in the bush?
> A. No, it wasn't my choice.[133]

129 *Prosecutor v. Dominic Ongwen*, ICC-02/04-01/15, ICC, Transcript 7 December 2016, 14 [hereafter Ongwen Transcript Date].

130 Ongwen Transcript 6 December 2016 (n 116), 33.

131 *Ibid.*, 34.

132 *Prosecutor v. Dominic Ongwen*, ICC-02/04-01/15-1719-Red, ICC, Public Redacted Version of "Prosecution Closing Brief", 24 February 2020, paras 162, 174.

133 Ongwen Transcript 17 November 2015 (n 116), 38.

Q. You've told us that you became pregnant and gave birth to two children. Did you have any choice about whether you were going to have babies or not?
A. No, I didn't have any choice.[134]

Q. Madam Witness, you said earlier that Ongwen did not sleep with you for about a month. Can you tell us, did he start to sleep with you again after a month?
A. Yes. I recall that it was after a month that he started having sexual intercourse with me again.
Q. How long did this continue for?
A. Well, it went on for a long time 'til I had – I gave birth.
Q. Did you feel you had a choice with regards to the child?
A. No. If it's up to me, no, I wasn't yet ready to have a child.
Q. Did you feel you had a choice as to whether to have children or not?
A. No. I don't believe that I was mature enough to have children at that time. I believe I should have had children much later.[135]

In emphasising the question of the victim's choice over whether or not to bear a child, the OTP did not appear to be directly addressing an evidential issue. While the elements of the crime of forced pregnancy requires that the perpetrator confined a woman who has *forcibly* been made pregnant,[136] each of the victims in this case were impregnated through acts of rape, which were also charged in the case, the elements of which would necessarily meet the condition of forcible impregnation.[137] From an evidential perspective in this case, the elements of the crime would therefore be fulfilled by proving the occurrence of rape resulting in pregnancy, followed by the confinement of the victim. Rather than being an evidential issue therefore, the particular emphasis on the victims' lack of choice over whether or not to bear children appears instead to have contributed to the construction of a normative narrative around the crime that is emphatic and unambiguous about the idea that it hinges upon the violation of an individual's ability to exercise reproductive agency and choice.

The nature of the discussion of the issue of contraception, and whether or not the victims had access to it in the bush, further reinforces this normative

134 Ongwen Transcript 16 November 2015 (n 116), 26.
135 Ongwen Transcript 18 September 2015 (n 116), 43–44.
136 Article 7(1)(g)-4, ICC Elements of Crimes.
137 See Cottier and Mzee (n 4), 499.

account of the crime. During defence questioning, a witness was asked whether women had access to herbal contraceptive medicines and whether this was 'something the women used on their own accord or their husbands made them take the medicines to stop them from becoming pregnant?'[138] This witness stated that women had access to traditional Acholi medicine which prevented them from becoming pregnant.[139] By contrast, the OTP asked a witness whether LRA 'wives' were able to take any measures to prevent themselves from getting pregnant. This witness said 'no, you cannot refuse or you cannot determine pregnancy because there was no contraception, there was no family planning, so we did not – you could not prevent pregnancies. In Uganda now people are able to get contraceptive, but in the bush when you become pregnant, you become pregnant and you have your child.'[140]

This factual dispute over whether or not women had access to contraception of some form in the bush seems to serve as a further device through which to contest whether or not the victims in this case were able to exercise some kind of reproductive agency or choice. It carries the implication that, if women had access to contraception but became pregnant in any case, it may ultimately have been their choice to do so. In a context in which abducted women became pregnant through repeated rapes in overwhelmingly coercive circumstances from which they were prevented through violence from escaping,[141] raising the question of whether or not the victims of these crimes had access to contraception seems to underscore the idea that, fundamentally, the normative crux of the crime of forced pregnancy, and the wrong invoked by it, relates to the violation of the victim's reproductive autonomy and choice.

4.2 *Harms*

Aside from the prominent emphasis on the violation of the victim's choice over whether or not to bear children, the nature of the harm experienced by victims of forced pregnancy in more concrete, tangible terms, i.e. in terms of the impact on and implications for victims of this violation of their reproductive choice, features surprisingly little in the discourse around forced pregnancy that emerged during the course of proceedings in the *Ongwen* case.[142] During the confirmation of charges hearings, the OTP identified in limited

138 Ongwen Transcript 5 April 2017 (n 116), 45.

139 *Ibid.*

140 Ongwen Transcript 13 September 2017 (n 116), 16.

141 Ongwen Confirmation of Charges (n 106), para 102–135.

142 Some testimony may have taken place in closed session, and may not therefore be available in the public record of proceedings.

form some of the harms that were experienced by the victims of forced pregnancy. It explained that '[m]any of [the forced wives] became pregnant without any choice in the matter, and some gave birth to numerous children who were themselves then ingested into the ranks of the LRA. Not only was the physical effect upon such girls and women devastating, but there were long-lived mental effects as well.'[143]

Here, the OTP pointed in general terms toward physical and mental harms experienced by victims of forced pregnancy, without elaborating on how it understood such harms specifically as they relate to forced pregnancy. One expert witness elaborated on the infliction of psychological trauma on victims of sexual and gender-based crimes, including forced pregnancy, noting the presence of 'PTSD, depression, anxiety, and dissociation; loss of perceived control; shame; increased sexual risk/vulnerability; erosion of traditional cultural, parental, and familial protective factors; and impaired psychosocial development and functioning of children who are products of rape/forced pregnancy.'[144]

The OTP's account of the harm inflicted by forced pregnancy expanded more fully on the stigmatising effects of forced marriage and pregnancy on both the victim and their child. The OTP recounted that '[f]or those who survived, even after their escape or release, they had to live – they still have to live with the stigma of being an LRA wife, a perversion of the true meaning of that word. [...] And there's a whole category of other victims: The children born in captivity resulting from these forced marriages, who sometimes face hostility and taunts as a result of their parentage.'[145] The role of social stigma was also the dominant theme in expert witness testimony on the impact of forced pregnancy on victims. An expert witness explained that:

> Women who become pregnant following incidents of rape [...] face the scorn of their community. [...] In Uganda, forced pregnancy causes the mother and child stigma in their communities. Children of forced pregnancies serve as a symbol and reminder of the history of atrocities committed by the LRA, and are therefore subjects of blame, scorn, rejection in their communities, often being automatically labelled as a criminal, rebel, or murderer. [...] [C]hildren born of LRA-forced pregnancies are deeply affected by their biological origins and subsequent treatment by

143 Ongwen Transcript 21 January 2016 (n 116), 14.

144 *Prosecutor v. Dominic Ongwen*, ICC-02/04-01/15-1720-Conf, ICC, Public redacted version of Common Legal Representative of Victims' Closing Brief, 28 February 2020, para 109.

145 Ongwen Transcript 21 January 2016 (n 116), 14.

> society. […] [I]nequities [are noted] in relation to children's access to health, education, and employment.[146]

During closing statements, the legal representative for victims highlighted the harms experienced by victims of forced pregnancy in similar terms:

> Women and girls returning from the bush who had a child had to bear a special burden and were specially discriminated against. And some even just for the fact of being abducted and being a women or a girl were stigmatised or excluded. P-352 stated that she faced stigma from her community, her family and her husband's family after returning from the bush. Girls or women who escaped and brought back their children from the bush were subject to a particular stigma and isolation. You may remember P-422, who explained the difficulties for women and girls who returned from the bush with children, since they were viewed, the children, as the children of LRA commanders.[147]

These accounts of the social stigmatisation of victims of forced pregnancy are embedded within the experience of stigmatisation experienced by victims of abduction and forced marriage more generally. Indeed, while each of these accounts refer to stigmatisation experienced by the mother and the child upon return to their communities, they focus in particular on the stigmatisation of the children born of forced pregnancy, or speak in general terms about the stigmatisation of women and girls returning from the bush. In this sense, due to the factual circumstances addressed in this case, the possible social harms experienced by victims of forced pregnancy in particular are folded into, and in this way perhaps obscured, by the narrative around the wider experience of abduction and forced marriage in which the forced pregnancy took place, or are to some extent eclipsed by a greater focus on the social harms experienced by the victim's child.

Beyond the issue of social stigma, the statements of witnesses highlighted by the legal representative of victims during closing statements point briefly towards some of the more specific, individualised harms attached to experiences of forced pregnancy. For instance, once witness referred to the particular physical risks and harms that related to experiencing pregnancy and childbirth in these circumstances, stating that '[i]t was a very terrible time for me as I gave

146 Ongwen Transcript 11 March 2020 (n 116), 38.

147 *Ibid.*, 14.

birth in the bush. It was a very hard time for me as I was helped by my co-wife who was not even an expert in the field of giving birth.'[148] In addition, the economic implications of becoming a parent without having chosen to do so are evident in the statement of another witness:

> I gave birth to two sons with Dominic Ongwen and I am taking care of them without anyone to help me since I have no source of become [sic – income] because I am jobless. I feel I have lost my dignity as a woman because I was forced into sexual intercourse by a rebel and I could not do anything to defend myself that I even gave birth to two sons.[149]

The legal representative for victims also referred to the testimony of an expert witness which outlined the impact of the abduction of children by the LRA on their education, in which the particular circumstances of women and girls who returned from the bush having borne children was highlighted. The expert witness testified that the abductions 'actually disrupted a lot of education for children. There are some children who were abducted, for example, the girls, some of them came back with children. Some of them did not have children but they did not – they are no longer interested in education, so this also interfered with this – with their education.'[150]

The testimony of one witness captures several of these wider dimensions to the harm experienced by victims of forced pregnancy, giving meaning to the more abstract normative narrative around reproductive choice by spelling out some of the implications for the individual of this violation of their reproductive choice. For this reason, this testimony is worth quoting at length.

> Q. Madam Witness, you became pregnant as a result of this sexual encounter and you have a child out of this encounter. How has this experience impacted on your life?
>
> A. All these things, all the things that happened to me, have had a very negative impact on my life. It's caused me a lot of problems. I'm a young person, but I now have a child. And that causes me a lot of worry and a lot of stress as to how I'm going to be able to take care of my child. And up to now, I still worry. I'm now grown up, but I still worry about how I'm going to take care of my child.

148 *Ibid.*, 38.

149 *Ibid.*

150 *Ibid.*, 16.

Q. You were distributed as a wife to the commander and he fathered a child with you. Did he ever marry you?

A. No, he did not marry me.

Q. According to page 1 of your statement where you indicate your tribe, according to your culture what is the fate of a child born of an unmarried mother?

A. In my culture, a child that is born out of wedlock is known as the mother's child. You as the mother have to take care of your child, the child is your responsibility. The child does not have a home. So the child belongs to the mother. It's the mother's sole responsibility.

Q. Is this responsibility greater if the child is a boy as opposed to the child being a girl?

A. Yes, it is. Because, if it's a boy, it's more difficult to take care of a boy than to take care of a girl, because as a girl, when a girl grows up, she goes, she gates [sic] married and she leaves. But a boy will always stay with you, so it's more difficult to take care of a boy than it is take care of a girl.

Q. Is it easy for your family to provide land for your son?

A. No, it's not. Because my parents do not have the means to do that, to enable me to get land so that they can give it to that child. It's not easy.

Q. You have moved on in your life and you are in a relationship. What impact has it had on you and the children?

A. My new relationship, this is it, let me explain it: The man that I'm with right now from time to time complains, he complains about my other child. He says that when I – he sees that child that child is more or less the same age as me, so when he looks at that child and he looks at me, then he says I'm an older person than I claim to be. But that's not true, because I had the child when I was young. He does not want that child, so the child stay with my parents. I'm with that man and the children that I've had with him. So it's extremely painful for me that I'm separated from my child. It's very painful for me.

Q. Are you able to provide for this child?

A. Not really, I do not have the means. But when I get anything, when I harvest something or when I get some money I sent the money to my parents so that it can help them take care of my child. But I do not have substantial means and I'm not able to provide enough assistance.

Q. Can you openly support this child?

A. No. That's not how I do it. I do not do it openly. I give it secretly. I send the money secretly so that my partner or husband does not know that I'm sending money to my parents to help my other child.[151]

In addition to the stigma the witness and her child experienced from her new partner, this testimony speaks to a multi-dimensional account of the harms she experienced as a result of forced pregnancy. It highlights the economic implications for this witness as an individual who does not have the means to support a child alone, in addition to the economic implications for the child themselves due to the family's inability to provide him with economic security. The testimony also highlights the significant emotional distress experienced by the witness due to her separation from her child as a result of rejection by a new partner, and her concerns over how she will ultimately be able to provide for the child. In this way, this testimony begins to spell out what it may mean in material terms for an individual's reproductive choice to have been violated in this way, highlighting in this case the impact it can have on the victim and the child's economic security, as well as the particularly complex emotional dimensions to a victim's relationship to a child born of forced impregnation.

Aside from these relatively brief references to the impact of forced pregnancy on victims, along with the more general emphasis on the social stigma experienced by them, the narratives that emerged around forced pregnancy during the course of the *Ongwen* case do not provide a more elaborate account of the nature of the particularised harms inflicted by the crime of forced pregnancy. The dominant normative narrative that emerged during the course of proceedings ultimately related to the violation of the victim's reproductive choice, providing a more principled, abstract normative account of the crime than one rooted in the material harms experienced by victims as a result of the violation of this choice.

5 Conclusion

Analysing the historical roots of the criminalisation of forced pregnancy and enforced sterilization in the Rome Statute, the conceptual implications of how these crimes were defined, and how forced pregnancy has subsequently been addressed in the *Ongwen* trial reveals the significant process of normative evolution that has taken place in how crimes of reproductive violence are

151 Ongwen Transcript 30 November 2017 (n 116), 27–32.

conceptualised. Of each of the crimes examined in this study, the criminalisation of forced pregnancy and enforced sterilization represents the most pronounced development in this respect; from a wider normative environment in which such acts were not only not considered wrongful outside of the context of genocide, but were to some extent normalised and tolerated as a means to facilitate the enjoyment of other human rights through the population control framework, to a contemporary discourse that explicitly centralises the reproductive autonomy and rights of the individual as the principles that are invoked by the criminalisation of forced pregnancy.

The particularly radical dimension of this evolution relates to the change in the place of the individual, primarily women, in relation to matters of reproduction that it represents. The analysis of how reproductive matters initially emerged in international affairs through the population control paradigm, with its unambiguous concern with collective (governmental) regulation of the reproductive lives of individuals, illustrates how at this stage, the individual themselves was conceptually peripheral to the dominant concern with limiting fertility and controlling population growth. This same collective concern was evident in how forms of reproductive violence had been addressed indirectly in international criminal law – as intrinsically, and exclusively, linked to the targeting of groups and their ability reproduce. Tying in with the increasing prominence of the human rights discourse on sexual and reproductive health, and therefore the growing conceptualisation of the reproductive sphere as one governed by individual rights, the 1990s saw a significant normative shift in terms of how acts such as forced pregnancy and enforced sterilization came to be understood as acts of violence that violate individual rights.

The process of codifying these crimes in the Rome Statute nevertheless reflected an ongoing ambivalence over more emphatic recognition of reproductive rights. Their ultimate definitions captured the tension between the emerging notion that individuals are entitled to exercise agency and autonomy in their reproductive lives, with interference with this autonomy through force or coercion therefore constituting crimes in their own right, versus the continuing insistence among some states that individual reproductive choice be subordinated to wider social imperatives rooted in cultural, religious and gendered norms.

Against this normative background, the emphatic emphasis in the *Ongwen* case on reproductive rights, autonomy and choice, in the explicit statements rooting the criminalisation of forced pregnancy in reproductive autonomy and rights and in the narrative advanced during proceedings centralising the violation of the victims' choice, represents a remarkable move beyond the conceptual constraints imposed on the definition of the crime. In addition, what is particularly remarkable about this normative emphasis on reproductive rights, autonomy and choice is how the *Ongwen* case has, to date, addressed in much more limited terms the nature of the more tangible harms experienced by the victims of forced pregnancy. Without spelling out more fully how violations of reproductive autonomy impact on and inflict tangible harms on victims, the *Ongwen* case has instead constructed a normative account of the criminalisation of forced pregnancy as fundamentally, and almost exclusively, about protecting reproductive rights and the principle of reproductive autonomy. In addition, in invoking an unqualified right to reproductive autonomy in relation to forced pregnancy, this case has constituted a significant normative shift in how acts of reproductive violence are constructed in international criminal law, in a way that breaks unequivocally from the concern with protecting the reproduction and therefore the existence of groups, to foreground instead the individual and their right to exercise agency in their reproductive life as the subject protected by the crime.

CHAPTER 6

Conclusion

This book has explored the normative dimensions of the individual acts that constitute international crimes from the perspective of understanding international criminal law as a system of meaning that does not simply reflect a natural, predetermined order, but contributes to constructing the world in its own image. Drawing on a Durkheimian understanding of the relationship between law and society, the book has conceptualised the normative dimensions of criminal wrongs as being both declarative and constitutive of a society's collective consciousness. It has built on scholarship that has used this co-constitutive conception of the relationship between law and society to demonstrate how international criminal justice can be understood to function as a mechanism for continuously reaffirming the existence of an international society through the performative expression of its punitive feelings, and has sought to develop this reasoning at the more granular level of the acts criminalised by international criminal law. The book has sought in this way to demonstrate how international criminal justice not only performatively reconstitutes the international society on behalf of which it claims to speak but, in casting certain acts as 'public', criminal wrongs, also performatively constitutes a set of norms or values as their referent that are so central to that society's identity and how it defines itself that their violation requires public condemnation.

The book has sought to demonstrate how this constitutive conception of criminal wrongs is especially relevant to understanding the normative dimensions of the criminal acts that constitute international crimes because of how international criminal law exists outside of the structuring legal and normative framework of a state. Without an external framework on which to hang the normative meaning of or justification for the criminalisation of these acts, the normative contents of international criminal wrongs must be actively constituted in meaning making processes that exceed those embedded within the state. The aim of the substantive chapters of this book has ultimately therefore been to trace these processes of normative meaning making in relation to the criminalisation of attacks on cultural property, pillage, sexual violence and reproductive violence.

In embedding these processes of meaning making within a wider theoretical conception of crimes as both manifesting and constituting a set of fundamental norms or values shared by the society that the criminal justice system is understood to represent, the normative dimensions of these criminal acts

 | DOI:10.1163/9789004687844_008

have been approached as the products both of processes of social definition as well as of ongoing processes of construction and reconstitution in practice. In adopting this approach, the book has deviated to some extent from an exclusively Durkheimian conception of criminal law as the manifestation of a society's collective consciousness in terms of how it has also sought to recognise how a society's moral order, of which criminal law is understood to be an expression, is not static, unchanging and apolitical, but is instead shaped and instituted by dominant social forces.[1]

The approach adopted in this study, of combining an account of the normative history of a crime with an analysis of the normative implications of its contemporary definition, along with how it has been discursively constructed through practice, has therefore sought to capture a more flexible conception of how criminal law can be understood as both a manifestation and reconstitution of a particular moral order. The analysis has sought to reveal in this sense how the crimes analysed are products of socially, politically and historically situated conditions, and has supplemented Durkheim's more static conception of collective consciousness with recognition of how actors and institutions also contribute to tangibly constructing and shaping their normative meaning through practice.

1 Making Crimes Mean

The analysis of the crimes of attacks on cultural property, pillage, sexual violence and reproductive violence have substantiated this understanding of the normative dimensions of the criminal acts that constitute international crimes. Each chapter has revealed how these crimes emerged from a particular set of historical and conceptual conditions which led to this conduct emerging as abhorrent. In the cases of attacks on cultural property and pillage, these forms of conduct came to be understood as wrong, and ultimately to be prohibited, during a period in which wider ideas were emerging in Europe about limiting the unnecessary use of force during war. Within this wider normative context, particular veneration had also come to be accorded to art, culture and historic monuments during the Renaissance and Enlightenment, while the commitment to the sanctity of private property emerged as a central pillar of the liberal philosophy that came to dominate in Europe in the 18th century.

1 David Garland, *Punishment and Modern Society: A Study in Social Theory* (University of Chicago Press), 53.

These ideas formed the wider conceptual conditions in which prohibitions on attacking cultural property and pillage came to be incorporated into early codifications of the laws of war during the late 19th century.

Although often lumped together under the same conceptual umbrella, the analysis of the criminalisation of sexual violence and reproductive violence revealed altogether distinct normative histories. Similar to prohibitions on attacking cultural property and pillage, international prohibitions on sexual violence have long historical roots which can also be traced in part to the emergence of the principle of necessity in regulating the conduct of war. Early prohibitions on rape nevertheless also emerged from a social context in which women constituted the property of male relatives, which therefore manifested in the codification of honour-based conceptions of rape in international humanitarian law that reflected an understanding of the wrong of the act as emanating from the violation of male ownership of female chastity.

The same patriarchal social conditions ensured that an understanding of forms of reproductive violence as wrongful emerged much later in international discourses, which ultimately only began to take place in the 1990s. Prior to the emergence of a human rights discourse on sexual and reproductive health, in which the reproductive sphere was increasingly constructed as one governed by individual rights, a confluence of patriarchal norms positioning the reproductive functions of women as naturally subject to the control of partners, families, or communities, along with the dominance of the population control paradigm in international discourses ensured that acts of reproductive violence were not generally considered wrongful unless they formed part of an attack on the existence of a group. The criminalisation of acts of reproductive violence as war crimes and crimes against humanity in the Rome Statute was in this sense both a reactive response to evidence of acts of forced pregnancy reported to have taken place in the former Yugoslavia but also a product of the relatively-newly emerged and far from settled notion that coercively interfering with an individual's reproductive capacity could be considered wrongful.

The unique historical roots of these crimes reveal how they each emerged as a result of a process of social definition through which a particular set of social, political and historical conditions in the dominant European order rendered the acts in question repugnant and catalysed their prohibition in early codifications on the laws of war or, in the case of acts of reproductive violence, their criminalisation in the Rome Statute. While not yet translated into the not-yet-existing framework of international criminalisation, at their normative roots, each of these criminal acts can be understood in this sense to constitute a manifestation of the discrete temporal, social and moral orders from which they emerged.

Once codified as acts constituting international crimes, the nature of the definitions of these criminal acts provides an additional component to how their normative dimensions can be understood. Examining how the definitions of these crimes invoke certain norms, principles or values through the nature of the conduct that they capture in the abstract has provided part of an answer to the question of what public wrongs are constituted through the criminalisation of these acts. The analysis revealed how, at the definitional level, the crimes of attacking cultural property and pillage invoke a conception of the norms or values protected by the crime that, for the most part, reflect their normative roots. In the case of attacks on cultural property, the dual normative roots of the crime have been reflected in a degree of fluctuation between definitions that invoke a civilian use justification for the criminalisation of these acts, versus other definitions that invoke a more cultural-value oriented conception of the reasons for their criminalisation. In this sense, the nature of the public wrong invoked by the definitions of the crime of attacks on cultural property relates to both the infliction of civilian suffering by attacking buildings with a civilian character during armed conflict, but also to the wrong of damaging or destroying cultural property because of the separate idea that culture, and its physical embodiments, is valuable in its own right. More straightforwardly, the definitions of pillage codified in different statutes and developed through the case law in general reflect the normative roots of the crime, invoking a public wrong that is rooted in the violation of the rights to property during armed conflict.

The definitions of the crimes of forced pregnancy and enforced sterilization similarly capture the normative environment from which they emerged in terms of how they invoke a public wrong that rests on the violation of a circumscribed individual entitlement to agency and autonomy in one's reproductive life in a specific set of circumstances. This tempered and situation-specific invocation of an individual right to reproductive choice embodies in the definitions of these crimes the tension in the wider social order between the relatively recent emergence of the notion that individuals have a right to reproductive choice versus the ongoing resistance to this normative development in many social and cultural contexts.

By contrast, the definitions of the crimes of rape and sexual violence developed through the case law of the ad hoc tribunals and codified in the Rome Statute are distinct to the other crimes examined in this book in terms of how they do not straightforwardly invoke a public wrong that reflects the normative history and roots of the international prohibition of these forms of violence. The definitions of these crimes instead marked a departure from the honour-based conceptions of the wrong of rape from which the prohibition of rape and sexual violence initially emerged, and which subsequently shaped how these norms were codified in international humanitarian law. The definitions of rape and sexual violence developed in international criminal law ultimately construct accounts of the public wrong attached to these crimes that are rooted in, on the one hand, the infliction of physical violence and bodily harm on the victim and, on the other hand, the violation of their individual right to exercise sexual agency and autonomy.

While the substance of the norm against rape in general terms may not have changed substantially from the prohibitions of attacks on honour contained in international humanitarian law, the reasons why acts of sexual violence are considered wrongful have in this sense evolved significantly to reflect the changing social order in which women have been increasingly understood as subjects with an individual right not to experience non-consensual interference with their bodily autonomy or in their sexual lives. In a similar way, the later criminalisation of forms of reproductive violence can be partly understood as a manifestation of the wider social shift away from normalising control over women's reproductive functions towards the emerging notion that women are entitled to exercise agency and autonomy in their reproductive lives. The analysis has in this way revealed how the definitions of the crimes of sexual violence and reproductive violence codified and developed in international criminal law epitomise a more flexible conception of an international collective consciousness in terms of how these crimes mirror and reconstitute the changing position of women in the dominant social and moral order.

Finally, expanding on this more flexible conception of collective consciousness, the analysis of the discourse in decisions and during the course of proceedings has substantiated the significance of practice for understanding the normative dimensions of these crimes, revealing how the actors and institutions engaged in prosecutions further contribute to constructing and shaping their normative meaning. This is evident in how the normative themes and narratives that emerge in the case law and during the course of proceedings around each of these crimes build on and, to varying extents, differ from the conceptual nature of their definitions, as well as from their normative roots.

For instance, while the different definitions of the crime of attacks on cultural property reflect the dual normative roots of this prohibition, invoking both civilian use and cultural value rationales for the protection of cultural property during armed conflict, the case law and the discourse during proceedings construct an exclusively cultural value justification for its criminalisation. In addition, the analysis of the discourse in decisions and during proceedings has further revealed a significant degree of evolution in the nature of how cultural value has been constructed in practice, reflecting a turn away from a traditional object-centric, internationalist conception towards an account of cultural value that also captures a functionalist, local and people-oriented approach. Illustrating the centrality of practice in developing the normative meaning of crimes, this evolution was particularly pronounced in the *Al Mahdi* case at the ICC, in which, despite the civilian use rationale for the protection of cultural property invoked by the Rome Statute definition of the crime, a multifaceted account of a cultural value justification for its criminalisation was advanced, including a particular emphasis on a functionalist and local account of cultural value that sought to invoke a living connection between people and buildings.

Similarly, while less complex and varied than those constructed around attacks on cultural property, the normative themes and narratives constructed around the crime of pillage go further in the extent to which they depart from the conceptual basis invoked by the definition of the crime. While the early cases at the ICTY reflected relatively limited engagement with the normative dimensions of the criminalisation of pillage beyond appealing to its normative roots in the protection of rights to property under international humanitarian law, the analysis revealed how the cases at the SCSL and the ICC pivoted towards a narrative that centralised the use value of pillaged property in ensuring the subsistence and survival of civilians. This narrative is somewhat at variance with the ownership rights model of the definition applied at these courts and the wrong of the violation of the right to private property during armed conflict that it invokes. In the same way, the centrality of reproductive rights and the principles of reproductive autonomy and choice in the normative narratives constructed around forced pregnancy in the judgments and during the proceedings in the *Ongwen* case deviate from the more circumscribed account of these principles invoked by the definition and drafting history of the crime.

Crimes of rape and sexual violence constitute somewhat of an exception to this pattern. Perhaps due to the fact that the definitions themselves underwent significant transformation through their development in the case law of the ICTY and ICTR and their codification in the Rome Statute, the analysis revealed that the narratives constructed around these crimes in decisions map more closely on to the definition applied in a particular case. Thus, the early ICTY and ICTR case law on rape, which was characterised by an evolving debate over the relevance of the element of consent for the definition of the crime, also directly invoked the associated principle of sexual autonomy. By contrast, the case law of the ICC, where the definition of rape follows a coercive circumstances model, has constructed a normative discourse around crimes of sexual violence that follows the conceptual model of understanding rape as a form of physical violence and aggression that violates bodily integrity.

At the same time, despite the identification of sexual autonomy as a principle protected by the criminalisation of rape in certain decisions of the ICTY and ICTR, the discourse in decisions and during proceedings at each of the courts and tribunals overwhelmingly constructs an account of the individualised harms inflicted by sexual violence that focusses on the physical, on bodily injury and suffering, or on the social harms of shame and stigma. This has resulted in the exclusion of the sexual dimensions of the harms experienced by individuals, despite some limited allusions to harms of this nature during the conduct of proceedings, and has ultimately resulted in the construction of a normative account of crimes of sexual violence in the case law that reproduces elements of the underlying logic of an honour-based narrative and elides how such crimes violate and may impact on sexual subjectivity. In this way, the narratives constructed around crimes of sexual violence do not follow the same pattern as the other crimes analysed in the sense that they do not depart from the conceptual nature of their definitions to the same extent. However, similar to the other crimes, the analysis of crimes of sexual violence nevertheless also exposes the process of construction and meaning making that takes place through practice in illustrating the inclusion and exclusion of perspectives involved in how the narratives around these crimes are constructed.

In this respect, by centralising the discourses and narratives constructed in legal decisions and during trial proceedings for understanding how the criminalisation of these acts has been imbued with meaning, the approach applied in this book has demonstrated how the normative meanings of these acts are actively produced, rather than being natural or given. In doing so, this book has sought to demonstrate not only what the public wrongs constituted through these individual criminal acts are, but also, importantly, how they are formed. In this way, this study has sought to expose how the themes and narratives constructed in legal decisions and during proceedings form a central part of how international criminal law performatively invokes and reconstitutes a set of norms and values shared by the international society on whose behalf it claims to speak.

1.1 *Meaning Making as Continuum*

The discursive and narrative expressivist approach adopted in this research has in this way also illustrated the value of conceptualising the process of meaning making that takes place through practice in holistic terms. This process is comprehensive of the different dimensions of the legal process in each case as well as the aggregation of meaning that accumulates through sequences of cases and decisions engaging with and building on one another. The diversity of normative themes articulated through the trial process and reflected in the factual, legal and normative narratives contained in decisions, as well as how these have developed and evolved over time, highlights how the process of meaning making that imbues criminal acts with meaning transcends the normative statements offered in any particular judgment.

Instead, the process captured by this approach suggests that the normative meaning making that takes place with respect to these criminal acts can be understood to involve multiple steps in which meaning is generated at different points and on an ongoing basis. This first involves the criminalisation of an act that has come to be identified as wrongful, with the initial normative implications of how it has been defined in legal terms. This is followed subsequently by a process of construction during the trial process which fleshes out the normative meaning of a crime through the testimonies of victims and witnesses and the construction of factual and normative narratives by prosecution and defence. Within these individual trial processes, micro-level processes of meaning making take place in how discrete narratives constructed during proceedings necessarily involve inclusions and exclusions, with individual witnesses and parties to proceedings framing their narrative of events to meet the evidential requirements of the definition of the crime and the requirements of the legal process. The overarching narratives constructed by prosecution and defence during a trial, for instance in opening or closing statements, in turn involve acts of decontextualisation and recontextualisation, in which certain witness testimonies and other evidence is selected and recounted by parties to proceedings in support of their overall narrative of the case.

This multiplicity of narratives during proceedings is then further decontextualised and recontextualised in the judicial discourse that emerges from the trial, in the decisions required at different stages of proceedings, such as the confirmation of charges decision, the trial, sentencing and appeals judgments and, in some instances, reparations decisions. In these decisions, the profusion of testimonies recounted during proceedings and the factual and normative narratives constructed by the parties are in turn summarised, may be reinterpreted, and are reframed according to the relevant legal and procedural framework to form the basis of a decision. The nature of these narratives, and therefore the form that this meaning making takes, at times also differs according to the stage of proceedings. The process of adjudication may reflect a perspective that is centred on the perpetrator, sentencing decisions may reflect greater focus on the impact of the perpetrator's crimes, centralising the issues of gravity and the harm inflicted on victims, while reparations practices engage most fully with the nature of the harms experienced by victims, usually offering the most expansive, holistic and victim-centred account of a crime. For instance, while each of the themes identified in the discourse around these crimes are to varying extents woven into each of the different stages of proceedings in each case, the analysis of the crime of pillage revealed how the use value of pillaged property – its role in daily lives and in ensuring the subsistence and survival of civilians – emerged particularly emphatically in the more harm and victim-focussed phases of sentencing and reparations in the *Katanga* and *Ongwen* cases at the ICC.[2]

The analysis of the crime of attacks on cultural property reflects a similar pattern, in which the various dimensions of the cultural value of the city of Dubrovnik and the mausoleums in Timbuktu, and therefore the nature of the particular harms inflicted by the destruction of property of such value, are expounded most fully in the sentencing decision in the *Jokić* case at the ICTY and the *Al Mahdi* case at the ICC respectively.[3] In the *Al Mahdi* case in particular, the reparations order constructed the most comprehensive account of cultural value in how, in addition to the other dimensions of cultural value captured throughout the trial, the Reparations Order also emphasised the emotional dimension of the relationship between people and cultural heritage, extensively citing the testimonies of individual victim applicants that testified to the emotional distress and harm they suffered as a result of the destruction of the mausoleums.[4] In this way, the nature of the stage of proceedings and the different interests at stake are revealed to also contribute to shaping how the legally relevant interest or harm is identified and constructed during proceedings and in the judicial discourse, and how the normative meaning attributed to the crime is therefore constructed.

All of this also takes place against the backdrop of previous decisions that address the same crimes. The normative meaning attributed to a criminal act and the narrative constructed around it in a particular decision is in this sense not static and isolated, but also forms part of an interconnected conversation between sequences of decisions. While sometimes implicit, this often also takes place explicitly, such as in the evolving jurisprudence on the definition of rape at the ICTY and ICTR, in which different chambers entered into conversation with one another to offer an evolving normative conception of the crime as an act of bodily violence and aggression versus one that centralised the principle of sexual autonomy.[5] In a similar fashion, in its analysis of the reparation required for the moral harm inflicted by the destruction of the mausoleums in Timbuktu, the Trial Chamber in the *Al Mahdi* case at the ICC drew

2 See Chapter 3, section 3(b).
3 See Chapter 2, sections 3 and 4.
4 See Chapter 2, section 3(d)(iii).
5 See discussion in Chapter 4, section 2.

on some of the object-centric narratives of cultural value that were advanced in decisions addressing the attack on Dubrovnik at the ICTY, which emphasised the authenticity and inherent value of historical buildings.[6] Seen from this perspective, the analysis of these criminal acts has exposed how their normative meanings are not generated in isolation, in a particular judgment or indeed exclusively in judgments, but can be better understood as taking place at different points throughout the different stages of the legal process and in a multiplicity of interconnected cases.

Fundamentally, then, this book has demonstrated how the normative dimensions of the individual acts that constitute international crimes can be understood as ongoing processes of construction and meaning making. It has illustrated how certain historical, social and conceptual conditions allowed these acts to emerge as repugnant, while the acts of criminalisation, prosecution and judgment contribute to a constitutive and continuing process of normative meaning making that performatively calls into existence a certain set of internationally-shared norms and values, which figure into the representational work that international criminal justice does in the world. In this respect, adopting an approach that understands the normative dimensions of these acts holistically in terms of an ongoing process of construction and discursive meaning making has revealed a greater degree of diversity to the representational aspects of international criminal justice than is often acknowledged.

1.2 *Diversity of Interests*

This book began by highlighting how an understanding of the nature of the violence captured by international crimes as direct, physical violence and bodily harm that violates corresponding basic security rights to life, physical security and bodily integrity figures centrally in many of the philosophical theorisations of the categories of international crimes, and forms the basis of some foundational critiques of the field. The analysis of the crimes of attacks on cultural property, pillage, crimes of sexual violence and crimes of reproductive violence has nevertheless revealed how the normative dimensions of the acts that constitute international crimes can be understood as more complex than this dominant interpretation on two levels. Firstly, on a basic level, the nature of the rights, interests or values invoked by the definitions of the criminal acts analysed in this book and how they have been interpreted in the case law go far beyond the typical 'attacks on "basic security rights"'[7] conceptualisation of

6 See discussion in Chapter 2, section 3(c).

7 Asad G. Kiyani, 'International Crime and the Politics of Criminal Theory: Voices and Conduct of Exclusion', (2015) 48(1) *New York University Journal of International Law and Politics*, 185.

international crimes. In this respect, the analysis has revealed how these acts have been interpreted as protecting the specifically cultural dimensions of cultural property, as protecting both liberal individual rights to private property but also communal or collective rights to property, and as protecting individual rights to sexual and reproductive autonomy, the right to decide freely and responsibly on the number and spacing of children, the right to health and the right to family.

At a second level, in adopting a narrative expressivist and discursive approach to capture the continuum of meaning making that takes place throughout the legal process, the analysis has also offered an additional layer to how these acts can be normatively conceptualised. Understanding the normative dimensions of the criminal acts that constitute international crimes in these terms reveals not only that they are more normatively diverse than the basic security rights paradigm suggests but that, taken individually, they can also be understood as normatively varied and complex in their own right. This book in this way also complicates the notion that the normative dimensions of a criminal act can be boiled down to the protection of a static or immutable right, value or legal good or the prevention of a specific and clear-cut type of harm.

In this respect, the analysis has for instance revealed how the criminalisation of attacks on cultural property has been understood to engage universalist notions of cultural value and the inherent value of a cultural object in its material existence, but also to protect its social meaning, the social and religious practices that surround such property, and its role in the emotions, memories, identities and social fabric of individuals and communities. Similarly, while individual rights to private property as well as community rights to communal property have been invoked to justify the criminalisation of pillage, prosecutions have nevertheless also transcended the property rights paradigm. They have increasingly downplayed the element of ownership and instead centralised the use value of objects in the livelihoods, subsistence and survival of civilians, in addition to at times highlighting the particular cultural role and significance of certain items within a particular community.

The same normative diversity is evident in the analysis of the crimes of sexual violence and reproductive violence. Thus, the criminalisation of sexual violence has been identified as protecting the values of physical and moral integrity, human dignity and sexual autonomy and integrity, while condemnation for the violation of a conjugal order in which sexual violation inflicts shame and stigma on victims is nevertheless also implicitly interwoven into the discourses of decisions and proceedings. The crime of forced pregnancy has similarly been identified to protect an individual right to personal and reproductive autonomy, the right to decide freely and responsibly on the number and spacing of children, the right to health and the right to family, while the violation of the victims' agency and choice has featured centrally in trial narratives.

Seen from this perspective, the assumption that the acts that constitute international crimes are normatively limited to violations of basic security rights appears reductive both in terms of the nature of the rights that are identified as well as in terms of the utility of conceptualising the normative dimensions of these acts exclusively through the lens of protecting specific and discrete rights, interests or legal goods, or preventing precise and clear-cut harms. Instead, what is revealed is a diverse, dynamic and evolving normative picture in which acts are interpreted from multiple perspectives. Some of these perspectives reflect a normative conception of these criminal acts as rooted in liberal conceptions of individual rights, while others at times reflect some more contextualised, social or communitarian elements in the nature of the rights identified to attach to or the harms identified as having been inflicted by these acts. In this sense, the representational work of international criminal justice in performatively invoking a set of internationally-shared norms and values on behalf of a notional international society can be seen at times to transcend the 'basic security rights' paradigm in the diversity and complexity of how the normative dimensions of these acts are constructed in practice.

1.3 *Foundation Building*

Understanding the normative dimensions of the acts that constitute international crimes in these terms as an ongoing process of construction and discursive meaning making in practice in this way not only reveals a greater degree of normative diversity to these acts than the basic security rights paradigm suggests, but also underscores the lack of a settled or coherent extrinsic normative framework from which they derive their normative content. In this respect, the analysis of the process of meaning making that surrounds the criminal acts analysed in this book resonates with Sarah Nouwen's doubt over the prospect of identifying any normative essence to the category of international crime,[8] and with David Luban's conclusion that 'the atrocities and humiliations that count as crimes against humanity are, in effect, the ones that turn our stomachs, and no principle exists to explain what turns our stomachs.'[9] By

8 Sarah Nouwen, 'International Criminal Law: Theory All Over the Place' in Anne Orford and Florian Hoffman (eds), *The Oxford Handbook of the Theory of International Law* (Oxford University Press 2016), 751.

9 David Luban, 'A Theory of Crimes Against Humanity', (2004) 29(1) *Yale Journal of International Law*, 101.

demonstrating how each of the criminal acts analysed in this book emerged as the product of specific historical, social, and political conditions, and how their normative meaning is continually shaped and reconstituted in practice, this study in this way ultimately also suggests that no clear unifying foundations can be understood to underlie these acts. At the same time, this approach goes further than Luban's conclusion that no principle exists that explains what turns our stomachs, to suggest that 'what turns our stomachs' is in itself not a settled and unchanging category. Instead, this analysis has demonstrated how 'what turns our stomachs' is contingent on the configuration of a particular social and moral order, which is in turn reflected in and reconstituted by the criminal justice system that emerges from it.

This constitutive understanding of the normative dimensions of the acts that constitute international crimes and, importantly, the unsettled and changeable understanding of their normative foundations that comes with it, is underscored by the somewhat inconsistent and not always coherent character of the process of construction and meaning making that takes place through practice. In particular, the disjunct identified between the normative histories of these crimes and what their definitions conceptually invoke versus the narratives constructed around them in practice reveals a degree of malleability to the nature of their normative meanings. Similarly, some of the values or principles invoked in practice as constituting the normative basis of these crimes, such as moral integrity in relation to crimes of sexual violence, do not in themselves have a clear or transparent meaning, while others, such as human dignity, are so broad as to explain little as to the normative basis of the criminalisation of the particular act in question. In a similar way, the human right to private property, while codified in some domestic and regional human rights treaties, is straightforwardly invoked as a basis for the crime of pillage in the case law, despite not enjoying a settled or unambiguous status under international human rights law.

In addition, the fact that the normative narratives constructed around some crimes differ not only from what their definitions conceptually invoke, but also between courts and cases, further exposes this normative malleability and the lack of a settled, clear or universal normative meaning attributed to them even within the internal practices of international criminal law. This is demonstrated for instance in the shift from emphasising rights to property in relation to pillage at the ICTY compared to the emphatically humanitarian focus of the narratives constructed around this crime at the ICC and SCSL. It is also evident in the evolution in the conception of cultural value that is constructed around the crime of attacking cultural property between the ICTY and the *Al Mahdi* case at the ICC, as well as in the abandonment at the ICC of the early language on sexual autonomy that emerged from the ICTY and the ICTR. These discursive shifts reveal how the actors involved in the processes of prosecution and judgment have a degree of leeway in terms of how they go about explaining or justifying the criminalisation of these acts.

Taken as a whole, the nature of these processes of meaning making, which reflect a not always coherent and somewhat ad hoc and unsystematic exposition of the normative dimensions of these criminal acts, underscore how their normative foundations are not fixed, static or immutable, existing extrinsically to the framework of international criminal law, but are better understood as being constituted internally through practice. In this respect, despite not always being necessary for the purposes of the legal reasoning in a particular decision, the attempts to justify or explain the criminalisation of an act in normative terms, evidenced by statements like those describing the crime of attacking cultural property as representing 'a violation of values especially protected by the international community'[10] or describing the crime of forced pregnancy as 'grounded in the woman's right to personal and reproductive autonomy',[11] seems to reflect an impulse to construct normative foundations to the criminalisation of these acts that do not pre-exist these statements.

This constructive role of practice in relation to the substance of the law itself is well-recognised and relatively uncontroversial. In particular with respect to the decisions of the ad hoc tribunals, for instance, which operated with limited jurisprudence and vague statutes, judges are widely understood to have been required to address significant gaps and ambiguities in the law. As a result, these judgments are often seen to have represented a balancing act between the judicial function of delivering a verdict and the role of judges as developers of international criminal law.[12] Judges have in this respect been described as having 'resorted to expansive legal interpretations trying to fill the gap left open by a Swiss cheese corpus of international law.'[13] The approach adopted in this book reveals how the processes of meaning making that take place with respect to the normative dimensions of the acts that constitute international crimes can be understood in similar terms. In the absence of an extrinsic normative framework through which to justify or explain the criminalisation of

10 *Prosecutor v. Miodrag Jokić*, IT-01-42/1-S, ICTY, Sentencing Judgment, 18 March 2004, para 46.

11 *Prosecutor v. Dominic Ongwen*, ICC-02/04-01/15, ICC, Trial Judgment, 4 February 2021, para 2717 [hereafter Ongwen Trial Judgment].

12 Rosa Aloisi and James Meernik, *Judgment Day: Judicial Decision Making at the International Criminal Tribunals* (Cambridge University Press 2017), 11.

13 *Ibid.*

particular acts of violence at the international level, the processes of meaning making that take place through practice, whether through decisions themselves or through the discourses that emerge during proceedings, can ultimately be understood to function as a means through which the field builds its own normative foundations.

Recognising in this way how the normative foundations of these acts are malleable and built internally through practice is not a purely theoretical matter, relating only to how these acts can be understood in normative or representational terms, but also carries certain legal implications. In a similar way to some of the legality concerns raised with respect to the more expansive interpretations that characterised in particular the case law of the ad hoc tribunals, which have been criticised for how they 'took a toll on the right of individual defendants to a sufficiently foreseeable, accessible, and specific penal law',[14] exposing how the normative foundations of these acts are constructed and transformed through practice may also raise questions for procedural fairness and the principle of legality. In particular, the shifting and malleable nature of the normative foundations of these acts may impact on the foreseeability of the law, the principle of strict construction and the consistency and predictability of sentencing.

In this respect, revealing some of the changes that have taken place in how the normative dimensions of the crimes of attacks on cultural property, pillage, sexual violence and reproductive violence are constructed in practice has also exposed instances where these normative shifts are linked to or manifest through changes in how the legal elements of a crime have been interpreted. For example, in *Kordić and Čerkez* at the ICTY, the Trial and Appeals chambers arrived at differing conclusions as to the scope of the offence of destruction or wilful damage to institutions dedicated to religion or education based ultimately on different interpretations of cultural value.[15] Based on its analysis of the rules governing the protection of cultural property during armed conflict, the Trial Chamber included educational institutions within the scope of the offence on the grounds that they 'are undoubtedly immovable property of great importance to the cultural heritage of peoples in that they are without exception centres of learning, arts, and sciences, with their valuable collections of books and works of arts and science.'[16]

14 Sergey Vasiliev, 'The making of international criminal law' in Catherine Brölmann and Yannick Radi (eds), *Research Handbook on the Theory and Practice of International Lawmaking* (Edward Elgar 2016), 393.

15 See Chapter 2, section 3(a).

16 *Prosecutor v. Dario Kordić and Mario Čerkez*, IT-95-14/2-T, ICTY, Trial Judgment, 26 February 2001, para 360.

Adopting a more hierarchical and internationalist interpretation of cultural value, the Appeals Chamber by contrast rejected the notion that educational institutions could be considered of great importance to the cultural heritage of peoples on the basis that cultural or spiritual heritage is limited to 'objects whose value transcends geographical boundaries, and which are unique in character and are intimately associated with the history and culture of a people.'[17] It went on to stress that the adjective 'cultural' used in Article 53 of Additional Protocol I 'applies to historic monuments and works of art and cannot be construed as applying to all institutions dedicated to education such as schools.'[18] In this way, the Trial and Appeals chambers' disagreement over whether the scope of the offence captured educational institutions hinged upon the difference in their approaches to the nature of cultural value. Thus, how these chambers interpreted the normative dimensions of this crime, in other words, how they understood what can be considered culturally valuable and therefore to be correctly protected by the offence, ultimately shaped their conclusions as to its legal scope.

While in this instance the Appeals Chamber in *Kordić and Čerkez* ultimately favoured a more restrictive interpretation of the crime, in other instances, shifts in how the normative dimensions of a crime are constructed have had the opposite effect. The interpretation of the term 'attack' in the Rome Statute's language of 'intentionally directing attacks against' cultural property in the *Al Mahdi* case represents a particularly contentious example of where this has taken place.[19] Expanding the traditional interpretation of attack as an act of violence against an adversary that takes place during the conduct of hostilities, the Trial Chamber in *Al Mahdi* determined that:

> [T]he element of 'direct[ing] an attack' encompasses any acts of violence against protected objects and will not make a distinction as to whether it was carried out in the conduct of hostilities or after the object had fallen under the control of an armed group. [...] This reflects the special status of religious, cultural, historical and similar objects [...] international humanitarian law protects cultural objects as such from crimes committed both in battle and out of it.[20]

---

17 *Prosecutor v. Dario Kordić and Mario Čerkez*, IT-95-14/2-A, ICTY, Appeal Judgment, 17 December 2004, para 91–92.

18 *Ibid.*, para 92.

19 See Chapter 2, section 2(b).

20 *Prosecutor v. Ahmad Al Faqi Al Mahdi*, ICC-01/12-01/15, ICC, Judgment and Sentence, 27 September 2016, para 15 [hereafter Al Mahdi Judgment and Sentence].

This more expansive interpretation of attack has nevertheless been criticised by some commentators in relation to the factual circumstances in the *Al Mahdi* case, who have suggested that 'the term "attack" is not the word that would be used to describe the demolition or destruction of structures, using implements that are not weapons or military in nature, and where armed adversaries are not to be found within hundreds of kilometres.'[21] In this decision, the normative conception of the crime applied by the Chamber in this way again proved pivotal for shaping its legal interpretation. The Chamber used its understanding of the crime as centring on the cultural value of the protected property, stressing its 'special status' as distinct from the protections accorded to civilian objects in general and in contrast to the more civilian use rationale invoked by the definition of the crime in the Rome Statute,[22] to ultimately broaden the nature of the conduct captured by the offence to the extent that some commentators have questioned whether this interpretation violated the principle of strict construction in the Rome Statute.[23]

Similar developments were revealed by the analysis of the element of ownership in the definition of the crime of pillage, which has been interpreted in increasingly expansive terms in the case law of the ICC and the SCSL.[24] Various decisions have interpreted the elements of intending to deprive an owner of property without their consent in broad terms, at times brushing aside the factual questions of ownership and consent,[25] and at others developing somewhat nebulous interpretations of the element of ownership, such as the assertion by the Trial Chamber in *Ntaganda* that it would consider 'the person who had the property under him or her as the 'owner'.'[26] The underlying normative transformation from the individual ownership rights model reflected in the ICC definition of pillage to the emphatically use value narrative constructed around it, and evidenced in the wider analysis of the crime, has in this way resulted, in a similar way to the expansion of the term attack in relation to attacks on cultural property, in a widening and loosening of the legal elements of the crime, which may similarly implicate the principles of foreseeability and strict construction.

21 William Schabas, 'Al Mahdi Has Been Convicted of a Crime He Did Not Commit', (2017) 49 *Case Western Reserve Journal of International Law*, 78.
22 See discussion in Chapter 2, section 2(b).
23 Schabas (n 21), 77.
24 See Chapter 3, section 3(c).
25 See Chapter 3, section 3(c).
26 *Prosecutor v. Bosco Ntaganda*, ICC-01/04-02/06, ICC, Trial Judgment, 8 July 2019, para 1034.

Perhaps the most well-recognised example of where the normative conception of a crime has produced legal effects in shaping the nature of its definition is the evolution of the definition of rape in the case law of the ad hoc tribunals.[27] Following the adoption of different definitions of rape in the early case law of the ad hoc tribunals, in *Kunarac*, the Trial Chamber straightforwardly based its inclusion of the element of consent in its definition of the crime on its identification of sexual autonomy as 'the basic principle which is truly common'[28] to the crime of rape in national jurisdictions. The evolving definition of rape in the case law of the ad hoc tribunals, which, as demonstrated in the analysis, reflected and was partly driven by different conceptions of the nature of the wrong attached to this crime as an act of physical violence and aggression or as a violation of sexual autonomy,[29] has nevertheless been problematised for failing to adhere to the principle of legality. Roelof Haveman has, for instance, highlighted how the three definitions of rape developed in the case law during this period 'were only determined when the verdicts were given after the statements of evidence were recorded. This result[ed] in the suspect being highly curtailed of the possibility to defend himself.'[30]

Differing normative conceptions of a crime have also figured into some chambers' reasoning on the question of gravity for the purposes of establishing jurisdiction and for sentencing, in particular in relation to attacks on cultural property. In this respect, the varying approaches to cultural value identified in the narratives of different cases have ultimately produced different legal outcomes by shaping the analysis of the gravity of a crime. In *Hadžihasanović and Kubura* at the ICTY, the Trial Chamber determined that vandalism to the interior of a monastery was of sufficient gravity to constitute the offence of damage or destruction to institutions dedicated to religion, and to therefore fall within the court's jurisdiction, on the basis that 'special attention is paid to certain property, namely religious buildings, owing to their spiritual value. [...] The Chamber considers that the seriousness of the crime of destruction of or damage to institutions dedicated to religion must [...] take much greater account of the spiritual value of the damaged or destroyed property than the

27 See Chapter 4, section 2(b)-(d).

28 *Prosecutor v. Dragoljub Kunarac et al.*, IT-96-23-T & IT-96-23/1-T, ICTY, Trial Judgment, 22 February 2001, para 457 [hereafter Kunarac Trial Judgment].

29 See Chapter 4, section 2.

30 Roelof Haveman, 'Rape and Fair Trial in Supranational Criminal Law', (2002) 9(3) *Maastricht Journal of European and Comparative Law*, 264. See similarly Jessica Lynn Corsi, 'An Argument for Strict Legality in International Criminal Law', (2018) 49(4) *Georgetown Journal of International Law*, 1321–1381.

material extent of the damage or destruction.'[31] In this way, the Chamber's particular intangible understanding of the value of religious property, and therefore of that which is normatively protected by the crime, proved operative in its conclusion that it could exercise jurisdiction over the act of vandalism in this case.

Similarly illustrating how differing conceptions of the normative dimensions of a crime can shape the analysis of its gravity, and can in this way affect legal outcomes, in sentencing, the Trial Chamber in *Al Mahdi* identified a higher degree of gravity to the destruction of the mausoleums in Timbuktu based in particular on an internationalist conception of cultural value. The Chamber explained that 'all the sites but one [...] were UNESCO World Heritage sites and, as such, their attack appears to be of particular gravity as their destruction does not only affect the direct victims of the crimes, namely the faithful inhabitants of Timbuktu, but also people throughout Mali and the international community.'[32] In this way, the internationalist dimensions of the Chamber's approach to the issue of cultural value, and therefore to how this crime was constructed in normative terms, also fed into the reasoning on Al Mahdi's sentence. Each of these examples ultimately demonstrate how recognising that the normative foundations of these acts are not rooted in a static and unchanging extrinsic framework, but are instead constructed and transformed internally through an ongoing process of meaning making in practice is not free of consequence in legal terms, but can also shape outcomes in ways that may ultimately implicate aspects of procedural fairness and the principle of legality.

2 International Criminal Wrong as Flexible and Dynamic

Taken together, understanding the normative dimensions of the acts that constitute international crimes in terms of a process of meaning making that takes place throughout the different stages of a continuum of cases, through which the field constructs its normative foundations internally through practice and produces a diversity of normative themes and interests in the process, ultimately points towards a more flexible and dynamic conception of wrong in international criminal law than is captured by the harm-based theories of criminalisation or theories of legal goods discussed at the beginning of this book.

---

31 *Prosecutor v. Enver Hadžihasanović and Amir Kubura*, IT-01-47-T, ICTY, Trial Judgment, 15 March 2006, para 63. For discussion see Chapter 2, section 3(a).

32 Al Mahdi Judgment and Sentence (n 20), para 80. For discussion see Chapter 2, section 3(b).

By revealing how the normative meanings of these criminal acts are constantly being discursively produced, re-constituted and transformed in practice, this book has illustrated how their normative dimensions are not given, settled or unchanging, and offers instead an account of wrongs in international criminal law as socially constructed, dynamic and pluralistic.

2.1 *Legal and Normative Pluralism*

The character of these wrongs as socially constructed and pluralistic is ultimately inherent to the nature of international criminal law in particular, but also to criminal law more generally. The normative pluralism that emerges in the nature of the harms, values or interests identified in the analysis of each of the crimes in this book, the way that they transform over time and the pluralism that characterises how they are articulated, in directly normative terms as relevant harms or protected rights, values or interests, or more implicitly, through the legal, factual and normative narratives that are constructed in the discourse, can be understood as a product of the inherently pluralistic character of international criminal law. Pluralism in international criminal law has been described as 'impossible to deny, prevent, or halt.'[33] International criminal law's pluralist character is variously identified in the 'irreducibly pluralistic environment'[34] in which it operates, in the plethora of its enforcement institutions, the diversity of substantive and procedural rules they apply, and the multiplicity of approaches and interpretations reflected in the body of case law that results from this institutional, jurisdictional and situational variety.[35]

At a more foundational level, pluralism has also been understood to characterise 'the building blocks that constitute the normative structure'[36] of international criminal law, which reflect diverging values, rationales and normative identities. This emerges partly from the legal-cultural diversity of the domestic criminal law traditions from which international criminal law draws, but also from the diversity of the normative, methodological, and ideological foundations of the field.[37] In this respect, international criminal law has been described as reconciling 'at least three dimensions: the 'universalist'

33 Elies van Sliedregt, 'International Criminal Law and Legal Pluralism' in Paul Schiff Berman (ed), *The Oxford Handbook of Global Legal Pluralism* (Oxford University Press 2020), 576.

34 Alexander K.A. Greenawalt, 'The Pluralism of International Criminal Law', (2011) 86(3) *Indiana Law Journal*, 1068.

35 Elies van Sliedregt and Sergey Vasiliev, 'Pluralism: A New Framework for International Criminal Justice' in Elies van Sliedregt and Sergey Vasiliev (eds), *Pluralism in International Criminal Law* (Oxford University Press 2014), 4–6, 14.

36 *Ibid.*, 29.

37 *Ibid.*, 29–34.

aspirations of public international law, the 'humanist' dimensions of human rights law and the legality and fairness-oriented foundations of criminal law.'[38] Elies van Sliedregt and Sergey Vasiliev explain how the 'conflicting premises, ambitions, and aspirations at the heart'[39] of international criminal law partly originate in this way from the plurality of the legal fields from which it draws its normative contents. In terms of substantive law, they therefore highlight how, for instance, the general international law dimensions of international criminal law pull in a state-centred direction, its criminal law dimensions centralise principles of strict legality, while its humanitarian and human rights law dimensions may tend to favour more progressive victim-centred or humanitarian interpretations.[40]

In this respect, the analysis of the normative dimensions of the criminal acts examined in this book reveals how they often reflect and reconstitute the legally pluralist character of the field as a whole, in how the wrongs invoked frequently draw explicitly on international criminal law's legally pluralist roots in different bodies of law. For instance, pillage was initially framed in the case law of the ICTY as normatively rooted in international humanitarian law's rules 'aimed at protecting property rights in times of armed conflict.'[41] The Trial Chamber in *Kunarac* at the ICTY conducted a review of domestic criminal law on rape to inform its conclusion that the relevant principle to be protected by this crime is sexual autonomy.[42] At the ICC, the Appeals Chamber in *Ongwen* referred to the Convention on the Elimination of All Forms of Discrimination Against Women and the International Covenant on Economic, Social and Cultural Rights in its interpretation of the crime of forced pregnancy as protecting the right to decide freely and responsibly on the number and spacing of children and the right to health.[43] The Trial Chamber also relied on the decisions of the African Commission on Human and Peoples' Rights and the Inter-American Court of Human Rights to inform its conclusion that the right to property encompasses both individual and communal property with respect

38 Carsten Stahn and Larissa van den Herik, 'Fragmentation', Diversification and '3D' Legal Pluralism: International Criminal Law as the Jack-in-the-Box?' in Carsten Stahn and Larissa van den Herik (eds), *The Diversification and Fragmentation of International Criminal Law* (Brill Nijhoff 2012), 23–24.

39 van Sliedregt and Vasiliev (n 35), 32.

40 *Ibid.*, 32–33. See also Vasiliev (n 14), 375.

41 *Prosecutor v. Zdravko Mucić et al.*, IT-96-21-T, ICTY, Trial Judgment, 16 November 1998.

42 Kunarac Trial Judgment (n 27), para 457.

43 *Prosecutor v. Dominic Ongwen*, ICC-02/04-01/15 A, ICC, Appeal Judgment, 15 December 2022, para 1056–1058.

to the crime of pillage.[44] These examples make explicit how a pluralistic conception of the wrong that attaches to the criminal acts that constitute international crimes partly emerges from and in turn reconstitutes the field's legally pluralist structural foundations.

The analysis also reveals how the foundational pluralism of values, rationales and normative identities that characterise international criminal law manifests in the diverse nature of how wrongs are articulated. The normative dimensions of the acts analysed have been varyingly articulated in terms of rights, such as a right to private property, a right to reproductive autonomy, to health or to family,[45] in terms of protected interests, such as the protection of cultural property or individual sexual autonomy,[46] or in terms of harms, such as those of shame and stigma experienced by victims of sexual violence and the harm to the conjugal order of their communities, the harm to the social fabric of communities inflicted by the destruction of cultural property, or the harm to civilians' ability to survive inflicted by the pillaging of their property.[47]

The nature of these narratives also illustrates some of the interplay between the normative dimensions of the acts that constitute international crimes and the wider crime categories within which they are embedded, in terms of how some narratives have been shaped by the context of armed conflict or other form of large-scale violence in which an act took place. This is evident, for instance, in the emphasis on the subsistence and survival of civilians in relation to the war crime of pillage or in the centrality of the injury to a community's conjugal order through the sexual violation of its members in the case of the war crime and crime against humanity of sexual violence. In other instances, a more stand-alone normative conception of a criminal act is offered that is less reliant on the context required by the category of crime to which it belongs, such as when the normative conception of an act is articulated in terms of the protection of a right or interest.

These diverse ways of constructing the normative dimensions of these acts ultimately capture some of the pluralist normative identities of the field, reflecting influences from domestic criminal law theory, such as in the identification of particular protected interests, as well as a pull towards more victim-oriented and humanitarian considerations in the increasingly comprehensive

---

44 Ongwen Trial Judgment (n 11), para 2766.

45 See Chapter 3, section 2; Chapter 2, section 3(a); Chapter 4, section 2(d) and section 3(a)(ii).

46 See Chapter 2, section 3(a); Chapter 4, section 2(d).

47 See Chapter 4, section 3(b)(iii); Chapter 2, section 3(d)(ii); Chapter 3, sections 3(b) and 4(a).

and nuanced nature of the harms that are articulated during proceedings and in judgment, sentencing and, in particular, reparation. The analysis of the crimes of attacks on cultural property, pillage, sexual violence and reproductive violence has in this way exposed how the meaning making processes through which the normative foundations of these acts are constructed through practice in turn reproduce the field's structural pluralism at a normative level, producing a correspondingly pluralistic account of the wrongs that attach to these acts.

2.2 *Criminal Wrong as Socially and Politically Situated*

At the same time, the nature of the flexible and dynamic wrongs that emerge through the process of being continually discursively produced, re-constituted and transformed in practice, while partly reflecting the legally pluralist structures of international criminal law as a field, may also relate at a more fundamental level to the inherently socially constructed nature of the concept of 'wrong' in criminal law more generally. The wider theoretical framework adopted in this research, drawing on a Durkheimian understanding of criminal wrongs as both declarative and constitutive of a society's collective consciousness, foregrounded in the first instance how criminal wrongs are products of processes of social definition. The analysis of the crimes nevertheless also sought to move beyond Durkheim's static and homologous conception of collective consciousness by tracing some of the specific historical, social and political conditions in which these acts came to be understood as wrong in a Western-dominated international order as well as how their normative meanings are constructed and transformed in practice in an ongoing process of meaning making that both reflects and reconstitutes wider changes in this dominant social and moral order.

This co-constitutive relationship between changes in the dominant order and the nature of how wrongs are identified and constructed in international criminal law is best illustrated by the analysis of the crimes of sexual and reproductive violence. From its honour-based prohibition in international humanitarian law to its construction in international criminal law in terms of individual physical integrity and bodily and sexual autonomy, but not more fully in terms of sexual subjectivity, the nature of how the wrong attached to sexual violence is conceptualised has transformed alongside the changes in the position of women in the wider social and moral order. Similarly mapping on to these tectonic social shifts in gender roles and relations, the criminalisation of acts of reproductive violence took place in the context of a turn away from the population control paradigm in international discourses, towards a more individual rights-based understanding of the reproductive sphere, with the invocation of an individual's right to reproductive autonomy in the *Ongwen* case reflecting an emphatic consolidation of this shift.

While perhaps less evidently mapping on to such profound social changes, the analysis of the crimes of attacking cultural property and pillage nevertheless reflect a similar dynamic. The practice around the crime of attacks on cultural property has evolved in a way that reflects wider developments in the field of heritage studies towards a more local, community-oriented and intangible understanding of cultural value.[48] Similarly, the practice on pillage has moved away from its historical roots in an emphatically-liberal individualist protection for property rights during armed conflict to reflect the more humanitarian and victim-oriented concern with subsistence and survival characteristic of the rise of the human security paradigm in the international order.[49]

The analysis of the normative dimensions of each of these crimes can in this sense be understood as paradigmatic of a conception of criminal wrong that is socially constructed and politically situated. In the domestic context, Lindsay Farmer exposes the inherently constructed and contingent nature of the concept of 'wrong' and its relationship to criminal law through a useful illustrative discussion of the distinction between the categories of *malum in se* and *malum prohibitum.*[50] In his analysis of this distinction, Farmer highlights how the notion of *malum in se*, with its invocation of inherent wrong independent of law, implies a conception of wrongfulness that is 'obvious', as opposed to crimes *mala prohibita*, which are crimes that are only wrong because they are prohibited by law. Farmer illustrates in this way how the notion of *mala in se* implies a category of 'core' or 'paradigmatic' crimes by virtue of the idea that their wrongfulness is more readily identified than those of *mala prohibita* crimes, which instead constitute the periphery of criminal law.[51] Approaching

48 For an overview of these developments see Angela M. Labrador and Neil Asher Silberman 'Introduction: Public Heritage as Social Practice' in Angela M. Labrador and Neil Asher Silberman (eds), *The Oxford Handbook of Public Heritage Theory and Practice* (Oxford University Press 2018), 1–18.

49 For an overview of the shift in the international order during the post-Cold War period from privileging state security to human security see Ruti G. Teitel, *Humanity's Law* (Oxford University Press 2012).

50 Lindsay Farmer, 'Criminal Wrongs in Historical Perspective' in R.A. Duff et al. (eds), *The Boundaries of the Criminal Law* (Oxford University Press 2010), 220. For other examples of literature addressing criminal wrong in similar terms see Richard L. Gray, 'Eliminating the (Absurd) Distinction Between Malum In Se and Malum Prohibitum Crimes', (1995) 73(3) *Washington University Law Quarterly*, 1369–1398; David Brown, 'Criminalisation and Normative Theory', (2013) 25(2) *Current Issues in Criminal Justice*, 605–625.

51 Farmer (n 50), 218.

the notion of criminal wrong from a historical perspective, Farmer uses this notion of 'core' or 'paradigmatic' crimes to highlight how in reality:

> [T]he core is in fact always changing, either because crimes which were regarded as central or paradigmatic are no longer treated as such (eg treason, blasphemy) or because central features of 'core' crimes change in ways which shift the meaning and social significance of the crime. [...] [T]he content of the idea of non-trivial harm or wrong is going to be highly dependent on the temporally contingent social meaning of certain actions.[52]

On this basis, Farmer concludes by calling for 'a richer account not only of what count as legal wrongs but of how these legal wrongs are linked to social, political, and legal order.'[53]

While understanding criminal law as in this way 'explicable largely as the result of exercises of political power at particular points in history'[54] is common in more sociologically or criminologically oriented scholarship on domestic criminal law, the 'context-free and abstract arguments of some [criminal law] philosophy',[55] which have informed many of the theorisations of international crimes offered in the scholarship to date,[56] have tended not to address this more socially and politically-informed dimension of what constitutes a wrong and its relationship to criminal law.[57]

The absence of the political from the discussion on the nature of the forms of violence that constitute international crimes is arguably somewhat characteristic of international criminal law and much of the rhetoric that surrounds it. This rhetoric often reflects a heavily natural law flavour in the vocabulary of 'atrocities that deeply shock the conscience of humanity' and the commonplace notion that 'the nature of the acts which international criminal law has traditionally dealt with [...] tend to reflect [...] the minimum content of natural law, exist[ing] at a liminal point in criminal law.'[58] In a similar way, while not

52 *Ibid.*, 220.

53 *Ibid.*, 237.

54 Andrew Ashworth and Jeremy Horder, *Principles of Criminal Law* (Oxford University Press 2009), 2.

55 Brown (n 50), 619.

56 For an overview see Introduction, section 1.

57 Farmer (n 50), 216–217.

58 Robert Cryer and Albert Nell, 'The philosophy of international criminal law' in Alexander Orakhelashvili (ed), *Research Handbook on the Theory and History of International Law* (Edward Elgar 2020), 207.

always made explicit, a strong undercurrent of understanding the core international crimes as reflecting some form of *mala in se*, as intrinsically bad, evil or morally wrong, capturing conduct that could be considered 'so evil that not prosecuting it was viewed as wrongful',[59] shaped the field at its inception and often continues to animate how international crimes are conceptualised.[60]

This general tendency is also reflected in how the nature of the acts that constitute international crimes are commonly understood as resting on a set of given and self-evident, or in Farmer's words 'obvious',[61] wrongs, which characterises the popular discourse around the field as well as the spectrum of harm-based and protected legal goods or interests theories of international crimes discussed in the introduction to this book.[62] This in turn produces a discourse around international crimes that elides the relationship between criminal wrong and the wider social, political and moral order which constitutes international criminal law and is constituted by it, and which emerges particularly clearly in the analysis of the crimes of sexual and reproductive violence in this study, but is also reflected in those of attacks on cultural property and pillage.

The analysis of the crimes in this book in this way underscores the relevance to international criminal law of a socially constructed and contingent conception of wrong, which recognises the relationship between transformations in social and political relations and how 'particular moral concepts of wrong themselves change over time.'[63] Understanding the normative dimensions of

59 Patrick Keenan, 'Doctrinal Innovation in International Criminal Law: Harms, Victims, and the Evolution of the Law', (2020) 42(2) *University of Pennsylvania Journal of International Law*, 433.

60 Corsi (n 30), 1367. See also Carsten Stahn, *A Critical Introduction to International Criminal Law* (Cambridge University Press 2019), 19–22; William A. Schabas, 'International crimes' in David Armstrong (ed), *Routledge Handbook of International Law* (Routledge 2009), 272–274.

61 Farmer (n 50), 218.

62 For instance, Larry May describes the normative contents of crimes against humanity as limited to 'basic rights to security and subsistence', David Luban describes them as acts that violate 'basic moral decency' while for Massimo Renzo they are acts that violate 'basic human rights.' Kai Ambos refers to rights to life, human dignity and physical integrity as legal goods protected by the crimes against humanity, war crimes and genocide, while the wider philosophical literature on war crimes has overwhelmingly focussed on acts involving violence to life and person. See Introduction, section 1. Larry May, *Crimes Against Humanity: A Normative Account* (2005 Cambridge University Press), 21; David Luban, 'A Theory of Crimes Against Humanity', (2004) 29(1) *Yale Journal of International Law*, 119; Massimo Renzo, 'Crimes Against Humanity and the Limits of International Law', (2012) 31(4) *Law and Philosophy*, 453; Kai Ambos, 'The Overall Function of International Criminal Law: Striking the Right Balance Between the Rechtsgut and the Harm Principles', (2015) 9(2) *Criminal Law and Philosophy*, 66.

63 Farmer (n 50), 237. See also Gray (n 50), 1369–1398.

the criminal acts that constitute international crimes in the terms proposed by this book, as an ongoing, flexible and dynamic process of meaning making that constitutes and is constituted by a pluralistic and socially constructed conception of wrong goes some way towards exposing this relationship. This, in turn, contributes in a small way to exposing some of the foundational politics of international crimes, which are often masked by the enduring strength of a naturalistic understanding of the wrongs that make up their constituent parts.

2.3 *Legitimation*

In understanding the nature of criminal wrong in international criminal law as socially constructed and dynamic, it is important to recall the co-constitutive relationship between criminal law and society outlined at the beginning of this book, in which criminal law is understood to be both 'generated by and productive of social order.'[64] In this respect, the constructed and contingent character of criminal wrong can be understood to operate in two directions; transformations in the dominant social and political order create the conditions in which certain acts come to be understood as wrongful and therefore to be criminalised, at the same time as the institutions and practices of criminal justice also play a role in reasserting and reconstituting what is seen as wrongful and how these wrongs are understood.

In reflecting on the latter aspect of how criminal wrongs are constituted and reshaped through practice, which the analysis of the criminal acts in this book has exposed, it is worth returning to Frédéric Mégret's call for supplementing a Durkheimian conception of international criminal law with attention to the practices of the actors and institutions of international criminal justice as a means of uncovering some of 'the power that lies behind and constitutes the criminal-justice system.'[65] In this respect, Mégret's emphasis on the practices of these actors highlights how the themes and narratives that emerge through practice and constitute the process of meaning making that imbues the criminal acts analysed in this book with their normative meaning are partly a product of the agency of the actors and institutions engaged in the system of criminal justice. In other words, the normative discourses that emerge in practice and construct a particular account of the wrong attaching to a criminal act are not transcendent, emerging from nowhere, but are instead the product of the conscious or unconscious choices of the individuals and actors involved in these cases. As noted by Kjersti Lohne, since 'only individuals – not

---

64 Farmer (n 50), 237.

65 Frédéric Mégret, 'Practices of Stigmatization', (2013) 76 *Law and Contemporary Problems*, 293. For discussion see Chapter 1, section 2.

institutions and laws – have intentions, the actors inhabiting those institutions and prescribing those laws become key to understanding the developments of these very same institutions and laws.'[66]

Understanding the nature of the processes of meaning making and the construction of normative foundations that take place through practice as in this way a product of the agency of the actors involved in the justice system raises the question of their motivations and the power they exercise in pursuing particular narratives. While the motivations and reasoning of particular actors in constructing certain narratives was beyond the scope of this research, and may not even or always be a product of conscious reflection, taken as a whole, the nature of some of the themes and narratives identified in this research are nevertheless suggestive of a certain self-interested dynamic that may reflect a concern with legitimating the charges in a particular case in normative terms.

In particular, digging into the fine grain of the normative themes and narratives that have emerged through the case law and during proceedings reveals a tendency to rhetorically invoke harm or injury to the human person, usually in the form of invoking the life, physical security and bodily integrity paradigm, in terms of how the harms inflicted by and the wrongs underlying these criminal acts have been constructed. This is particularly the case with respect to the crimes against property of attacking cultural property and pillage, that do not directly involve injury to the human person in these terms.

While the normative discourse around attacks on cultural property is varied, constructing a multifaceted account of the nature of what can be understood to be valuable about cultural property, in the *Al Mahdi* case at the ICC, in which this crime was the sole charge, the functionalist, people-oriented approach featured heavily, in particular in the narrative constructed by the OTP. The OTP's narrative during proceedings appeared in this respect to seek to personify the destroyed mausoleums, casting them as living entities through invoking a profound connection between the buildings and a 'persons' deepest inner self'[67] and 'the very core of their being.'[68] Seeking in this way to situate the crime of attacks on cultural property within the wider normative universe of international criminal law, the OTP explained that the common denominator that unites international crimes relates to how they 'inflict irreparable damage

---

66 Kjersti Lohne, 'Towards a Sociology of International Criminal Justice' in Morten Bergsmo et al. (eds), *Power in International Criminal Justice* (Torkel Opsahl Academic EPublisher 2020), 54.

67 *Prosecutor v. Ahmad al-Faqi al-Mahdi*, ICC-01/12-01/15, ICC, Transcript 23 August 2016, 90 [hereafter Al Mahdi Transcript Date].

68 Al Mahdi Transcript 24 August 2016 (n 67), 7.

to the human person in his or her body, mind, soul and identity',[69] going on to describe the crime of attacking cultural property as one that 'affects the soul and spirit of a people.'[70]

The OTP made explicit this justificatory aspect of its reasoning in therefore arguing that 'such an attack [...] falls into the category of crimes that destroy the roots of an entire people and profoundly and irremediably affects its social practices and structures. This is precisely why such acts constitute a crime under Article 8(2)(iv) of the Rome Statute.'[71] The precise nature of how the OTP constructed the cultural value of the mausoleums in the *Al Mahdi* case, as being a living part of the people themselves, appears in this way to have functioned to legitimise pursuing a case involving a sole charge of the destruction of a building by discursively elevating it in gravity it to one that ultimately can be understood to have inflicted damage to the human person.

In a similar fashion, in marked contrast to the ownership rights model of the definition of the crime, the narratives constructed around charges of pillage at the SCSL and the ICC have been emphatic in their emphasis on the implications of the loss of property for the life and physical security of victims in impoverished communities 'where victims lived on a subsistence basis.'[72] Pillaged property has been described as 'essential to [the civilian population's] survival',[73] with victims left 'without basic necessities'[74] and having 'suffered a great deal as a result of the attackers having stolen the food [...] many people suffered from intense hunger.'[75] These types of descriptions that explain the nature of the harm inflicted by pillage on victims, in these instances in terms of the threat to their subsistence and survival, are nevertheless absent when pillaged items have not fit as easily into the normative framework of threats to survival and subsistence, such as in the numerous instances where charges have also included the theft of items such as televisions, radios or watches.[76]

69 Al Mahdi Transcript 1 March 2016 (n 67), 12.

70 *Ibid.*

71 *Ibid.*, 13.

72 *Prosecutor v. Issa Hassan Sesay et al.* (*RUF Case*), SCSL-04-15-T, SCSL, Sentencing Judgment, 8 April 2009, para 172–176.

73 *Prosecutor v. Germain Katanga*, ICC-01/04-01/07, ICC, Judgment pursuant to article 74 of the Statute, 7 March 2014, para 1665.

74 *Prosecutor v. Jean-Pierre Bemba Gombo*, ICC-01/05-01/08, ICC, Judgment pursuant to Article 76 of the Statute, 21 June 2016, para 51–53.

75 *Prosecutor v. Dominic Ongwen*, ICC-02/04-01/15, ICC, Sentence 6 May 2021, para 201.

76 See *Prosecutor v. Jean-Pierre Bemba Gombo*, ICC-01/05-01/08, ICC, Judgment pursuant to Article 74 of the Statute 21 March 2016, para 502, 509, 547, 646; *Prosecutor v. Bosco Ntaganda*, ICC-01/04-02/06, ICC, Trial Judgment, 8 July 2019, para 514, 1035, 1042; *Prosecutor v. Bosco Ntaganda*, ICC-01/04-02/06, ICC, Sentencing Judgment, 7 November

The normative narrative constructed around the crime of pillage in these cases ultimately remains silent on the nature of the harm inflicted by the loss of items of this nature or the wrong that can be understood to underlie the charges for pillaging these types of property.

Similar to the nature of the narrative constructed around cultural value in the *Al Mahdi* case, this implies that the form taken by the normative narrative constructed around charges of pillage may have been, in part, driven by a justificatory impulse on the part of the actors involved in these cases since, where it is possible to discursively situate the act within the paradigm of basic security rights, the OTP and the chambers in these cases rely on this framework to normatively justify the prosecution of acts that, in themselves, do not involve direct harm or injury to the human person in these terms. By contrast, in the absence of such a clear link to the basic security rights paradigm, the normative dimensions of these acts are left unaddressed. The elevating of crimes against property to those involving harm to the human person that characterises the OTP's discourse in the *Al Mahdi* case and the decisions on pillage at the ICC and SCSL may in this way suggest that the nature of how actors explain and justify certain charges, in other words, what normative narratives they choose to construct about particular criminal acts, may be driven, at least in part, by an impulse to legitimate their pursuit of charges in a particular case.

Although not involving crimes against property, the analysis of the treatment of forced pregnancy in the *Ongwen* case at the ICC also supports this reasoning. In contrast to the narratives around crimes against property that seek to centralise harm to the human person, the OTP and the Trial Chamber made little mention of the significant physical demands of pregnancy and the profound violation of bodily integrity inherent in being forced to carry a pregnancy to term without having chosen to do so. Instead, the narrative constructed around this crime by both the OTP and the Trial Chamber relied almost exclusively on a principled account of the wrong of the crime as rooted in protections for reproductive rights and, in particular, a right to reproductive autonomy and choice. The physical nature of the harms inflicted on victims of these acts have so far gone almost unremarked in the narratives constructed in this case. This may be because pregnancy and motherhood are represented

---

2019, para 139; *Prosecutor v. Alex Tamba Brima et al.* (*AFRC Case*), SCSL-04-16-T, SCSL, Trial Judgment, 20 June 2007, para 1426; SCSL, *Prosecutor v. Moinina Fofana and Allieu Kondewa* (*CDF Case*), SCSL-04-14-T, SCSL, Trial Judgment, 2 August 2007, para 460; *Prosecutor v. Issa Hassan Sesay et al.* (*RUF Case*), SCSL-04-15-T, SCSL, Trial Judgment, 2 March 2009, para 1535, 1594; *Prosecutor v. Charles Ghankay Taylor*, SCSL-03-01-T, SCSL, Trial Judgment, 18 May 2012, para 1939.

almost universally in the dominant social order as positive 'life affirming experiences – as the greatest achievements of a woman's life.'[77] It is possible that the physical demands of pregnancy may therefore be difficult to conceive of as injuries or harms when nevertheless experienced by an individual without their choice. Since the reasoning of the actors involved in trials in choosing to construct certain narratives did not form part of this research, it is difficult to assess why this more abstract and principled normative meaning was attributed to the crime in this case. It is also important to note that, of all four crimes analysed, to date, only one case has involved charges for crimes of reproductive violence, with the result that the meaning making processes around these crimes remain in their early stages.

At the same time, it may still be possible to speculate that this principled emphasis on reproductive autonomy and rights similarly formed part of a process of legitimation on the part of the OTP and the chambers involved in this case. The emphasis on reproductive rights, autonomy and choice in both the OTP's narrative of the case and the invocation of these principles by the Trial and Appeals Chambers can perhaps partly be interpreted as a response to the consistent calls among civil society and some states for greater gender-sensitivity in international criminal law.[78] The significance of being the first case to involve charges for forced pregnancy may in this sense have encouraged the actors involved in this case to construct a normative narrative that reflects the increasing gender-sensitivity of some quarters of the dominant social and moral order and, in doing so, to legitimate their progressive credentials on such issues. In this sense, the two aspects to understanding how criminal wrongs are socially constructed – as both the product of how notions of wrong are constructed and change in wider society, but also as a product of the role that institutions and practices of criminal justice in turn play in reasserting, transforming and reconstituting how wrongs are understood – are evidently not divorced from one another. Rather, the wider social and moral order not only provides the social context from which wrongs emerge but may also feed back into how actors involved in cases construct justificatory narratives that they believe may resonate with and be perceived as legitimate more widely.

While the reasons behind the construction of particular normative narratives by the actors engaged in the practice of international criminal justice was

77 Rosemary Grey, 'Reproductive Crimes in International Criminal Law' in Indira Rosenthal, Valerie Oosterveld and Susana SáCouto (eds), *Gender & International Criminal Law* (Oxford University Press, forthcoming), 33.

78 For an overview see Louise Chappell, *The Politics of Gender Justice at the International Criminal Court: Legacies and Legitimacy* (Oxford University Press 2016).

not ultimately the focus of this research, reflecting in this way on the nature of some of the narratives revealed through the analysis contained in this book nevertheless suggests that there may be a degree of self-justification at play on the part of the actors engaged in their construction, in which certain narratives are pursued as a means of legitimating the choices in a particular case. This points towards an element of inward-looking self-interest in shaping how the foundational normative aspects of these acts are constructed. In other words, if the normative foundations of these criminal acts can be understood, as proposed by this book, as being constructed internally through an ongoing process of meaning making in practice, the particular interests of the actors engaged in this process may contribute to shaping the outcomes of what these foundations end up being.

Although the nature of the research conducted for this book does not allow for more expansive or definitive conclusions to be drawn in this respect, reflecting on the interests at play in the process of meaning making that takes place in practice exposes some of the implications of understanding the normative dimensions of the criminal acts that constitute international crimes in these terms. This raises questions for further reflection as to the power exercised by the actors that shape how wrong is constructed in international criminal law and, in doing so, may not only shape the legal outcomes in a particular case, but also contribute to shaping the nature of the internationally shared norms and values that are performatively invoked through international criminal justice.

Ultimately, this book has not sought to take a normative position on the nature of the norms or values called into existence through the international criminalisation and prosecution of attacks on cultural property, pillage, sexual violence and reproductive violence. The more modest aim in conducting this analysis was instead to expose what some of these norms and values may be, and the nature of the processes through which they come to be. The book has in this respect offered a more granular but also a more socially and politically situated understanding of the normative dimensions of the acts that constitute international crimes, which reveals a more complex, dynamic and diverse normative picture than is captured by their typical characterisation as violations of basic security rights in some form. In doing so, this book has ultimately sought to lay some of the groundwork to enable a more particularised and transparent conversation about some of the representational work that international criminal justice does in the world.

Appendix 1

Decisions

Attacks on Cultural Property

Case name	Case number	Decision	Date
International criminal tribunal for the former yugoslavia (ICTY)			
Babić, Milan	IT-03-72-S	Sentencing Judgment	29 June 2004
Babić, Milan	IT-03-72-A	Judgment on Sentencing Appeal	18 July 2005
Blaškić, Tihomir	IT-95-14-T	Trial Judgment	3 March 2000
Blaškić, Tihomir	IT-95-14-A	Appeal Judgment	29 July 2004
Brđanin, Radoslav	IT-99-36-T	Trial Judgment	1 September 2004
Brđanin, Radoslav	IT-99-36-A	Appeal Judgment	3 April 2007
Jokić, Miodrag	IT-01-42/1-S	Sentencing Judgment	18 March 2004
Jokić, Miodrag	IT-01-42/1-A	Appeal Judgment	30 August 2005
Hadžihasanović, Enver & Kubura, Amir	IT-01-47-T	Trial Judgment	15 March 2006
Hadžihasanović, Enver & Kubura, Amir	IT-01-47-A	Appeal Judgment	22 April 2008
Karadžić, Radovan	IT-95-5/18-T	Trial Judgment	24 March 2016
Karadžić, Radovan	IT-9S-S118-AR98bis.l	Appeal Judgment	11 July 2013
Kordić, Dario & Čerkez, Mario	IT-95-14/2-T	Trial Judgment	26 February 2001
Kordić, Dario & Čerkez, Mario	IT-95-14/2-A	Appeal Judgment	17 December 2004
Krajišnik, Momčilo	IT-00-39-T	Trial Judgment	27 September 2006
Krajišnik, Momčilo	IT-00-39-A	Appeal Judgment	17 March 2009

 | DOI:10.1163/9789004687844_009

Case name	Case number	Decision	Date
Martić, Milan	IT-95-11-T	Trial Judgment	12 June 2007
Martić, Milan	IT-95-11-A	Appeal Judgment	8 October 2008
Mladić, Ratko	IT-09-92-T	Trial Judgment	22 November 2017
Naletilić, Mladen & Martinović, Vinko	IT-98-34-T	Trial Judgment	31 March 2003
Naletilić, Mladen & Martinović, Vinko	IT-98-34-A	Appeal Judgment	3 May 2006
Plavšić, Biljana	IT-00-39&40/1-S	Sentencing Judgment	27 February 2003
Prlić, Jadranko et al.	IT-04-74-T	Trial Judgment	29 May 2013
Prlić, Jadranko et al.	IT-04-74-A	Appeal Judgment	29 November 2017
Stanišić, Mićo & Župljanin, Stojan	IT-08-91-T	Trial Judgment	27 March 2013
Stanišić, Mićo & Župljanin, Stojan	IT-08-91-A	Appeal Judgment	30 June 2016
Strugar, Pavle	IT-01-42-T	Trial Judgment	31 January 2005
Strugar, Pavle	IT-01-42-A	Appeal Judgment	17 July 2008
International Criminal Court (ICC)			
al-Mahdi, Ahmad al-Faqi	ICC-01/12-01/15	Judgment and Sentence	27 September 2016
al-Mahdi, Ahmad al-Faqi	ICC-01/12-01/15	Reparations Order	17 August 2017

Pillage

Case name	Case number	Decision	Date
International triminal tribunal for the former yugoslavia (ICTY)			
Blaškić, Tihomir	IT-95-14-T	Trial Judgment	3 March 2000
Blaškić, Tihomir	IT-95-14-A	Appeal Judgment	29 July 2004

Case name	Case number	Decision	Date
Brđanin, Radoslav	IT-99-36-T	Trial Judgment	1 September 2004
Brđanin, Radoslav	IT-99-36-A	Appeal Judgment	3 April 2007
Gotovina, Ante et al.	IT-06-90-T	Trial Judgment	15 April 2011
Gotovina, Ante et al.	IT-06-90-A	Appeal Judgment	16 November 2012
Hadžihasanović, Enver & Kubura, Amir	IT-01-47-T	Trial Judgment	15 March 2006
Hadžihasanović, Enver & Kubura, Amir	IT-01-47-A	Appeal Judgment	22 April 2008
Jelisić, Goran	IT-95-10-T	Trial Judgment	14 December 1999
Jelisić, Goran	IT-95-10-A	Appeal Judgment	5 July 2001
Kordić, Dario & Čerkez, Mario	IT-95-14/2-T	Trial Judgment	26 February 2001
Kordić, Dario & Čerkez, Mario	IT-95-14/2-A	Appeal Judgment	17 December 2004
Martić, Milan	IT-95-11-T	Trial Judgment	12 June 2007
Martić, Milan	IT-95-11-A	Appeal Judgment	8 October 2008
Mucić, Zdravko et al.	IT-96-21-T	Trial Judgment	16 November 1998
Mucić, Zdravko et al.	IT-96-21-A	Appeal Judgment	20 February 2001
Mucić, Zdravko et al.	IT-96-21-T bis-R117	Sentencing Judgment	9 October 2001
Mucić, Zdravko et al.	IT-96-21-Abis	Judgment on Sentence Appeal	8 April 2003
Naletilić, Mladen & Martinović, Vinko	IT-98-34-T	Trial Judgment	31 March 2003
Naletilić, Mladen & Martinović, Vinko	IT-98-34-A	Appeal Judgment	3 May 2006
Simić, Blagoje et al.,	IT-95-9-T	Trial Judgment	17 October 2003

Case name	Case number	Decision	Date
Simić, Blagoje	IT-95-9-A	Appeal Judgment	28 November 2006
Tadić, Duško	IT-94-1	Decision on the Defence Motion for Interlocutory Appeal on Jurisdiction	2 October 1995
Special Court for Sierra Leone (SCSL)			
Brima, Alex Tamba et al.	SCSL-04-16-T	Trial Judgment	20 June 2007
Brima, Alex Tamba et al.	SCSL-04-16-T	Sentencing Judgment	19 July 2007
Brima, Alex Tamba et al.	SCSL-2004-16-A	Appeal Judgment	22 February 2008
Fofana, Moinina & Kondewa, Allieu	SCSL-04-14-T	Trial Judgment	2 August 2007
Fofana, Moinina & Kondewa, Allieu	SCSL-04-14-T	Sentencing Judgment	9 October 2007
Fofana, Moinina & Kondewa, Allieu	SCSL-04-14-A	Appeal Judgment	28 May 2008
Sesay, Issa Hassan et al.	SCSL-04-15-T	Trial Judgment	2 March 2009
Sesay, Issa Hassan et al.	SCSL-04-15-T	Sentencing Judgment	8 April 2009
Sesay, Issa Hassan et al.	SCSL-04-15-A	Appeal Judgment	26 October 2009
Taylor, Charles Ghankay	SCSL-03-01-T	Trial Judgment	18 May 2012
Taylor, Charles Ghankay	SCSL-03-01-T	Sentencing Judgment	30 May 2012
Taylor, Charles Ghankay	SCSL-03-01-A	Appeal Judgment	26 September 2013
International Criminal Court (ICC)			
Bemba Gombo, Jean-Pierre	ICC-01/05-01/08	Decision Pursuant to Article 61(7)(a) and (b) of the Rome Statute on	15 June 2009

Case name	Case number	Decision	Date
		the Charges of the Prosecutor Against Jean-Pierre Bemba Gombo	
Bemba Gombo, Jean-Pierre	ICC-01/05-01/08	Judgment pursuant to Article 74 of the Statute	21 March 2016
Bemba Gombo, Jean-Pierre	ICC-01/05-01/08	Decision on Sentence pursuant to Article 76 of the Statute	21 June 2016
Bemba Gombo, Jean-Pierre	ICC-01/05-01/08 A	Judgment on the appeal of Mr Jean-Pierre Bemba Gombo against Trial Chamber III's "Judgment pursuant to Article 74 of the Statute"	8 June 2018
Katanga, Germain & Ngudjolo Chui, Mathieu	ICC-01/04-01/07	Decision on the confirmation of charges	30 September 2008
Katanga, Germain	ICC-01/04-01/07	Judgment pursuant to article 74 of the Statute	7 March 2014
Katanga, Germain	ICC-01/04-01/07	Order for Reparations pursuant to Article 75 of the Statute	24 March 2017

Case name	Case number	Decision	Date
Katanga, Germain	ICC-01/04-01/07 A3 A4 A5	Judgment on the appeals against the order of Trial Chamber II of 24 March 2017 entitled "Order for Reparations pursuant to Article 75 of the Statute"	8 March 2018
Ngudjolo Chui, Mathieu	ICC-01/04-02/12	Judgment pursuant to article 74 of the Statute	18 December 2012
Ngudjolo Chui, Mathieu	ICC-01/04-02/12 A	Judgment on the Prosecutor's appeal against the decision of Trial Chamber II entitled "Judgment pursuant to article 74 of the Statute"	7 April 2015
Ntaganda, Bosco	ICC-01/04-02/06	Decision Pursuant to Article 61(7)(a) and (b) of the Rome Statute on the Charges of the Prosecutor Against Bosco Ntaganda	9 June 2014
Ntaganda, Bosco	ICC-01/04-02/06	Trial Judgment	8 July 2019

Case name	Case number	Decision	Date
Ntaganda, Bosco	ICC-01/04-02/06	Sentencing Judgment	7 November 2019
Ongwen, Dominic	ICC-02/04-01/15	Decision on the confirmation of charges against Dominic Ongwen	23 March 2016
Ongwen, Dominic	ICC-02/04-01/15	Trial Judgment	4 February 2021

Sexual Violence

Case name	Case number	Decision	Date
International criminal tribunal for the former yugoslavia (ICTY)			
Banović, Predrag	IT-02-65/1-S	Sentencing Judgment	28 October 2003
Bralo, Miroslav	IT-95-17-S	Sentencing Judgment	7 December 2005
Bralo, Miroslav	IT-95-17-A	Judgment on Sentencing Appeal	2 April 2007
Brđanin, Radoslav	IT-99-36-T	Trial Judgment	1 September 2004
Brđanin, Radoslav	IT-99-36-A	Appeal Judgment	3 April 2007
Češić, Ranko	IT-95-10/1-S	Sentencing Judgment	11 March 2004
Delić, Rasim	IT-04-83-T	Trial Judgment	15 September 2008
Đorđević, Vlastimir	IT-05-87/1-T	Trial Judgment	23 February 2011
Đorđević, Vlastimir	IT-05-87/1-A	Appeal Judgment	27 January 2014
Furundžija, Anto	IT-95-17/1-T	Trial Judgment	10 December 1998
Furundžija, Anto	IT-95-17/1-A	Appeal Judgment	21 July 2000

Case name	Case number	Decision	Date
Haradinaj, Ramush et al.	IT-04-84-T	Trial Judgment	3 April 2008
Haradinaj, Ramush et al.	IT-04-84bis-T	Trial Judgment (retrial)	29 November 2012
Haradinaj, Ramush et al.	IT-04-84-A	Appeal Judgment	19 July 2010
Karadžić, Radovan	IT-95-5/18-T	Trial Judgment	24 March 2016
Krajišnik, Momčilo	IT-00-39-T	Trial Judgment	27 September 2006
Krajišnik, Momčilo	IT-00-39-A	Appeal Judgment	17 March 2009
Krstić, Radislav	IT-98-33-T	Trial Judgment	02 August 2001
Krstić, Radislav	IT-98-33-A	Appeal Judgment	19 April 2004
Kunarac, Dragoljub et al.	IT-96-23-T& IT-96-23/1-T	Trial Judgment	22 February 2001
Kunarac, Dragoljub et al.	IT-96-23& IT-96-23/1-A	Appeal Judgment	12 June 2002
Kvočka, Miroslav et al.	IT-98-30/1-T	Trial Judgment	2 November 2001
Kvočka, Miroslav et al.	IT-98-30/1-A	Appeal Judgment	28 February 2005
Martić, Milan	IT-95-11-T	Trial Judgment	12 June 2007
Martić, Milan	IT-95-11-A	Appeal Judgment	8 October 2008
Mladić, Ratko	IT-09-92-T	Trial Judgment	22 November 2017
Mrkšić, Miroslav et al.	IT-95-13/1-T	Trial Judgment	27 September 2007
Mrkšić, Miroslav et al.	IT-95-13/1-A	Appeal Judgment	5 May 2009
Mucić, Zdravko et al.	IT-96-21-T	Trial Judgment	16 November 1998
Mucić, Zdravko et al.	IT-96-21-A	Appeal Judgment	20 February 2001
Mucić, Zdravko et al.	IT-96-21-T bis-R117	Sentencing Judgment	9 October 2001
Mucić, Zdravko et al.	IT-96-21-Abis	Judgment on Sentence Appeal	8 April 2003

Case name	Case number	Decision	Date
Nikolić, Dragan	IT-94-2-S	Sentencing Judgment	18 December 2003
Nikolić, Dragan	IT-94-2-A	Judgment on Sentencing Appeal	4 February 2005
Plavšić, Biljana	IT-00-39&40/1-S	Sentencing Judgment	27 February 2003
Prlić, Jadranko et al.	IT-04-74-T	Trial Judgment	29 May 2013
Prlić, Jadranko et al.	IT-04-74-A	Appeal Judgment	29 November 2017
Rajić, Ivica	IT-95-12-S	Sentencing Judgment	8 May 2006
Šainović, Nikola et al.	IT-05-87-T	Trial Judgment	26 February 2009
Šainović, Nikola et al.	IT-05-87-A	Appeal Judgment	23 January 2014
Šešelj, Vojislav	IT-03-67-T	Trial Judgment	31 March 2016
Sikirica, Duško	IT-95-8-S	Sentencing Judgment	13 November 2001
Simić, Blagoje et al.	IT-95-9-T	Trial Judgment	17 October 2003
Simić, Blagoje	IT-95-9-A	Appeal Judgment	28 November 2006
Simić, Milan	IT-95-9/2-S	Sentencing Judgment	17 October 2002
Stakić, Milomir	IT-97-24-T	Trial Judgment	31 July 2003
Stakić, Milomir	IT-97-24-A	Appeal Judgment	22 March 2006
Stanišić, Jovica & Simatović, Franko	IT-03-69-T	Trial Judgment	30 May 2013
Stanišić, Jovica & Simatović, Franko	IT-03-69-A	Appeal Judgment	9 December 2015
Stanišić, Mićo & Župljanin, Stojan	IT-08-91-T	Trial Judgment	27 March 2013
Stanišić, Mićo & Župljanin, Stojan	IT-08-91-A	Appeal Judgment	30 June 2016
Tadić, Duško	IT-94-1	Trial Judgment	7 May 1997
Tadić, Duško	IT-94-1-T	Sentencing Judgment	14 July 1997

Case name	Case number	Decision	Date
Tadić, Duško	IT-94-1-A	Appeal Judgment	15 July 1999
Tadić, Duško	IT-94-1-A and IT-94-1-Abis	Judgment in Sentencing Appeals	26 January 2000
Todorović, Stevan	IT-95-9/1-S	Sentencing Judgment	31 July 2001
Zelenović, Dragan	IT-96-23/2-S	Sentencing Judgment	4 April 2007
Zelenović, Dragan	IT-96-23/2-A	Judgment on Sentencing Appeals	31 October 2007
International Criminal Tribunal for Rwanda (ICTR)			
Akayesu, Jean-Paul	ICTR-96-4-T	Trial Judgment	2 September 1998
Akayesu, Jean-Paul	ICTR-96-4-A	Appeal Judgment	1 June 2001
Bagilishema, Ignace	ICTR-95-1A-T	Trial Judgment	7 June 2001
Bagilishema, Ignace	ICTR-95-1A-A	Appeal Judgment	3 July 2002
Bagosora, Théoneste et al.	ICTR-98-41-T	Judgment and Sentence	18 December 2008
Bagosora, Théoneste et al.	ICTR-98-41-A	Appeal Judgment	14 December 2011
Bikindi, Simon	ICTR-01-72-T	Trial Judgment	2 December 2008
Bikindi, Simon	ICTR-01-72-A	Appeal Judgment	18 March 2010
Bisengimana, Paul	ICTR-00-60-T	Judgment and Sentence	13 April 2006
Bizimungu, Casimir	ICTR-99-50-T	Judgment and Sentence	30 September 2011
Bizimungu, Augustin	ICTR-00-56B-A	Appeal Judgment	30 June 2014
Gacumbitsi, Sylvestre	ICTR-2001-64-T	Trial Judgment	17 June 2004
Gacumbitsi, Sylvestre	ICTR-2001-64-A	Appeal Judgment	7 July 2006
Gatete, Jean-Baptiste	ICTR-2000-61-T	Judgment and Sentence	31 March 2011

Case name	Case number	Decision	Date
Gatete, Jean-Baptiste	ICTR-00-61-A	Appeal Judgment	9 October 2012
Hategekimana, Ildephonse	ICTR-00-55B-T	Judgment and Sentence	6 December 2010
Hategekimana, Ildephonse	ICTR-00-558-A	Appeal Judgment	8 May 2012
Kajelijeli, Juvénal	ICTR-98-44A-T	Trial Judgment	1 December 2003
Kajelijeli, Juvénal	ICTR-98-44A-A	Appeal Judgment	23 May 2005
Kamuhanda, Jean de Dieu	ICTR-95-54A-T	Trial Judgment	22 January 2004
Kamuhanda, Jean de Dieu	ICTR-99-54A-A	Appeal Judgment	19 September 2005
Karemera, Édouard & Ngirumpatse, Matthieu	ICTR-98-44-T	Trial Judgment	2 February 2012
Karemera, Édouard & Ngirumpatse, Matthieu	ICTR-98-44-A	Appeal Judgment	29 September 2014
Mpambara, Jean	ICTR-01-65-T	Trial Judgment	11 September 2006
Mugenzi, Justin & Mugiraneza, Prosper	ICTR-99-50-A	Appeal Judgment	4 February 2013
Muhimana, Mikaeli	ICTR- 95-1B-T	Trial Judgment	28 April 2005
Muhimana, Mikaeli	ICTR- 95-1B-A	Appeal Judgment	21 May 2007
Musema, Alfred	ICTR-96-13-T	Judgment and Sentence	27 January 2000
Musema, Alfred	ICTR-96-13-A	Appeal Judgment	16 November 2001
Muvunyi, Tharcisse	ICTR-2000-55A-T	Trial Judgment	12 September 2006
Muvunyi, Tharcisse	ICTR-2000-55A-A	Appeal Judgment	29 August 2008
Nchamihigo, Siméon	ICTR-01-63-T	Trial Judgment	12 November 2008
Nchamihigo, Siméon	ICTR-2001-63-A	Appeal Judgment	18 March 2010

Case name	Case number	Decision	Date
Nahimana, Ferdinand et al.	ICTR-99-51-T	Trial Judgment	3 December 2003
Nahimana, Ferdinand et al.	ICTR-99-52-A	Appeal Judgment	28 November 2007
Ndindabahizi, Emmanuel	ICTR-2001-71-I	Judgment and Sentence	15 July 2004
Ndindabahizi, Emmanuel	ICTR-01-71-A	Appeal Judgment	16 January 2007
Ndindiliyimana, Augustin et al.	ICTR-00-56-T	Judgment and Sentence	17 May 2011
Ndindiliyimana, Augustin et al.	ICTR-00-56-A	Appeal Judgment	11 February 2014
Ngirabatware, Augustin	ICTR-99-54-T	Judgment and Sentence	20 December 2012
Ngirabatware, Augustin	MICT-12-29-A	Appeal Judgment	18 December 2014
Niyitegeka, Eliézer	ICTR-96-14-T	Judgment and Sentence	16 May 2003
Niyitegeka, Eliézer	ICTR-96-14-A	Appeal Judgment	9 July 2004
Nizeyimana, Ildéphonse	ICTR-2000-55C-T	Judgment and Sentence	19 June 2012
Nizeyimana, Ildéphonse	ICTR-00-55C-A	Appeal Judgment	29 September 2014
Nyiramasuhuko, Pauline et al.	ICTR-98-42-T	Trial Judgment	24 June 2011
Nyiramasuhuko, Pauline et al.	ICTR-98-42-A	Appeal Judgment	14 December 2015
Nzabirinda, Joseph	ICTR-2001-77-T	Sentencing Judgment	23 February 2007
Nzabonimana, Callixte	ICTR-98-44D-T	Judgment and Sentence	31 May 2012
Nzabonimana, Callixte	ICTR-98-44D-A	Appeal Judgment	29 September 2014
Renzaho, Tharcisse	ICTR-97-31-T	Judgment and Sentence	14 July 2009
Renzaho, Tharcisse	ICTR-97-31-A	Appeal Judgment	1 April 2011

Case name	Case number	Decision	Date
Rugambarara, Juvénal	ICTR-00-59-T	Sentencing Judgement	16 November 2007
Rukundo, Emmanuel	ICTR-2001-70-T	Trial Judgment	27 February 2009
Rwamakuba, André	ICTR-98-44C-T	Trial Judgment	20 September 2006
Semanza, Laurent	ICTR-97-20-T	Judgment and Sentence	15 May 2003
Semanza, Laurent	ICTR-97-20-A	Appeal Judgment	20 May 2005
Extraordinary Chambers in the Courts of Cambodia (ECCC)			
Kaing, Guek Eav (Duch)	001/18-07-2007/ ECCC/TC	Trial Judgment	26 July 2010
Kaing, Guek Eav (Duch)	001/18-07-2007-ECCC/SC	Appeal Judgment	3 February 2012
Nuon, Chea & Samphan, Khieu	002/19-09-2007/ ECCC/TC	Trial Judgment	7 August 2014
Nuon, Chea & Samphan, Khieu	002/19-09-2007-ECCC/SC	Appeal Judgment	23 November 2016
Nuon, Chea & Samphan, Khieu	002/19-09-2007/ ECCC/TC	Trial Judgment	16 November 2018
Special Court for Sierra Leone (SCSL)			
Brima, Alex Tamba et al.	SCSL-04-16-T	Trial Judgment	20 June 2007
Brima, Alex Tamba et al.	SCSL-04-16-T	Sentencing Judgment	19 July 2007
Brima, Alex Tamba et al.	SCSL-2004-16-A	Appeal Judgment	22 February 2008
Fofana, Moinina & Kondewa, Allieu	SCSL-04-14-T	Trial Judgment	2 August 2007
Fofana, Moinina & Kondewa, Allieu	SCSL-04-14-T	Sentencing Judgment	9 October 2007
Fofana, Moinina & Kondewa, Allieu	SCSL-04-14-A	Appeal Judgment	28 May 2008
Sesay, Issa Hassan et al.	SCSL-04-15-T	Trial Judgment	2 March 2009
Sesay, Issa Hassan et al.	SCSL-04-15-T	Sentencing Judgment	8 April 2009

Case name	Case number	Decision	Date
Sesay, Issa Hassan et al.	SCSL-04-15-A	Appeal Judgment	26 October 2009
Taylor, Charles Ghankay	SCSL-03-01-T	Trial Judgment	18 May 2012
Taylor, Charles Ghankay	SCSL-03-01-T	Sentencing Judgment	30 May 2012
Taylor, Charles Ghankay	SCSL-03-01-A	Appeal Judgment	26 September 2013
International Criminal Court (ICC)			
al-Hassan Ag Abdoul Aziz	ICC-01/12-01/18	Rectificatif à la Décision relative à la confirmation des charges portées contre Al Hassan Ag Abdoul Aziz Ag Mohamed Ag Mahmoud	30 September 2019
Bemba Gombo, Jean-Pierre	ICC-01/05-01/08	Decision Pursuant to Article 61(7) (a) and (b) of the Rome Statute on the Charges of the Prosecutor Against Jean-Pierre Bemba Gombo	15 June 2009
Bemba Gombo, Jean-Pierre	ICC-01/05-01/08	Judgment pursuant to Article 74 of the Statute	21 March 2016
Bemba Gombo, Jean-Pierre	ICC-01/05-01/08	Decision on Sentence pursuant to Article 76 of the Statute	21 June 2016
Bemba Gombo, Jean-Pierre	ICC-01/05-01/08 A	Judgment on the appeal of Mr Jean-Pierre Bemba Gombo against	8 June 2018

Case name	Case number	Decision	Date
		Trial Chamber III's "Judgment pursuant to Article 74 of the Statute"	
Blé Goudé, Charles	ICC-02/11-02/11	Decision on the confirmation of charges against Charles Blé Goudé	11 December 2014
Gbagbo, Laurent	ICC-02/11-01/11	Decision on the confirmation of charges against Laurent Gbagbo	12 June 2014
Gbagbo, Laurent & Blé Goudé, Charles	ICC-02/11-01/15	Reasons for oral decision of 15 January 2019 on the Requête de la Défense de Laurent Gbagbo afin qu'un jugement d'acquittement portant sur toutes les charges soit prononcé en faveur de Laurent Gbagbo et que sa mise en liberté immédiate soit ordonnée, and on the Blé Goudé Defence no case to answer motion	16 July 2019
Katanga, Germain & Ngudjolo Chui, Mathieu	ICC-01/04-01/07	Decision on the confirmation of charges	30 September 2008
Katanga, Germain	ICC-01/04-01/07	Judgment pursuant to article 74 of the Statute	7 March 2014

Case name	Case number	Decision	Date
Katanga, Germain	ICC-01/04-01/07	Order for Reparations pursuant to Article 75 of the Statute	24 March 2017
Katanga, Germain	ICC-01/04-01/07 A3 A4 A5	Judgment on the appeals against the order of Trial Chamber II of 24 March 2017 entitled "Order for Reparations pursuant to Article 75 of the Statute"	8 March 2018
Muthaura, Francis Kirimi et al.	ICC-01/09-02/11	Decision on the Confinnation of Charges Pursuant to Article 61(7) (a) and (b) of the Rome Statute	23 January 2012
Lubanga Dyilo, Thomas	ICC-01/04-01/06	Decision on the confirmation of charges	29 January 2007
Lubanga Dyilo, Thomas	ICC-01/04-01/06	Judgment pursuant to Article 74 of the Statute	14 March 2012
Lubanga Dyilo, Thomas	ICC-01/04-01/06 A 5	Judgment on the appeal of Mr Thomas Lubanga Dyilo against his conviction	1 December 2014
Lubanga Dyilo, Thomas	ICC-01/04-01/06 A A 2 A 3	Judgment on the appeals against the "Decision establishing the principles and procedures to	3 March 2015

Case name	Case number	Decision	Date
		be applied to reparations" of 7 August 2012 with amended order for reparations	
Ngudjolo Chui, Mathieu	ICC-01/04-02/12	Judgment pursuant to article 74 of the Statute	18 December 2012
Ngudjolo Chui, Mathieu	ICC-01/04-02/12 A	Judgment on the Prosecutor's appeal against the decision of Trial Chamber II entitled "Judgment pursuant to article 74 of the Statute"	7 April 2015
Ntaganda, Bosco	ICC-01/04-02/06	Decision Pursuant to Article 61(7)(a) and (b) of the Rome Statute on the Charges of the Prosecutor Against Bosco Ntaganda	9 June 2014
Ntaganda, Bosco	ICC-01/04-02/06	Trial Judgment	8 July 2019
Ntaganda, Bosco	ICC-01/04-02/06	Sentencing Judgment	7 November 2019
Ongwen, Dominic	ICC-02/04-01/15	Decision on the confirmation of charges against Dominic Ongwen	23 March 2016
Ongwen, Dominic	ICC-02/04-01/15	Trial Judgment	4 February 2021

Reproductive Violence

Case name	Case number	Decision	Date
Extraordinary chambers in the courts of cambodia (ECCC)			
Nuon, Chea & Samphan, Khieu	002/19-09-2007-ECCC/OCIJ	Second Request for Investigative Actions Concerning Forced Marriages and Forced Sexual Relations	15 July 2009
An, Ao & Tith, Yim	004/07-09-2009-ECCC-OCIJ	Consolidated Decision on the Requests for Investigative Action Concerning the Crime of Forced Pregnancy and Forced Impregnation	13 June 2016
International Criminal Court (ICC)			
Ongwen, Dominic	ICC-02/04-01/15	Decision on the confirmation of charges against Dominic Ongwen	23 March 2016
Ongwen, Dominic	ICC-02/04-01/15	Trial Judgment	4 February 2021
Ongwen, Dominic	ICC-02/04-01/15 A	Appeal Judgment	15 December 2022

Appendix 2

Keywords

Crime	Keywords
Attacks on cultural property	religi / cultur / histor / mosque / church / mekte / worship / sacr / library / bridge / Mostar / Dubrovnik / mausoleum / tomb
Pillage	pillag / plunder / loot / steal / stole / theft / thieve / rob / spoliation / booty / property / belonging / goods / consent / pay / paid
Sexual violence	rape / sex / vagina / penis / breast / genital / anus / penetrat / oral / anal / nudity / naked / undress / intercourse / consent / shame / virgin / inhuman / outrage / prostitution / enslavement / indecent
Reproductive violence	pregnan / born / birth / produc / bab / child / contracepti / choice / choose / autonomy

 | DOI:10.1163/9789004687844_010

Appendix 3

Transcripts

Attacks on Cultural Property

Case name	Case number
International criminal tribunal for the former yugoslavia (ICTY)	
Babić, Milan	IT-03-72
Blaškić, Tihomir	IT-95-14
Brđanin, Radoslav	IT-99-36
Jokić, Miodrag	IT-01-42/1
Hadžić, Goran	IT-04-75
Hadžihasanović, Enver & Kubura, Amir	IT-01-47
Karadžić, Radovan	IT-95-5/18
Kordić, Dario & Čerkez, Mario	IT-95-14/2
Krajišnik, Momčilo	IT-00-39
Martić, Milan	IT-95-11
Milošević, Slobodan	IT-02-54
Mladić, Ratko	IT-09-92
Naletilić, Mladen & Martinović, Vinko	IT-98-34
Plavšić, Biljana	IT-00-39&40/1
Prlić, Jadranko et al.	IT-04-74
Stanišić, Mićo & Župljanin, Stojan	IT-08-91
Strugar, Pavle	IT-01-42
International Criminal Court (ICC)	
al-Mahdi, Ahmad al-Faqi	ICC-01/12-01/15

Pillage

Case name	Case number
International Criminal Tribunal for the Former Yugoslavia (ICTY)	
Blaškić, Tihomir	IT-95-14
Brđanin, Radoslav	IT-99-36

 | DOI:10.1163/9789004687844_011

Case name	Case number
Gotovina, Ante et al.	IT-06-90
Hadžihasanović, Enver & Kubura, Amir	IT-01-47
Jelisić, Goran	IT-95-10
Kordić, Dario & Čerkez, Mario	IT-95-14/2
Martić, Milan	IT-95-11
Mucić, Zdravko et al.	IT-96-21
Naletilić, Mladen & Martinović, Vinko	IT-98-34
Simić, Blagoje et al.,	IT-95-9
Special Court for Sierra Leone (SCSL)	
Brima, Alex Tamba et al.	SCSL-04-16
Fofana, Moinina & Kondewa, Allieu	SCSL-04-14
Sesay, Issa Hassan et al.	SCSL-04-15
Taylor, Charles Ghankay	SCSL-03-01
International Criminal Court (ICC)	
Bemba Gombo, Jean-Pierre	ICC-01/05-01/08
Katanga, Germain	ICC-01/04-01/07
Ntaganda, Bosco	ICC-01/04-02/06
Ongwen, Dominic	ICC-02/04-01/15

Sexual Violence

Case name	Case number
International Criminal Tribunal for the Former Yugoslavia (ICTY)	
Brđanin, Radoslav	IT-99-36
Đorđević, Vlastimir	IT-05-87/1
Furundžija, Anto	IT-95-17/1
Haradinaj, Ramush et al.	IT-04-84
Karadžić, Radovan	IT-95-5/18
Krajišnik, Momčilo	IT-00-39
Kunarac, Dragoljub et al.	IT-96-23 & 23/1
Kvočka, Miroslav et al.	IT-98-30/1
Martić, Milan	IT-95-11
Milošević, Slobodan	IT-02-54
Mladić, Ratko	IT-09-92

Case name	Case number
Mucić, Zdravko et al.	IT-96-21
Plavšić, Biljana	IT-00-39 & 40/1
Šainović, Nikola et al.	IT-05-87
Stanišić, Mićo & Župljanin, Stojan	IT-08-91
Stakić, Milomir	IT-97-24
Tadić, Duško	IT-94-1
Zelenović, Dragan	IT-96-23/2
International Criminal Tribunal for Rwanda (ICTR)	
Akayesu, Jean-Paul	ICTR-96-4
Bizimungu, Casimir	ICTR-99-50
Bagosora, Théoneste et al.	ICTR-98-41
Gacumbitsi, Sylvestre	ICTR-2001-64
Hategekimana, Ildephonse	ICTR-00-55B
Kajelijeli, Juvénal	ICTR-98-44A
Karemera, Édouard & Ngirumpatse, Matthieu	ICTR-98-44
Muhimana, Mikaeli	ICTR- 95-1B
Muvunyi, Tharcisse	ICTR-2000-55A
Ndindiliyimana, Augustin et al.	ICTR-00-56
Nizeyimana, Ildéphonse	ICTR-2000-55C
Semanza, Laurent	ICTR-97-20
Extraordinary Chambers in the Courts of Cambodia (ECCC)	
Kaing, Guek Eav (Duch)	001/18-07-2007/ECCC
Nuon, Chea & Samphan, Khieu	002/19-09-2007/ECCC
Special Court for Sierra Leone (SCSL)	
Brima, Alex Tamba et al.	SCSL-04-16
Fofana, Moinina & Kondewa, Allieu	SCSL-04-14
Sesay, Issa Hassan et al.	SCSL-04-15
Taylor, Charles Ghankay	SCSL-03-01
International Criminal Court (ICC)	
al-Hassan Ag Abdoul Aziz	ICC-01/12-01/18
Bemba Gombo, Jean-Pierre	ICC-01/05-01/08
Katanga, Germain	ICC-01/04-01/07
Lubanga Dyilo, Thomas	ICC-01/04-01/06
Ntaganda, Bosco	ICC-01/04-02/06
Ongwen, Dominic	ICC-02/04-01/15

Reproductive Violence

Case name	Case number
International Criminal Court (ICC)	
Ongwen, Dominic	ICC-02/04-01/15

Bibliography

Table of Cases

ICTY

Prosecutor v. Tihomir Blaškić, IT-95-14-T, ICTY, Trial Judgment, 3 March 2000.

Prosecutor v. Radoslav Brđanin, IT-99-36-T, ICTY, Trial Judgment, 1 September 2004.

Prosecutor v. Radoslav Brđanin, IT-99-36-A, ICTY, Appeal Judgment, 3 April 2007.

Prosecutor v. Ranko Češić, IT-95-10/1-PT, ICTY, Third Amended Indictment, 26 November 2002.

Prosecutor v. Ranko Češić, IT-95-10/1-S, ICTY, Sentencing Judgment, 11 March 2004.

Prosecutor v. Vlastimir Đorđević, IT-05-87/1-T, ICTY, Trial Judgment, 23 February 2011.

Prosecutor v. Vlastimir Đorđević, IT-05-87/1-A, ICTY, Appeal Judgment, 27 January 2014.

Prosecutor v. Anton Furundžija, IT-95-17/1-T, ICTY, Trial Judgment, 10 December 1998.

Prosecutor v. Dragan Gagović et al., IT-96-23, ICTY, Indictment, 19 June 1996.

Prosecutor v. Ante Gotovina et al., IT-06-90-T, ICTY, Trial Judgment, 15 April 2011.

Prosecutor v. Enver Hadžihasanović and Amir Kubura, IT-01-47-T, ICTY, Trial Judgment, 15 March 2006.

Prosecutor v. Ramush Haradinaj et al., IT-04-84-T, ICTY, Trial Judgment, 3 April 2008.

Prosecutor v. Goran Jelisić, IT-95-10-T, ICTY, Trial Judgment, 14 December 1999.

Prosecutor v. Miodrag Jokić, IT-01-42/1-S, ICTY, Sentencing Judgment, 18 March 2004.

Prosecutor v. Radovan Karadžić, IT-95-5/18-T, ICTY, Trial Judgment, 24 March 2016.

Prosecutor v. Dario Kordić and Mario Čerkez, IT-95-14/2-T, ICTY, Trial Judgment, 26 February 2001.

Prosecutor v. Dario Kordić and Mario Čerkez, IT-95-14/2-A, ICTY, Appeal Judgment, 17 December 2004.

Prosecutor v. Momčilo Krajišnik, IT-00-39-T, ICTY, Trial Judgment, 27 September 2006.

Prosecutor v. Dragoljub Kunarac et al., IT-96-23-T & IT-96-23/1-T, ICTY, Trial Judgment, 22 February 2001.

Prosecutor v. Dragoljub Kunarac et al., IT-96-23&IT-96-23/1-A, ICTY, Appeal Judgment, 12 June 2002.

Prosecutor v. Zoran Kupreškić et al., IT-95-16-T, ICTY, Trial Judgment, 14 January 2000.

Prosecutor v. Miroslav Kvočka et al., IT-98-30/1-T, ICTY, Trial Judgment, 2 November 2001.

Prosecutor v. Milan Martić, IT-95-11-T, ICTY, Trial Judgment, 12 June 2007.

Prosecutor v. Ratko Mladić, IT-09-92-T, ICTY, Trial Judgment, 22 November 2017.

Prosecutor v. Zdravko Mucić et al., IT-96-21-T, ICTY, Trial Judgment, 16 November 1998.

Prosecutor v. Mladen Naletilić and Vinko Martinović, IT-98-34-T, ICTY, Trial Judgment, 31 March 2003.

Prosecutor v. Biljana Plavšić, IT-00-39&40/1-S, ICTY, Sentencing Judgment, 27 February 2003.

Prosecutor v. Jadranko Prlić et al., IT-04-74-T, ICTY, Trial Judgment, 29 May 2013.

Prosecutor v. Nikola Šainović et al., IT-05-87-T, ICTY, Trial Judgment, 26 February 2009.

Prosecutor v. Nikola Šainović et al., IT-05-87-A, ICTY, Appeal Judgment, 23 January 2014.

Prosecutor v. Blagoje Simić et al., IT-95-9-T, ICTY, Trial Judgment, 17 October 2003.

Prosecutor v. Milomir Stakić, IT-97-24-T, ICTY, Trial Judgment, 13 July 2003.

Prosecutor v. Mićo Stanišić and Stojan Župljanin, IT-08-91-T, ICTY, Trial Judgment, 27 March 2013.

Prosecutor v. Pavle Strugar, IT-01-42-T, ICTY, Trial Judgment, 31 January 2005.

Prosecutor v. Duško Tadić, IT-94-1, ICTY, Decision on the Defence Motion for Interlocutory Appeal on Jurisdiction, 2 October 1995.

Prosecutor v. Duško Tadić, IT-94-1-T, ICTY, Opinion and Judgment, 7 May 1997.

Prosecutor v. Dragan Zelenović, IT-96-23/2-S, ICTY, Sentencing Judgment, 4 April 2007.

ICTR

Prosecutor v. Jean-Paul Akayesu, ICTR-96-4-T, ICTR, Trial Judgment, 2 September 1998.

Prosecutor v. Jean-Paul Akayesu, ICTR-96-4-T, ICTR, Appeal Judgment, 1 June 2001.

Prosecutor v. Théoneste Bagosora et al., ICTR-98-41-T, ICTR, Trial Judgment, 18 December 2008.

Prosecutor v. Théoneste Bagosora et al., ICTR-98-41-A, ICTR, Appeal Judgment, 14 December 2011.

Prosecutor v. Sylvestre Gacumbitsi, ICTR-2001-64-A, ICTR, Appeal Judgment, 7 July 2006.

Prosecutor v. Ildephonse Hategekimana, ICTR-00-55B-T, ICTR, Judgment and Sentence, 6 December 2010.

Prosecutor v. Juvénal Kajelijeli, ICTR-98-44A-T, ICTR, Judgment and Sentence, 1 December 2003.

Prosecutor v. Édouard Karemera and Matthieu Ngirumpatse, ICTR-98-44-T, ICTR, Judgment and Sentence, 2 February 2012.

Prosecutor v. Mikaeli Muhimana, ICTR-95-1B-T, ICTR, Judgment and Sentence, 28 April 2005.

Prosecutor v. Tharcisse Muvunyi, ICTR-00-55, ICTR, Judgment and Sentence, 12 September 2006.

Prosecutor v. Augustin Ndindiliyimana et al., ICTR-00-56-T, ICTR, Trial Judgment, 17 May 2011.

Prosecutor v. Ildéphonse Nizeyimana, ICTR-2000-55C-T, ICTR, Judgment and Sentence, 19 June 2012.

Prosecutor v. Laurent Semanza, ICTR-97-20-T, ICTR, Trial Judgment, 15 May 2003.

SCSL

Prosecutor v. Alex Tamba Brima et al. (*AFRC Case*), SCSL-04-16-T, SCSL, Trial Judgment, 20 June 2007.

Prosecutor v. Alex Tamba Brima et al. (AFRC *Case*), SCSL-04-16-T, SCSL, Sentencing Judgment, 19 July 2007.

Prosecutor v. Moinina Fofana and Allieu Kondewa (CDF *Case*), SCSL-04-14-T, SCSL, Trial Judgment, 2 August 2007.

Prosecutor v. Moinina Fofana and Allieu Kondewa (CDF *Case*), SCSL-04-14-A, SCSL, Appeal Judgment, 28 May 2008.

Prosecutor v. Issa Hassan Sesay et al. (RUF *Case*), SCSL-04-15-T, SCSL, Trial Judgment, 2 March 2009.

Prosecutor v. Issa Hassan Sesay et al. (RUF *Case*), SCSL-04-15-T, SCSL, Sentencing Judgment, 8 April 2009.

Prosecutor v. Charles Ghankay Taylor, SCSL-03-01-T, SCSL, Trial Judgment, 18 May 2012.

Prosecutor v. Charles Ghankay Taylor, SCSL-03-01-T, SCSL, Sentencing Judgment, 30 May 2012.

Prosecutor v. Charles Ghankay Taylor, SCSL-03-01-A, SCSL, Appeal Judgment, 26 September 2013.

ECCC

Prosecutor v. Ao An and Yim Tith (*Case 004*), 004/07-09-2009-ECCC-OCIJ, ECCC, Consolidated Decision on the Requests for Investigative Action Concerning the Crime of Forced Pregnancy and Forced Impregnation, 13 June 2016.

Prosecutor v. Nuon Chea and Samphan Khieu (*Case 002/02*), 002/19-09-2007-ECCC/OCIJ, ECCC, Second Request for Investigative Actions Concerning Forced Marriages and Forced Sexual Relations, 15 July 2009.

Prosecutor v. Nuon Chea and Khieu Samphan (*Case 002/02*), 002/19-09-2007/ECCC/TC, ECCC, Trial Judgment, 16 November 2018.

ICC

Prosecutor v. Al Hassan Ag Abdoul Aziz Ag Mohamed Ag Mahmoud, ICC-01/12-01/18, ICC, Rectificatif à la Décision relative à la confirmation des charges, 30 September 2019.

Prosecutor v. Ahmad Al Faqi Al Mahdi, ICC-01/12-01/15, ICC, Judgment and Sentence, 27 September 2016.

Prosecutor v. Ahmad Al Faqi Al Mahdi, ICC-01/12-01/15, ICC, Reparations Order, 17 August 2017.

Prosecutor v. Jean-Pierre Bemba Gombo, ICC-01/05-01/08, ICC, Decision Pursuant to Article 61(7)(a) and (b) of the Rome Statute on the Charges of the Prosecutor Against Jean-Pierre Bemba Gombo, 15 June 2009.

Prosecutor v. Jean-Pierre Bemba Gombo, ICC-01/05-01/08, ICC, Judgment pursuant to Article 74 of the Statute, 21 March 2016.

Prosecutor v. Jean-Pierre Bemba Gombo, ICC-01/05-01/08, ICC, Judgment pursuant to Article 76 of the Statute, 21 June 2016.

Prosecutor v. Laurent Gbago and Charles Blé Goudé, ICC-02/11-01/1, ICC, Dissenting Opinion Judge Herrera Carbuccia – Reasons for oral decision of 15 January 2019 on the Requête de la Défense de Laurent Gbagbo afin qu'un jugement d'acquittement portant sur toutes les charges soit prononcé en faveur de Laurent Gbagbo et que sa mise en liberté immédiate soit ordonnée, and on the Blé Goudé Defence no case to answer motion, 16 July 2019.

Prosecutor v. Germain Katanga and Mathieu Ngudjolo Chui, ICC-01/04-01/07, ICC, Decision on the Confirmation of Charges, 30 September 2008.

Prosecutor v. Germain Katanga, ICC-01/04-01/07, ICC, Judgment pursuant to article 74 of the Statute, 7 March 2014.

Prosecutor v. Germain Katanga, ICC-01/04-01/07, ICC, Decision on sentence pursuant to article 76 of the Statute, 23 May 2014.

Prosecutor v. Germain Katanga, ICC-01/04-01/07, ICC, Order for Reparations pursuant to Article 75 of the Statute, 24 March 2017.

Prosecutor v. Bosco Ntaganda, ICC-01/04-02/06, ICC, Trial Judgment, 8 July 2019.

Prosecutor v. Bosco Ntaganda, ICC-01/04-02/06, ICC, Sentencing Judgment, 7 November 2019.

Prosecutor v. Dominic Ongwen, ICC-02/04-01/15, ICC, Decision on the confirmation of charges against Dominic Ongwen, 23 March 2016.

Prosecutor v. Dominic Ongwen, ICC-02/04-01/15-1719-Red, ICC, Public Redacted Version of "Prosecution Closing Brief", 24 February 2020.

Prosecutor v. Dominic Ongwen, ICC-02/04-01/15-1720-Conf, ICC, Public redacted version of Common Legal Representative of Victims' Closing Brief, 28 February 2020.

Prosecutor v. Dominic Ongwen, ICC-02/04-01/15, ICC, Trial Judgment, 4 February 2021.

Prosecutor v. Dominic Ongwen, ICC-02/04-01/15, ICC, Sentence, 6 May 2021.

Prosecutor v. Dominic Ongwen, ICC-02/04-01/15, ICC, Defence Appeal Brief Against the Convictions in the Judgment of 4 February 2021, 19 October 2021.

Prosecutor v. Dominic Ongwen, ICC-02/04-01/15 A, ICC, Appeal Judgment, 15 December 2022.

Application Under Regulation 46(3), Prosecution's Request for a Ruling on Jurisdiction under Article 19(3) of the Statute, ICC, 9 April 2018.

Other

African Commission on Human and Peoples' Rights v. Republic of Kenya, Application No. 006/2012, African Commission on Human and Peoples' Rights, Judgment, 26 May 2017.

Case of the Mayagna (Sumo) Awas Tingni Community v. Nicaragua, Series C No. 79, Inter-American Court of Human Rights, Judgment, 31 August 2001.

Trial of the Major War Criminals before the International Military Tribunal, Volume 1, 14 November 1945-1 October 1946.

Trial of German Major War Criminals, Proceedings of the International Military Tribunal sitting at Nuremberg, Germany, Part 22 (22nd August 1946 to 1st October 1946).

United States v. Krauch et al. (*IG Farben Case*), Trials of War Criminals Before the Nuremberg Military Tribunals Under Control Council No. 10, Volume VIII.

United States v. Krupp et al. (*The Krupp case*), Trials of War Criminals Before the Nuremberg Military Tribunals Under Control Council Law No. 10, Volume IX.

Wainwright v. the UK, Application no. 12350/04, European Court of Human Rights, 26 September 2006.

X and Y v. the Netherlands, Application no. 8978/80, European Court of Human Rights, Judgment, 26 March 1985.

Transcripts

ICTY

Prosecutor v. Tihomir Blaškić, IT-95-14, ICTY, Transcripts: 21 April 1998, 29 April 1998, 16 July 1998, 17 July 1998.

Prosecutor v. Radoslav Brđanin, IT-99-36, ICTY, Transcripts: 28 March 2002, 21 November 2002.

Prosecutor v. Ante Gotovina et al., IT-06-90, ICTY, Transcripts: 11 March 2008.

Prosecutor v. Goran Hadžić, IT-04-75-T, ICTY, Transcripts: 20 June 2013, 16 September 2014.

Prosecutor v. Enver Hadžihasanović and Amir Kubura, IT-01-47, ICTY, Transcripts: 17 December 2003.

Prosecutor v. Miodrag Jokić, IT-01-42/1-S, ICTY, Transcripts: 4 December 2003.

Prosecutor v. Radovan Karadžić, IT-95-5/18, ICTY, Transcript: 8 December 2011, 9 December 2011.

Prosecutor v. Dario Kordić and Mario Čerkez, IT-95-14/2, ICTY, Transcripts: 10 July 2000.

Prosecutor v. Momčilo Krajišnik, IT-00-39, ICTY, Transcripts: 4 February 2004, 29 June 2005, 20 October 2004, 31 October 2005.

Prosecutor v. Dragoljub Kunarac et al., IT-96-23 & 23/1, ICTY, Transcripts: 30 March 2000, 3 April 2000, 4 April 2000, 14 April 2000, 25 April 2000, 26 April 2000, 18 May 2000, 11 September 2000, 12 September 2000, 20 November 2000.

Prosecutor v. Miroslav Kvočka et al., IT-98-30/1, ICTY, Transcripts: 5 September 2000, 4 October 2000.

Prosecutor v. Milan Martić, IT-95-11, ICTY, Transcripts: 31 March 2006, 26 May 2006, 26 June 2006.

Prosecutor v. Slobodan Milošević, IT-02-54, ICTY, Transcripts: 29 October 2001, 15 February 2002, 7 March 2002, 8 April 2000, 9 April 2002, 10 April 2002, 16 July 2002, 8 October 2002, 18 December 2002, 11 March 2003, 3 July 2003, 8 July 2003, 16 September 2003, 23 October 2003, 27 October 2005.

Prosecutor v. Ratko Mladić, IT-09-92, ICTY, Transcripts: 1 July 1996, 16 October 2013, 18 March 2014, 6 December 2016.

Prosecutor v. Ratko Mladić and Radovan Karadžić, IT-95-18-R61 & IT-95-5-R61, ICTY, Transcripts: 1 July 1996, 2 July 1996, 8 July 1996, 11 July 1996.

Prosecutor v. Zdravko Mucić et al., IT-96-21, ICTY, Transcripts: 17 March 1997, 4 September 1997.

Prosecutor v. Biljana Plavšić, IT-00-39 & 40/1, ICTY, Transcripts: 16 December 2002.

Prosecutor v. Jadranko Prlić et al., IT-04-74-T, ICTY, Transcripts: 4 May 2006, 15 May 2006, 22 May 2006, 24 May 2006, 4 December 2006, 22 February 2007, 17 May 2007, 22 May 2007, 21 July 2008, 13 October 2008, 5 May 2009, 20 May 2009, 3 November 2009, 13 January 2010.

Prosecutor v. Nikola Šainović et al., IT-05-87, ICTY, Transcripts: 23 August 2006, 24 August 2006.

Prosecutor v. Pavle Strugar, IT-01-42-T, ICTY, Transcripts: 25 October 2001, 23 February 2003, 16 December 2003, 18 December 2003, 13 January 2004, 20 January 2004, 21 January 2004, 28 January 2004, 4 February 2004, 5 February 2004, 24 February 2004, 31 March 2004, 3 May 2004, 4 May 2004, 4 June 2004, 8 September 2004, 8 December 2004, 23 April 2008.

Prosecutor v. Duško Tadić, IT-94-1, ICTY, Transcripts: 19 July 1996.

ICTR

Prosecutor v. Jean Paul Akayesu, ICTR-96-4-I, ICTR, Transcripts: 3 November 1997.

Prosecutor v. Sylvestre Gacumbitsi, ICTR-01-64-T, ICTR, Transcripts: 6 August 2003.

Prosecutor v. Mika Muhimana, ICTR-95-1B-T, ICTR, Transcripts: 15 April 2004.

Prosecutor v. Tharcisse Muvunyi, ICTR-00-55-A.T, ICTR, Transcripts: 22 June 2005.

Prosecutor v. Augustin Ndindiliyimana et al., ICTR-00-56-T, ICTR, Transcripts: 5 April 2005, 10 October 2005, 20 June 2005.

Prosecutor v. Ildephonse Nizeyimana, ICTR-00-55C-T, ICTR, Transcripts: 17 February 2011.

SCSL

Prosecutor v. Alex Tamba Brima et al. (*AFRC Case*), SCSL-2004-16-T, SCSL, Transcripts: 27 July 2005, 7 December 2006.

Prosecutor v. Issa Hassan Sesay et al. (*RUF Case*), SCSL-2004-15-T, SCSL, Transcripts: 27 July 2003, 1 February 2005, 2 March 2006, 4 August 2008.

Prosecutor v. Charles Ghankay Taylor, SCSL-2003-01-T, SCSL, Transcripts: 7 October 2008, 29 January 2009.

ICC

Prosecutor v. Ahmad al-Faqi al-Mahdi, ICC-01/12-01/15, ICC, Transcripts: 1 March 2016, 22 August 2016, 23 August 2016, 24 August 2016, 17 August 2017.

Prosecutor v. Jean-Pierre Bemba Gombo, ICC-01/05-01/08, ICC, Transcripts: 14 January 2009, 22 November 2010, 29 November 2010, 1 December 2010, 17 January 2011, 24 January 2011, 1 March 2011, 15 March 2011, 2 February 2011, 8 February 2011, 26 June 2012, 14 September 2012, 16 May 2016, 17 May 2016, 11 January 2018.
Prosecutor v. Germain Katanga, ICC-01/04-01/07, ICC, Transcripts: 30 November 2010, 5 May 2014, 6 May 2014.
Prosecutor v. Germain Katanga and Mathieu Ngudjolo Chui, ICC-01/04-01/0736, ICC, Transcripts: 7 July 2008.
Prosecutor v. Thomas Lubanga Dyilo, ICC-01/04-01/06, ICC, Transcripts: 6 March 2009.
Prosecutor v. Bosco Ntaganda, ICC-01/04-02/06, ICC, Transcripts: 11 April 2007, 18 November 2015, 3 February 2017, 1 March 2017, 1 April 2017, 28 August 2018, 20 September 2019.
Prosecutor v. Dominic Ongwen, ICC-02/04-01/15, ICC, Transcripts: 16 September 2015, 18 September 2015, 16 November 2015, 17 November 2015, 21 January 2016, 22 January 2016, 25 January 2016, 6 December 2016, 7 December 2016, 5 April 2017, 13 September 2017, 7 November 2017, 8 November 2017, 30 November 2017, 24 January 2018, 21 February 2018, 3 May 2018, 28 May 2018, 10 March 2020, 11 March 2020.

International Instruments

African Charter on Human and Peoples' Rights, 27 June 1981.
American Convention on Human Rights, 22 November 1969.
Arab Charter on Human Rights, 22 May 2004.
Convention (IV) respecting the Laws and Customs of War on Land and its annex: Regulations concerning the Laws and Customs of War on Land, The Hague, 18 October 1907.
Convention (IV) relative to the Protection of Civilian Persons in Time of War, Geneva, 12 August 1949.
Convention on the Prevention and Punishment of the Crime of Genocide, 9 December 1949.
Convention for the Protection of Cultural Property in the Event of Armed Conflict with Regulations for the Execution of the Convention, 14 May 1954.
Convention on the Elimination of All Forms of Discrimination against Women, 18 December 1979.
Elements of the Crimes, International Criminal Court, 10 September 2002.
Instructions for the Government of Armies of the United States in the Field ('Lieber Code'), 24 April 1863.
Project of an International Declaration concerning the Laws and Customs of War, Brussels, 27 August 1874.
Protocol I to the European Convention Human Rights, 20 March 1952.

Protocol to the African Charter on Human and Peoples' Rights on the Rights of Women in Africa, 11 July 2003.

Protocol Additional to the Geneva Conventions of 12 August 1949, and relating to the Protection of Victims of International Armed Conflicts (Protocol I), 8 June 1977.

Protocol Additional to the Geneva Conventions of 12 August 1949, and relating to the Protection of Victims of Non-International Armed Conflicts (Protocol II), 8 June 1977.

Rome Statute of the International Criminal Court, 18 July 2002.

Statute of the International Criminal Tribunal for the Former Yugoslavia, 25 May 1993.

Statute of the International Criminal Tribunal for Rwanda, 8 November 1994.

Treaty on the Protection of Artistic and Scientific Institutions and Historic Monuments ('the Roerich Pact'), Washington, 15 April 1935.

UN Documents

UN, Beijing Declaration and Platform for Action, Fourth World Conference on Women 4 to 15 September 1995, Beijing, A/CONF.177/20.

UN, Diplomatic Conference of Plenipotentiaries on the Establishment of an International Criminal Court 15–17 July 1998, Summary records of the plenary meetings and of the meetings of the Committee of the Whole – Volume II.

UNFPA, Programme of Action Adopted at the International Conference on Population and Development 5–13 September 1994, Cairo, A/CONF.171/13.

UN Population Division, Proclamation of Teheran, Final Act of the International Conference on Human Rights 22 April – 13 May 1968, A/CONF. 32/41.

UN Population Division, UN World Population Conference 19 to 30 August 1974, Bucharest, World Population Plan of Action (WPPA), E/CONF, 60/L. 55.

UN Population Division, Second Conference on Population 6 to 14 August 1984, Mexico, Recommendations for the Further Implementation of the World Population Plan of Action Adopted in the World Population Conference, E/CONF.76/19.

UN Security Council, Final Report of the Commission of Experts Established Pursuant to Security Council Resolution 780 (1992), 27 May 1994, S/1994/674.

UN War Crimes Commission, Law Reports of Trial of War Criminals, Volume XV, Digest of Laws and Cases (1947).

Secondary Sources

Academic Literature

Agger, Inger and Jensen, Søren Buus, 'The Psychosexual Trauma of Torture' in John P. Wilson and Beverly Raphael (eds), *International Handbook of Traumatic Stress Syndromes* (Plenum Press 1993), 685–702.

Alcoff, Linda Martín, *Rape and Resistance* (Polity 2018).

Aloisi, Rosa and Meernik, James, *Judgment Day: Judicial Decision Making at the International Criminal Tribunals* (Cambridge University Press 2017).

Altunjan, Tanja, *Reproductive Violence and International Criminal Law* (T.M.C. Asser Press, 2021).

Amann, Diane Marie, 'Group Mentality, Expressivism, and Genocide', (2002) 2(2) *International Criminal Law Review*, 93–143.

Ambos, Kai, 'Punishment without a Sovereign? The Ius Puniendi Issue of International Criminal Law: A First Contribution towards a Consistent Theory of International Criminal Law', (2013) 33(2), *Oxford Journal of Legal Studies*, 293–315.

Ambos, Kai, *Treatise on International Criminal Law: Volume I: Foundations and General Part* (Oxford University Press 2013).

Ambos, Kai, *Treatise on International Criminal Law: Volume II: The Crimes and Sentencing* (Oxford University Press 2014).

Ambos, Kai, 'The Overall Function of International Criminal Law: Striking the Right Balance Between the Rechtsgut and the Harm Principles', (2015) 9(2) *Criminal Law and Philosophy*, 301–329.

Amy, Jean-Jacques, 'Certificates of virginity and reconstruction of the hymen', (2008) 13(2) *European Journal of Contraception & Reproductive Health Care*, 111–113.

Anghie, Antony and Chimni, B.S., 'Third World Approaches to International Law and Individual Responsibility in Internal Conflicts', (2003) 2(1) *Chinese Journal of International Law*, 77–103.

Arnold, Roberta and Wehrenberg, Stefan, '9. Paragraph 2(b)(ix): Intentionally directing attacks against protected buildings' in Otto Triffterer and Kai Ambos (eds), *Rome Statute of the International Criminal Court: A Commentary* (Beck/Hart 2016), 416–421.

Ashworth, Andrew and Horder, Jeremy, *Principles of Criminal Law* (Oxford University Press 2009).

Askin, Kelly Dawn, *War Crimes Against Women: Prosecution in International War Crimes Tribunals* (Martinus Nijhoff 1997).

Ba, Oumar, 'Contested Meanings: Timbuktu and the prosecution of destruction of cultural heritage as war crimes', (2020) 63(4) *African Studies Review*, 743–762.

Bassiouni, M. Cherif, *Introduction to International Criminal Law* (Martinus Nijhoff 2014).

Bentwich, Norman, *The Law of Private Property in War, with a Chapter on Conquest* (Sweet and Maxwell 1907).

Bhandar, Brenna, *Colonial Lives of Property: Law, Land and Racial Regimes of Ownership* (Duke University Press 2018).

Bianchi, Andrea, *International Law Theories: An Inquiry into Different Ways of Thinking* (Oxford University Press 2016).

Blake, Janet, 'On defining the cultural heritage', (2000) 49(1) *International and Comparative Law Quarterly*, 61–85.

Blank, Hanne, *Virgin: The Untouched History* (Bloomsbury 2008).

Blommaert, Jan, *Discourse: A Critical Introduction* (Cambridge University Press 2005).

Boon, Kristen, 'Rape and Forced Pregnancy under the ICC Statute: Human Dignity, Autonomy and Consent', (2000) *Columbia Human Rights Law Review*, 625–675.

Brammertz, Serge, Kevin C. Hughes, Alison Kipp and William B. Tomljanovich, 'Attacks against Cultural Heritage as a Weapon of War: Prosecutions at the ICTY', (2016) 14 *Journal of International Criminal Justice*, 1143–1174.

Bridgewater, Pamela D., 'Ain't I A Slave: Slavery, Reproductive Abuse, and Reparations', (2005) 14(1) *UCLA Women's Law Journal*, 89–161.

Brilmayer, Lea and Chepiga, Geoffrey, 'Ownership or Use – Civilian Property Interests in International Humanitarian Law', (2008) 49(2) *Harvard International Law Journal*, 413–446.

Brosché, Johan, Mattias Legnér, Joakim Kreutz and Akram Ijla, 'Heritage under attack: motives for targeting cultural property during armed conflict', (2017) 23(3) *International Journal of Heritage Studies*, 248–260.

Brown, David, 'Criminalisation and Normative Theory', (2013) 25(2) *Current Issues in Criminal Justice*, 605–625.

Brown, Sara, 'Female Perpetrators of the Rwandan Genocide' (2014) 16(3) *International Feminist Journal of Politics*, 448–469.

Bruner, Jerome, 'The Narrative Construction of Reality', (1991) 18(1) *Critical Inquiry*, 1–21.

Buck, Kerrin Geoffrey, 'Displacement and dispossession: redefining forced displacement and identifying when forced displacement becomes pillage under international humanitarian law', (2017) 2(1) *Journal of International Humanitarian Action*, 1–18.

Buffon, Veronica and Allison, Christine, 'The gendering of victimhood: Western media and the Sinjar genocide', (2016) 4(2) *Kurdish Studies*, 176–196.

Bull, Hedley, *The Anarchical Society: A Study of Order in World Politics* (Columbia University Press 2012).

Buss, Doris, "Rethinking 'Rape as a Weapon of War'", (2009) 17(2) *Feminist Legal Studies*, 145–163.

Buss, Doris, 'Performing Legal Order: Some Feminist Thoughts on International Criminal Law', (2011) 11 *International Criminal Law Review*, 409–423.

Cahill, Ann, *Rethinking Rape* (Cornell University Press 2011).

Carcano, Andrea, 'The Criminalization and Prosecution of Attacks Against Cultural Property' in Fausto Pocar, Marco Pedrazzi and Micaela Frulli (eds), *War Crimes and the Conduct of Hostilities: Challenges to Adjudication and Investigation* (2013 Edward Elgar), 78–88.

Carpenter, Robyn Charli, 'Forced maternity, children's rights and the genocide convention: A theoretical analysis', (2000) 2(2) *Journal of Genocide Research*, 213–244.

Carpenter, Robyn Charli, 'Surfacing Children: Limitations of Genocidal Rape Discourse', (2000) 22(2), *Human Rights Quarterly*, 428–477.

Casaly, Paige, 'Al Mahdi before the ICC: Cultural Property and World Heritage in International Criminal Law', (2016) 14 *Journal of International Criminal Justice*, 1199–1220.

Cassese, Antonio, *International Law* (Oxford University Press 2005).

Chappell, Louise, 'Women's Rights and Religious Opposition: The Politics of Gender at the International Criminal Court' in Yasmeen Abu-Laban (ed), *Gendering the Nation State: Canadian and Comparative Perspectives* (UCB Press, 2008), 139–164.

Chappell, Louise, *The Politics of Gender Justice at the International Criminal Court: Legacies and Legitimacy* (Oxford University Press 2016).

Charlesworth, Hilary, 'Feminist Methods in International Law', (1999) 93(2) *American Journal of International Law*, 379–394.

Chehtman, Alejandro, *The Philosophical Foundations of Extraterritorial Punishment* (Oxford 2010).

Chinkin, Christine, 'Gender-related Violence and International Criminal Law and Justice', in Antonio Cassese, Dapo Akande and Guido Acquaviva (eds), *The Oxford Companion to International Criminal Justice* (Oxford University Press 2009), 75–81.

Christensen, Mikkel Jarle, 'The emerging sociology of international criminal courts: Between global restructurings and scientific innovations', (2015) 63(6) *Current Sociology*, 825–849.

Christie, Nils, *A Suitable Amount of Crime* (Routledge 2004).

Clark, Janine Natalya, 'The First Rape Conviction at the ICC: An Analysis of the Bemba Judgment', (2016) 14(3) *Journal of International Criminal Justice*, 667–687.

Clark, Janine Natalya, 'The Destruction of Cultural Heritage in Armed Conflict: The 'Human Element' and the Jurisprudence of the ICTY', (2018) 18 *International Criminal Law Review*, 36–66.

Clarke, Adele E., *Situational Analysis: Grounded Theory After the Postmodern Turn* (SAGE Publications 2005).

Colby, Elbridge, 'The Military Value of the Laws of War', (1926) 15 *Georgetown Law Journal*, 24–34.

Cole, Alison, 'Prosecutor v. Gacumbitsi: The New Definition for Prosecuting Rape under International Law', (2008) 8 *International Criminal Law Review*, 55–85.

Cole, Alison, 'International Criminal Law and Sexual Violence: An Overview' in Clare McGlynn and Vanessa Munro (eds), *Rethinking Rape Law: International and Comparative Perspectives* (Routledge 2010), 47–60.

Conaghan, Joanne, 'The Essence of Rape', (2019) 39(1) *Oxford Journal of Legal Studies*, 151–182.

Conway, Heather and Stannard, John, 'Property and Emotions', (2015) 8(1) *Emotion Review*, 38–43.

Copelon, Rhonda, 'Surfacing Gender: Re-Engraving Crimes Against Women in Humanitarian Law', (1994) 5(2) *Hastings Journal of International Law*, 243–266.

Corrêa, Sonia and Reichmann, Rebecca Lynn, *Population and Reproductive Rights: Feminist Perspectives from the South* (Zed Books 1994).

Corrias, Luigi D.A. and Gordon, Geoffrey M., 'Judging in the Name of Humanity: International Criminal Tribunals and the Representation of a Global Public', (2015) 13 *Journal of International Criminal Justice*, 97–112.

Corsi, Jessica Lynn, 'An Argument for Strict Legality in International Criminal Law', (2018) 49(4) *Georgetown Journal of International Law*, 1321–1382.

Cottier, Michael and Mzee, Sabine, 'Article 8(e) War crime of forced pregnancy', in Otto Triffterer and Kai Ambos (eds), *Rome Statute of the International Criminal Court: A Commentary* (2016 Beck/Hart), 497–500.

Craig, Elaine, *Troubling Sex: Towards a Legal Theory of Sexual Integrity* (UBC Press 2012).

Cryer, Robert, 'The Doctrinal Foundations of International Criminalization' in M. Cherif Bassiouni (ed), *International Criminal Law, Volume 1: Sources, Subjects and Contents* (Martinus Nijhoff 2008), 107–128.

Cryer, Robert, Håkan Friman, Darryl Robinson, and Elizabeth Wilmshurst, *An Introduction to International Criminal Law and Procedure* (Cambridge University Press 2014).

Cryer, Robert and Nell, Albert, 'The philosophy of international criminal law' in Alexander Orakhelashvili (ed), *Research Handbook on the Theory and History of International Law* (Edward Elgar 2020), 200–239.

d'Aspremont, Jean, 'Critical histories of international law and the repression of disciplinary imagination', (2019) 7(1) *London Review of International Law*, 89–115.

Davis, Angela Y., *Women, Race and Class* (First Vintage Books 1983).

Dean, Carolyn, 'Empathy, Pornography, and Suffering', (2003) 14(1) *Differences*, 88–124.

deGuzman, Margaret, 'An Expressive Rationale for the Thematic Prosecution of Sex Crimes' in Morten Bergsmo (ed), *Thematic Prosecution of International Sex Crimes* (Torkel Opsahl Academic EPublisher 2012), 13–44.

deGuzman, Margaret, 'Choosing to Prosecute: Expressive Selection at the International Criminal Court', (2012) 33(2) *Michigan Journal of International Law*, 265–320.

Dehaibi, Laura, 'Liberal Property and Lived Property: A Critique of Abstract Universalism in the Human Right to Property' (PhD Dissertation, McGill University 2020).

Demko, Daniela, 'An Expressive Theory of International Punishment for International Crimes' in Florian Jeßberger and Julia Geneuss (eds), *Why Punish Perpetrators of Mass Atrocities? Purposes of Punishment in International Criminal Law* (Cambridge University Press 2020), 176–195.

De Silva, Nicole, 'International Courts' Socialization Strategies for Actual and Perceived Performance' in Theresa Squatrito, Oran R. Young, Andreas Follesdal and Geir Ulfstein (eds), *The Performance of International Courts and Tribunals* (Cambridge University Press 2018), 288–321.

de Vattel, Emer, *The Law of Nations, Book 3* (Liberty Fund Inc. 2008).

Dolan, Chris, 'Victims who are men', in Fionnuala Ní Aoláin et al. (eds), *The Oxford Handbook of Gender and Conflict* (Oxford University Press 2018), 86–102.

Dolan, Chris, Maria Eriksson Baaz and Maria Stern, 'What is sexual about conflict-related sexual violence? Stories from men and women survivors', (2020) 96(5) *International Affairs,* 1151–1168.

Dörmann, Knut, *Elements of War Crimes under the Rome Statute of the International Criminal Court: Sources and Commentary* (Cambridge University Press 2009).

Dörmann, Knut, 'Intentionally directing attacks against civilians not taking direct part in hostilities' in Otto Triffterer and Kai Ambos (eds), *Rome Statute of the International Criminal Court: A Commentary* (Beck/Hart 2016), 355–362.

Douglas, Lawrence, *The Memory of Judgment* (Yale University Press 2001).

Dowds, Eithne, *Feminist Engagement with International Criminal Law: Norm Transfer, Complementarity, Rape and Consent* (Hart Publishing 2020).

Dowds, Eithne, 'Towards a Contextual Definition of Rape: Consent, Coercion and Constructive Force', (2020) 83(1) *Modern Law Review,* 35–63.

Drake, Alyson, 'Aimed at Protecting Ethnic Groups or Women? A Look at Forced Pregnancy under the Rome Statute', (2012) 18(3) *William and Mary Journal of Women and the Law,* 595–623.

Drumbl, Mark, 'Introduction to International Criminal Law by M Cherif Bassiouni', (2005) 99 *American Journal of International Law,* 287–290.

Drumbl, Mark, *Atrocity, Punishment and International Law* (Cambridge University Press 2007).

Drumbl, Mark, 'The Expressive Value of Prosecuting and Punishing Terrorists: Hamdan, the Geneva Conventions, and International Criminal Law', (2007) 75(5–6) *George Washington Law Review,* 1165–1199.

Dubber, Markus Dirk, 'Theories of Crime and Punishment in German Criminal Law', (2005) 53(3) *American Journal of Comparative Law,* 679–707.

Duff, Antony *Punishment, Communication and Community* (Oxford University Press 2003).

Duff, Antony, *Answering for Crime: Responsibility and Liability in the Criminal Law* (Hart 2007).

Duff, Antony, 'Authority and Responsibility in International Criminal Law' in Samantha Besson and John Tasioulas (eds), *The Philosophy of International Law* (Oxford University Press 2010), 589–604.

Duranti, Marco, *The Conservative Human Rights Revolution: European Identity, Transnational Politics, and the Origins of the European Convention* (Oxford University Press 2017).

Durkheim, Emile, *The Division of Labour in Society* (Palgrave Macmillan 2013).

du Toit, Louise, 'From Consent to Coercive Circumstances: Rape Law Reform on Trial', (2012) 28(3), *South African Journal on Human Rights,* 380–404.

du Toit, Louise, *A Philosophical Investigation of Rape: The Making and Unmaking of the Feminine Self* (Routledge 2009).

du Toit, Louise and le Roux, Elisabet, 'A feminist reflection on male victims of conflict-related sexual violence', (2021) 28(2), *European Journal of Women's Studies*, 115–128.

Dworkin, Andrea, *Life and Death: Unapologetic Writings on the Continuing War Against Women* (The Free Press 1997).

Eager, Paige Whaley, 'From Population Control to Reproductive Rights: Understanding Normative Change in Global Population Policy (1965–1994)', (2004) 18(2) *Global Society*, 145–173.

Edwards, Christie J, 'Forced Contraception as a Means of Torture' in Center for Human Rights and Humanitarian Law, *Gender Perspectives on Torture: Law and Practice* (American University Washington College of Law, Washington, DC 2018), 139–160.

Ehlert, Caroline, *Prosecuting the Destruction of Cultural Property in International Criminal Law With a Case Study on the Khmer Rouge's Destruction of Cambodia's Heritage* (Martinus Nijhoff 2014).

Ehrlich, Susan, 'Text trajectories, legal discourse and gendered inequalities', (2012) 3(1) *Applied Linguistics Review*, 47–73.

Ehrlich, Susan and Romaniuk, Tanya, 'Text Trajectories and Gendered Inequalities in Institutions' in Jo Angouri and Judith Baxter (eds), *The Routledge Handbook of Language, Gender, and Sexuality* (Routledge 2021), 354–367.

Elander, Maria, 'The Victim's Address: Expressivism and the Victim at the Extraordinary Chambers in the Courts of Cambodia', (2013) 7 *International Journal of Transitional Justice*, 95–115.

Elander, Maria, *Figuring Victims in International Criminal Justice: The Case of the Khmer Rouge Tribunal* (Routledge 2018).

Elliott, H. Wayne, 'The Third Priority: The Battlefield Dead', (1996) 7 *Army Lawyer*, 3–20.

Elliott, Ingrid, Kivlahan, Coleen and Rahhal, Yahya, 'Bridging the Gap Between the Reality of Male Sexual Violence and Access to Justice and Accountability', (2020) 18 *Journal of International Criminal Justice*, 469–498.

Elliot, Rosemary and Mistry, Zubin, 'Introduction: Gender and Reproduction', (2020) 32(3) *Gender and History*, 509–522.

Engle, Karen, 'Feminism and its (Dis)Contents: Criminalizing Wartime Rape in Bosnia and Herzegovina', (2005) 99(4) *The American Journal of International Law*, 778–816.

Engle, Karen, *The Grip of Sexual Violence in Conflict: Feminist Interventions in International Law* (Stanford University Press 2020).

Eriksson Baaz, Maria and Stern, Maria, *Sexual Violence as a Weapon of War? Perceptions, Prescriptions, Problems in the Congo and Beyond* (Zed Books 2013).

Eriksson Baaz, Maria and Stern, Maria, 'Curious erasures: the sexual in wartime sexual violence', (2018) 20(3) *International Feminist Journal of Politics*, 295–314.

Farmer, Lindsay, 'Criminal Wrongs in Historical Perspective' in R.A. Duff, Lindsay Farmer, S.E. Marshall, Massimo Renzo, and Victor Tadros (eds), *The Boundaries of the Criminal Law* (Oxford University Press 2010), 214–237.

Feilchenfeld, Ernst H., *The International Economic Law of Belligerent Occupation* (Rumford Press 1942).

Feinberg, Joel, 'The Expressive Function of Punishment' in Joel Feinberg (ed), *Doing and Deserving: Essays in the Theory of Responsibility* (Princeton University Press 1970), 95–118.

Feinberg, Joel, *Harm to Others* (Oxford University Press 1984).

Feinberg, Joel, *The Moral Limits of the Criminal Law: Harm to Others* (Oxford University Press 1984).

Feldman, David, *Civil Liberties and Human Rights in England and Wales,* (Oxford University Press 2002).

Ferrell, Jeff, 'Cultural Criminology and the Politics of Meaning', (2013) 21(3) *Critical Criminology*, 257–271.

Fisher, Kirsten, *Moral Accountability and International Criminal Law – Holding Agents of Atrocity Accountable to the World,* (Routledge 2013).

Francioni, Francesco, 'The Human Dimension of International Cultural Heritage Law: An Introduction', (2011) 22(1), *European Journal of International Law*, 9–16.

Francioni, Francesco, 'The Evolving Framework for the Protection of Cultural Heritage in International Law' in Silvia Borelli and Federico Lenzerini (eds), *Cultural Heritage, Cultural Rights, Cultural Diversity New Developments in International Law* (Brill-Nijhoff 2012), 1–25.

Franke, Katherine M., 'Gendered Subjects of Transitional Justice,' (2006) 15(3) *Columbia Journal of Gender and Law*, 813–828.

Franzki, Hannah, 'Criminal trials, economic dimensions of state crime, and the politics of time in international criminal law: a German-Argentine constellation' (PhD dissertation, Birkbeck University of London, 2018).

Freidel, Frank, *Francis Lieber: Nineteenth-century Liberal* (Louisiana State University Press 1947).

Frigo, Malio, 'Cultural property v. cultural heritage: A "battle of concepts" in international law?', (2004) 86(854) *International Review of the Red Cross*, 367–378.

Frulli, Micaela, 'The Criminalization of Offences against Cultural Heritage in Times of Armed Conflict: The Quest for Consistency', (2011) 22(1) *European Journal of International Law*, 203–217.

Gamboni, Dario, *The Destruction of Art: Iconoclasm and Vandalism since the French Revolution* (Reaktion Books 1997).

Garland, David, *Punishment and Modern Society: A Study in Social Theory* (University of Chicago Press 1990).

Gebhard, Julia and Trimiño Mora, Diana, 'Reproductive Rights, International Regulation' in *Max Planck Encyclopaedia of Public International Law* (Oxford University Press 2013).

Gewirth, Alan, 'Human Dignity as the Basis of Rights' in Michael J. Meyer and William A. Parent (eds), *The Constitution of Rights: Human Dignity and American Values* (Cornell University Press 1992), 10–28.

Gewirtz, Paul, 'Narrative and Rhetoric in the Law' in Peter Brooks and Paul Gewirtz (eds), *Law's Stories: Narrative and Rhetoric in the Law* (Yale University Press 1996), 2–13.

Gibney, Ed and Wyatt, Tanya, 'Rebuilding the Harm Principle: Using an Evolutionary Perspective to Provide a New Foundation for Justice', (2020) 9(3) *International Journal for Crime, Justice and Social Democracy*, 100–115.

Glasius, Marlies, 'Do International Criminal Courts Require Democratic Legitimacy?', (2012) 23(1) *European Journal of International Law*, 43–66.

Glasius, Marlies, 'It Sends a Message': Liberian Opinion Leaders' Responses to the Trial of Charles Taylor', (2015) 13(3) *Journal of International Criminal Justice*, 419–447.

Glendinning, Miles, *The Conservation Movement: A History of Architectural Preservation Antiquity to Modernity* (Routledge 2013).

Gorris, Ellen Anna Philo, 'Invisible victims? Where are male victims of conflict-related sexual violence in international law and policy?', (2015) 22(4) *European Journal of Women's Studies*, 412–427.

Gottlieb, Yaron, 'Criminalizing Destruction of Cultural Property: A Proposal for Defining New Crimes under the Rome Statute of the ICC', (2005) 23(4) *Penn State International Law Review*, 857–896.

Graber, Doris Appel, *The Development of the Law of Belligerent Occupation 1863–1914: A Historical Survey* (Columbia University Press 1949).

Graf, Sinja, 'To Regain Some Kind of Human Equality: Theorizing the Political Productivity of "Crimes Against Humanity"', (2019) 15(3) *Law, Culture and the Humanities*, 744–763.

Gray, Harriet, Maria Stern and Chris Dolan, 'Torture and sexual violence in war and conflict: The unmaking and remaking of subjects of violence', (2020) 46(2) *Review of International Studies*, 197–216.

Gray, Richard L., 'Eliminating the (Absurd) Distinction Between Malum In Se and Malum Prohibitum Crimes', (1995) 73(3) *Washington University Law Quarterly*, 1369–1398.

Green, Stuart, 'Looting, Law and Lawlessness', (2007) 81(4) *Tulane Law Review*, 1129–1174.

Greenawalt, Alexander K.A., 'The Pluralism of International Criminal Law', (2011) 86(3) *Indiana Law Journal*, 1063–1130.

Grewal, Kiran, 'Rape in Conflict, Rape in Peace: Questioning the Revolutionary Potential of International Criminal Justice for Women's Human Rights', (2010) 33 *Australian Feminist Law Journal*, 57–79.

Grewal, Kiran, 'International Criminal Law as a Site for Enhancing Women's Rights? Challenges, Possibilities, Strategies', (2015) 23(2) *Feminist Legal Studies*, 149–165.

Grey, Rosemary, 'The ICC's First 'Forced Pregnancy' Case in Historical Perspective' (2017) 15 *Journal of International Criminal Justice*, 905–930.

Grey, Rosemary, *Prosecuting Sexual and Gender-Based Crimes at the International Criminal Court: Practice, Progress and Potential* (Cambridge University Press 2019).

Grey, Rosemary, 'Reproductive Crimes in International Criminal Law' in Indira Rosenthal, Valerie Oosterveld and Susana SáCouto (eds), *Gender & International Criminal Law* (Oxford University Press, forthcoming).

Grotius, Hugo, *The Rights of War and Peace Book III* (Liberty Fund 2005).

Hall, Christopher K, Joseph Powderly and Niamh Hayes, 'Article 7(1)(g) Rape ... or any other form of sexual violence of comparable gravity' in Otto Triffterer and Kai Ambos (eds), *Rome Statute of the International Criminal Court: A Commentary* (Beck/Hart 2016), 206–226.

Hall, Stuart, 'The Work of Representation' in Stuart Hall (ed), *Representation: Cultural Representations and Signifying Practices* (SAGE Publications 2003), 13–74.

Hansen, Randall and King, Desmond, *Sterilized by the State Eugenics, Race, and the Population Scare in Twentieth-Century North America* (Cambridge University Press 2014).

Haque, Adil Ahmad, 'Criminal Law and Morality at War' in R.A. Duff and Stuart Green (eds), *Philosophical Foundations of Criminal Law* (Oxford University Press 2011), 481–506.

Haque, Adil Ahmad, 'International Crime: In Context and In Contrast' in R.A. Duff, Lindsay Farmer, S.E. Marshall, Massimo Renzo, and Victor Tadros (eds), *The Structures of the Criminal Law* (Oxford University Press 2011), 106–133.

Harcourt, Bernard, 'The Collapse of the Harm Principle', (1999) 90 *Journal of Criminal Law and Criminology*, 109–194.

Harding, Sarah K., 'Value, Obligation and Cultural Heritage', (1999) 31(2) *Arizona State Law Journal*, 291–354.

Haveman, Roelof, 'Rape and Fair Trial in Supranational Criminal Law', (2002) 9(3) *Maastricht Journal of European and Comparative Law*, 263–277.

Hayes, Niamh, 'Creating a Definition of Rape in International Law: The Contribution of the International Criminal Tribunals' in Shane Darcy and Joseph Powderly (eds), *Judicial Creativity at the International Criminal Tribunals* (Oxford University Press 2011), 129–158.

Henckaerts, Jean-Marie and Doswald-Beck, Louise, *ICRC Customary International Humanitarian Law Volume I: Rules* (Cambridge University Press 2009).

Henry, Nicola, 'The Fixation on Wartime Rape: Feminist Critique and International Criminal Law', (2014) 23(1) *Social and Legal Studies*, 93–111.

Heri, Corina, 'The Human Right to Land, for Peasants and for All: Tracing the Social Function of Property to 1948', (2020) 20 *Human Rights Law Review*, 433–452.

Herring, Jonathan and Wall, Jesse, 'The Nature and Significance of the Right to Bodily Integrity', (2017) 76(3) *Cambridge Law Journal*, 566–588.

Hillyard, Paddy and Tombs, Steve, 'Beyond Criminology?' in Paddy Hillyard et al. (eds), *Beyond Criminology: Taking Harm Seriously* (Pluto Press 2004), 10–29.

Hirsch, Moshe, 'Introduction: Sociological Perspectives on International Tribunals', (2020) 34(2) *Temple International & Comparative Law Journal*, 193–201.

Houge, Anette Bringedal, 'Narrative expressivism: A criminological approach to the expressive function of international criminal justice', (2019) 19(3) *Criminology and Criminal Justice*, 277–293.

Husak, Douglas, *Overcriminalization: The Limits of the Criminal Law* (Oxford University Press 2008).

ICRC, *Commentary on the Geneva Conventions of 12 August 1949, Volume IV* (1958).

ICRC, *Commentary on the Protocol Additional to the Geneva Conventions of 12 August 1949, and relating to the Protection of Victims of Non-International Armed Conflicts (Protocol II) 8 June 1977* (1987).

ICRC, *Commentary on Convention (III) relative to the Treatment of Prisoners of War 1949* (2020).

Inal, Tuba, *Looting and Rape in Wartime: Law and Change in International Relations* (University of Pennsylvania Press 2013).

Jarvis, Michelle, 'Overview: The Challenge of Accountability for Conflict-related Sexual Violence Crimes' in Serge Brammertz and Michelle Jarvis (ed), *Prosecuting Conflict-Related Sexual Violence at the ICTY* (Oxford University Press 2016), 1–18.

Joachim, Jutta M., *Agenda Setting, the UN, and NGOs: Gender Violence and Reproductive Rights* (Georgetown University Press 2007).

Jokilehto, Jukka, *A History of Architectural Conservation* (Butterworth-Heinemann 2002).

Jones, Siân, 'Negotiating Authentic Objects and Authentic Selves: Beyond the Deconstruction of Authenticity', (2010) 15(2) *Journal of Material Culture*, 181–203.

Jørgensen, Nina H.B., *The Elgar Companion to the Extraordinary Chambers in the Courts of Cambodia* (Edward Elgar 2018).

Kaleck, Wolfgang, *Double Standards: International Criminal Law and the West* (Torkel Opsahl Academic EPublisher 2015).

Keenan, Patrick, 'Conflict Minerals and the Law of Pillage', (2014) 14(2) *Chicago Journal of International Law*, 524–558.

Keenan, Patrick, 'Doctrinal Innovation in International Criminal Law: Harms, Victims, and the Evolution of the Law', (2020) 42(2) *University of Pennsylvania Journal of International Law*, 407–444.

Keller, Reiner and Clarke, Adele E., 'Situating SKAD in interpretive inquiry', in Reiner Keller, Anna-Katharina Hornidge and Wolf J. Schünemann (eds) *The Sociology of Knowledge Approach to Discourse Investigating the Politics of Knowledge and Meaning-making* (Routledge 2018), 48–72.

Kelly, Tobias, *This Side of Silence: Human Rights, Torture, and the Recognition of Cruelty* (University of Pennsylvania Press 2013).

Kendall, Sara and Nouwen, Sarah, 'Representational practices at the International Criminal Court: the gap between juridified and abstract victimhood', (2013) 76(3–4) *Law and Contemporary Problems*, 235–262.

Kinsella, Helen, *The Image before the Weapon: A Critical History of the Distinction between Combatant and Civilian* (Cambridge University Press 2011).

Kirby, Paul, 'How is rape a weapon of war? Feminist International Relations, modes of critical explanation and the study of wartime sexual violence', (2012) 19(4) *European Journal of International Relations*, 797–821.

Kiyani, Asad G., 'International Crime and the Politics of Criminal Theory: Voices and Conduct of Exclusion', (2015) 48(1) *New York University Journal of International Law and Politics*, 129–208.

Kolb, Robert, 'The main epochs of modern international humanitarian law since 1864 and their related dominant legal constructions' in Kjetil Mujezinović Larsen, Camilla Guldahl Cooper and Gro Nystuen (eds), *Searching for a 'Principle of Humanity' in International Humanitarian Law* (Cambridge University Press 2012), 23–71.

Krause, Catarina and Alfreðsson, Guðmundur S., 'Article 17' in Guðmundur S. Alfreðsson and Asbjørn Eide (ed), *The Universal Declaration of Human Rights: A Common Standard of Achievement* (Martinus Nijhoff 1999), 359–378.

Krever, Tor, 'International Criminal Law: An Ideology Critique', (2013) 26(3) *Leiden Journal of International Law*, 701–723.

Labadi, Sophia, *UNESCO, Cultural Heritage, and Outstanding Universal Value: Value-Based Analyses of the World Heritage and Intangible Cultural Heritage Conventions* (Alta Mira Press 2013).

Labrador, Angela M. and Silberman, Neil Asher 'Introduction: Public Heritage as Social Practice' in Angela M. Labrador and Neil Asher Silberman (eds), *The Oxford Handbook of Public Heritage Theory and Practice* (Oxford University Press 2018), 1–18.

Lagodny, Otto, 'The Case of Substantial Criminal Law before the Bars of Constitutional Law – An Overview from the Perspective of the German Legal Order', (1999) 7(3) *European Journal of Crime, Criminal Law and Criminal Justice*, 761–781.

La Haye, Eve, 'The Prohibition of Pillage in International Humanitarian Law' in Nina H. B. Jørgensen (ed), *The International Criminal Responsibility of War's Funders and Profiteers* (Cambridge University Press 2020), 189–200.

Lauterpacht, Hersch, 'The Problem of the Revision of the Law of War', (1952) 29 *British Year Book of International Law*, 360–382.

Lauterwein, Carl Constanin, *The Limits of Criminal Law: A Comparative Analysis of Approaches to Legal Theorizing* (Routledge 2010).

Laverty, Ciara, 'What is Sexual about Sexual Violence? Narratives from International Criminal Law', (2023) 21(2) *Journal of International Criminal Justice*, 383–404.

Laverty, Ciara and de Vos, Dieneke, 'Reproductive Violence as a Category of Analysis: Disentangling the Relationship between 'the Sexual' and 'the Reproductive' in Transitional Justice', (2021) 15 *International Journal of Transitional Justice*, 616–635.

Lemke, Jay L., *Textual Politics: Discourse and Social Dynamics* (Taylor and Francis 2005).

Le Moli, Ginevra, 'Three Circles of Dignity', (2019) 11 *Journal of Human Rights Practice*, 258–270.

Liss, Ryan, 'Crimes Against the Sovereign Order: Rethinking International Criminal Justice', (2019) 113(4) *American Journal of International Law*, 727–771.

Lixinski, Lucas, 'A Third Way of Thinking About Cultural Property', (2019) 44(2) *Brooklyn Journal of International Law*, 563–612.

Lixinski, Lucas, *International Heritage Law for Communities: Exclusion and Re-Imagination* (Oxford University Press 2019).

Lohne, Kjersti, 'Towards a Sociology of International Criminal Justice' in Morten Bergsmo, Mark Klamberg, Kjersti Lohne and Christopher B. Mahony (eds), *Power in International Criminal Justice* (Torkel Opsahl Academic EPublisher 2020), 47–78.

Lohne, Kjersti, 'Penal welfarism 'gone global'? Comparing international criminal justice to The Culture of Control', (2021) 23(1) *Punishment and Society*, 3–23.

Lostal, Marina, 'The Misplaced Emphasis on the Intangible Dimension of Cultural Heritage in the Al Mahdi Case at the ICC', (2017) 1(2) *Inter Gentes – The McGill Journal of International Law & Legal Pluralism*, 45–58.

Loughnan, Arlie, 'crime and sexual integrity' in Peter Crane and Joanne Conaghan (eds), *The New Oxford Companion to Law* (Oxford University Press 2009).

Loulanski, Tolina, 'Revising the Concept of Cultural Heritage: The Argument for a Functional Approach', (2006) 13 *International Journal of Cultural Property*, 207–233.

Luban, David, 'A Theory of Crimes Against Humanity', (2004) 29(1) *Yale Journal of International Law*, 85–167.

Luban, David, 'Fairness to Rightness: Jurisdiction, Legality, and the Legitimacy of International Criminal Law' in Samantha Besson and John Tasioulas (eds), *The Philosophy of International Law* (Oxford University Press 2010), 569–588.

Lundberg, Michael A., 'The Plunder of Natural Resources During War: A War Crime', (2008) 39(3) *Georgetown Journal of International Law*, 495–525.

Mackenzie, Megan, 'Securitizing Sex? Towards a Theory of the Utility of Wartime Sexual Violence', (2010) 12(2) *International Feminist Journal of Politics*, 202–221.

MacKinnon, Catharine, 'Feminism, Marxism, Method, and the State: Toward Feminist Jurisprudence', (1983) 8(4) *Signs*, 635–658.

MacKinnon, Catharine, *Toward a Feminist Theory of the State* (Harvard University Press 1989).

MacKinnon, Catharine, 'Defining Rape Internationally: A Comment on Akayesu', (2006) 44(3) *Columbia Journal of Transnational Law*, 940–958.

MacLachlan, Bonnie, 'Introduction' in Judith Fletcher and Bonnie MacLachlan (eds), *Virginity Revisited: Configurations of the Unpossessed Body* (University of Toronto Press 2007), 1–12.

Macleod, Christopher, 'Towards a Philosophical Account of Crimes Against Humanity', (2010) 21(2) *European Journal of International Law*, 281–302.

Madsen, Mikael Rask, 'The Sociology of International Law: An Introduction' in Richard Nobles and David Schiff (eds), *Law Society and Community: Socio-Legal Essays in Honour of Roger Cotterell* (Routledge 2014), 241–253.

Mardorossian, Carine M., 'Toward a new feminist theory of rape', (2002) 27 *Signs*, 743–775.

Marshall, Jill, *Personal Freedom Through Human Rights Law? Autonomy, Identity and Integrity Under the European Convention on Human Rights* (Martinus Nijhoff 2008).

Marshall, S.E. and Duff, R.A., 'Criminalisation and Sharing Wrongs' (1998) 11(1) *Canadian Journal of Law and Jurisprudence*, 7–22.

Matswetu, Vimbai Sharon and Bhana, Deevia, 'Humhandara and hujaya: Virginity, Culture, and Gender Inequalities Among Adolescents in Zimbabwe', (2018) 8(2) *SAGE Open*, 1–11.

Matthes, Erich Hatala, '"Saving Lives or Saving Stones?" The Ethics of Cultural Heritage Protection in War' (2018) 32(1), *Public Affairs Quarterly*, 67–84.

May, Larry, 'Mass Rape and the Concept of International Crime' in Carol A. L. Prager and Trudy Gover (eds), *Dilemmas of Reconciliation: Cases and Concepts* (Wilfrid Laurier University Press 2003), 137–168.

May, Larry, *Crimes Against Humanity: A Normative Account* (Cambridge University Press 2005).

May, Larry, *War Crimes and Just War* (Cambridge University Press 2007).

May, Larry, *Aggression and Crimes Against Peace* (Cambridge University Press 2009).

May, Larry, *Genocide a Normative Account* (Cambridge University Press 2012).

McAdams, Richard, *The Expressive Powers of Law: Theories and Limits*, (Harvard University Press 2015).

McGorrey, Paul, 'The Philosophy of Criminalisation: A Review of Duff et al.'s Criminalisation Series' (2018) 12(2) *Criminal Law and Philosophy*, 185–207.

McMahan, Jeff, 'War Crimes and Immoral Action in War' in R.A. Duff R.A. Duff, Lindsay Farmer, S.E. Marshall, Massimo Renzo, and Victor Tadros (eds), *The Constitution of the Criminal Law* (Oxford University Press 2013), 151–184.

McMillan, Nesam *Imagining the International: Crime, Justice, and the Promise of the Community* (Stanford University Press 2020).

Mégret, Frédéric, 'In Defense of Hybridity: Towards a Representational Theory of International Criminal Justice', (2005) 38(3) *Cornell International Law Journal*, 725–751.

Mégret, Frédéric, 'Practices of Stigmatization', (2013) 76 *Law and Contemporary Problems*, 287–318.

Mégret, Frédéric, 'In whose name? The ICC and the search for constituency' in Christian De Vos, Sara Kendall and Carsten Stahn (eds), *Contested Justice: The Politics and Practice of International Criminal Court Interventions* (Cambridge University Press 2015), 23–45.

Mégret, Frédéric, 'What Sort of Global Justice is 'International Criminal Justice'?', (2015) 13(1) *Journal of International Criminal Justice*, 77–96.

Meijers, Tim and Glasius, Marlies, 'Trials as Messages of Justice: What Should Be Expected of the International Criminal Court?', (2016) 30(4) *Ethics and International Affairs*, 429–447.

Merryman, John Henry, 'Two Ways of Thinking About Cultural Property', (1986) 80(4) *American Journal of International Law*, 831–853.

Merryman, John Henry and Elsen, Albert E., *Law, Ethics and the Visual Arts* (Kluwer Law International 2002).

Merryman, John Henry, Albert E. Elsen and Stephen K. Urice, *Law, Ethics, and the Visual Arts* (Kluwer Law International 2007).

Mibenge, Chiseche Salome, *Sex and International Tribunals: The Erasure of Gender from the War Narrative* (University of Pennsylvania Press, 2013).

Mill, John Stuart, 'On Liberty' in Joel Feinberg and Jules Coleman (eds), *Philosophy of Law* (Thomson Wadsworth 2008), 267–277.

Miller, Stephen M. and Miller, Jessica, 'Moral and legal prohibitions against pillage in the context of the 1899 Hague Convention and the South African War', (2019) 26(2) *War in History*, 185–203.

Miller, Zinaida, 'Anti-Impunity Politics in Post-Genocide Rwanda' in Karen Engle, Zinaida Miller, D. M. Davis (eds), *Anti-Impunity and the Human Rights Agenda* (Cambridge University Press 2017), 149–184.

Mir Puig, Santiago, 'Legal Goods Protected by the Law and Legal Goods Protected by the Criminal Law as Limits to the State's Power to Criminalize Conduct', (2008) 11(3) *New Criminal Law Review: An International and Interdisciplinary Journal*, 409–418.

Mohamed, Saira, 'Deviance, Aspiration and the Stories We Tell: Reconciling Mass Atrocity and the Criminal Law', (2015) 124(5) *Yale Law Journal*, 1628–1689.

Moyn, Samuel, *Not Enough: Human Rights in an Unequal World* (Belknap Press 2018).

Muehlenhard, Charlene L., Sharon Danoff-Burg and Irene G. Powch, 'Is Rape Sex or Violence? Conceptual Issues and Implications' in David Buss and Neil Malamuth (ed), *Sex, Power, Conflict: Evolutionary and Feminist Perspectives* (Oxford University Press 1996), 119–137.

Müller, Markus M., 'Cultural Heritage Protection: Legitimacy, Property, and Functionalism', (1998) 7(2) *International Journal of Cultural Property*, 395–409.

Munro, Vanessa E., 'Constructing Consent: Legislating Freedom and Legitimating Constraint in the Expression of Sexual Autonomy', (2008) 41(1) *Akron Law Review*, 923–956.

Munro, Vanessa E., 'From consent to coercion: Evaluating international and domestic frameworks for the criminalization of rape', in Clare McGlynn and Vanessa Munro (eds), *Rethinking Rape Law: International and Comparative Perspectives* (Routledge 2010), 17–29.

Nahlik, Stanisław Edward, 'Protection of Cultural Property' in Henry Dunant Institute (ed), *International Dimensions of Humanitarian Law* (Brill Nijhoff 1988), 203–216.

Neff, Stephen C., *Justice Among Nations: A History of International Law* (Harvard University Press 2014).

Nesiah, Vasuki, 'Missionary Zeal for a Secular Mission: Bringing Gender to Transitional Justice and Redemption to Feminism' in Sari Kouvo and Zoe Pearson (eds), *Feminist Perspectives on Contemporary International Law: Between Resistance and Compliance?* (Oxford: Hart, 2014), 137–158.

Ni Aoláin, Fionnuala, 'The Gender Politics of Fact-Finding in the Context of the Women, Peace and Security Agenda', *University of Ulster Transitional Justice Institute Research Paper* No. 14–08 (2014).

Niarchos, Catherine N., 'Women, War, and Rape: Challenges Facing the International Tribunal for the Former Yugoslavia', (1995) 17(4) *Human Rights Quarterly*, 649–690.

Niemi-Kiesiläinen, Johanna, Päivi Honkatukia and Minna Ruuskanen, 'Legal Texts as Discourses' in Åsa Gunnarsson, Eva-Maria Svensson (eds), *Exploiting the Limits of Law: Swedish Feminism and the Challenge to Pessimism* (Routledge 2007), 69–88.

Nouwen, Sarah, 'International Criminal Law: Theory All Over the Place' in Ann Orford and Florian Hoffman (eds), *The Oxford Handbook of the Theory of International Law* (Oxford University Press 2016), 738–761.

Nuotio, Kimmo, 'Theories of Criminalization and the Limits of Criminal Law: A Legal Cultural Approach' in R.A. Duff et al. (eds), *The Boundaries of the Criminal Law* (Oxford University Press 2010), 238–261.

O'Keefe, Roger, *The Protection of Cultural Property in Armed Conflict*, (Cambridge University Press 2009).

O'Keefe, Roger, 'Protection of Cultural Property' in ed. Andrew Clapham and Paola Gaeta, *The Oxford Handbook of International Law in Armed Conflict* (Oxford University Press 2014), 492–520.

Olson, Greta, 'On Narrating and Troping the Law: The Conjoined Use of Narrative and Metaphor in Legal Discourse' in Michael Hanne and Robert Weisberg (ed), *Narrative and Metaphor in the Law* (Cambridge University Press 2018), 19–36.

Oosterveld, Valerie, 'Sexual Violence Directed Against Men and Boys in Armed Conflict or Mass Atrocity: Addressing a Gendered Harm in International Criminal Tribunals', (2014) 10(1) *Journal of International Law and International Relations*, 107–128.

Otto, Diane, 'Feminist Approaches to International Law' in Anne Orford and Florian Hoffman (eds), *The Oxford Handbook of the Theory of International Law* (Oxford University Press 2016), 488–505.

Peršak, Nina, *Criminalising Harmful Conduct: The Harm Principle, its Limits and Continental Counterparts* (Springer 2007).

Petersen, Carole J, 'Reproductive Justice, Public Policy, and Abortion on the Basis of Fetal Impairment: Lessons from International Human Rights Law and the Potential Impact of the Convention on the Rights of Persons with Disabilities', (2015) 28(1) *Journal of Law and Health,* 121–163.

Petrovic, Jadranka, *The Old Bridge of Mostar and Increasing Respect for Cultural Property in Armed Conflict,* (Martinus Nijhoff 2012).

Phillips, Anne, *Our Bodies, Whose Property?* (Princeton University Press 2013).

Pizzarossa, Lucía Berro, 'Here to Stay: The Evolution of Sexual and Reproductive Health and Rights in International Human Rights Law', (2018) 7(3) *Laws*, 1–17.

Plante, Rebecca F., 'In Search of Sexual Subjectivities: Exploring the Sociological Construction of Sexual Selves' in Michael Kimmel (ed), *The Sexual Self: The Construction of Sexual Scripts* (Vanderbilt University Press 2007), 31–48.

Porter, Roy, 'Rape – Does It Have Historical Meaning?' in Sylvana Tomaselli and Roy Porter (ed), *Rape: An Historical and Cultural Enquiry* (Basil Blackwell 1989), 210–228.

Prott, Lyndel V. and O'Keefe, Patrick J., ''Cultural Heritage' or 'Cultural Property'?', (1992) 1(2) *International Journal of Cultural Property*, 307–320.

Prott, Lyndel V., 'The International Movement of Cultural Objects', (2005) 12(2) *International Journal of Cultural Property,* 225–248.

Pustogarov, Vladimir Vasilievich, 'Fyodor Fyodorovich Martens (1845–1909) – A Humanist of Modern Times', (1996) 312 *International Review of the Red Cross*, 300–314.

Rajkovic, Nikolas M. 'What is a "grave" international crime? The Rome Statute, Durkheim and the sociology of ruling outrages', (2020) 16(1) *Loyola University Chicago International Law Review,* 65–97.

Redlich, Fritz, *De Praeda Military: Looting and Booty 1500–1815* (Steiner 1956).

Reis, Harry T. and Sprecher, Susan, *Encyclopedia of Human Relationships* (SAGE 2009).

Renzo, Massimo, 'Crimes Against Humanity and the Limits of International Law', (2012) 31(4) *Law and Philosophy*, 443–476.

Riedlmayer, András, 'From the Ashes: The Past and Future of Bosnia's Cultural Heritage' in ed. Maya Schatzmiller, *Islam & Bosnia: Conflict Resolution and Foreign Policy in Multi-Ethnic States* (McGill Queen's Press 2002), 98–135.

Robinson, Darryl, 'The Identity Crisis of International Criminal Law', (2008) 21 *Leiden Journal of International Law*, 925–963.

Robinson, Darryl, 'International Criminal Law as Justice', (2013) 11(3) *Journal of International Criminal Justice*, 699–711.

Romay, Cecily, 'Women as Aliens: A Feminist Critique of the Public/Private Distinction in International Human Rights Law', (1993) 6 *Harvard Human Rights Journal*, 87–125.

Roseman, Mindy and Reichenbach, Laura, 'Global reproductive health and rights: reflecting on ICPD' in Laura Reichenbach and Mindy Roseman (eds), *Reproductive Health and Human Rights: The Way Forward* (University of Pennsylvania Press 2009), 3–20.

Roxin, Claus, *Strafrecht Allgemeiner Teil Band I: Grundlagen. Der Aufbau der Verbrechenslehre* (Beck 1997).

Saab, Anne, *Narratives of Hunger in International law: Feeding the World in Times of Climate Change* (Cambridge University Press 2019).

Sander, Barrie, 'The Expressive Limits of International Criminal Justice: Victim Trauma and Local Culture in the Iron Cage of the Law', (2019) 19(6) *International Criminal Law Review*, 1014–1045.

Sander, Barrie, 'The expressive turn of international criminal justice: A field in search of meaning', (2019) 32 *Leiden Journal of International Law*, 851–872.

Sander, Barrie, *Doing Justice to History: Confronting the Past in International Criminal Courts* (Oxford University Press 2021).

Sandholtz, Wayne, *Prohibiting Plunder: How Norms Change* (Oxford University Press 2007).

Savelsberg, Joachim J., 'The Representational Power of International Criminal Courts' in Morten Bergsmo et al. (eds), *Power in International Criminal Justice* (Torkel Opsahl Academic EPublisher 2020), 281–321.

Schabas, William 'International crimes' in David Armstrong (ed), *Routledge Handbook of International Law* (Routledge 2009), 268–280.

Schabas, William, *The International Criminal Court: A Commentary on the Rome Statute* (Oxford University Press 2016).

Schabas, William, 'Al Mahdi Has Been Convicted of a Crime He Did Not Commit', (2017) 49 *Case Western Reserve Journal of International Law*, 75–102.

Schipper, Friedrich T. and Frank, Erich, 'A Concise Legal History of the Protection of Cultural Property in the Event of Armed Conflict and a Comparative Analysis of the 1935 Roerich Pact and the 1954 Hague Convention in the Context of the Law of War', (2013) 9(1) *Archaeologies: Journal of the World Archaeological Congress*, 13–28.

Schmid, Evelyne, *Taking Economic, Social and Cultural Rights Seriously in International Criminal Law* (Cambridge University Press 2015).

Schomburg, Wolfgang and Peterson, Ines, 'Genuine Consent to Sexual Violence under International Criminal Law', (2007) 101(1) *The American Journal of International Law*, 121–140.

Schulhofer, Stephen, *Unwanted Sex: The Culture of Intimidation and the Failure of the Law* (Harvard University Press 2000).

Schulhofer, Stephen J., 'Reforming the Law of Rape', (2017) 35(2) *Law and Inequality*, 335–352.

Schulz, Philipp and Touquet, Heleen, 'Queering explanatory frameworks for wartime sexual violence against men', (2020) 96(5) *International Affairs*, 1169–1187.

Schünemann, Bernd, 'The System of Criminal Wrongs: The Concept of Legal Goods and Victim-based Jurisprudence as a Bridge between the General and Special Parts of the Criminal Code', (2004) 7(2) *Buffalo Criminal Law Review*, 551–582.

Schwarz, Kathryn, 'The Wrong Question: Thinking Through Virginity', (2002) 13(2) *Differences: A Journal of Feminist Cultural Studies*, 1–34.

Schwöbel-Patel, Christine, 'Spectacle in international criminal law: the fundraising image of victimhood', (2016) 4(2) *London Review of International Law*, 247–274.

Simić, Olivera and Collings, Jean, 'Defining Rape in War: Challenges and Dilemmas', (2018) 6(1) *Griffith Journal of Law and Human Dignity*, 184–228.

Sloane, Robert D, 'The Expressive Capacity of International Punishment: The Limits of the National Law Analogy and the Potential of International Criminal Law', (2007) 43(1) *Stanford Journal of International Law*, 39–94.

Sørensen, Marie Louise Stig and Viejo-Rose, Dacia, 'Introduction: The Impact of Conflict on Cultural Heritage: A Biographical Lens' in Marie Louise Stig Sørensen and Dacia Viejo-Rose (ed), *War and Cultural Heritage: Biographies of Place* (Cambridge University Press 2015), 1–17.

Stahn, Carsten and van den Herik, Larissa, 'Fragmentation', Diversification and '3D' Legal Pluralism: International Criminal Law as the Jack-in-the-Box?' in Carsten Stahn and Larissa van den Herik (eds), *The Diversification and Fragmentation of International Criminal Law* (Brill Nijhoff 2012), 21–90.

Stahn, Carsten, *A Critical Introduction to International Criminal Law* (Cambridge University Press 2019).

Stahn, Carsten, *Justice As Message: Expressivist Foundations of International Criminal Justice* (Oxford University Press 2020).

Steains, Cate, "Gender Issues" in Roy Lee (ed), *The International Criminal Court: The Making of the Rome Statute* (Kluwer Law International 1999), 357–390.

Stewart, Hamish, 'The Limits of the Harm Principle', (2010) 4(1) *Criminal Law and Philosophy*, 17–35.

Stolk, Sofia, *The Opening Statement of the Prosecution in International Criminal Trials: A Solemn Tale of Horror* (Routledge 2021).

Sunstein, Cass R, 'On the Expressive Function of Law', (1996) 144 *University of Pennsylvania Law Review*, 2021–2053.

Swaine, Aisling, 'Beyond Strategic Rape and Between the Public and Private: Violence Against Women in Armed Conflict', (2015) 37(3) *Human Rights Quarterly*, 755–786.

Tallgren, Immi, 'The Durkheimian Spell of International Criminal Law', (2013) 71(2) *Revue interdisciplinaire d'études juridiques*, 137–169.

Tallgren, Immi, 'The Voice of the International: Who is Speaking?', (2015) 13 *Journal of International Criminal Justice*, 135–155.

Teitel, Ruti G., *Humanity's Law* (Oxford University Press 2012).

Touquet, Heleen and Gorris, Ellen, 'Out of the shadows? The inclusion of men and boys in conceptualisations of wartime sexual violence', (2016) 24(47) *Reproductive Health Matters*, 36–46.

Turan, Gözde, 'Responsibility to prosecute' in an age of global governmentality: The international criminal court', (2016) 51 *Cooperation and Conflict*, 20–37.

van Banning, Theo R.G., *The Human Right to Property* (Intersentia 2002).

van den Herik, Larissa and Dam-de Jong, Daniëlla, 'Revitalizing the Antique War Crime of Pillage: The Potential and Pitfalls of Using International Criminal Law to Address Illegal Resource Exploitation during Armed Conflict', (2011) 22(3) *Criminal Law Forum*, 237–273.

van Sliedregt, Elies and Vasiliev, Sergey, 'Pluralism: A New Framework for International Criminal Justice' in Elies van Sliedregt and Sergey Vasiliev (eds), *Pluralism in International Criminal Law* (Oxford University Press 2014), 3–38.

van Sliedregt, Elies, 'International Criminal Law and Legal Pluralism' in Paul Schiff Berman (ed), *The Oxford Handbook of Global Legal Pluralism* (Oxford University Press 2020), 575–594.

Vasiliev, Sergey, 'The making of international criminal law' in Catherine Brölmann and Yannick Radi (eds), *Research Handbook on the Theory and Practice of International Lawmaking* (Edward Elgar 2016), 354–394.

Verrall, Saeeda, 'The Picture of Sexual Violence in the Former Yugoslavia Conflicts as Reflected in ICTY Judgments', in Serge Brammertz and Michelle Jarvis (ed), *Prosecuting Conflict-Related Sexual Violence at the ICTY* (Oxford University Press 2016), 299–334.

Viejo-Rose, Dacia and Sørensen, Marie Louise Stig, 'Cultural Heritage and Armed Conflict: New Questions for an Old Relationship' in Emma Waterton and Steve Watson (ed), *The Palgrave Handbook of Contemporary Heritage Research* (Palgrave Macmillan 2015), 281–296.

Viens, A.M., 'The Right to Bodily Integrity: Cutting Away Rhetoric in Favour of Substance' in Andreas von Arnauld, Kerstin von der Decken and Mart Susi (eds), *The Cambridge Handbook of New Human Rights: Recognition, Novelty, Rhetoric* (Cambridge University Press 2020), 363–377.

von Unger, Hella, Penelope Scott and Dennis Odukoya, 'Using SKAD to analyse classification practices in public health: methodological reflections on the research process' in Reiner Keller, Anna-Katharina Hornidge and Wolf J. Schünemann (eds), *The Sociology of Knowledge Approach to Discourse Investigating the Politics of Knowledge and Meaning-making* (Routledge 2018), 169–185.

Walasek, Helen, 'Destruction of the Cultural Heritage in Bosnia-Herzegovina: An Overview' in Helen Walasek (ed), *Bosnia and the Destruction of Cultural Heritage* (Ashgate 2015), 23–142.

Walasek, Helen, 'Introduction' in Helen Walasek (ed), *Bosnia and the Destruction of Cultural Heritage* (Ashgate 2015), 1–22.

Werner, Wouter G., 'Speech Act Theory and the Concept of Sovereignty: A Critique of the Descriptivistic and the Normativistic Fallacy', (2001) 14 *The Hague Yearbook of International Law*, 73–84.

Wetherell, Margaret, 'Themes in Discourse Research: The Case of Diana' in Margaret Wetherell et al. (eds), *Discourse Theory and Practice: A Reader* (Sage Publications 2002), 14–28.

Willems, Vera, 'International Courts and Tribunals and Their Linguistic Practices: A Communities of Practice Approach', (2017) 30 *International Journal for the Semiotics of Law*, 181–199.

Wilt, Harmen van der, 'On Regional Criminal Courts as Representatives of Political Communities: The Special Case of the African Criminal Court' in Kevin Jon Heller, Frédéric Mégret, Sarah Nouwen, Jens Ohlin, and Darryl Robinson, *The Oxford Handbook of International Criminal Law* (Oxford University Press 2020), 194–211.

Zampas, Christina and Gher, Jaime M., 'Abortion as a Human Right-International and Regional Standards', (2008) 8(2) *Human Rights Law Review*, 249–294.

Dubravka Žarkov, 'Sexual Violence Against Men in Contemporary Warfare' in Indira Rosenthal et al. (eds), *Gender and International Criminal Law* (Oxford University Press 2022), 101–123.

Zeidenstein, George, 'The Conundrum of Population and Reproductive Health Programs in the Early Twenty-First Century' in Laura Reichenbach and Mindy Jane Roseman (eds), *Reproductive Health and Human Rights: The Way Forward* (University of Pennsylvania Press 2009), 40–50.

Zipfel, Gaby, "Let Us Have a Little Fun": The Relationship between Gender, Violence and Sexuality in Armed Conflict Situations', (2013) 5 *RCCS Annual Review*, 32–45.

Blog Posts

de Vos, Dieneke, 'Can the ICC prosecute forced contraception?', *European University Institute Blog*, 14 March 2016 [available at https://me.eui.eu/dieneke-de-vos/blog/can-the-icc-prosecute-forced-contraception/ – accessed 11 February 2022].

Laverty, Ciara and de Vos, Dieneke, "Ntaganda' in Colombia: Intra-Party Reproductive Violence at the Colombian Constitutional Court', Opinio Juris, 25 February 2020, [available at – http://opiniojuris.org/2020/02/25/ntaganda-in-colombia-intra-party-reproductive-violence-at-the-colombian-constitutional-court/ – accessed 11 February 2022].

Starrenburg, Sophie, 'Who is the victim of cultural heritage destruction? The Reparations Order in the case of the Prosecutor v Ahmad Al Faqi Al Mahdi', *EJIL: Talk!*, 25 August 2017 [available at: https://www.ejiltalk.org/who-is-the-victim-of-cultural-heritage-destruction-the-reparations-order-in-the-case-of-the-prosecutor-v-ahmad-al-faqi-al-mahdi/ – accessed 11 February 2022].

NGO Reports

Drumbl, Mark, 'Accountability for Property Crimes and Environmental War Crimes: Prosecution, Litigation, and Development', International Centre for Transitional Justice, November 2009.

Lobato, Maria, 'Forced Pregnancy During the Khmer Rouge Regime: Acknowledging Forced Pregnancy as a Distinct Crime in the ECCC Proceedings', Cambodian Human Rights Action Coalition 2016.

Nowrojee, Binaifer, *Shattered Lives: Sexual Violence During the Rwandan Genocide and its Aftermath*, Human Rights Watch and FIDH, 1996.

Stewart, James G., *Corporate War Crimes: Prosecuting the Pillage of Natural Resources*, Open Society Institute, 2011.

News Articles

The Guardian, 'Destroying priceless art is vile and offensive – but it is not a war crime', 22 August 2016 [available at https://www.theguardian.com/artanddesign/jonathanjonesblog/2016/aug/22/ahmad-al-mahdi-war-crimes-the-hague-destroying-mausoleums-timbuktu#comment-81652909 – accessed 11 February 2022].

Maliweb, 'Détention d'un Malien à la CPI: De la poudre aux yeux?", 2 October 2015 [available at https://www.maliweb.net/societe/justice/detention-dun-malien-a-la-cpi-de-la-poudre-aux-yeux-1179012.html – accessed 11 February 2022].

Other

Final Record of the Diplomatic Conference Convened by the Swiss Federal Council for the Establishment of International Conventions for the Protection of War Victims and Held at Geneva from April 21st to August 12th 1949, Volume I.

Final Record of the Diplomatic Conference Convened by the Swiss Federal Council for the Establishment of International Conventions for the Protection of War Victims and Held at Geneva from April 21st to August 12th 1949, Volume II A.

ICC, Statement of the Prosecutor of the International Criminal Court, Fatou Bensouda, at the opening of Trial in the case against Mr Ahmad Al-Faqi Al Mahdi, 22 August 2016 [available at https://www.icc-cpi.int/Pages/item.aspx?name=otp-stat-al-mahdi-160822 – accessed 9 February 2022].

Song, Tianying, 'Legal Goods Protected by War Crimes', Centre of International Law Research and Policy Conference Paper, 26 August 2017 [available at https://www.cilrap.org/cilrap-film/170826-song/ – accessed 11 February 2022].

WHO, 'United Nations agencies call for ban on virginity testing', 17 October 2018 [available at https://www.who.int/news/item/17-10-2018-united-nations-agencies-call-for-ban-on-virginity-testing – accessed 11 February 2022].

WHO, OHCHR and UN Women, *Eliminating Virginity Testing: An Interagency Statement*, 2018 [available at https://apps.who.int/iris/bitstream/handle/10665/275451/WHO-RHR-18.15-eng.pdf?ua=1 – accessed 11 February 2022].

Index

Printed in the United States
by Baker & Taylor Publisher Services